Russia, the USSR,
and Eastern Europe
1975-1980

Russia, the USSR, and Eastern Europe

A Bibliographic Guide to
English Language Publications,
1975-1980

Stephan M. Horak

1982
Libraries Unlimited, Inc.
Littleton, Colorado

LIBRARIES UNLIMITED, INC.
P.O. Box 263
Littleton, Colorado 80160

Library of Congress Cataloging in Publication Data

Horak, Stephan M., 1920-
    Russia, the USSR, and Eastern Europe.

    Supplements: Russia, the USSR, and Eastern
Europe : a bibliographic guide to English language
publications, 1964-1974 / Stephan M. Horak. 1978.
    Includes index.
    1. Europe, Eastern--Bibliography. 2. Soviet
Union--Bibliography. 3. English imprints.
I. Title.
Z2483.H54 Suppl. [DJK9] 016.947   82-4603
ISBN 0-87287-297-1

TABLE OF CONTENTS

Part III
EASTERN EUROPE
(Including the GDR and the Balkan Peninsula)

INTRODUCTION

The present volume, a supplement to *Russia, the USSR, and Eastern Europe: A Bibliographic Guide to English Language Publications, 1964-1974*, published in 1978, extends its listing for the years 1975-1980. In addition, a limited number of works published in 1974 have been included which, for technical reasons, could not have been considered in the first volume. Their scholarly value warranted their inclusion in order not to deprive the user of the assistance this bibliography offers. It should be noted that some significant works published in 1980 are missing in the present volume. At the time of the completion of the manuscript, December 1981, the required information in the form of reviews in professional journals or other means were not available to the compiler. We hope to include the missing ones in a subsequent projected volume covering the years 1981-1985.

This volume comprises over 1,000 monographs in English, published in the United States and elsewhere, with only a few in foreign languages, those deemed essential on account of their contribution, especially in the absence of corresponding or similar works in English. Since over 75% of the books published in English for the period in question are here included, this selected bibliography should be seen as comprehensive as possible, especially when considering the quality of all the monographs published. Therefore, books which were repeatedly identified in professional journals as unsatisfactory by the academic standards have not been considered for inclusion. Nonetheless, we are aware that some valuable publications are absent due to either oversight on our part or unavailability of information at this time.

The present work, being a supplementary volume, is patterned in form, composition, and intention on its predecessor for the convenience of the users accustomed to the original arrangement. Apart from only a few new subdivisions, few changes have been made, especially in view of prevailing positive reviews and comments about the first volume, offered by numerous knowledgeable individuals to whom we extend our appreciation and thanks. The names of the reviewers have been omitted here; their identities can be traced through the information given in the sources of the reviews. Also, some periodicals previously consulted are not considered in this volume, especially those not exclusively concerned with Soviet and East European area studies or not popular enough to be found in most American university and public libraries. However, reference librarians should continue to consult such professional journals as *Library Journal, Choice, College & Research Libraries, RQ,* and *Wilson Library Bulletin*, where one might come across titles not listed elsewhere.

The selection of titles was generally based on the evaluation of the reviewers, experts in their respective fields and areas. Consequently, this volume, as much as the first one, should be seen as the product of a large collective input. The sources for those annotations derived from reviews are indicated. Other notations are mine, sometimes based on information supplied by the publishers or additional sources. All annotations offered in digest-form comprise basic information on the contents of the work, its special merit and contribution to the body of knowledge in a given field, and critical observations for the user's convenience and assistance. Considering the selective nature of the bibliography, the annotations are mostly positive as this was the main criterion in the selection of works listed.

The absence of information on prices in a small number of entries is mainly due to the publishers' failure to provide them for such sources as NUC, CBI, BPR, and *Books in Print*. This is especially true in the case of foreign publishers, including Canadian, and some ethnic American publishers.

Keeping in mind that two-thirds of the entries pertain to the Russian and Soviet Russian areas, it is easy to detect the prevalent concentration of Western scholarship at the expense, embarrassingly, of the non-Russian nationalities of the USSR and the East European countries. Perhaps the visibly disproportionate number of studies will stimulate greater interest among Western scholars involved in these areas of growing importance to provide the Western world with the critical information it is still lacking in this field.

My personal thanks go to the Faculty Research Council of Eastern Illinois University for granting me financial assistance to complete the task, to the Slavic librarians at the University of Illinois at the Urbana-Champaign campus, and to the publisher, Libraries Unlimited, Inc., for encouragement to continue my bibliographical work. Of course, my wife Marie Louise, as in the past, did her part in preparing the manuscript for the publisher. It is a satisfying experience to be indebted and grateful to those who make one's work possible.

S.M.H.

ABBREVIATIONS OF
PERIODICALS CONSULTED

AHR	*American Historical Review*
CRSN	*Canadian Review of Studies in Nationalism*
CSP	*Canadian Slavonic Papers*
GUIDE	*Guide to the Study of the Soviet Nationalities: Non-Russian Peoples of the USSR*
JBS	*Journal of Baltic Studies*
LJBR	*The Library Journal*
NP	*Nationalities Papers*
PR	*Polish Review*
RR	*Russian Review*
SEEJ	*Slavic and East European Journal*
SEER	*Slavonic and East European Review*
SR	*Slavic Review*
SS	*Soviet Studies*

Part I

GENERAL AND INTERRELATED THEMES

Chapter 1
GENERAL REFERENCE WORKS

1. **The American Bibliography of Slavic and East European Studies for 1975.** (1975) 224p. $15.00; **for 1976** (1976) 229p. $18.00; **for 1977** (1981) 272p. $35.00. David H. Kraus, Editor. Prepared at the Library of Congress for the American Association for the Advancement of Slavic Studies, Chicago, IL.
This bibliography seeks to present (on an annual basis) as complete a record as possible of North American publications in Slavic and East European studies. It includes works, primarily in English but also in other languages, which are of research or information value and which were published in North America or, if published elsewhere, were written, edited, or compiled by North Americans. The average number of entries per issue is 5,000. An author index and a bibliographical index are provided. This is a basic tool for anyone involved in East European studies.

2. Budurowycz, Bohdan. **Slavic and East European Resources in Canadian Academic and Research Libraries.** Research Collections in Canadian Libraries, vol. 4. Ottawa: National Library of Canada, 1976. xvi, 595p. $6.00, paper.
This book is intended as a guide to Slavic and East European resources in Canadian libraries for scholars, students, and librarians. Its primary purpose is to report on the extent of existing research collections and to draw recommendations for a well-planned and coordinated national collection policy. The survey gives a detailed descriptive analysis of resources in each of the 50 academic and 17 specialized libraries in 10 Canadian provinces. It analyzes the holdings for all the disciplines in the humanities and social sciences in all languages dealing with the USSR and all East European countries. This is a valuable reference guide to Slavic and East European collections in North America.
SR, 37:1:148-49

3. **Dictionary Catalog of the Slavonic Collection.** 2nd ed. rev. and enlarged. New York, Public Library. Slavonic Division. Boston: G. K. Hall, 1974. 44 vols. $2,900.00.
This second edition contains 724,000 cards and includes Roman and non-Roman alphabet language material (Baltic and Slavic), as well as Western language sources published before 1972.

4. Dwyer, Joseph D., ed. **Russia, the Soviet Union, and Eastern Europe: A Survey of Holdings at the Hoover Institution on War, Revolution and Peace.** Stanford: Hoover Institution Press, 1980. x, 233p. $18.95.
This volume offers a most comprehensive description of the Hoover Institution's holdings on the USSR and all East European countries, and includes monographs, documents, reference tools, journals, and newspapers that are arranged by countries and subdivided into major subject categories. Scholars will welcome publication of the *Survey*, which enables them to locate materials, especially within the interlibrary loan system.

5. Hnik, Thomas, ed. **European Bibliography of Soviet, East European and Slavonic Studies.** Vol. 1: 1975. Birmingham, England: University of Birmingham, 1977.

xxxvii, 437p. $12.00; Vol. 2: 1976. Birmingham, England: University of Birmingham, 1979. xxxviii, 479p. $22.00.

Two former bibliographies, *Soviet, East European and Slavonic Studies in Britain* (published by ABSEES) and *Travaux et publications parus en français en ... sur la Russie et l'URSS* (published in *Cahiers du monde russe et soviétique*), are combined in the annual listing of books, articles, and scholarly reviews published in Western Europe. Included also are American and Canadian authors whose works were published either in European journals or were available in European libraries. The bibliography covers mainly the humanities and social sciences. The author-subject index of personal names refers to numbered entries. The table of contents is arranged by countries and subdivided by subjects.

NP, 8:2:267-68

6. Horak, Stephan M. **Russia, the USSR, and Eastern Europe: A Bibliographic Guide to English Language Publications, 1964-1974.** Edited by Rosemary Neiswender. Littleton, CO: Libraries Unlimited, 1978. xiv, 488p. $25.00.

This volume is intended to update Paul Horecky's *Russia and the Soviet Union: A Bibliographic Guide to Western Publications* (1965) and his volumes on East Central and Southeastern Europe (1969). The 1,611 entries are annotated with excerpts from or adaptations of reviews in British, Canadian, and American journals devoted to Slavic and East European studies. Where no review could be found, annotations have been supplied by the compiler. Included in the three parts of the book are works on Russia, the USSR, and Eastern Europe. Only monographic publications are listed. Author-title and subject indexes are appended.

SR, 38:3:542

7. Hunter, Brian, comp. **Soviet-Yugoslav Relations, 1948-1972: A Bibliography of Soviet, Western, and Yugoslav Comment and Analysis.** Garland Reference Library in Social Science, vol. 18. New York: Garland Publishing, 1976. 223p. $20.00.

This volume includes a listing of periodical articles and books on Soviet-Yugoslav relations. The entries are annotated, and articles are arranged chronologically within each of three sections representing the Soviet, Yugoslav, and Western views. It contains author and subject indexes, a list of periodicals used, and a chronology of events.

8. Jones, David Lewis, comp. **Books in English on the Soviet Union, 1917-73: A Bibliography.** Garland Reference Library of Social Science, vol. 3. New York and London: Garland Publishing, 1975. xiv, 331p. $30.00.

This bibliography lists 4,585 books which deal with the Soviet Union "from the October Revolution of 1917 to the end of 1973." Only works in English are included, and they are arranged by subject with an index of names at the end of the book. The objective, though not explicitly stated, appears to be a comprehensive listing of books in the social sciences and humanities. Not comprehensive, yet nonselective, the usefulness of this bibliography remains limited.

SR, 36:1:123-24

9. Lewanski, Richard C., ed. **Eastern Europe and Russia/Soviet Union: A Handbook of West European Archival and Library Resources.** New York: K. G. Saur, 1980. xv, 317p. $75.00.

This guide provides information on more than 1,000 collections in 22 countries from Austria to the Vatican and including both Germanies, Great Britain, and Ireland. Arrangement follows directory format: alphabetical by country, within country by locality, and within locality by institution. The information was gathered by means of personal visits when possible, otherwise by questionnaire. The results are understandably of variable quality.

SR, 40:3:517

10. Palm, Charles G., and Dale Reed, comps. **Guide to the Hoover Institution Archives.** Foreword by W. Glenn Campbell. Hoover Bibliographical Series, 59. Stanford: Hoover Institution Press, 1980. xii, 418p. $50.00.

This work provides entries, arranged alphabetically into two sections, for "virtually all archival and manuscript material accessioned" through 1978. The first section deals with materials in the archives; the second describes the institute's microfilm collection of archival and manuscript material held in private or other repositories. This guide supersedes both Nina Almond and H. H. Fisher's *Special Collections in the Hoover Library on War, Revolution and Peace* (1940) and the special collections section of the 77-volume *Library Catalogs of the Hoover Institution* (G. K. Hall, 1969-1977). This publication is excellent for large libraries used by scholars doing research in these areas.

LJBR, 1980:24

11. Staar, Richard F., ed. **Yearbook on International Communist Affairs, 1980.** Stanford: Hoover Institution Press, 1980. xxxi, 486p. $35.00.

During the past decade and a half, the *Yearbook* has become an essential reference tool for scholars and students working in the area of Communist studies. This fourteenth issue updates through 1979 basic data on all 17 ruling parties and virtually all of the remaining 82 nonruling parties. As in earlier editions of the publication, each essay provides brief background information on the historical evolution of the party in question, including the organizational structure of the party; a discussion of internal party affairs and, in the case of the ruling parties, the most important domestic political developments; and an assessment of the foreign relations of the party. Each volume concludes with a useful bibliography of books on Communist affairs.

RR,ᵥ40:1:76

12. Valois, Paul, and Thomas Hnik, comps. **Soviet, East European and Slavonic Studies in Britain 1974: A Bibliography.** Issued with ABSEES: *Soviet and East European Abstract Series*, vol. VI, no. 4(48). Glasgow: Institute of Soviet and East European Studies for NASEES, 1975. 168p. £1.75.

This annual bibliography of British writings on Soviet, East European, and Slavonic studies appeared for the first time in 1972, covering publications from 1971. For continuity of this British series, see Hnik, Thomas, ed. *European Bibliography of Soviet, East European and Slavonic Studies*, entry 5.

13. Wynar, Lubomyr R. **Slavic Ethnic Libraries, Museums, and Archives in the United States: A Guide and a Directory.** With the assistance of Pat Kleeberger. Chicago: American Library Association, 1980. x, 164p. $17.50, paper.

The 14 Slavic ethnic groups are listed alphabetically, as are institutions appearing under these groups. Standard directory-type information is provided for each institution listed. Since the data were obtained from a survey, information is often incomplete or impossible to verify. The researcher might use this *Guide* for location of otherwise unavailable material.

Chapter 2
ECONOMICS

14. Adam, Jan. **Wage Control and Inflation in the Soviet Bloc Countries.** London: Macmillan, 1979. xx, 243p. £15.00.

The main concern of Adam's book is the Soviet-type incomes policy that forms an integral part of planning. The study is pioneering in the sense that it is one of surprisingly few Western contributions to the study of the subject. It covers systems of regulation of wages, bonuses and payments for plan overfulfillment in Eastern Europe, with stress on experiments by countries attempting to move away from the prototype system which first evolved in the Soviet Union and towards more flexible and decentralized arrangements. The last part assesses the effectiveness of wage regulation systems and anti-inflationary instruments. This book should be of interest to students of Soviet economics.

SS, 33:1:152-53

15. Birkos, Alexander S., and Lewis A. Tambs, comps. **East European and Soviet Economic Affairs: A Bibliography (1965-1973).** Littleton, CO: Libraries Unlimited, 1975. 170p. $10.00.

This bibliography of English-language books and articles published between 1965 and 1973 on the economics of Eastern Europe and the Soviet Union is intended primarily for instructors and students. Within each country listings are subdivided under the following topics: economic surveys, agriculture, banking, consumption and standard of living, economic planning, foreign trade, industry, investment, labor, prices, social insurance, and wages. The volume lists 1,168 entries.

CSP, 17:4:698

16. **Comecon: Progress and Prospects.** NATO-Directorate of Economic Affairs, series no. 6. Brussels: NATO-Directorate of Economic Affairs, 1977. 282p.

This volume presents the papers given at a 1977 colloquium sponsored by NATO's Directorate of Economic Affairs. The collection evaluates Comecon integration by treating such basic issues as: How well integrated is Comecon relative to full economic merger among its members? Has significant integration occurred since the 1971 Complex Program? What are the specific integrative features in Comecon? What is the role of the Soviet Union, which dominates the organization economically, politically, and militarily? The book provides a worthwhile analysis of the fundamental features of Comecon and should be of interest to both economists and political scientists.

SR, 38:3:512

17. Ellman, Michael. **Socialist Planning.** Cambridge, London, New York, Melbourne: Cambridge University Press, 1979. xviii, 300p. $35.00.

Ellman's treatment is perhaps most telling in relation to some key issues of economic planning. Well-chosen quotations highlight the extent to which the simplistic centralization/decentralization distinction may fail to throw light on contemporary developments in the Soviet planning system. The comparison of the bulk of planning work

in the USSR to the work of clerks in income tax offices in the West is illuminating. This book is a welcome addition to the literature and can be strongly recommended for economics undergraduates. The specialist, too, will discover much that is new and stimulating.
SEER, 58:4:626-27

18. Franscisco, Ronald A., Betty A. Laird, and Roy D. Laird, eds. **Agricultural Policies in the USSR and Eastern Europe.** Conclusion by Eugen Wädekin. Boulder, CO: Westview Press, 1980. xvii, 332p. Tables. $24.50.
Contributors to this volume see the agrarian problem in Communist systems as only the most conspicuous aspect of the more comprehensive problem of low efficiency — the price paid for the pursuit of ideological goals. The nations of Eastern Europe and the USSR seem destined to face, increasingly, a choice between satisfying citizen demand for improved diets and satisfying ideological imperatives. Between 1970 and 1979 enormous investments were made in the state and collective farms, but returns, especially in labor productivity, have been disappointing.

19. Hewett, Edward A. **Foreign Trade Prices in the Council for Mutual Economic Assistance.** Soviet and East European Studies Series. New York and London: Cambridge University Press, 1974. xii, 196p. $17.50.
The author's treatment of foreign trade pricing is an empirical approach to price formulation and analysis. He develops a general model to aid in an analysis of the importance of foreign trade prices as determinants in the movement of resources. His book is primarily for the specialist and in need of continual updating.
SR, 34:4:843-44

20. Holzman, Franklyn D. **International Trade under Communism — Politics and Economics.** New York: Basic Books, 1976. xvi, 239p. $10.00.
Holzman's arguments are so lucid and his explanations of institutional, political, and economic interactions so simple yet so complete that the complexities surrounding the Council for Mutual Economic Assistance (CMEA) are made accessible to the layperson. This book is must reading for all students of socialist economies.
SR, 38:2:315-16

21. Karcz, Jerzy F. **The Economics of Communist Agriculture: Selected Papers.** Edited and with an introductory essay by Arthur W. Wright. Studies in East European and Soviet Planning, Development, and Trade, no. 25. Bloomington, IN: International Development Institute, 1979. xiv, 494p. $22.50.
This volume is a memorial tribute to the scholarship of the late Jerzy F. Karcz, who died in 1970. The editor has arranged 19 articles and reviews into three sections. The first section contains items largely concerned with the background of collectivization. The remaining part of the book is divided into two sections, one on Soviet "command farming" and its reform, and another in which variants of socialist agriculture are compared and evaluated with regard to their performance and transferability to other developing nations. A cumulative index is provided, as are succinct summaries of other papers related to some of Karcz's writings.
SR, 39:1:133-34

22. Loeber, Dietrich André, comp. and ed. **East-West Trade: A Sourcebook on the International Economic Relations of Socialist Countries and Their Legal Aspects.**

4 vols. Dobbs Ferry, NY: Oceana Publications, 1976. 1424p. $150.00. (xlix, 424p.; xviii, 578p.; xviii, 547p.; xviii, 647p.).

The book will be useful primarily to legal experts on East-West trade and to anyone interested in the organization of foreign trade systems in socialist countries. It concentrates on two principal subjects: the organizations of intrasocialist and East-West relations, and the equality and discrimination in East-West economic relations. This volume can be highly recommended as a basic reference.

SR, 36:2:328-30

23. Nayyar, D., ed. **Economic Relations between Socialist Countries and the Third World.** Montclair, NJ: Allanheld, Osmun & Co., 1979. vii, 265p. $22.50.

This work consists of a collection of essays devoted to economic relations between the socialist countries of Eastern Europe and nonsocialist, less developed countries, with a special chapter devoted to relations between the latter and China. An introductory article is followed by case studies of Tanzania, Egypt, Ghana, Nigeria, India, and Pakistan, in turn followed by an analysis of the impact of Soviet oil. The usefulness of this book lies in the attempt to go beyond the simple presentation of valuable information on the dimensions, patterns, and other attributes of socialist aid and trade and into the realm of hypothesis testing. As far as data are concerned, a compact and clearly painted picture emerges, although nothing very new is to be found.

SEER, 58:4:628-29

24. Shlaim, Avi, and G. N. Yannopoulos, eds. **The EEC and Eastern Europe.** New York and London: Cambridge University Press, 1978. viii, 251p. $35.00.

This compendium of essays by scholars from Great Britain and West Germany addresses several aspects of this variable, from the processes of economic integration to the variegated forms of economic relations, such as coproduction and the scope of financial cooperation. These developments are traced, in most instances, up to 1977. The underlying Soviet approbation and motivation is explored, along with the post-1975 dialogue, albeit halting, between the EEC Commission and the CMEA Secretariat. These essays leave no doubt that the Soviet Union has altered its basic posture about East European dealings with Western countries, and indeed expects to be a beneficiary, while attempting to maintain relatively effective instruments of control over its CMEA partners.

SR, 40:1:130

25. Spulber, Nicolas, ed. **Organizational Alternatives in Soviet-Type Economies.** New York: Cambridge University Press, 1979. x, 290p. $29.95.

This work comprises 16 articles on the topic of what is wrong with the Soviet economic model and how these deficiencies can be remedied. The articles are supplemented by four excerpts from Soviet authors. The East European essays are grouped into four categories: bureaucracies, socialization and economic laws, planning methods, and planning goals. According to Spulber, the Soviet economic model is politically based, politically operated, and immune to effective reform for political reasons.

SR, 40:3:485-86

26. Wilczynski, J. **Technology in COMECON: Acceleration of Technological Progress through Economic Planning and the Market.** New York: Praeger Publishers, 1974. xviii, 379p. $22.50.

This book is full of information, including 59 tables and 8 diagrams about technology in Comecon countries (excluding Cuba) as seen from the viewpoint of an economist. The book will be useful mainly for reference and possibly as a textbook for certain courses.

SR, 35:1:152

Chapter 3

GOVERNMENT AND LAW

27. Bertsch, Gary K., and Thomas W. Ganschow, eds. **Comparative Communism: The Soviet, Chinese and Yugoslav Models.** San Francisco: W. H. Freeman, 1976. xi, 463p. $12.95, cloth; $6.95, paper.

The compilers of this volume have assembled a set of relevant readings intended primarily for undergraduate study. These are arranged in nine sections covering the ideological and cultural background, historical development, the political system, the economy, and foreign relations. The readings are taken from published books and articles and include no primary material. The selection of readings is quite a good one for the compiler's purposes, though Marxists and radicals would not be happy with it.

SR, 36:1:124-25

28. Rush, Myron. **How Communist States Change Their Rulers.** Ithaca, NY: Cornell University Press, 1974. 346p. $15.00.

In this book the concentration is on the Soviet Union and Soviet bloc countries of Eastern Europe. It gives a reliable, factual account of the successions in six countries, dealing with factional struggles, purges, and "plots against rulers." The author tends to see Soviet intervention in Eastern Europe as an effort to remove individual leaders rather than to inhibit or reverse unacceptable policies.

SR, 34:4:840-41

29. Simons, William B., ed. **The Constitutions of the Communist World.** Leyden, Holland: Sijthoff & Noordhoff, 1980. 662p. $92.00.

The volume presents translations into English of the texts of the current constitutions of all the Communist countries, including the USSR and Eastern Europe. Each constitution is preceded by a brief introduction. This is an updated volume to John Triska's *The Constitutions of the Communist-Party States* (1968).

30. Todd, Emmanuel. **The Final Fall: An Essay on the Decomposition of the Soviet Sphere.** Translated by John Waggoner. New York: Karz, 1979. xix, 236p. $12.50.

Todd's work is a penetrating, critical study of the sociopolitical system of the Soviet Union and East European allies. His approach is so novel and his analysis is so coherent that students of East European history should give special attention to his treatment of the issues and his provocative conclusions. As a historian, he believes that a closed society, like the Soviet Union, can only be studied by using conventional research methods combined with demographic statistics. This approach makes it possible to understand the behavior pattern of the entire society.

RR, 39:1:96-97

Chapter 4
INTERNATIONAL RELATIONS

31. Bromke, Adam, and Derry Novak, eds. **The Communist States in the Era of Détente, 1971-1977.** Oakville, Ontario: Mosaic Press, 1978. viii, 306p. $7.95, paper. The present volume, a collection of papers given at a conference in 1975, has been delayed in publication. It is nonetheless useful. The theme of the volume is détente as seen against the background of the conflict (should one say "contradictions") between the developed and underdeveloped world. The confrontation between the oil producers and the oil consumers, together with the conflict between Moscow and Peking, is seen in this book as the most dangerous factor threatening world peace.
    SEER, 58:4:633-34

32. Griffith, William E. **The Ostpolitik of the Federal Republic of Germany.** Cambridge, MA: The MIT Press, 1978. 325p. $25.00.
This is a very detailed study, virtually a chronology, of West German policy toward Eastern Europe and the Soviet Union from Adenauer's time to the present. There is a vast compendium of sources, including many German ones. The book also deals with American and Soviet foreign policies, primarily as they relate to Germany, for those who want to see who did what when in this area, and who wrote about it. It is a useful work. *Ostpolitik* appears to have been written in a great hurry. As a result, it makes difficult reading. Despite all the confusions, Griffith has made a valuable contribution to the study of the complexities of West German foreign policy overall.
    RR, 39:1:105-106

Chapter 5
LANGUAGE AND LITERATURE

33. Brecht, Richard D., and Catherine V. Chvany, eds. **Slavic Transformational Syntax.** Foreword by Horace G. Lunt. Michigan Slavic Materials, no. 10. Ann Arbor: Department of Slavic Languages and Literatures, University of Michigan, 1974. vi, 261p. paper.

This volume provides Slavic material of theoretical interest to general linguists and makes recent theoretical developments in general linguistics accessible to Slavicists already familiar with the data. This is a stimulating book, yet with admittedly tentative answers.

SR, 35:2:390-91

34. Cooper, Henry R., Jr., comp. **The Igor Tale: An Annotated Bibliography of Twentieth Century Non-Soviet Scholarship on the "Slovo o polku Igoreve."** Columbia Slavic Studies. White Plains, NY, and London: M. E. Sharpe and Mansell, 1978. vi, 130p. $20.00.

This work includes brief annotations describing 390 citations to the broad range of non-Soviet scholarship on the *Slovo o polku Igoreve* that was published between 1900 and 1976. The bibliography is divided into six main sections: bibliographies, texts, translations; commentaries; linguistic analyses; literary analyses; historical analyses; and reviews of Soviet scholarship. Roman Jakobson's fifth reconstruction of the *Slovo* is included in an appendix. A word and verse index, and title, author, coauthor, and reviewer indexes are appended. The work is indispensable to anyone studying Rus' literature.

SR, 38:3:544

35. de Bray, R. G. A. **Guide to the Slavonic Languages.** 3rd ed., revised and expanded. 3 vols. Vol. 1: *Guide to the South Slavonic Languages.* Vol. 2: *Guide to the West Slavonic Languages.* Vol. 3: *Guide to the East Slavonic Languages.* Columbus, OH: Slavic Publishers, 1980. Vol. 1. 399p. $24.95; Vol. 2. 483p. $27.95; Vol. 3. 254p. $22.95.

In the recently published volume 3, *Guide to the East Slavonic Languages*, the author has made substantial revisions to the sections on Russians and Ukrainians. (The Belorussian section was thoroughly revised for the 1969 edition.) The bibliography has also been brought up to date. In the Russian section, the introduction has been expanded to include an outline of the historical development of the language prior to the eighteenth century. The main changes in the Ukrainian section consist in a substantial rewriting of the pronunciation, correcting some earlier errors, and a complete rewriting of the dialects section in line with current thinking on their subdivision.

SEER, 59:4:589-90

36. Herman, Louis Jay, comp. and ed. **A Dictionary of Slavic Word Families.** New York and London: Columbia University Press, 1975. xvi, 667p. $20.00.

A unique cross between a root lexicon and a polyglot dictionary with prominent characteristics of an etymological dictionary, Herman's work is a comparative display of the vocabulary structure of the four major Slavic languages. Each of the 200 articles is headed by a list of the various Russian, Polish, Czech, and Serbo-Croatian allomorphs of a particular Slavic root.

SR, 35:1:187-88

37. Mihailovich, Vasa D., et al., comps. and eds. **Modern Slavic Literatures.** Vol. 2: *Bulgarian, Czecho-Slovak, Polish, Ukrainian, and Yugoslav Literatures: A Library of Literary Criticism.* New York: Frederick Ungar, 1976. xvi, 720p. $30.00.

This volume covers authors from the late nineteenth century to recent years. The chosen parts of literary criticisms deal with a particular writer's style, thematics, problematics or ideology reflected or prominent in a given work. Comparative criticism is also included. In most cases, the earlier writers are provided with evaluations from their own times as well as from contemporary days. This is a most effectual, serviceable, and singular volume that will be appreciated by many specialists, students, and laypersons.

NP, 6:2:214-15

38. Mihailovich, Vasa D., ed. **White Stones and Fir Trees: An Anthology of Contemporary Slavic Literatures.** Rutherford, NJ, and London: Fairleigh Dickinson University Press and Associated University Presses, 1977. 603p. $18.00.

The present volume reprints about 125 works previously published in the *Literary Review*, evenly divided among Yugoslavia, Soviet Russia, Poland, Czechoslovakia, and Bulgaria. In addition, there are five reprinted essays, plus a new general introduction by Professor Vasa D. Mihailovich, which presents a strong case for reading and studying Slavic literatures as a unit. The works are grouped by theme — "A Poet's World," "Love," "War," etc. Translations were made of works from five countries in nine languages. The book will be useful for courses in East European and world literature.

SR, 37:2:354-55

39. Terry, Garth M. **East European Languages and Literatures: A Subject and Name Index to Articles in English-Language Journals, 1900-1977.** Oxford and Santa Barbara, CA: Clio Press, 1978. xxvi, 276p. $47.50.

This is an invaluable reference work that provides something of a key to the nonmonograph English-language and French-Canadian contributions to the study and appreciation of the Slavonic, Hungarian, Rumanian, Baltic and Finnish languages and literatures since the beginning of the present century. Over 800 titles have been consulted. A name index includes both authors and *personalia* not rating entries in the main text. The work includes over 9,000 references.

SEER, 58:3:471-72

Chapter 6
POLITICAL THEORIES, NATIONALISM, COMMUNISM, RELIGION

40. Bociurkiw, Bohdan R., and John W. Strong, eds. **Religion and Atheism in the U.S.S.R. and Eastern Europe.** Toronto and Buffalo: University of Toronto Press, 1975. xviii, 412p. $17.50.

These papers, presented at an international symposium on religion and atheism in Communist societies held at Carleton University in April 1971, have been expanded, and, in some cases, updated to 1974 for this publication. The volume adds comparative dimensions to the existing literature by examining the status of religion in the Soviet Union and in all East European Communist countries.

SR, 38:3:500

41. Brown, Archie, and Jack Gray, eds. **Political Culture and Political Change in Communist States.** New York: Holmes & Meier, 1977. xiv, 286p. $24.00.

This is a book about the intriguing question of why nations respond differently to similar challenges, in this case, the Communist effort to create societies that conform to the presumed Marxist-Leninist ideal. The extremely uneven results of the bold experiment in social engineering are the problem to be analyzed and interpreted. The main thrust of the volume is found in the chapters on Yugoslavia, Poland, Hungary, and Czechoslovakia, for which the authors have assembled an impressive array of pertinent empirical data. The authors focus on the examination of those aspects of political culture that are not readily susceptible to such explanations.

SR, 37:4:681-82

42. DeGeorge, Richard T., and James P. Scanlan, eds. **Marxism and Religion in Eastern Europe: Papers Presented at the Banff International Slavic Conference, September 4-7, 1974.** Sovietica, vol. 36. Dordrecht, Holland, and Boston: D. Reidel, 1976. xvi, 181p. $25.00.

The subject matter of this volume, which is rich in substance, is both timely and exciting, and the high level of scholarship found here does not detract from the work's immediate interest. The section dealing with religion, and especially the unsatisfactory relationship between the state and cultural-religious institutions in Poland, Ukraine, Lithuania, and the predominantly Muslim provinces of the Soviet Union, is descriptive and factual, in one word — historical.

SR, 36:2:330-32

43. Hammond, Thomas T., and Robert Farrell, eds. **The Anatomy of Communist Takeovers.** Foreword by Cyril E. Black. New Haven and London: Yale University Press, 1975[1971]. xviii, 664p. $25.00.

With contributions by 30 American and foreign experts, this is the most convenient and comprehensive analysis yet available of the ways and means by which Communists have come to power in various countries or parts of countries since 1917. This volume is not a history of world Communism but of Communist takeovers. Since 1917, there were 22 successful Communist take-overs. All essays are abundantly footnoted and a brief bibliography of basic works on international Communism is given at the end of the volume.

SR, 35:4:743-44

44. Janos, Andrew C., ed. **Authoritarian Politics in Communist Europe: Uniformity and Diversity in One-Party States.** Berkeley: Institute of International Studies, University of California, Berkeley, 1976. xii, 196p. $3.75, paper.

The seven essays included in this volume stress the factors of continuity as well as of change. The general papers, in particular, are characterized by an effort to introduce concepts that bring the discussion of Communist-governed societies closer to the general methods of social science. This effort has met with uneven success in the different contributions. Among the contributors are: T. H. Rigby, Robert C. Tucker, Alfred G. Meyer, and Zygmunt Baumann with Andrew Janos' opening essay which offers an ambitious matrix of different types of authoritarian regimes.

SR, 37:4:682-83

45. Pinkus, Theo, ed. **Conversations with Lukács.** Cambridge, MA: MIT Press, 1975. 155p. $8.95.

György Lukács, the last universal Marxist, who died in 1970, is a legend and a classic today. This slim volume, translated from the German, is based on tape-recorded discussions with the octogenerian which took place over a four-day period in September 1966. Three West German interlocutors asked Lukács about his ideas on philosophy, literature, and the political and ideological problems of our time.

SR, 35:3:542-43.

46. Shapiro, Jane P., and Peter J. Potichnyj, eds. **Change and Adaptation in Soviet and East European Politics.** New York: Praeger Publishers, 1976. xii, 236p. Tables. $18.50.

This collection of papers, delivered at the Banff Conference in 1974, is divided into sections on political culture, censorship, and nationalities. The "nationalities" section deals with the lessons to be drawn from Russian-Ukrainian-Byelorussian relations from historiography and with involvement of Kazakhs in modernization in Central Asia.

SEER, 56:1:158

47. Simmonds, George W., ed. **Nationalism in the USSR and Eastern Europe in the Era of Brezhnev and Kosygin.** Detroit: University of Detroit Press, 1977. 534p. $12.00.

Simmonds has assembled in one volume the papers and proceedings presented at the conference held at the University of Detroit. It comprises contributions covering most of the major national minorities in the Soviet Union, four nationalities of Eastern Europe (Poles, Hungarians, Albanians, and Rumanians), and two national minority groups (Slovaks and Croatians). All the contributors believe that nationalism has reemerged as one of the major forces in Eastern Europe and the Soviet Union. The volume demonstrates that little is still known about the national processes and their demographic, socioeconomic, and sociopsychological underpinnings.

SR, 38:2:327-28

Chapter 7
SOCIOLOGY

48. Connor, Walter D. **Socialism, Politics, and Equality: Hierarchy and Change in Eastern Europe and the USSR.** New York: Columbia University Press, 1979. x, 389p. $20.00.

This volume's principal achievement is its presentation in reasonably systematic form of a considerable amount of data on prestige ratings, social mobility, income structure, and patterns of "cultural consumption" in Eastern Europe and the Soviet Union. In this sense, Connor provides a more comprehensive picture of socialist stratification systems and differences among them than did earlier studies that focused on a narrower range of socialist countries. This book will be welcomed by all those interested in the nature and dimensions of inequality in existing socialist systems.

    SR, 39:1:125-26

49. Connor, Walter D., and Zvi Y. Gitelman, et al. **Public Opinion in European Socialist Systems.** New York and London: Praeger Publishers, 1977. x, 197p. Tables. £12.50.

This work is an effort to broaden the study of Communist systems by analyzing the ways in which existing social structures modify, constrain, and even affect the policies of ruling regimes. Since polling public opinion is an essential step in the legitimation process of socialist states, most of the book is devoted to the nature and content of socialist opinion polling in particular and socialist survey research in general. In greater detail, the impact of opinion polling is discussed in Poland, Czechoslovakia, USSR, and Hungary.

    SR, 37:4:690-91

50. Jancar, Barbara Wolfe. **Women under Communism.** Baltimore and London: The Johns Hopkins University Press, 1978. xii, 291p. $16.00.

The countries covered in this study are the Soviet Union and East European bloc countries, including selective data from Yugoslavia. In addition, where information was available, Jancar discusses the condition of women in China. The book focuses on the multiple variables, the nature, and the texture of the environment as it affects the inability of women to achieve equality in Communist countries. Within this larger concern, two important questions are raised: 1) In light of women's great strides within the economy, why have they not moved into the higher reaches of society where policy is made? 2) Why is it that women haven't risen to approximately the same status level in every Communist country, even though differences exist in the cultural backgrounds and economic bases of these countries? Jancar's work is certainly a valuable addition to our understanding of women in the Communist world.

    SR, 39:1:128-29

51. Kaser, Michael. **Health Care in the Soviet Union and Eastern Europe.** Boulder, CO: Westview Press, 1976. vi, 278p. $30.00.

This study provides basic and indispensable information on the health services available to 9% of the world population, roughly 360 million people. It details the experience of 60 years of Soviet "socialized medicine," and the 30 years of experience for Bulgaria, Czechoslovakia, the German Democratic Republic, Hungary, Poland, and Rumania. The book is valuable not only because it is the only one of its kind available, but also because the accumulation of statistical data permits the comparative focus to be carried out within the Comecon nations, and between the Comecon and other nations.

SR, 37:1:143-45

52. Lane, David. **The Socialist Industrial State: Towards a Political Sociology of State Socialism.** Boulder, CO: Westview Press, 1976. 230p. $18.50.

A perennial difficulty comes to the fore in Lane's analysis—the problem connected with the notion of Communism as a generalized model of a socioeconomic system. Strictly speaking, there is no one model but, rather, a multitude of models. The author is aware of this, and he clearly demonstrates that the political sociology of Communist nations is a complex matter. The new term which he has coined, "State Socialism," is not meant to remove the difficulty but to supply a more suitable common denominator for observed phenomena. The book is a remarkable contribution to the literature on comparative Communism.

SR, 37:2:309-310

53. Musil, Jiří. **Urbanization in Socialist Countries.** White Plains, NY: M. E. Sharpe, 1980. xi, 185p. $20.00.

This is the most updated, rigorous, and comprehensive study offering an empirical analysis of the problems of urbanization in Eastern European countries. Original sources and data not available in the West enrich the value of this book.

Part II
RUSSIAN EMPIRE PRIOR TO 1917 AND USSR; NON-RUSSIAN REPUBLICS; JEWS

Chapter 8
RUSSIAN EMPIRE PRIOR TO 1917 AND USSR

GENERAL REFERENCE WORKS

Bibliographies and Serials

54. Dossick, Jesse John. **Doctoral Research on Russia and the Soviet Union, 1960-1975: A Classified List of 3,150 American, Canadian, and Statistical Analysis.** Garland Reference Library of Social Science, vol. 7. New York: Garland Publishing, 1976. xxiv, 345p. $18.00.
This represents the continuation of Dossick's 1959 published bibliography covering the period from 1876 to 1959. The dissertations are arranged in 21 broad subject groups with subdivisions. Indexes include the names of authors and Russian and Soviet personal names.

55. Grant, Steven, and John H. Brown. **The Russian Empire and Soviet Union: A Guide to Manuscripts and Archival Materials in the United States.** Boston: G. K. Hall, 1981. 550p. $75.00.
This outstanding guide describes and locates material from all 50 states and offers the broadest possible range of Russian and Soviet subjects, including politics; social, diplomatic and military history; economics; art; literature; religion; and music. In-depth annotations concerning collections are provided by the authors.

56. Thompson, Anthony. **Russia/U.S.S.R.: A Selective Annotated Bibliography of Books in English.** World Bibliographical Series, vol. 6. Oxford and Santa Barbara, CA: Clio Press, 1979. xiii, 287p. $21.00.
This bibliography is presented as "a selection of readable books on all aspects of a great federal country." Its 1,247 entries do not include periodical articles nor works in languages other than English, and the emphasis is on more recent publications in all fields. The book's arrangement by subject is well organized, its typographic layout excellent, and the index is thorough.
SEER, 59:1:158

57. Whitby, Thomas J., and T. Lorkovic, eds. and trans. **Introduction to Soviet National Bibliography.** Littleton, CO: Libraries Unlimited, 1979. 229p. $30.00.
This is a competent English translation of I. B. Gracheva and V. N. Frantskevich's work published in 1967, which forms the core of this new *Introduction*. The 1967 text is prefaced by Whitby's 48-page survey of Russian and Soviet national bibliography (before and after 1917), which is unique in its genre and should prove useful to non-Russophones in particular. Appendices include a glossary (by Marilyn Kann), a list of the various Book Chambers and of their publications, and a bibliography.
SEER, 59:1:153-54

Biographies

58. Howe, Irving. **Leon Trotsky.** Edited by Frank Kermode. New York: The Viking Press, 1978. x, 214p. $10.00.

Howe's *Leon Trotsky* is a sympathetic, but frankly critical, study of a man who combined brilliant insight with stubborn intransigence, who readily saw the errors of others but simultaneously became a prisoner of his own assumptions, who was a "mixture of the rigid and the flexible." In this book, Trotsky is shown anticipating the danger of the Bolshevik Party "substituting" itself for the working class. Later he wrote *Terrorism and Communism*, a manifesto of revolutionary degeneration. Although concerned with freedom of cultural expression, he did not hesitate to suppress trade-union independence nor the Kronstadt uprising in the sea of blood.

SR, 38:4:677-78

59. Lewytzkyj, Borys, and Juliusz Stroynowski, eds. **Who's Who in the Socialist Countries: A Biographical Encyclopedia of 10,000 Leading Personalities in 16 Communist Countries.** Munich and New York: VErlag Dokumentation K. G. Saur, 1978. xi, 736p. DM 198.00.

The editors have made a very ambitious and long-awaited effort to fill an existing void. The result is a monumental work containing some 10,000 entries with "over 4,000 listings for the Soviet Union alone," including all major changes in the Politburo and the Central Committee of the Communist Party, along with changes in leadership that occurred in 15 Union Republics as a result of the 25th Party Congress in February 1976. In addition, the work covers Albania, Bulgaria, Cambodia, China, Czechoslovakia, Cuba, the GDR, Hungary, Korea, Laos, Mongolia, Poland, Rumania, Vietnam, and Yugoslavia. The biographies contain information gathered as late as 1977. This work should appeal to those involved in specialized research and to the general public.

NP, 7:2:231-33

60. Warth, Robert D. **Leon Trotsky.** Twayne's World Leaders Series, 72. Boston: Twayne Publishers, G. K. Hall, 1977. 215p. $8.95.

Warth has tried, with considerable success, to cover the highlights of Trotsky's life and activities. Unfortunately, his book is too skimpy and too matter-of-fact to provide an alternative to Deutscher. He almost entirely ignores Trotsky's theoretical writings. The book can be recommended to students as supplementary reading only.

Handbooks and Encyclopedias

61. Berner, Wolfgang, et al., eds. **The Soviet Union 1976-77: Domestic, Economic, and Foreign Policy.** New York and London: Holmes & Meier, 1978. 270p. $24.50.

This yearbook, fourth in a series edited at the Bundesinstitut für ostwissenschaftliche und internationale Studien in Cologne, is a must purchase for university libraries. It provides the advanced specialist or neophyte with an authoritative survey of Soviet domestic and foreign policies in 1976-1977 and, for those wishing to delve deeper, an invaluable starting point for further research. Each chapter is rich in factual material and interpretation.

SR, 38:1:122-23

62. Davies, R. W., ed. **The Soviet Union.** London: George Allen & Unwin, 1978. 191p. Illus. $14.75.

This textbook is a handsome contribution to undergraduate education, prepared by a

British expert on the Soviet Union in the social sciences, humanities, and science. Chapters are integrated so that no undesirable overlap destroys the book's unity.
SR, 38:2:306-307

63. Lewytzkyj, Borys, ed. **The Soviet Union: Figures—Facts—Data** (Title also in German). Munich, New York, London, Paris: K. G. Saur, 1979. xxxvi, 614p. $49.00.

Using an encyclopedic approach with figures, names, and other data in tabular form, Lewytzkyj offers insight into all spheres of the USSR. Utilizing Soviet sources as well as some Western ones, the volume covers such diverse areas as size of the territories-republics, population, structure of administration, party and state apparatus, economy, science, and education. Description is offered in English, German, and Russian, making this most useful guide a universal reference source. *The Soviet Union* provides within its 14 main subject headings 450 different items ranging from contemporary data as of 1976 to 1917 to information dating back to the tsarist Russian census of 1897, as in the case of the population.
NP, 8:2:251-52

64. Scherer, John L., ed. **USSR Facts and Figures Annual.** 4 vols. Gulf Breeze, FL: Academic International Press, 1977- . Vol. 1: 1977. xii, 320p. $35.00; Vol. 2: 1978. xv, 559p. $51.00; Vol. 3: 1979. x, 308p. $38.50; Vol. 4: 1980. x, 391p. $42.50.

Based on data drawn both from Western and Soviet sources, this annual statistical handbook presents information on contemporary Soviet life divided topically into 15 sections. Original sources are footnoted for data presented in tabular form. Statistics for U.S. production levels, military capabilities, and other economic and sociological indicators are provided selectively for purposes of comparison. Volume 1 concentrates on the period 1974-76; volume 2 covers 1977 and contains a survey of the events of the year in the Soviet Union. Volume 3 is extremely broad, covering government, parties, administration, institutions, armed forces, economy, social services. There are some historical series of economic data. It is a useful, wide-ranging reference annual. Volume 4 updates much of the information in previous volumes.

Libraries, Archives, and Museums

65. Grant, Steven A., comp. **Scholars' Guide to Washington, D.C. for Russian/Soviet Studies.** Kennan Institute for Advanced Russian Studies of the Woodrow Wilson International Center for Scholars. Washington, DC: Smithsonian Institution Press, 197. xii, 404p. $19.95, cloth. $5.95, paper.

This volume, the first in a projected series of guides developed by the Kennan Institute of the Wilson Center, brings together information on the many and varied research collections in the Washington, DC area which contain material of interest to scholars in the field of Russian and Soviet studies. The guide is divided into three sections: collections, organizations, and appendices. In the first section, Grant describes all types of libraries, archives, and manuscript depositories; museums and galleries; collections of music, maps, and films; and data banks. The organizations section lists various types of associations, cultural and exchange organizations, U.S. and foreign government agencies, research centers, and publications and media. In addition to names, addresses, telephone numbers, and interlibrary loan information, entries include discussion of holdings, publications, and subject strengths. Appendices include US-USSR bilateral agreements, Washington area meetings, bookstores, and housing and other services. Indexes are supplied for names of institutions and organizations, personal papers, library subject strength, and subject. Grant also provides a bibliography of union lists, guides, and directories.

    SR, 37:3:550

66. Grimsted, Patricia Kennedy. **Archives and Manuscript Repositories in the USSR: Moscow and Leningrad.** Supplement 1: Bibliographical Addenda. Bibliotheca Slavica, 9. Zug, Switzerland: Inter Documentation Company, 1976. xiv, 203p. S.Fr. 37.50.

Like Grimsted's original handbook/directory (Princeton, 1972), this selective bibliographic supplement is admirably conceived and executed. A number of prerevolutionary books and articles are included, and the coverage extends through 1973 (with some 1974 imprints). Of special interest is the inclusion of about 150 catalogs and descriptions of collections of medieval Slavic manuscripts and early Russian historical documents. Entries are conveniently coordinated with those in the original volume, and IDC order numbers are cited for items available on microfiche. The bibliographic accuracy, excellent annotations, appropriate indexes (author-title and subject), and other auxiliary features make the book a model for scholarly bibliography in the Slavic field.

    SR, 37:3:550

Description and Travel

67. **The Moscovia of Antonio Possevino, S.J.** Translated, annotated, and with an introduction by Hugh F. Graham. UCIS Series in Russian and East European Studies, no. 1. Pittsburgh: University Center for International Studies, University of Pittsburgh, 1977. xxxii, 180p. $20.00.

Graham offers the "Moscovia" in a most attractive and usable form, in the company of a helpful introduction, explanatory notes, and a fragment translated from the Muscovite transcript of Possevino's representations at the court of Ivan IV. Possevino's account is quite astute and illuminating in areas that have little to do with Ivan or religion. He provides a sober estimate of Moscow's population and of the nature of its urban life. This interesting source is ideally suited for the various uses of teaching or research.

    SR, 39:1:111-13

68. Smith, Hedrick. **The Russians.** New York: Quadrangle/The New York Times Book Company, 1976. xiv, 527p. $12.50.

69. Kaiser, Robert G. **Russia: The People and the Power.** New York: Atheneum, 1976. xiv, 499p. $12.95.

Two American reporters who have spent several years in Moscow offer the general reader a picture of the Soviet Union that is reasonably balanced but clearly reflects the spirit of our time. These two books cover much the same ground but with differences of emphasis and style. Smith, in particular, captures the look, sound, and mood of Russians with extraordinary immediacy. Kaiser's book is more discursive, with themes recurring at various points. Occasionally he touches on such issues as moral conduct and how it grows out of social context. These books are written with admiration and sympathy for the Russian people and a sharp awareness of the controlling aspects of the Soviet system.

    SR, 36:4:685-86

ANTHROPOLOGY AND FOLKLORE

70. Alexander, Alex E. **Russian Folklore: An Anthology in English Translation.** Belmont, MA: Nordland, 1975. 400p. $16.95.

This anthology is ushered in with a foreword by William E. Harkins, followed by examples of all the major genres of Russian folklore: ceremonial poetry connected with the calendar, wedding ceremonials and chants, funeral laments, charms, proverbs, folktales, *byliny*, historical songs, ballads, religious verses, songs of serfdom, love lyrics, and the chastushki. Each group is preceded by a brief discussion of the genre. The texts are well chosen and are typical of the genres. The translations render the originals faithfully and read well. Alexander's impressive work is a must for students in the fields of folklore, literature, and Russian culture in general.

    RR, 35:2:220-21

71. Gellner, Ernest, ed. **Soviet and Western Anthropology.** New York: Columbia University Press, 1980. xxv, 285p. $37.50.

The book is the result of a conference at Burg Wartenstein, Germany in 1976 that brought together Soviet scholars and their Western counterparts. It deals specifically and in depth with the reconstruction of primitive society, the application of anthropology to the modern world and to ethnicity, the relationship of Marxism to anthropology and history, and the contribution of linguistics, psychology, and demography to anthropology. The book shows the important and critical differences between the perceptions of Soviet ethnographers, on the one hand, and British, American, and French social anthropologists, on the other. This book has shown the way for effective crossboundary communication and thereby has done a valuable service.

    CSP, 23:2:221-22

72. Oinas, Felix J., and Stephen Soudakoff, eds. and trans. **The Study of Russian Folklore.** Indiana University Folklore Institute, Monograph Series, vol. 25. Slavistic Printings and Reprintings, Textbook Series, 4. The Hague: Mouton, 1976. x, 341p. Dfl. 48.

The editors present a readable introduction to the chief problems and genres of Russian folklore. The collection includes a number of key studies by leading Soviet specialists, past and present, among them such familiar names as V. M. Zhirmunskii, A. M. Astakhova, V. Ia. Propp, and others. Each article is preceded by an editorial commentary giving its background and placing it in context. While heavily emphasizing *byliny*, the volume also includes pieces on folk tales, riddles, songs, and fairy tales.

    SR, 36:1:161

73. Reeder, Roberta, ed. and trans. **Down along the Mother Volga: An Anthology of Russian Folk Lyrics.** Introduction by V. Ia. Propp. Philadelphia: University of Pennsylvania Press, 1975. xx, 246p. $12.50.

This publication consists of two separate parts: a translation of V. Ia. Propp's essay on Russian folk lyrics and a selection of translations of Russian folk lyrics, classified by subject matter and genre. A list of Propp's sources and a selected bibliography are included in the volume, which must be considered a useful, though limited, contribution.

    SR, 35:2:391-92

74. Shoolbraid, G. M. H. **The Oral Epic of Siberia and Central Asia.** Uralic and Altaic Series, vol. 111. Bloomington: Indiana University Publications, 1975. 176p. $12.00.

The first three chapters of this book touch lightly and generally on epics and their historical underpinnings, the Buryat-Mongol epics, and Turkic epics. Considerably more space is devoted to analyzing a few Buryat *uligers* (epics) than to all the epics of the Turkic nationalities of the Soviet East. Stories for a selection of epics found in Soviet Asia occupy the remainder of the text. Short synopses of the main action are provided for nine out of ten oral epics represented in the book.

75. Warner, Elizabeth A. **The Russian Folk Theatre.** Slavistic Printings and Reprintings, 104. The Hague and Paris: Mouton, 1977. xviii, 257p. DM 75.00.

This is a well-documented presentation of an important topic derived from little-known primary and secondary sources. In addition to its numerous interesting and valuable insights, this study also identifies many new areas for future research in the study of both folklore and Russian drama. The book is divided into four parts: Ritual Drama, The Puppet Theater, Non-Ritual Drama, and The Folk Actor and His Act. The study also provides an excellent model for future study of Russian folklore.

SR, 38:1:163-64

THE ARTS

Architecture

76. Berton, Kathleen. **Moscow: An Architectural History.** New York: St. Martin's Press, 1977. v, 256p. $16.95.

Berton, a Canadian student of Russian studies who lived in Moscow for several years, has divided her subject according to Moscow's historical epochs — the medieval era, the seventeenth century, the eighteenth century, and the tumult of the twentieth century. Essentially, the work is intended for the general reader who is interested in architecture but also has an appetite for the panorama of Russian history. The fine maps preceding each chapter allow the reader to orient himself spatially as well as chronologically. This is a readable, informative book about Moscow's past and its architecture. The modest black-and-white illustrations are quite adequate, although several key edifices are not represented.

SR, 39:1:165-66

77. **Moscow: Monuments of Architecture: Eighteenth-the First Third of the Nineteenth Century.** 2 vols. Introduction by M. Ilyin. Translated by I. Ivyanskaya. Moscow: "Iskusstvo," 1975. Vol. 1: 114p. Illus. 3.20 rubles; Vol. 2: 356p. Photographs. 12.52 rubles.

Moscow's classical architecture had its origins early in the reign of Catherine II, who encouraged construction of new buildings to replace the clutter of the marketplace and the deteriorating churches, palaces, and government buildings. The nobility who flocked to Moscow after their emancipation by Peter in the early 1760s also contributed to the spurt of classical building. Both volumes add to the knowledge of the architectural artifacts of Moscow and its environs, especially those structures in the mode of classicism.

SR, 38:1:161-62

78. Staar, S. Frederick. **Melnikov: Solo Architect in a Mass Society.** Princeton, NJ: Princeton University Press, 1978. xvii, 277p. Plates. $25.00.

This is one of the very few books that treat progressive Soviet architecture of the 1920s, and it is the first monograph to be published on Konstantin Stepanovich Mel'nikov (1890-1974). Staar's publication is an indispensable life and work study of this exciting artist, and it can also be read as a general survey of the various architectural movements in Soviet Russia in the 1920s and 1930s. In his chronological survey of Mel'nikov's life and work, Staar depends to a large extent on archival sources and rare published materials.

SEER, 57:4:594-96

Fine Arts

79. Birkos, Alexander S., comp. **Soviet Cinema: Directors and Films.** Hamden, CT: Archon Books, 1976. x, 344p. $17.50.

Over 100 Soviet film directors and a selected list of more than 1,500 of their films produced in the USSR from 1918 through 1975 are listed and described here. Although the book offers useful information, it is often incomplete.

80. Bowlt, John E., ed. and trans. **Russian Art of the Avant-Garde: Theory and Criticism, 1902-1934.** The Documents of 20th Century Art Series. New York: The Viking Press, 1976. xi, 360p. Illus. $20.00.

This is not a history of the Russian avant-garde but a useful collection and translation of selected theoretical statements, written between 1902 and 1934 by Russian artists, mainly easel painters. Through the artists' own words, the reader is able to witness the image of art change dramatically from a harbinger of a new religion to the revolutionary construction of a new society – the artist as priest giving way to the artist as engineer. The volume includes an introductory essay, biographical data, illustrations, and a 40-page bibliography of works in Russian and Western languages.

SR, 36:1:162-64

81. Bowlt, John E. **The Silver Age: Russian Art of the Early Twentieth Century and the "World of Art" Group.** Newtonville, MA: Oriental Research Partners, 1979. 365p. $25.00.

Bowlt's book is the most comprehensive study in English of the "World of Art" movement, which existed from 1898 to 1906. The author stresses the need for a new and critical examination of the "World of Art" in order to rectify the distortions created by the Soviet art historians. Approximately one-half of the book is devoted to the history of the movement. The author studies the "World of Art's" turn from Diaghilev's tutelage, its allegiance to Makovskii's *Apollon* after 1906, the subsequent evolution of the second "World of Art" society (1910-24), and the émigré "Le monde artiste" of the 1920s.

CSP, 22:3:429-30

82. Douglas, Charlotte. **Swans of Other Worlds: Kazimir Malevich and the Origins of Abstraction in Russia.** Ann Arbor, MI: UMI Research Press, 1979. x, 147p. $23.95.

This study is an interesting account of Russian avant-garde artistic activities and movements from 1908 to 1915 and of the diverse theoretical origins of Malevich's idea of Suprematism. Douglas points out the importance of Nikolai Kulbin's publications and exhibits of Impressionist painters, including the exhibits of Vladimir Izbelskii, among others, in the general formation of avant-garde principles. This is an informative and illuminating study of Malevich's artistic evolution.

RR, 40:2:227-28

83. Karginov, German. **Rodchenko.** London: Thames & Hudson, 1979. 270p. Illus. $24.95.

The activities of Alexander Rodchenko (1891-1956) exemplified the multifaceted nature of the aesthetic revolution that paralleled the political and social upheaval brought about by the October Revolution. Rodchenko built on the total break with traditional pictorial aesthetics carried out by Malevich and Tatlin and pioneered new functional "constructivist" forms of art in political posters, photography, theater, furniture, advertising, book design, and illustration. Over 200 illustrations document each phase and aspect of Rodchenko's work.

SR, 39:2:359

84. Marshall, Herbert. **The Pictorial History of the Russian Theatre.** Introduction by Harold Clurman. New York: Crown Publishers, 1977. xvi, 208p. Photographs. $14.95.

This book adds valuable visual material to already known historical information as well as providing detailed descriptions of many theatrical troupes in existence in Moscow and Leningrad. It contains over 500 black-and-white photographs and prints of stage sets, play scenes, graphic works, and portraits of theater personalities. A short section summarizes the history of the theater up to the year 1900. The main part of the book discusses the histories of various theatrical endeavors in both cities. The book is intended for a general rather than a specialized audience, but no Russian scholar should be without it.

SR, 38:3:541

85. Nilsson, Nils Ake, ed. **Art, Society, Revolution: Russia, 1917-1921.** Atlantic Highlands, NJ: Humanities Press, 1980. 271p. $25.00.

Nine contributors to this volume discuss topics like: "Spring 1918, The Arts and the Commissars," "Mandelstahm and the Revolution," "The Intelligentsia Debate in Russia, 1917-1918," "Russian Futurism, 1917-1919," "Scythian Theory and Literature," and "Agitation, Propaganda and the Cinema: The Search for New Solutions, 1917-1921." All of the essays are informative and well written.

86. Taylor, Richard. **The Politics of the Soviet Cinema, 1917-1929.** New York and London: Cambridge University Press, 1979. xvi, 214p. $19.95.

Taylor focuses on the opportunities and problems confronting film industry executives, including intraindustry relations and dealings with other Soviet and Communist executives. His treatment of the material and organizational problems that beset the Soviet film industry at the beginning is particularly useful, and his examination of film revenues and taxes is enlightening.

SR, 39:2:360

87. Valkenier, Elizabeth. **Russian Realist Art: The State and Society: The Peredvizhniki and Their Tradition.** Studies of the Russian Institute, Columbia University. Ann Arbor, MI: Ardis, 1977. xvi, 251p. Illus. $7.50.

Valkenier's book is the first monograph in English to describe the Realist school of painting in Russia during the second half of the nineteenth century. This study, therefore, is a pioneering effort and it merits particular acknowledgment. The author gives particular attention to the derivation of the Russian Realist idea by discussing the general effect on Russian art of the genre painter of the 1840s, the influence of the new generation of social thinkers on artistic awareness, the decline of the Imperial Academy of Fine Arts in 1863, and the establishment of the Artel and then of the Association of Traveling Art Exhibits in 1870. Addenda include an extensive bibliography and documentary information on the program and intentions of the Artel and ATAE.

SR, 37:3:545-46

88. Williams, Robert C. **Artists in Revolution: Portraits of the Russian Avantgarde, 1905-1925.** Bloomington and London: Indiana University Press, 1977. x, 242p. Illus. $15.00.

This book explores the "intersection of innovative and revolutionary art" in Russia between 1905 and 1925 through a series of biographical studies of outstanding figures in the arts. In considering the careers of several artists, the author attempts to identify a "moment of innovation" in the life of each artist and to investigate the social and psychological factors that contributed to his break with the past. The volume presents a rich collection of information, including material on once popular, but now little known, intellectual sources, such as Claude Braydon's *Primer of Higher Space* and its impact — albeit indirect — on Malevich.

    SR, 38:1:158-59

THE ECONOMY

Bibliographies

89. Kazmer, Daniel R., and Vera. **Russian Economic History: A Guide to Information Sources.** Detroit: Gale Research Company, 1977. x, 520p. $18.00.

This is an annotated bibliography of books, pamphlets, and articles in English on the Russian economy. The work covers both Imperial Russia and the Soviet Union and is both a unique and a welcome tool for the student of Russia. It supersedes and updates the bibliographies by Harry Schwartz, which relate only to the Soviet period, and that by David Shapiro that covers pre-revolutionary Russia, though the latter is broader in its coverage in that it is not confined to economic aspects. Each chapter is divided roughly into four sections. Three chronological sections, listing works covering periods up to 1860, 1860 to 1917, and since 1917, are preceded by a general section on the topic. Within each section, works are listed alphabetically by the author.

90. White, Paul M., comp. **Soviet Urban and Regional Planning: A Bibliography with Abstracts.** London: Mansell, 1979. ix, 276p. £12.95.

This is a classified bibliography of books and articles in English, French, and German, including both Soviet material published in English and Western translations of Russian material as well as Western studies. The compiler contributes an introduction on the theory and practice of Soviet planning.

    SS, 32:4:613

General Studies

91. Bergson, Abram. **Productivity and the Social System — The USSR and the West.** Cambridge, MA: Harvard University Press, 1978. xi, 256p. $17.50.

Bergson's ultimate concern is with economic merit, a major aspect of which is economic efficiency. The latter concept is not easily measurable operationally, though strong inferences about it can be drawn on the basis of what is measurable, i.e., productivity. These are all comparative, rather than absolute, concepts and Bergson approaches an evaluation of the performance of the Soviet economy (and to a lesser extent of other Soviet-type economies as well) by a variety of comparisons with non-socialist economies. He employs fairly systematically the United States, Great Britain, France, Western Germany, Italy and Japan as benchmarks in evaluating comparative resource productivity, rates of productivity increase, consumption per capita and its increase, and so on.

    SS, 31:4:600-601

92. Brada, Josef C., ed. **Quantitative and Analytical Studies in East-West Economic Relations.** Studies in East European and Soviet Planning, Development and Trade, no. 24. Bloomington: International Development Research Center, Indiana University, 1976. xiv, 133p. Tables. Charts. $6.00, paper.

International trade models are difficult to apply to socialist economies because the peculiarities of those systems, particularly central planning, violate basic assumptions. Yet those assumptions are not unreasonable for socialists to hold: economic rationality and differential response to factor endowments. The models need not be abandoned, only modified. The authors of papers in this volume appropriately adjust traditional international trade models for socialist system differences and test them empirically. The adjustments are not substantial, and traditional models apply very well to socialist systems.

    SR, 36:2:322-24

93. Hunter, Holland, ed. **The Future of the Soviet Economy: 1978-1985.** Boulder, CO: Westview Press, 1978. xiv, 177p. $16.00.

This collection consists of five essays based on papers presented at the national convention of the AAASS in 1977, along with an introduction and summary by Professor Hunter. The central themes of the essays are that resource and demographic constraints will make continued Soviet economic growth more and more dependent on increasing productivity and international trade and that traditional Soviet economic strategies, policies, and institutions are not conducive to raising productivity.

    SR, 39:3:507-508

94. Katsenelinboigen, Aron. **Soviet Economic Thought and Political Power in the USSR.** New York: Pergamon Press, 1980. xiv, 213p. $25.00.

This book describes the development of mathematical economics in the USSR, but not in terms of the people involved and the political significance of the field for the future of the Soviet system. The author grew up in the movement and was himself a contributor to its progress until he immigrated to the United States with his family in 1973. He provides vivid sketches of the men and women involved in reviving economics in the USSR after Stalin died. The book will be useful for all students of postwar Soviet economic thought.

    RR, 40:2:209

95. Krylov, Constantin A. **The Soviet Economy: How It Really Works.** Lexington, MA: Lexington Books, 1979. xiv, 255p. $17.95.

This work focuses on an issue that is crucial to every society — the appropriate role of the state. Every economy needs to determine what things shall be done by the government and what things by individuals responding to market incentives. Krylov describes the organization of the institutions of central planning and administrative allocation of the contemporary Soviet economy, and he relates the functioning of these institutions to the familiar economic outcomes of the system — *tolkachi, shturmovshchina, vsedomstvennost', ochkovtiratel'stvo.* In the process, the reader acquires a keen sense of the limitations of administrative allocation as a mechanism for organizing economic activity.

    RR, 39:1:103-104

96. Nove, Alec. **The Soviet Economic System.** London: George Allen & Unwin, 1977. 399p. Tables. $23.25.

The author notes in his preface that the main difference between this and his earlier work is organizational. *The Soviet Economic System* integrates the treatment of both structure and problems as each sector of the Soviet economy is discussed. The sequence of coverage is traditional, beginning with planning and management, moving to the various sectors of the

Soviet economy, and ending with a general assessment of the Soviet economy. In addition to the citation of references in the text, a brief bibliography of works on the Soviet economy is presented. This book is descriptive, problem-oriented, and based heavily upon cited Russian-language sources.

SR, 39:1:131-32

Economic History

97. Bushkovitch, Paul. **The Merchants of Moscow, 1580-1650.** Cambridge: Cambridge University Press, 1980. xii, 212p. $16.95.

Because of the absence of an adequate history of Russian trade, the author has found it necessary to devote considerable attention to the context in which the trade of the Moscow merchants took place. An initial description of Moscow and its merchants is followed by a description of trade in seventeenth-century Russia trade routes, the status of foreign merchants, the toll system, and by three chapters discussing the foreign trade along those routes (the most important of which was the route through Archangel and the Baltic). Moscow's role in the internal market, especially in salt production and trade, and the relationship between the Moscow merchants and the state, make up the rest of the monograph.

RR, 40:2:181-82

98. Carr, Edward Hallett. **A History of Soviet Russia: Foundations of a Planned Economy, 1926-1929,** vol. 3, parts 1 and 2. New York: Macmillan, 1976. Part 1: x, 313p. Part 2: 330p. $17.50, each volume.

While volumes 1 and 2 of *Foundations of a Planned Economy, 1926-1929*, dealt in great detail with domestic matters, these two parts of volume 3 review Soviet relations with the capitalist world and developments within the Communist parties of seven capitalist countries. All libraries and all serious students of Soviet history will want to have these volumes.

99. Crisp, Olga. **Studies in the Russian Economy before 1914.** New York: Barnes & Noble, Harper & Row, 1976. xii, 278p. $25.00.

This is a collection of essays. All but one have been previously published (although almost all have been revised for this volume), but not always in publications that are easily accessible. The most significant chapter in the volume is the lead essay, "The Patterns of Industrialization in Russia, 1700-1914." This is a very important book, essential to a correct understanding of the Russian economy in the last century of tsardom.

SR, 36:3:501-502

100. Davies, R. W. **The Industrialization of Soviet Russia.** Vol. 1: *The Socialist Offensive: The Collectivization of Soviet Agriculture, 1929-1930.* Vol. 2: *The Soviet Collective Farm, 1929-1930.* Cambridge, MA: Harvard University Press, 1980. Vol. 1: xxii, 491p. Tables. $35.00; Vol. 2: x, 216p. Tables. $18.50.

Davies' book deals essentially with economic problems. There is a thorough use of Soviet sources, supplemented only occasionally by outside sources such as émigré writings, and all sources are used with appropriate caution. Many new points of detail in the collectivization emerge from the two volumes, but the story as hitherto known is not substantially altered. This study is a worthy continuation of E. H. Carr's works.

Economic Theory and Planning

101. Howard, David H. **The Disequilibrium Model in a Controlled Economy.** Lexington, MA: Lexington Books, 1980. xi, 112p. $20.50.
The author adapts the Barro and Grossman model to Soviet conditions, testing its predictions. In the spirit of the disequilibrium literature, Howard is mainly concerned with exploring the intermarket effects of, in this case, excess final demand. The book is well written in a clear style; however, it will appeal only to those with some attachment to the formal world of disequilibrium modeling.
    SS, 33:2:314-15

102. Katsenenlinboigen, Aron. **Studies in Soviet Economic Planning.** White Plains, NY: M. E. Sharpe, 1978. xvi, 229p. Tables. $22.50.
This book will be of great interest to all students of socialist systems and economic planning. Perhaps the most stimulating section, from both descriptive and analytical points of view, is chapter 6, which discusses incentive schemes.
    SEER, 58:3:467-68

103. Lewin, Moshe. **Political Undercurrents in Soviet Economic Debates: From Bukharin to the Modern Reformers.** Princeton, NJ: Princeton University Press, 1974. xix, 373p. $16.50.
This book focuses on the political aspects and ideas of the Soviet economic debates of the 1920s and 1960s. The author attempts to show the similarity of certain themes developed in the earlier period, notably by Bukharin, with those developed in the later period by the most representative modern Soviet economic reformers. The reformers' vision of socialism is at sharp variance with the coercive, monolithic, "civil-war model" used by Stalin. The book is challenging, well written, and of interest for all scholars in the Soviet field.
    SR, 35:4:745-47

104. Nove, Alec. **Political Economy and Soviet Socialism.** London: George Allen & Unwin, 1979. 249p. £10.00.
This volume is a collection of papers written over the last 12 years. There is one single cohesive piece pointing out the core problems of Soviet socialism — going from the Russian past, through the Russians' application of Marx's general economic theory to the specific conditions of their semi-European and semi-Asiatic country, to the contemporary Soviet economic problems as well as the meaning of Soviet studies. Nove's book is intentionally provocative, and this is a most fascinating political-economic contribution to Soviet studies.
    SS, 31:4:601-603

105. Ryavec, Karl W. **Implementation of Soviet Economic Reforms: Political, Organizational, and Social Processes.** New York: Praeger Publishers, 1975. xiii, 360p. $21.50.
This book explores what the process of economic reform tells us about the politics of the USSR and about pluralism in the steering and running of the world's largest hierarchical organization. The focus is on how change was initiated, implemented, amended, or held up by various groups. The research involved is thorough and competent, drawing on the full range of Western and Soviet sources and using the insights of a host of Western writings on various aspects of politics and administration theory. It is also comprehensive in that it deals with all aspects of the Soviet manager's environment.
    CSP, 18:3:361-62

106. Thornton, Judith, ed. **Economic Analysis of the Soviet-Type System.** New York and London: Cambridge University Press, 1976. viii, 372p. Figures. Tables. $37.50.
This is an ambitious book that gathers a representative, if not completely comprehensive, set of papers analyzing planned economies of the Soviet type, using concepts and approaches familiar in the analysis of market economies. It is also a stimulating book, one to admire and to learn from, but one to argue with here and there. Its underlying rationale — that, despite institutional differences from market economies, it is possible to use the tools and models of modern economics to explain planned economies — is certainly validated, and it contains many hints of the kinds of new insights this endeavor can provide.
SR, 37:2:314

107. Zauberman, Alfred. **The Mathematical Revolution in Soviet Economics.** London: Oxford University Press, 1975. xiv, 62p. $9.00.
Zauberman argues that mathematical economics has influenced the theory of Soviet planning more than its practice. The author believes that mathematical economics creates an ongoing revolution, a cognitive revolution, opening communication between Soviet and other scholars. The method brings fresh viewpoints to outdated planners because it introduces rational choice and scarcity prices into a system that had neither.
SR, 35:2:355-56

108. Zauberman, Alfred. **Mathematical Theory in Soviet Planning: Concepts, Methods, Techniques.** Toronto: Oxford University Press, 1976. xiv, 464p. $49.75.
Zauberman catalogues the very substantial contributions of Soviet mathematicians and economists to the theory of economic planning. He relates their work to that of Western counterparts and one is impressed with the confluence of methodology despite divergent ideological origins. The book has value as a reference tool for the mathematical economist interested in Soviet planning.
CSP, 19:4:518

Agriculture

109. McCauley, Martin. **Khrushchev and the Development of Soviet Agriculture: The Virgin Land Programme 1953-1964.** London: Macmillan, 1976. xiii, 232p. $30.00.
Although the main focus of this study is the virgin land program, it does incorporate a review of Khrushchev's agricultural policies as a whole with their political implications. Historical perspective is provided in the introductory chapters that trace the eastward expansion of the agricultural frontier during both tsarist and Soviet times prior to the Khrushchev period. The book concludes with a brief assessment of land productivity in the virgin land areas in the post-Khrushchev period and an examination of various alternatives to cropland expansion, particularly the problem of intensifying agriculture in the more humid sectors of the European USSR.
CSP, 20:4:577-78

110. Osofsky, Stephen. **Soviet Agricultural Policy: Toward the Abolition of Collective Farms.** Praeger Special Studies in International Economics and Development. New York: Praeger Publishers, 1974. xi, 300p. $20.00.
The purpose of this book is "to probe for the major problem areas in the kolkhoz" and to do so largely in terms of political analysis. The author covers a wide range of problems, such as labor force utilization, organizational issues, the private sector, farm size, party influence, land rent, and cost/price issues. The author's recommendations in dealing with

the existing problems are familiar—less control from above and more incentives from below.

SR, 34:4:835-36

111. Shaffer, Harry G., ed. **Soviet Agriculture: An Assessment of Its Contribution to Economic Development.** New York and London: Praeger Publishers, 1977. xviii, 167p. Tables. $17.50.

This book comprises four pieces on Soviet agriculture by authors using widely differing ideological and analytical frames of reference. The objective is to offer readers a wide spectrum of views on Soviet agriculture based upon the reasonable supposition that Soviet agriculture is both important and controversial.

SR, 38:2:314-15

112. Solomon, Susan Gross. **The Soviet Agrarian Debate: A Controversy in Social Science, 1923-1929.** Boulder, CO: Westview Press, 1977. xvi, 309p. $15.25.

The author not only reexamines the theses of the organizational school, led by A. Chayanov, but she finds new perspectives as well. She does this in two ways—on the one hand, she emphasizes the true scientific contribution of the agrarian Marxists; on the other, she analyzes the debate from a sociological point of view. In particular, the author focuses both on the solidarity and divisions which appear in a specifically scientific milieu and on their impact on the context of rural studies. This work should capture the attention not only of historians of Soviet Russia, but of everyone engaged in studying the theory of peasant decision making.

SR, 38:4:676-77

113. Vainshtein, Sevyan. **Nomads of South Siberia: The Pastoral Economies of Tuva.** Cambridge: Cambridge University Press, 1980. x, 289p. $39.50.

Written by a Soviet anthropologist, this is the most detailed account of Inner Asian pastoralism available to the Western reader. The author draws on archival sources and his own extensive fieldwork over the last 25 years to describe the economy of the nomadic pastoralists of Tuva, a region that borders Mongolia and the USSR. He details the migratory movements, the husbandry of the different herds, and technology of the peoples of this region. He reaches some conclusions on the rise of the state among the nomads of Central Asia.

Industry, Production, Transportation

114. Amann, Ronald, and Julian Cooper, eds. **The Technological Level of Soviet Industry.** New Haven and London: Yale University Press, 1977. xxxii, 575p. Tables. Figures. $30.00.

This book does not provide a simple conclusion concerning the comparative technological level of Soviet industry, but it is a storehouse of approaches to, and facts about, innovation in the Soviet economy. It presents much evidence for—and counterexamples to refute—some of the generalizations current in our thinking about the ability of the Soviet system to generate technical progress.

SR, 38:3:504-506

115. Berliner, Joseph S. **The Innovation Decision in Soviet Industry.** Cambridge, MA and London: The MIT Press, 1976. xii, 561p. $35.00.

Berliner's methodology subjects virtually every Soviet newspaper article, journal paper, civil-service manual, technical monograph, and scholarly book published in the decade after 1965 to the closest scientific scrutiny for evidence, specific or general, on what hinders or promotes change of process or technique. His book shows that the Kremlin might be wise to call for its own domestic cost-benefit analysis at a time when the growth of national income has sunk to 3.5%.

    SR, 37:2:311-13

116. Campbell, Robert W. **Trends in the Soviet Oil and Gas Industry.** Baltimore and London: The Johns Hopkins University Press, 1976. xvi, 125p. Tables. Figures. $10.00.

This compact, succinct book is a useful companion to the author's *Economics of Soviet Oil and Gas* (1968) by updating the data base of the earlier work and reviewing the most important developments since 1965. Separate chapters deal with Soviet energy policy, exploration, drilling, oil production, oil transport, oil refining, the gas industry, the economic reform in oil and gas, and Soviet participation in world energy markets. This is a valuable book for both serious students of Soviet energy policy and more general readers.

    SR, 36:4:696

117. Dewdney, John C. **The USSR.** Studies in Industrial Geography, vol. 3. Boulder, CO: Westview Press, 1976. xvi, 262p. Tables. $19.50.

Dewdney provides a useful review of the development and distribution of the leading sectors of the Soviet industrial economy. The text contains a substantial amount of factual information in an encyclopedic manner and encompasses the environmental, resource, transport, and population factors related to industrialization in the USSR. The book also examines specific industrial sectors and regional contrasts in Soviet industry, thereby being a convenient source for selected industrial data.

    SR, 36:3:511

118. Green, Donald W., and Christopher I. Higgins. **Sovmod I: A Macroeconomic Model of the Soviet Union.** Preface by Richard P. Foster. Foreword by Lawrence R. Klein and Herbert S. Levine. New York: Academic Press, Harcourt Brace Jovanovich, 1977. xxii, 312p. Tables. Appendices. $22.50.

This is a substantial piece of empirical research that uncovers dozens of regularities in the performance of the Soviet economy — some obvious, some puzzling, and some, quite possibly, spurious. The results represent a new and interesting set of data about a planned economy that itself needs to be explained by some adequate theory. The Sovmod data bank will be a valuable research tool if it is made available to scholars of the Soviet economy.

    SR, 38:3:501-503

119. North, Robert N. **Transport in Western Siberia: Tsarist and Soviet Development.** Vancouver: University of British Columbia Press and The Centre for Transportation Studies, 1979. viii, 364p. $22.00.

The author has rightly not attempted to divorce transport from the rest of the economy with which it is so inextricably linked. The book remains a well-written, abundantly illustrated, scholarly, and penetrating analysis of Siberian development that few could read without profit.

    SS, 32:2:313-14

120. Stowell, Christopher E., assisted by Neal Weigel, with chapters by Edward Maguire and Erast Borisoff. **Soviet Industrial Import Priorities: With Marketing Considerations for Exporting to the USSR.** New York: Praeger Publishers, 1975. xxxii, 508p. Tables. Charts. Appendices. $30.00.

The authors are all associated with WJS, Inc., a well-known export management and consulting firm dealing primarily in Soviet and Chinese markets, and this volume is directed at U.S. businessmen interested in the Soviet market. The businessman or scholar interested in description and analysis of selected facets of Soviet technology will find this handbook very valuable and useful.

SR, 35:4:747-48

121. Symons, Leslie, and Colin White, eds. **Russian Transport: An Historical and Geographical Survey.** London: G. Bell & Sons, 1975. xxiv, 192p. Maps. Tables. £7.25.

The first essay is an analysis of the impact of Russian railway construction on the grain market in the 1860s and 1870s. Russian railways facilitated grain exports, encouraged regional specialization, and altered the domestic pattern of grain supply. The second contribution in the book is a history of railways and economic development in Turkestan before 1917. This work is a welcome addition to the sparse Western literature on Russian and Soviet transportation.

SR, 35:4:749

122. Treml, Vladimir G., ed. **Studies in Soviet Input-Output Analysis.** New York and London: Praeger Publishers, 1977. xx, 446p. Tables. Figures. $23.50.

This collection is a product of the well-known research project on Soviet input-output data and analyses that has long been in progress at Duke University. The entire project is concerned primarily with how Soviet input-output data can be used by U.S. researchers, rather than with the role of input-output in Soviet planning. The book will be very useful for those needing a complete version of the input-output table in value units for the USSR in 1966 and for those requiring detailed information about and analysis of Soviet work in the input-output area.

SR, 37:3:512-13

Labor and Trade Unions

123. Grandstaff, Peter J. **Interregional Migration in the USSR: Economic Aspects, 1959-1970.** Durham, NC: Duke University Press, 1980. 188p. $14.75.

This book, dealing with the testing of general migration formulations in the Soviet context, is a most reasonable approach to the study of migration in the USSR because there is considerable generality in demographic processes in that country. Grandstaff demonstrates an excellent grasp of demographic and statistical techniques and uses data judiciously. He determines that despite assertions of fundamental differences between migration in Soviet and market economic systems, existing generalizations concerning migration processes in the market economies accurately describe much of recent Soviet experience — the volume of migrants is high; agricultural occupations are of low prestige; and the attractiveness of urban living and industrial working conditions contribute to the high rate of rural-to-urban migration throughout the USSR.

124. Kahan, Arcadius, and Blair A. Ruble, eds. **Industrial Labor in the USSR.** New York: Pergamon Press, 1979. xv, 421p. $32.50.

This volume is the result of a conference on Soviet industrial labor held at the Kennan

Institute in September 1977. The topics discussed are: characteristics of the industrial labor force, labor unions, standards of living, politics, and the worker as hero in Soviet literature. This book should become an integral part of the library of all serious students of the Soviet economy.

RR, 39:3:378-79

Resources and Their Utilization

125. Conolly, Violet. **Siberia Today and Tomorrow: A Study of Economic Resources, Problems and Achievements.** New York: Taplinger Publishing Company, 1976. 248p. Illus. Maps. $20.00.

The author's purpose is to present a balanced account of the Siberian economy with attention to readers interested in the region but unfamiliar with the Russian language. This balance is achieved by judicious reporting of success and failure, of great hopes and grave problems, and by drawing upon journalistic accounts of local tribulations to enliven production statistics. The book is probably the best of its kind on today's market.

SR, 36:2:325-26

126. Dienes, Leslie, and Theodore Shabad. **The Soviet Energy System.** Washington, DC: V. H. Winston & Sons, 1979. Distributed by Halsted Press. vii, 298p. £12.00.

This book provides information on the energy industry, with chapters on the production of oil, gas, and solid fuels, and ample coverage of the electricity sector, including hydroelectric and nuclear power. The most original section is that on energy consumption in the USSR, a subject which has received comparatively little coverage in the West. The authors claim that Soviet fuel usage is inefficient. The book performs a valuable service in drawing together a mass of information in a well-written and easily readable form.

SS, 32:4:609-610

127. Goldman, Marshall I. **The Enigma of Soviet Petroleum: Half-Full or Half-Empty?** London: George Allen & Unwin, 1980. 214p. $19.95.

The author discusses various aspects of the Soviet oil industry as it might affect Western economies. He argues in favor of supplying the Soviets with the new technology in order to keep Eastern Europe from competing in world oil markets, which could become detrimental for the economies of the Western industrialized states.

Finance and Credit

128. Garvy, George. **Money, Financial Flows and Credit in the Soviet Union.** National Bureau of Economic Research Studies in International Economic Relations, 7. Cambridge, MA: Ballinger Publishing Co., 1977. xii, 223p. £11.00.

Garvy observes that "Western analysts (have) generally tended to assign money and credit a subordinate role in achieving policy objectives in socialist countries." Hence, he finds, they either virtually ignore money or conclude that monetary management has been notably successful. He notes that the system's inability to allocate resources efficiently, to provide incentives to increase productivity, and to respond to developments not anticipated in plans has been recognized. The book describes in detail contemporary banking and public financial institutions.

SEER, 58:1:147-48

Consumption

129. Vyas, Arvind. **Consumption in a Socialist Economy: The Soviet Industrialization Experience, 1929-37.** Foreword by Maurice Dobb. New Delhi, India: People's Publishing House, 1978. xii, 239p. Tables. Rs. 50.

This book evaluates the policies implemented by the Soviet leadership during the First and Second Five-Year Plans. In the first section, Vyas develops a model that examines the relationship between consumption and accumulation. The second section shows the analytical framework as applied to the actual Soviet experience. He takes two planning problems into account simultaneously—an inadequate supply of food and a lack of productivity capacity in the investment sector. This book is a valuable teaching aid and can also be recommended to those who are interested in the problems of a country on the eve of rapid industrialization.

  SR, 39:2:311-12

Foreign Economic Policy

130. Goldman, Marshall I. **Détente and Dollars: Doing Business with the Soviets.** New York: Basic Books, 1975. x, 337p. $15.00.

This book is intended to provide a perspective on the causes of the abrupt changes in U.S.-Soviet trade during the period 1971 to 1974. The issues it raises for both the public and the behavior of American business firms, and on its further prospects, offer case studies of important examples of Soviet trading activities with the United States—grain purchases and the Soviet effort to purchase an air traffic control system from U.S. firms.

  SR, 35:3:539-40

131. Holliday, George D. **Technology Transfer to the USSR, 1928-1937 and 1966-1975: The Role of Western Technology in Soviet Economic Development.** Boulder, CO: Westview Press, 1979. xiv, 225p. $18.50.

The author, an analyst of Soviet-bloc trade and finance for the Congressional Reference Service of the Library of Congress, argues in this compact and well-researched book that the current Soviet leadership has adopted a strategy of "technological interdependence" with the West. Holliday provides the best description to date on the process of technical transfer in the Soviet motor vehicle industry.

  SR, 39:4:694-95

132. Kirchner, Walther. **Studies in Russian-American Commerce, 1820-1860.** Studien zur Geschichte Osteuropas, vol. 19. Leiden: E. J. Brill, 1975. xii, 265p. Tables. Illus. Appendices. Dfl. 68.

In aggregate, Russian-American commerce in the 40 years before the American Civil War was declining and relatively unimportant, although each nation bought from or supplied to the other significant amounts of cotton, sugar, tobacco, hemp and flax and their products, and, to a lesser extent, iron and tallow. About half of this volume is a valuable discussion of trade and shipping statistics. The remainder concerns port conditions, the chief entrepreneurs engaged in trade, and the treaty of 1832.

  SR, 36:4:679

133. Klinghoffer, Arthur Jay. **The Soviet Union and International Oil Products, 1977.** New York: Columbia University Press, 1977. ix, 389p. $16.50.

The central question in Klinghoffer's book is the interaction between the USSR's trade in oil and its general foreign policy operations. At one time, the question was how oil import needs influenced foreign policy. When the USSR became a net exporter at the end of the 1950s, the question was how the country could use oil exports to further foreign policy goals. The author stipulates that the main objectives and criteria in oil trade are economic, that is, to earn foreign exchange. But taking that as given, he then examines the many ways and cases in which the USSR has used oil trade to further political goals as well. The book is very useful in view of the present situation, since it reveals so clearly what political leverage it gives the USSR in world affairs to have large oil exports.

CSP, 20:2:269-70

134.   Knoppers, Jake V. Th. **Dutch Trade with Russia from the Time of Peter I to Alexander I: A Quantitative Study in Eighteenth Century Shipping.** 3 vols. Occasional Papers, no. 1, 1976. Montreal: Centre Interuniversitaire d'Etudes Européennes/Interuniversity Centre for European Studies, 1976. Vol. 1: xxii, 404p. Maps. Vol. 2: iv, 334p. (pp. 405-738). Tables and Graphs. Vol. 3: ii, 129p. (pp. 739-867). Paper.

These three study volumes, utilizing the primary sources of Russia and Holland in regard to commercial resources, could be enormously valuable in educating the reader about this complex problem. The main emphasis in this study is on the presentation and analysis of ship movements as an indicator of developments and changes, both absolute and relative, in the maritime commerce between these two countries. The author's good historio-graphical summary and lengthy bibliographical compendium attest to his substantial contribution, for he has digested and quantified masses of Dutch archival source materials. He also provides interesting and informative details about individual Russian ports.

SR, 39:2:297-301

135.   Stevens, Christopher. **The Soviet Union and Black Africa.** New York: Holmes & Meier, 1976. xiv, 236p. Tables. $24.00.

This study is noteworthy for its richness of detail. The chapters dedicated to the patterns of trade and aid are a laudable feature of the study and, through numerous tables and charts, offer the reader a lucid and perceptive assessment of such topics as cost-benefit calculations, the effectiveness of foreign aid, and the adaptability of Soviet economic endeavors to conditions in technologically backward regions that are not always receptive to economic programs and formulas designed in Moscow. It is regrettable that attempts to relate economic pursuits to political objectives receive only casual treatment.

SR, 37:1:141-42

136.   Turpin, William Nelson. **Soviet Foreign Trade: Purpose and Performance.** Lexington, MA: Lexington Books, 1977. xi, 172p. $15.00.

The purpose of this monograph is to test the received Western view of the object of Soviet foreign trade with developed capitalist states—that imports are limited to those inputs urgently required for development and that exports are constrained by the necessity to meet the import bill. In developing this thesis, the author examines the organizational structure of the foreign trade system and the reasons for the creation of its institutional peculiarities. Turpin advocates the creation of a Western organization "to control and to perform trade with the Soviet Union in the interest of attaining political benefits."

SEER, 58:1:148-49

EDUCATION AND CULTURE

Bibliographies

137. Yoo, Yushin, comp. **Soviet Education: An Annotated Bibliography and Reader's Guide to Works in English, 1893-1978.** Introduction by Ivan Lubachko. Westport, CT: Greenwood Press, 1980. 200p. $37.50.

The 1,587 citations in this fully annotated bibliography are arranged under 66 topical headings. An author index is also included. This work, however, is not comprehensive, considering the fact that only two percent of the citations are pre-1950 imprints. Nellie Apanasewicz's *Education in the U.S.S.R.* (GPO, 1974) is still the best English-language bibliography available.

History of Education

138. Black, Joseph L. **Citizens for the Fatherland: Education, Educators, and Pedagogical Ideals in Eighteenth-Century Russia.** East European Monographs, 53. Boulder, CO: *East European Quarterly*, 1979. 273p. $16.50. Distributed by Columbia University Press, New York.

The unifying theme of this volume is epitomized by its appendix, a 54-page translation by Elizabeth Gorky of *Book on the Duties of Man and Citizen*, a civil catechism introduced into Russian schools in 1786. Covering a range of subjects from the nature of sovereignty to the organization of a domestic household and the treatment of constipation, the catechism was aimed at molding Russian pupils into loyal, obedient, contented, and well-behaved subjects. By clarifying the theoretical background of Catherine's educational reforms, Black has brought the whole educational issue more clearly into view.

RR, 39:3:362-63

139. Fitzpatrick, Sheila, ed. **Cultural Revolution in Russia, 1928-1931.** Bloomington and London: Indiana University Press, 1978. 309p. $17.50.

This volume consists of papers presented at a conference held in New York in November 1974 on the theme of Soviet society and culture during the first five-year plan. During these years of forced collectivization and industrialization, all social groups were in a state of flux and shock, while at the same time, the power of the state machine and Stalin grew relentlessly. The early formative years—1921 to 1931—were a period of great experimentation when the party leadership was feeling its way towards a new social order. With the license and encouragement of the leadership, Communist writers, scientists, educationalists, and others launched an all-out war against the "bourgeois specialists" and sought to build society in their own revolutionary image.

SS, 31:2:300-303

140. McClelland, James C. **Autocrats and Academics: Education, Culture, and Society in Tsarist Russia.** Chicago and London: University of Chicago Press, 1979. xiv, 150p. $14.00.

This author argues that the tsarist state founded the educational system in order to promote change, but always insisted on keeping control, thus minimizing the impact of much change. Russia's educators, the academic intelligentsia, contested the state for control of the system, but basically agreed on the sort of education to be offered. McClelland concludes, despite the continuous struggle between them for control of the system, it was more important that the autocracy and the academic intelligentsia agree in fostering Western educational models, than that they recognize that "the model itself may have been inappropriate" for Russia.

SR, 40:1:111

Institutions and Organizations

141. Dunstan, John. **Paths to Excellence and the Soviet School.** Windsor, England: NFER Publishing Company, 1978. 302p. $21.00. Distributed by Humanities Press, Atlantic Highlands, NJ.

This is an outstanding piece of scholarly reporting on a complex subject about which the educational profession is poorly informed. Extensively researched in original sources, meticulously documented, and carefully interpreted, this book provides the most complete coverage in any language of educational opportunities provided for what may be called the "Soviet children of privilege." Dunstan's work is of prime interest and is essential to a full understanding of what is transpiring today in the USSR in the area of social values and organizational innovations in the mammoth Soviet school system.

SR, 39:1:137-39

Special Studies and Physical Education

142. Fitzpatrick, Sheila. **Education and Social Mobility in the Soviet Union, 1921-1934.** New York: Cambridge University Press, 1979. x, 355p. $32.50.

This monograph's important subject is the education and social mobility in the early 1930s of the new Soviet elite, which included Khrushchev, Brezhnev, and Kosygin. Much of the book is incidental to that subject and becomes a highly detailed study of the twists and turns of educational policy in the 1920s and early 1930s. The book is organized into three general sections: the first discusses the history of Soviet education under Narkompros in the 1920s, the second deals with the cultural revolution of Stalin's first Five-Year Plan (1928-1932), with its attempt to mobilize and educate workers and peasants for the new society, and the third section treats the restoration of order in education in 1932-1934.

SR, 39:3:500-501

143. Fleron, Frederic J., ed. **Technology and Communist Culture: The Socio-Cultural Impact of Technology under Socialism.** New York and London: Praeger Publishers, 1977. xii, 520p. Tables. $27.50.

Fleron has performed a valuable service in assembling for publication a number of papers from the 1975 Bellagio Conference on Technology and Communist culture, the major focus of which was "the extent to which particular aspects of imported machine technology and technical rationality have proven to be more or less incompatible with the goal cultures of Communist society and the ways in which these societies have attempted to deal with this problem by means of selective adaptation of foreign technology and innovative indigenous developments." The articles are grouped into three sections, covering Marxist perspectives on technology, technology transfer and innovation, and the impact of technology in socialist countries. This is an extremely important work for students of comparative Communism and modernization.

SR, 38:2:325-26

144. Kreusler, Abraham A. **Contemporary Education and Moral Upbringing in the Soviet Union.** Ann Arbor, MA: University Microfilms International, 1976. viii, 243p. $14.50.

This book consists of two parts—the first deals with the structure and general features of the Soviet educational system; the second and larger part deals with the main aspects of education. The focus of the book is on the political and ideological aims and contents of the different forms of education, such as collective education within schools and youth organizations.

SR, 37:2:315

145. Riordan, James. **Sport in Soviet Society: Development of Sport and Physical Education in Russia and the USSR.** New York and London: Cambridge University Press, 1977. x, 435p. $21.50.

Riordan obviously has intimate knowledge of Soviet sports, providing a wealth of factual information and literary references in this book. His topic is modern sport—its organization, major periods, and influences in historical development. He also elaborates on the relationship of Soviet top sports to foreign policy.

SR, 39:2:324-25

146. Shneidman, N. Norman. **The Soviet Road to Olympus: Theory and Practice of Soviet Physical Culture and Sport.** Toronto: The Ontario Institute for Studies in Education, 1978. x, 180p. + 4pp. photographs. $9.95, paper.

The emphasis in this book is directed toward sports organization and a description of programs of athletics and physical education. Shneidman lays out such phenomena as training programs, qualification criteria of different sports, and levels of performance. This book is mainly of interest to sports practitioners and sports scientists.

SR, 39:2:324-26

147. Walker, Gregory. **Soviet Book Publishing Policy.** New York and London: Cambridge University Press, 1978. xvi, 164p. $15.95.

Walker, head of the Slavonic section of the Bodleian Library in Oxford, gives an overview of Soviet publishing, going beyond organizational description into detailed reporting of practices. The book contains fresh and valuable information on many aspects, including pricing, author's fee scales, editorial procedure, management problems, and the book trade. He makes clear that Soviet publishing is a tool of political and ideological influence.

SR, 38:3:506-507

GEOGRAPHY AND DEMOGRAPHY

Bibliographies

148. Harris, Chauncy D., comp. **Guide to Geographical Bibliographies and Reference Works in Russian or on the Soviet Union.** Chicago: University of Chicago, Department of Geography, 1975. xviii, 478p. Maps. $5.00, paper.

This work contains 2,660 bibliographies and reference materials (for example, statistical compilations, maps, atlases, and encyclopedias) conveniently organized into seven parts. The first five parts cover Soviet publications. Part 6 lists reference works and bibliographies in Western languages (predominantly English). Also included are maps of statistical, sponsoring institutions, and administrative units of the USSR.

SR, 35:1:137-38

General and Regional

149. Lydolph, Paul E. **Geography of the USSR.** Elkhart Lake, WI: Misty Valley Publishing, 1979. ix, 522p. $17.95.

This is a companion volume to the author's previous book of the same title, which covered the country by regions. This new volume treats the subject matter by topics, aiming to illustrate geographical principles using the USSR as an example and to analyze spatial distributions in the USSR using modern geographical methods. This book is intended to develop generalizations about the country as a whole rather than to provide detailed descriptions of individual places.

SS, 31:4:622

Population, Ethnology

150. Bater, James H. **The Soviet City: Ideal and Reality.** London: Edward Arnold; Beverly Hills, CA: Sage Publications, 1980. 196p. $18.95.

Bater presents, principally for students, an introduction to Soviet planning and its results in cities of the Soviet Union. He is concerned both with the major principles underlying Soviet planning and with the real conditions of Soviet life. The author concludes that many urban problems are rooted in inadequate financial resources of city governments and the inability of city Soviets and planners to overcome the very strong economic and political positions of ministries engaged in industrial production. The book provides a good, brief, balanced synthesis of what is known about the plans and realities in Soviet cities.

RR, 40:1:71-72

151. Besemeres, John F. **Socialist Population Politics: The Political Implications of Demographic Trends in the USSR and Eastern Europe.** White Plains, NY: M. E. Sharpe, 1980. 384p. $25.00.

This is a solid, well-documented, and well-researched book dealing with the current and pending shifts in the population of the USSR, Poland, and Yugoslavia. The author shows the growing political impact of Muslim demographic explosions in the USSR, manpower and migration problems, and differential demographic politics in their ethnic perspective as well as in relation to international politics. The book should be required reading for students of Soviet and East European affairs.

152. Chinn, Jeff. **Manipulating Soviet Population Resources.** New York: Holmes & Meier, 1977. viii, 163p. Tables. $22.50.

The author's objective is to examine Soviet population policy under the assumption that, in a planned economy, population growth and distribution are elements of public policy and hence are subsumed within the overall framework of national economic planning. He focuses on population growth and population distribution. This study will be of interest to anyone working in the general area of Soviet population.

SR, 38:2:318-19

153. Coale, Ansley J., Barbara A. Anderson, and Erna Härm. **Human Fertility in Russia since the Nineteenth Century.** Princeton, NJ: Princeton University Press, 1979. xxvi, 285p. $16.50.

As a demographic reconstruction of trends in human fertility among the diverse population of nineteenth-century Russia and the present-day Soviet Union, this study can be described as a useful footnote to other works on the historical demography of Europe already published under the auspices of the Office of Population Research, Princeton University. This monograph confirms the broad generalization about the impact of rapid industrialization on the declining fertility of the mainly Slavic and Baltic nationalities of the Soviet Union. It does not explain the unexpected rise in birth rates among the natives of Central Asia and the nearly stationary fertility rate among the Islamic populations of the Caucasus. The data are based on Russian and Soviet censuses published in the past 80 years.

SR, 39:4:676-77

154. Lewis, Robert A., and Richard H. Rowland. **Population Redistribution in the USSR: Its Impact on Society, 1897-1977.** Praeger Special Studies. New York: Holt, Rinehart & Winston, 1979. xx, 485p. $34.95.

This work offers a wealth of detailed information on changes of population both over time and from regional to rural/urban standpoints. In contending that "population change relates primarily to modernization, and not directly to political systems, or to cultural or historical factors unique to any one country," the authors find themselves contradicted by the results of their own research. Data on regional population redistribution show a tremendous gap in natural increases between the Moslem and the non-Moslem areas of the USSR. The difference is due primarily to a different attitude towards birth control, which in turn reflects religious allegiances.

SS, 33:1:154

Climatology and Ecology

155. Komarov, Boris (pseud.). **The Destruction of Nature in the Soviet Union.** White Plains, NY: M. E. Sharpe, 1980. x, 150p. $15.00.

This book offers for the first time information from a Soviet citizen about ecological and environmental problems in the Soviet Union. A well-written, informed, and cogently argued report, it was sent to the West in 1978 as a *samizdat* manuscript.

156. Lydolph, Paul E. **The Climate of the Soviet Union.** World Survey of Climatology, vol. 7. Amsterdam and New York: Elsevier Scientific Publishing Company, 1977. xii, 443p. Illus. $81.75.

Lydolph has performed a valuable and long overdue service in compiling a comprehensive reference on climatic factors in the Soviet Union. Approximately half of the book consists of maps and charts that cover a diverse range of subjects. Most of the figures are collected from a large number of Soviet sources. The collection and organization of the figures themselves make the book worthwhile not only to climatologists but to economists, political scientists, and agronomists who deal with events controlled by and related to climate.

SR, 36:4:696-97

Natural Resources

157. Shabad, Theodore, and Victor L. Mote. **Gateway to Siberian Resources (The BAM).** Washington, DC: Scripta Publishing Co., Scripta Technica, 1977. viii, 189p. $15.95.

The prime physical project going on now in the Soviet Union is the construction of the "Baikal-Amur Mainline," or BAM, over 2,000 miles from the upper Lena River to the lower Amur and the Pacific. This book is a model of the value of wide-ranging geographical analysis of the interplay and significance of such questions. The detailed analysis of the project itself "as a catalyst for the development of Pacific Siberia" is the best available, maintaining a good balance between the environmental, historical, and resource details and problems of the specific region, and how BAM fits into the wider context. This book is a landmark in the geographical analysis of a major project such as BAM.

SR, 38:1:129

Special Studies

158. Anderson, Barbara A. **Internal Migration during Modernization in Late Nineteenth-Century Russia.** Princeton, NJ: Princeton University Press, 1980. xxv, 222p. $18.00.
Arguing that poverty and overcrowding did not automatically induce people to depart from familiar surroundings, Anderson postulates a series of cultural influences as the key to migration patterns in late nineteenth-century Russia. The most modern provinces sent migrants to large northern cities, while the more traditional agricultural provinces contributed more to Siberian agricultural migration. The author finds little or no correlation between migration rates and population pressure. Urban migrants were drawn from provinces whose populations were growing more slowly, and even Siberian migrants came initially from provinces with relatively low growth.
    CSP, 23:3:350-51

159. Bater, James H. **St. Petersburg: Industrialization and Change.** Montreal: McGill-Queen's University Press, 1976. xxvi, 469p. $32.00.
Bater describes St. Petersburg's "transition from a court-administrative centre to an industrial-commercial complex" under the impact of rapid industrialization. To examine this change, the author focuses his meticulous analysis of conditions in St. Petersburg on two widely separated times: the late 1860s and the years immediately preceding World War I. Characterized by sizable economic growth and well documented by contemporary statistical surveys, these periods "constitute as happy a marriage between available sources and comparable years as is feasible." The result of this work is by far the best study of St. Petersburg yet produced — a compendium of invaluable information, much of it tellingly presented in the book's 20 graphs, 49 tables, 62 illustrations, and 72 maps.
    CSP, 21:1:110-11

160. Gibson, James R. Mikos Pinther, cartographer. **Imperial Russia in Frontier America: The Changing Geography of Supply of Russian America, 1784-1867.** New York: Oxford University Press, 1976. xiv, 256p. Illus. Maps. $10.00.
This is a study of the costly, uncertain, and ultimately unresolved search for a reliable, inexpensive food base for the colonies. The Russian-American Company originally supplied its colonies from Siberia. The trans-Pacific route was later supplemented by equally costly circumnavigations from Kronstadt. Ultimately, however, it was local supply which was essential.
    SR, 36:1:114

161. Lincoln, W. Bruce. **Petr Petrovich Semenov-Shanskii: The Life of a Russian Geographer.** Newtonville, MA: Oriental Research Partners, 1980. x, 118p. $11.00.
With remarkable economy, Lincoln summarizes the career and contributions of Russia's foremost nineteenth-century geographer, Semenov-Tian-Shanskii. Apart from his influence in the Imperial Russian Geographical Society, Semenov's main contributions were to improve the collection and interpretation of social statistics and to develop the regional approach to Russian geography founded by Karl Theodore Hermann and his pupil, K. I. Arsenev. His voluminous publications (listed chronologically in an appendix) included the monumental *Geografichesko-statisticheskii slovar rossiiskoi imperii* (1863-65).
    RR, 40:2:191

GOVERNMENT AND STATE

Law

To 1917

162. Kleimola, Ann M. **Justice in Medieval Russia: Muscovite Judgment Charter (Pravye gramoty) of the Fifteenth and Sixteenth Centuries.** Transactions of the American Philosophical Society, new series, vol. 65, part 6, October 1975. Philadelphia: American Philosophical Society, 1975. 93p. $5.00, paper.

Kleimola has written a most interesting study based on the trial records and court judgments of the middle Moscovite period. She employs the available documentation to demonstrate that the quality of evidence most frequently determined the decisions. The records are complete for the fifteenth century, but not yet for the sixteenth. This study stands as the most comprehensive examination of Muscovite trial procedures and the ways in which decisions were reached, giving an additional insight into the history of Muscovite development.

    SR, 35:4:728-29

163. Wortman, Richard S. **The Development of a Russian Legal Consciousness.** Chicago and London: University of Chicago Press, 1976. xii, 345p. $20.00.

Wortman explains how an entirely new legal ethos emerged in Russia during the first half of the nineteenth century. By the mid-nineteenth century, a new type of noble judicial official—the very antithesis of his eighteenth-century counterpart—had emerged in Russia's courts and central judicial administration. In this book, Wortman has provided us with a sensitive and thought-provoking account of the Russian bureaucratic mind as it developed within the judicial and administrative agencies before the judicial reform of 1864. His book is one of the most impressive works on the Russian bureaucracy yet to appear.

    SR, 36:2:296

1917 to the Present

164. Balz, Manfred Wilhelm. **Invention and Innovation under Soviet Law: A Comparative Analysis.** Lexington, MA: Lexington Books, D. C. Heath, 1975. xii, 187p. $15.00.

Balz has written an exhaustive and thoughtful study of Soviet methods of encouraging invention within a socialist framework, giving special attention to developments since Soviet adherence to the Paris Convention for the protection of industrial property in 1964 and revision of Soviet law in 1973. Soviet law is expected to attract increasing Western attention as joint ventures are introduced. From a legal viewpoint, this study is admirably written; from a sociological viewpoint, the broader social ramifications of patent law are left unexplored.

    SR, 36:2:320

165. Barry, Donald D., et al., eds. **Contemporary Soviet Law: Essays in Honor of John N. Hazard.** The Hague: Martinus Nijhoff, 1974. xxvi, 242p. Dfl. 52.50.

The Festschrift consists of 10 essays authored by leading Western scholars in Soviet law. Among the topics discussed are: "Criminal Law and Social Control," "Law and Political

Dissent in the Soviet Union," "Samizdat under Soviet Law," and "Soviet Labor Law Reform since the Death of Stalin."

SR, 35:2:352-54

166. Barry, Donald D., George Ginsbury, and Peter B. Maggs, eds. **Soviet Law after Stalin.** Part I: *The Citizen and the State in Contemporary Soviet Law.* Leyden: A. W. Sijthoff, 1977. xv, 303p. $36.00. Part 2: *Social Engineering through Law.* Alphen aan den Rijn: Sijthoff & Noordhoff, 1978. xiv, 335p. $48.00.

These books represent two parts of a planned three-volume series on legal developments in the USSR after 1953 to which more than a dozen prominent North American and West European scholars have contributed articles. Unlike many other collective works, these volumes are remarkably consistent both in structure and content; in addition, they have the virtue of being the first reasonably comprehensive, systematic guides to Soviet law in English. They will no doubt be an enormous aid to students both of the Soviet Union and of comparative law.

RR, 40:2:211-14

167. Cameron, George Dana, III. **The Soviet Lawyer and His System: A Historical and Bibliographic Study.** Michigan International Business Studies, no. 14. Ann Arbor: Division of Research, Graduate School of Business Administration, University of Michigan, 1978. xii, 198p. Tables. Figures. $9.00, paper.

This book mainly includes reviews and evaluations of English-language literature as well as translations from the Russian on the various aspects of the function of lawyers in the USSR. It may serve as a useful primer on the Soviet legal system and its professionals and as a supplemental text in courses on the Soviet government and in broad-gauged comparative law courses. The work is also a bibliographical resource.

NP, 9:1:147-48

168. Chenoweth, Don W. **Soviet Civil Procedure: History and Analysis.** Transactions of The American Philosophical Society, vol. 67, part 6, October 1977. Philadelphia: The American Philosophical Society, 1977. 55p. $6.00, paper.

This is a welcome addition to the meager literature in the field of civil procedure. The author reviews the salient features in the development and elaboration of Soviet theory and practice in that important sphere, and he assesses the highlights of the record to date with completeness, accuracy, and lucidity. The study is well documented and good use is made of Soviet primary and secondary sources.

SR, 38:2:313

169. Feldbrugge, F. J. M., ed. **The Constitutions of the USSR and the Union Republics: Analysis, Texts, Reports.** Alphen aan den Rijn: Sijthoff & Noordhoff, 1979. xv, 366p. Dfl. 150.

This volume deals with the USSR Constitution and 15 union republic constitutions, offering a lengthy introductory profile by G. Ginsburgs and S. Pomorski; the parallel texts of the 1936 and 1977 USSR Constitutions so that changes and similarities may be directly compared; translations of Brezhnev's speeches. The introductory profile explores the ideological, policy, historical, and socialist community dimensions of the USSR.

SEER, 59:1:143-44

170. Newcity, Michael A. **Copyright Law in the Soviet Union.** New York and London: Praeger Publishers, 1978. x, 213p. $16.50.

The author of this book, a member of the New York bar, has produced a substantial study of copyright law in the Soviet Union. He begins with a historical survey of domestic copyright law from 1828 to 1973, when the USSR joined the University Copyright Convention. One of his interesting contributions is the account of how the Soviet Union joined. A concluding section reviews developments since accession to the copyright convention. Newcity concludes that political considerations will continue to becloud publishing relations.

SR, 38:3:506-507

Politics and Government, Special Studies

171. Ulrdricks, Teddy J. **Diplomacy and Ideology: The Origins of Soviet Foreign Relations, 1917-1930.** London: Sage, 1979. 239p. $22.50.

This book's focus is not on the foreign relations or policies of the Soviet state but rather on the apparatus that was expected to manage them, i.e., the foreign affairs Komissariat. Soviet archives were inaccessible for a project of this sort, but the author has made diligent use of Soviet publications and American, British, and West German sources, including a wide variety of archival records. Especially interesting are Ulrdricks' biographical data on some 650 officials of the Soviet diplomatic service during the period 1917-1930.

RR, 39:3:373

172. Vanneman, Peter. **The Supreme Soviet: Politics and the Legislative Process in the Soviet Political System.** Publications of the Consortium for Comparative Legislative Studies. Durham, NC: Duke University Press, 1977. xii, 256p. $11.75.

This book falls into two parts: the introduction and chapter 10, which contain the major theses; and nine chapters of useful descriptive material on the Supreme Soviet. The results of research, found in chapters 1 through 9, are as extensive as any available on the Supreme Soviet. The author's principal finding is that the Supreme Soviet is extending its influence over state and mass organs, and power relations are shifting, which may signal development toward democracy and the rule of law. However, the argument is flawed in several instances and ways.

SR, 37:2:308-309

173. White, Stephen. **Political Culture and Soviet Politics.** London: Macmillan; New York: St. Martin's Press, 1979. xi, 234p. $22.50.

This book advances the argument that the study of political culture in Communist states is a good test to change political culture, and the magnitude of the effort to accomplish it is uniquely high in Communist countries. White's two chapters on traditional Russian political culture are masterful summary interpretations of popular perceptions of and attitudes towards the state, which, in fact, remained unchanged from tsarist times.

To 1917

174. Haimson, Leopold H., ed. **The Politics of Rural Russia, 1905-1914.** Bloomington and London: Indiana University Press, 1979. x, 309p. $19.50.

This collection of essays grew out of a 1968 graduate seminar at Columbia University. Drawing heavily on archival materials, the investigators make full use of the latest Soviet scholarship in this field. In addition to an introduction and a thoughtful concluding chapter by Haimson, contributions include essays on the gentry and the zemstvo in 1905-1907, the Octobrist Party, the Nationalist Party, the State Council, the United Nobility, and the peasantry in the elections to the Fourth Duma.

SR, 39:2:303-304

175. Hazard, J. N., P. B. Maggs, and W. E. Butler, eds. **The Soviet Legal System.** Vol. 1: *Fundamental Principles and Historical Commentary.* 3rd ed. New York: Oceana Publications, Inc., 1977. 608p. $17.50. Vol. 2: *Selected Contemporary Legislation and Documents,* edited by W. E. Butler. New York: Oceana Publications, Inc., 1978. 733p. $40.00.

The student of Soviet law today cannot complain of a lack of materials in English. One of the most objective resources has always been Hazard's translation of selected original sources, mainly from the reports of the highest courts, and this has now been supplemented by a skillful retranslation into English by Butler of the All-Union fundamental legislation, which had previously been made available in a version published in the USSR (even that is not always now obtainable).

    SS, 31:2:278-84

176. Pinter, W. M., and D. K. Rowney, eds. **Russian Officialdom: The Bureaucratization of Russian Society from the Seventeenth to the Twentieth Century.** London: Macmillan, 1980. xvii, 396p. £20.00.

This collection of essays is arranged in chronological order and deals with such topics as "Administration for Development: The Emerging Bureaucratic Elite, 1920-1930" and "Evolution of Leadership Selection in the Central Committee, 1917-1927." The seventeenth to nineteenth centuries are well covered, making the book unique as a comprehensive survey of the evolution of Russian and Soviet officialdom.

·177. Ransel, David L. **The Politics of Catherinian Russia: The Panin Party.** New Haven and London: Yale University Press, 1975. x, 327p. $17.50.

This book is about court politics. It offers a serious attempt to explain not only what happened but what it meant. Panin's Imperial Council project was an attempt to assure that he would continue to be consulted by the empress when it appeared that rival factions were in the ascendancy. This is a major contribution to the study of eighteenth-century Russia.

    SR, 35:1:125-26

178. Sawicki, Stanislaw J. **Soviet Law and Housing Law: A Historical and Comparative Study.** Foreword by John Hazard. New York and London: Praeger Publishers, 1977. xxvi, 199p. £13.05.

This study focuses on two important areas of Soviet law: land and housing. Sawicki devotes two chapters to the ownership and use of land, topics that have been in dispute throughout much of tsarist and Soviet history. The rest of the work deals exclusively with housing law. Discussed in great detail is the history of Soviet housing legislation, cooperative and private housing, rents, landlord (the state) and tenant relations, leasing and subleasing of rooms, apartments, and homes, housing exchanges, and eviction procedures.

    SR, 39:2:319-20

179. Smith, Gordon B. **The Soviet Procuracy and the Supervision of Administration.** Documentation Office for East European Law, University of Leyden. Alphen aan den Rijn: Sijthoff & Noordhoff, 1978. xii, 154p. Dfl. 55.

The Soviet Procuracy is a singular and remarkable institution having no direct analogue in Western legal systems. With a lineage in Russian experience dating back to the Petrine era, the Procuracy in its Soviet incarnation has retained the essential features prescribed by Lenin in 1922. The author believes the general supervision function of the Procuracy will continue to expand in the Soviet legal system. Students of Soviet law, government, and economics will find that this excellent monograph offers a new insight into their areas of concern.

SEER, 58:1:145-47

180. Solomon, Peter H., Jr. **Soviet Criminologists and Criminal Policy: Specialists in Policy-Making.** London: Macmillan, 1978. x, 253p. £10.00.
The purpose of this work is to determine the nature of the participation of Soviet criminal-law scholars and criminologists in the making of policy towards crime. The first part of the book traces the development of the participation of criminologists in the period 1938-1963. The central part focuses on the 1960s by investigating the contribution of criminologists in three areas of policy and legislation on crime: crime prevention, alcoholism and hooliganism, and parole and recidivism reforms. The third part of the book reviews the results of these investigations and discusses their significance. The author rests his work on more than 50 personal interviews with leading Soviet criminal lawyers, criminologists, and law enforcement officials.

SS, 31:3:448-50

181. Szamuely, Tibor. **The Russian Tradition.** Edited with an introduction by Robert Conquest. New York: McGraw-Hill, 1975. xii, 443p. $12.50.
Szamuely offers in this erudite book an interpretation of the Russian political tradition. The organization of the book follows the author's view that the Russian tradition had two mutually hostile but intimately related strands—the absolutist state brought to clear definition by Ivan IV, and the revolutionary movement created by the intelligentsia in the nineteenth century. The thesis is as follows: After a period of gestation during the Mongol conquest, the Russian state emerged as a synthesis of oriental despotism, Muscovite patrimonialism (bondage of all classes), and Byzantine caesaropapism.

SR, 35:3:528-29

182. Szeftel, Marc. **The Russian Constitution of April 23, 1906: Political Institutions of the Duma Monarchy.** Studies Presented to the International Commission for the History of Representative and Parliamentary Institutions, no. 61. Brussels, 1976. 517p.
With this impressive monograph, Marc Szeftel brings to completion his monumental investigation into Russia's constitutional development during the last years of the empire. Based upon a meticulous analysis of all the extant sources, juridical as well as historical, it gives the first detailed objective portrait in any language of a political system that was more than usually ambivalent, in that it sought to reconcile the fundamentally antagonistic principles of bureaucratic absolutism and representative government.

SEER, 57:2:302-304

1917 to the Present

183. Barry, Donald D., and Carol Barner-Barry. **Contemporary Soviet Politics: An Introduction.** Englewood Cliffs, NJ: Prentice-Hall, 1978. x, 406p. $8.95, paper.
The Barrys have produced a good textbook—the material is condensed to a manageable 300 pages, the narratives flow smoothly, the major subject bases are touched, and none of the primary schools of thought about Communist governments should react with substantial chagrin. The book is aimed at the undergraduate student.

SR, 37:3:510-11

184. Berner, Wolfgang, et al., eds. **The Soviet Union 1973: Domestic Policy, Economics, Foreign Policy.** Translated by Hannes Adomeit and Edwina Moreton. New York: Holmes & Meier, 1975. xx, 190p. $15.95.

This volume represents an interdisciplinary effort by 35 contributors. A brief appendix contains information on the composition of the ruling bodies of the Soviet government and Communist Party, ambassadorial appointments, and the numerical strength of foreign Communist parties. The yearbook lists the main events that took place in the Soviet Union in 1973 in a wide variety of fields. Topics on defense and dissidents are included.

SR, 35:4:738

185. Besançon, Alain. **The Soviet Syndrome.** New York: Harcourt Brace Jovanovich, 1978. 103p. $8.95.

The author of this book warns that even after 50 years of economic difficulties and intellectual irresolution, the Soviet Union remains committed as ever to its ideology of Communist expansion. This commitment is disguised by Soviet pragmatic fluctuations between bold offensives and strategic retreats, alternating between war communism and détente. In his thought-provoking publication, Besançon offers an unfashionable and shocking overview of Soviet history. All in all, he has provided a clear and pungent inquiry into the problems confronting the West in trying to understand Soviet thinking and actions.

NP, 9:1:145-46

186. Bialer, Seweryn. **Stalin's Successors: Leadership, Stability, and Change in the Soviet Union.** Cambridge: Cambridge University Press, 1980. v, 312p. $19.95.

This study offers a comprehensive, careful, and convincing account of the Soviet political system. It is a well-documented piece of scholarship not to be ignored by experts or students of the Soviet Union. The author is one of the most perceptive observers of Soviet politics, society, and foreign policy.

187. Bortoli, Georges. **The Death of Stalin.** Translated from the French by Raymond Rosenthal. New York: Praeger Publishers, 1975. vii, 214p. + 16pp. photographs. $8.95.

This is an original and useful book that comprehensively portrays Soviet life during the five months from the Nineteenth Party Congress to Stalin's death in March 1953. The book also reviews the condition of all classes of the population (peasants, workers, managers, government and party leaders), the economy, religious life, and status of national minorities, and special features of Stalinism, and the curious imperialistic-messianic role of the Soviet Union.

SR, 35:2:340

188. Cocks, Paul, et al., eds. **The Dynamics of Soviet Politics.** Russian Research Center Studies, 76. Cambridge, MA, and London: Harvard University Press, 1976. x, 427p. $17.50.

This book is framed by two "think pieces," one by Adam Ulam on the continuing need for scholarly examination of the Soviet system, and the other by Zbigniew Brzezinski, who takes up the question of the influence of Russian history and social change on Soviet politics. Brzezinski finds that political processes in the Soviet Union have a viability of their own and are not merely the outcome of other forces. Essays are of superior quality, and this anthology will be of considerable interest and use to both students and scholars.

SR, 37:1:136-37

189. Cohen, Stephen F., Alexander Rabinowitch, and Robert Sharlet, eds. **The Soviet Union since Stalin.** Introduction by Alexander Rabinowitch. Bloomington: Indiana University Press, 1980. 342p. $22.50.

Topics in this compilation range from the development of pluralism within the Soviet party apparatus, to the problems of ethnicity, to foreign policy. Particularly refreshing is the treatment of emergent issues in the Soviet Union, like feminism and environmental concerns. The general quality of essays is high. This volume can serve well as supplementary text in undergraduate courses.

190. Colton, Timothy J. **Commissars, Commanders, and Civilian Authority: The Structure of Soviet Military Politics.** Cambridge, MA: Harvard University Press, 1979. viii, 365p. $25.00.

Colton argues in his study that the military party organs of the Soviet Union, for the most part, are not in conflict with the regular military staff and command. He concludes that the tensions between the political officers and the military commanders have been minimal except in the days of the civil war. Even during the purge of the military in the late 1930s, there was little conflict; in fact, both groups of officers suffered equally in the purge. The persistence of this relationship is both surprising and a warning that, with the party and military working together in basic harmony, the Soviet system is likely to remain relatively stable.

RR, 39:2:259-60

191. Friedgut, Theodore H. **Political Participation in the USSR.** Princeton, NJ: Princeton University Press, 1979. xv, 353p. $18.50.

This thoughtful and well-researched monograph makes an important contribution to the already considerable body of literature examining citizen participation in a Communist Party-dominated political system. In fact, the monograph deals almost exclusively with political participation in Soviet local government. In spite of some shortcomings, it remains a book which all serious students of Soviet politics should read closely.

RR, 39:1:255-56

192. Hill, Ronald J. **Soviet Political Elites: The Case of Tiraspol.** New York: St. Martin's Press, 1977. x, 226p. $16.95; London: Martin Robertson, 1977. x, 226p. £7.85.

From 1967 to 1968, as a member of the British-Soviet academic exchange, Hill was able to study at the Moldavian Academy of Sciences. This unusual assignment enabled him to pursue his investigation of a single medium-sized city, Tiraspol. His candid description of this investigation tells us a great deal about the possibilities for local research in the USSR, along with the stringent limitations. Like all case studies, Hill's work provides a mine of evidence. Its excellent use of statistical tables, charts, and maps are very helpful. Above all, the extraordinarily skillful combination of conceptual frameworks, general data concerning the Soviet system, and rich new material make the book a model for other investigations.

SR, 38:1:124-25

193. Hough, Jerry F. **Soviet Leadership in Transition.** Washington, DC: The Brookings Institution, 1980. xi, 175p. $11.95.

Hough has brought forth massive amounts of evidence on the objective characteristics of Soviet officials, based upon his unrivaled absorption in Soviet sources. He demonstrates that Soviet officialdom is composed of four major age cohorts ("generations") distinguishable not only by age, but also by the crucial experiences that shaped their general notions about the Soviet political order and the outside world, by the type and extent of education they received, and by their relative size and distribution within the establishment. The author feels that generational turnover will have a major impact on the values and perspectives ascendant among Soviet policy-makers.

RR, 40:2:210-11

194. Hough, Jerry F. **The Soviet Union and Social Science Today.** Russian Research Center Studies, 77. Cambridge, MA, and London: Harvard University Press, 1977. xviii, 275p. $16.50.

This book is essentially a barrage of argument and evidence designed to provoke critical reexamination by Sovietologists of the assumptions and methods of their research. The author hopes to encourage more realistic understanding of the Soviet Union and thereby more appropriate American policies toward that country. The book has two distinct but interrelated themes: the first is that the studies of Soviet politics and social science have much to learn from each other, and the second is that faulty assumptions and methodology have led to a serious underestimate of the degree of pluralism and participation in the Soviet system. Hough supports his arguments with much new research of his own, which would make rewarding reading even if one does not agree with any of the author's major conclusions.

SR, 37:3:507-509

195. Hough, Jerry F., and Merle Fainsod. **How the Soviet Union Is Governed.** Cambridge, MA, and London: Harvard University Press, 1979. [Cambridge, MA, 1953, 1963, under the title *How Russia Is Ruled* by Merle Fainsod]. xiv, 679p. $18.50.

This is, in fact, the third edition of Fainsod's book under the editorship of, and with some revisions made by, Jerry Hough. Regrettably, this book offers too many easy generalizations and misconceptions.

196. MacAuley, Mary. **Politics and the Soviet Union.** Harmondsworth, England, and New York: Penguin Books, 1977. 352p. $3.95, paper.

Parts 1 and 2 of this book trace the evolution of the system to the late Stalin era; even part 3, which is devoted to description and analysis of the contemporary political system, conveys a picture both of the flow of major events and the broad changes in the system over the last quarter-century. At each stage, the reader is invited to consider the central issues confronting the Soviet leadership and the alternatives available and visible to them. This is the best introduction to Soviet politics available in English.

SR, 37:3:509-510

197. Medvedev, Roy A., and Zhores A. Medvedev. **Khrushchev: The Years in Power.** Translated by Andrew W. Durkin. New York: Columbia University Press, 1976. xv, 198p. $10.95.

The Medvedev brothers have made several of the most important contributions to knowledge of Soviet history and politics, and, although this book is not as good as some of their earlier works, it is informative and provocative. It offers valuable confirmation of pessimistic Western diagnoses of the chronic ills of Soviet agriculture, resulting from decades of Stalin's incredible mismanagement. The book will interest serious students of Soviet affairs and might be useful as supplementary reading in courses on Soviet politics.

SR, 36:2:312-13

198. Mehnert, Klaus. **Moscow and the New Left.** Translated from German by Helmut Fischer. Berkeley: University of California Press, 1975. xii, 275p. $12.50.

This short but valuable study of the new leftists of the 1960s examines an interesting episode. The Soviet leaders disowned widespread protest against capitalist society because of echoes of protest in its own. It is the reviewer's opinion that Soviet leaders reveal their lack of confidence in their own society by the gingerly way in which they treat protest in capitalist society.

SR, 36:3:512-13

199.   Morton, Henry W., and Rudolf L. Tökés, eds. **Soviet Politics and Society in the 1970s.** Studies of the Russian Institute, Columbia University. New York: The Free Press, 1974. xxvi, 401p. $12.95.

This volume contains a central theme – the overall responsiveness and adaptiveness of the Soviet political system when confronted with social change. Contributions concern politics and social change, including articles on dissent, cotton politics in Soviet Central Asia, and women in Soviet politics. This is a book that lies in the mainstream of contemporary political science.

SR, 35:2:361-62

200.   Nove, Alec. **Stalinism and After.** London: George Allen & Unwin, 1975. 205p. $7.50, paper.

This book provides an excellent introduction to the political system of the USSR, portraying the modern political order as an outgrowth of pre-revolutionary historical conditions. Nove's analysis of the origins of Stalinism emphasizes that the economic and political conditions created by the civil war and the early years of NEP seemed to favor the dominance of Stalin and his tough-minded cohorts over the more intellectual segments of the Bolshevik leadership. This survey includes the ideological and policy orientations of both the Khrushchev and Brezhnev regimes.

SR, 35:4:744-45

201.   Reshetar, John S., Jr. **The Soviet Polity: Government and Politics in the USSR.** 2nd ed. New York: Harper & Row, 1978. xi, 413p. $8.95, paper.

This is an updated and expanded version of the first edition (1971), including 12 chapters, rather than 10. With some regrouping of material, there is now a chapter devoted specifically to the economy and social services, one on law and the judiciary, and a separate chapter on political socialization and education. This is a text on Soviet government that can be recommended for its readable length, depth, and precision of preparation.

RR, 39:1:92-93

202.   Rigby, T. H., Archie Brown, and Peter Reddaway, eds. **Authority, Power and Policy in the USSR.** New York: St. Martin's Press, 1980. xi, 207p. $22.50.

This is a collection of essays dedicated to Leonard Shapiro on the occasion of his seventieth birthday. In a theoretical essay, Rigby attempts to employ Weberian categories for an understanding of the Soviet system. Alec Nove grapples with the subject: What is the connection between central planning and Stalinist-type totalitarianism? He believes that while centralized planning did not create the one-party state, it greatly increased the size of bureaucracy and the all-pervasive power of dictatorship. Peter Reddaway writes on Soviet policy towards dissent in the past 15 years, while Archie Brown examines the changing power of the General Secretary. Overall, the volume is a credible Festschrift for a great scholar.

RR, 40:3:347-48

203. Rigby, T. H. **Lenin's Government: Sovnarkom 1917-1922.** New York and London: Cambridge University Press, 1979. xvi, 320p. + 4pp. plates. $34.50.

This thorough work focuses on the uppermost government institution in Russia, the Council of People's Commissars (Sovnarkom), from its inception amid the tumult of the October Revolution to its eclipse by the organs of the party while Lenin lay dying in 1923. Rigby details the creation of the Sovnarkom and its imposition of control over the old administration in Petrograd, the transfer of the seat of government to Moscow and the development there of its machinery or policy decision and execution, and the personalities of Sovnarkom's members and their relations with Lenin as Russia's government institutions evolved and then deteriorated under the stresses of civil war and one-party rule. The author weaves a number of theses into a compelling revisionist picture not only of the specific institutions of government decision making, but of the emerging character of the Soviet regime as a whole.

SR, 39:2:308-309

204. Rosenfeldt, Neils Erik. **Knowledge and Power: The Role of Stalin's Secret Chancellery in the Soviet System of Government.** Copenhagen University, Institute of Slavonic Studies, no. 5. Copenhagen: Rosenkilde and Bagger, 1978. 219p. 80D.Kr., paper.

A special merit of this study is the author's historical approach to the problem of the exclusive concentration of power, treating the autocracy and its organs as features that evolved from the time Stalin set his staff up in the Central Committee's already-existing Secret Department when he became general secretary in 1922. The Special Sector may have emerged within it, or outside of it, by 1928 or by 1934, when its existence was officially recognized in the materials of the Seventeenth Party Congress on the reorganization of the Central Committee apparatus.

SR, 39:2:309-311

205. Sharlet, Robert. **The New Soviet Constitution of 1977: Analysis and Text.** Brunswick, OH: King's Court Communications, 1978. x, 132p. $2.95, paper.

Sharlet has provided the American student of Soviet law and politics with a compact and useful reference work on the "Brezhnev" constitution. The volume consists of two principal sections, analysis of the new constitution, followed by a translation of the document.

SR, 38:2:313

206. Simons, William B., ed. **The Soviet Codes of Law.** Alphen aan den Rijn, Netherlands: Sijthoff & Noordhoff, 1980. xxxviii, 1239p. $92.50.

The law reforms of the late 1950s and early 1960s in the Soviet Union resulted in the enactment of new legislation in virtually every major field of Soviet law — initially at the federal level and, in most cases, subsequently at the constituent union republic level. This volume is the first complete compilation of translations in English of the codes of law of the Russian Republic, and also those federal codes where there is federal jurisdiction in that particular field.

207. Tarschys, Daniel. **The Soviet Political Agenda: Problems and Priorities, 1950-1970.** White Plains, NY: M. E. Sharpe, 1979. viii, 217p. $20.00.

This is a short, interesting book, unsatisfactory in some ways but well worth reading by those who teach and study Soviet politics. The substance of the book is an analysis of the content of *Pravda* editorials for 1950, 1960, and 1970. The purpose of the analysis is to examine the changing political agenda between 1950 and 1970, that is, the political leadership's perception of political priorities and the methods of dealing with them.

SR, 39:4:691

208. Tolstoy, Nikolai. **The Secret Betrayal: 1944-1947.** New York: Charles Scribner's Sons, 1978. 503p. $14.95.
This book tells of the forced repatriation by British and American authorities of several million Russians, Ukrainians, and Cossacks stranded in Western Europe in 1944 and early 1945. Some of these people had fought alongside the Axis powers in the hope of liberating their homelands from Soviet Communism. When they arrived in the Soviet Union, they met a fate that they had fearfully anticipated—most were either summarily shot by NKVD officials, tortured and eventually hanged, or sent to prison work camps in the Soviet Arctic where few have survived. This book is an important contribution to the literature of "Big Three" diplomacy during World War II.

209. Valenta, Jiri. **Soviet Intervention in Czechoslovakia 1968: Anatomy of a Decision.** Baltimore: The Johns Hopkins University Press, 1979. xii, 208p. $12.00.
Valenta, who fled his native country in the wake of the 1968 upheavals, has produced a thoroughly readable, dispassionate account of the complex processes of decision making in the Soviet Union that ultimately led to the fateful determination that military intervention in Czechoslovakia was unavoidable. The study is a model of scholarship. The author has canvassed just about all the documentary material relevant to his subject and has conducted a number of interviews with participants and participant observers in the events to fill in gaps in the literature and buttress his knowledge.
RR, 39:3:385-86

Communism, Communist Party

210. Dallin, Alexander, ed. **The Twenty-Fifth Congress of the CPSU: Assessment and Context.** Stanford: Hoover Institution Press, 1977. xii, 127p. $5.95.
This volume resulted from a conference held at Stanford University to review the record of the Twenty-Fifth Congress. There are nine essays ranging from science policy to the economy and foreign policy. This is a useful summary that should stimulate readers to delve more deeply into some of the problems touched on at the conference.
SEER, 27:1:145-46

211. Ryavec, Karl W., ed. **Soviet Society and the Communist Party.** Amherst: University of Massachusetts Press, 1978. xviii, 220p. $15.00.
This collection of eight original essays is the end product of two conferences at which the nature of the Soviet Communist Party and its capability for managing change in society were examined. All but one of the essays is concerned with the post-Stalin period, and most focus on the post-Khrushchev years. Several authors offer some tentative, near-term projections based on trends that they have observed in some depth.
SR, 39:3:508-509

212. Service, Robert. **The Bolshevik Party in Revolution: A Study in Organizational Change 1917-1923.** New York: Barnes & Noble, 1979. 246p. Maps. $24.50.
The author provides a comprehensive answer to the question: How did the Bolshevik party emerge in the period 1917-1923 to dominate state administration? He starts with a picture of great disarray, rent at all levels by major differences of outlook, and neglectful of organizational tasks and responsibilities. In this analysis, a Stalinist party is shown to have developed as much or more from local pressures after 1917 as from pressures from above. The Orgburo and the burgeoning Secretariat were responses to practical needs. This process paralleled efforts to streamline the state apparatus, and thus the party prepared

itself for an easy transition to actually exercising state authority when Sovnarkom was ready to release it, according to the reviewer of this book.

RR, 39:1:84-86

213. Wesson, Robert G. **Lenin's Legacy: The Story of the CPSU**. Histories of Ruling Communist Parties series. Stanford, CA: Hoover Institution Press, 1978. xviii, 318p. Appendices. $7.50, paper.

Wesson uses the supreme leadership of the party as the main theme of his book, which is basically divided into four sections, devoted respectively to Lenin, Stalin, Khrushchev, and Brezhnev. This is a readable and up-to-date synthesis of writings in English. It contains tables showing Politburo and Secretariat membership in 1977, party membership since 1905, ethnic composition, percent of female membership, age distribution, social status, number of local party organs, educational level of party members, and a short bibliographical note.

SR, 38:2:305-306

Police Terror, Espionage, Propaganda

214. Carmichael, Joel. **Stalin's Masterpiece: The "Show Trials" and Purges of the Thirties — The Consolidation of the Bolshevik Dictatorship.** London: Weidenfield & Nicolson, 1976. viii, 238p. £6.95.

Between August 1936 and the end of 1938, literally all of the old Bolshevik leaders were brought before the court, and accused of treason and espionage, to which they ardently confessed and were sentenced and immediately executed or else they perished in camps. This book is full of plausible assumptions and intelligent questions. First, it presents a short but clear historical perspective, going back to the Bolshevik putsch in October 1917. Second, it explains the significance of "Trotskyism" during the trials and, finally, Carmichael, perhaps less successfully, attempts to penetrate the motive behind Stalin's macabre "masterpiece." On balance, the book is an important contribution to our understanding and knowledge of the show trials.

CSP, 19:3:377-78

215. Conquest, Robert. **Kolyma — The Arctic Death Camps.** London: Macmillan, 1978. 256p. £6.95.

This book is concerned with the forced labor camps in the basins of the river Kolyma and Indigirka, North Eastern Siberia, in the period of Stalinism, roughly from 1930 to 1954. A considerable part of the book is devoted to the presentation of the conditions of work and death in the Kolyma camps. According to the author's calculations, the number of slave-laborers working at any one time in Kolyma was between 300,000 to 500,000 in the period 1944 to 1954 and probably somewhat lower in the previous years. During the quarter of a century of Stalinist industrialization, probably about three million people lost their lives in the Kolyma slave camps.

216. Dolgun, Alexander, with Patrick Watson. **Alexander Dolgun's Story: An American in the Gulag.** New York: Alfred A. Knopf, 1975. viii, 370p. $10.00.

Dolgun — an American citizen and clerk in the American embassy in Moscow, who was arrested in 1948, released from Gulag in 1956, and allowed to leave the USSR in 1971 — survived the worst of Stalin's prisons, in part by playing teasing games with the interrogators. His story is the implicit lesson to be learned from the volume — that Stalinism is farce as well as tragedy.

SR, 35:2:340-41

217. Gerson, Lennard D. **The Secret Police in Lenin's Russia.** Philadelphia: Temple University Press, 1976. xvi, 332p. + 8pp. photographs. $15.00.
This book is clearly written, meticulously documented, and as unbiased as a man of evident humanist sympathies can make a discussion of such a grim subject. Gerson emphasizes Lenin's personal role in sponsoring and encouraging the Cheka, particularly in its ruthless disregard for procedure (or, precisely, for everything we associate with the rule of law). The reviewer expresses the opinion that this fatal tendency in the Soviet system goes back to its origins. By 1922 the basic spheres of Cheka activity—secret informer networks, concentration camps, praetorian internal troops, and frontier guards—had been firmly established.
> SR, 36:2:302-303

218. Glaser, Kurt, and Stefan T. Possony. **Victims of Politics: The State of Human Rights.** New York: Columbia University Press, 1979. xvi, 614p. Illus. $35.00.
This book recounts instances of human rights violations under such rubrics as racial discrimination; class, caste, and sex discrimination; discrimination against entire cultures; language, religions; mass expulsions; slavery, forced labor; torture; and genocide. The authors draw on examples from a variety of countries but focus heavily on the USSR.
> SR, 39:3:510-11

219. Powell, David E. **Antireligious Propaganda in the Soviet Union.** Cambridge, MA: MIT Press, 1975. x, 206p. $25.00.
The author has marshaled a large number of tables, graphs, and maps to analyze the ideological warfare waged by the Soviet regime against the dwindling band of religious believers. His data attest to the enormous resources expended in this effort: tens of thousands of propagandists, reams of literature, stocks of films and museum displays. Yet the data also support the ironic conclusion that, in Powell's words, antireligious propaganda appears to be "an exercise in futility and self-deception ... an instrument that stimulates and reinforces the religious convictions it aims to destroy."
> CSP, 18:1:103-104

220. Trepper, Leopold. **The Great Game: Memoirs of the Spy Hitler Couldn't Silence.** New York: McGraw-Hill, 1977. xii, 442p. Photographs. $10.95.
The author of this book was the organizer from 1938 to 1942 of a Soviet spy network covering Brussels, Paris, and Berlin. The Gestapo called it *die rote Kapelle*, and it is familiar to newspaper and thriller readers as the Red Orchestra. By ethnic origin, Trepper is a Polish Jew, born near Cracow in 1904. He joined the Communist Party in Palestine in 1925 and was an active militant there and in France until 1932, when he went to Moscow. In 1938 he founded his spy network in Brussels for the Red Army intelligence. This book shows as false several prevalent notions about the nature of espionage and Communism. Though the author feels aggrieved, with good reason, he tries hard to tell the truth.
> SR, 37:1:130-31

Dissent Movement

221. Barghoorn, Frederick C. **Détente and the Democratic Movement in the USSR.** New York and London: The Free Press and Collier Macmillan, 1976. x, 229p. $12.95.
Barghoorn examines post-Khrushchev foreign policy from the new and unique perspective provided by the critical voices of dissent. His sources are the part of the broad spectrum of dissent that has articulated demands for greater civil liberties and human rights. In specific, the author discusses views of Sakharov, Solzhenitsyn, Amalrik, Galanskov, and Roy

Medvedev. He recommends continued pressure by individuals and groups in America on behalf of those struggling for human rights in the USSR.

SR, 36:2:310-11

222. Dunlop, John B. **The New Russian Revolutionaries.** Belmont, MA: Nordland Publishing Company, 1976. 344p. $18.50.

In early 1967, the KGB uncovered an oppositionist organization consisting of barely a score of members, who were arrested and brought to trial. The group called itself All-Russian Social-Christian Union for the Liberation of the People, and its members were known as the Berdiaevites, having derived their intellectual inspiration from Nikolai Berdiaev's *The New Middle Ages.* The author has reconstructed the biographies of the main leaders, chronicled the life and collapse of the organization, described the arrests, trials, and imprisonments of the members, and provided a summary of the main programmatic tenets and of their intellectual sources. In his conclusion, Dunlop points to a similarity between the Decembrists and the new Russian revolutionaries.

SR, 39:1:124-25

223. Fireside, Harvey. **Soviet Psychoprisons.** Foreword by Zhores Medvedev. New York: Norton, 1979. 201p. $11.95.

This volume adds much recent useful and significant information on the subject of Soviet psychoprisons. The historical background of psychiatric interment of dissidents, the internal politics of the Soviet psychiatric profession, recent organized dissident efforts to stop the practice, and other features are all useful complements to our present knowledge. Fireside's volume is a useful mode of delegitimating the barbaric policy both in the USSR and elsewhere, and perhaps its broadest value lies therein.

NP, 9:1:144-45

224. Grigorenko, Peter G. **The Grigorenko Papers: Writings by General P. G. Grigorenko and Documents on His Case.** Introduction by Edward Crankshaw. Boulder, CO: Westview Press, 1976 [Amsterdam: Alexander Herzen Foundation, 1973]. viii, 187p. $12.50.

The life of Peter Grigorenko is similar to the kind of model life that Soviet journalists so love to describe in feature stories under a heading like, "From a Farm Laborer to a General." Just when Grigorenko's career had progressed to its logical end—retirement—a new and seemingly unexpected life began for him: organization of an underground union to fight for the revival of Leninism, then came his arrest, reduction to the ranks and declaration of insanity, release and participation in the human rights movement, rearrest, and almost five years in KGB prisons and prison psychiatric hospitals. At the age of 70, he became one of the founders of the Helsinki Group.

SR, 37:2:316-17

225. Harasowska, Marta, and Orest Olhovych, eds. **The International Sakharov Hearing.** Baltimore: Smoloskyp Publishers, 1977. 335p. $8.95.

The Common Committee of East European Exiles in Denmark sponsored a public hearing in Copenhagen in October 1975 on human rights in the USSR. The oral testimony of 24 Soviet émigrés who testified at that hearing is reproduced in this volume. Testimony, focusing on the period 1965 to 1975, is grouped under four headings: "Political Oppression and the Persecution of Dissidents," "The Fight against Religion and the Suffering of the Faithful," "The Abuse of Psychiatry," and "The Oppression of Non-Russian Nationalities in the Soviet Union." The book brings to light many important and interesting allegations that warrant verification.

SR, 38:4:689-90

226. Haynes, Victor, and Olga Semyonova, eds. **Workers against the Gulag: The New Opposition in the Soviet Union.** London: Pluto Press, 1979. 129p. £1.95.
The author of this book is angry, resentful. He documents case after case of illegal dismissal, discrimination, victimization, and imprisonment in the Soviet Union. The Novocherkassk riots are touched on and there is much on trade unions, strikes, and protests, with the authors arguing that every Soviet citizen should have the right to emigrate should he/she so wish. A considerable amount of documentation is provided on the Free Trade Union Association of Soviet Working People which came into being in late 1977.
SEER, 58:3:478

227. Medvedev, Roy A., ed. **The Samizdat Register.** W. W. Norton, 1977. viii, 314p. $10.95.
This volume offers selections from the first three issues of the journal *The Twentieth Century*, providing an opportunity for a Western audience to overhear the debate between Marxist dissenters and their conservative rivals regarding Soviet past and present reality.
SR, 38:1:133-34

228. Meerson-Aksenov, Michael, and Boris Shragin, eds. **The Political, Social and Religious Thought of Russian "Samizdat": An Anthology.** Translated by Nickolas Lupinin. Belmont, MA: Nordland Publishing Company, 1977. 624p. $29.50.
This anthology is a pathbreaker because it consists of essays by men who are recognized as professional intellectuals in a full sense, that is, as men of thought, many of whom have academic training in philosophy and other humanities. The volume is subdivided into the following subsections: "Socialism with a Human Face," "Personality, Freedom, and Responsibility," "The Human Rights Movement," "The Debate over the Democratic Movements," "The Debate over the National Renaissance in Russia," "Revolutionary Democracy," and "The Jewish Question in the USSR." This book should be on the list of required reading for professors dealing with the Soviet Union.
NP, 7:2:226-27

229. Podrabinek, Alexander. **Punitive Medicine.** Ann Arbor, MI: Karoma Publishers, 1980. 237p. $12.95.
This is an English translation of the Russian text published by Khronika Press in 1979. Podrabinek discusses material available to him at the time of writing (1976 to 1977), examining the historical, legal, and medical aspects of incarceration in general and special psychiatric hospitals, with numerous references to individual cases and personal reports.

230. Rubenstein, Joshua. **Soviet Dissidents: Their Struggle for Human Rights.** Beacon, NY: Beacon House, 1980. 288p. $12.95.
This study provides a good history of the Soviet dissident movement from its roots in the Khrushchev years to Andrei Sakharov's exile from Moscow. The book, which is based upon interviews as well as documentary sources, offers insights into the motives and the philosophies of leading dissidents. Rubenstein describes the variety of groups criticizing the Soviet regime and its policies. The book is especially valuable for the layperson concerned with human rights or current affairs.
LJBR, 1980:368

231. Sakharov, Andrei D. **My Country and the World.** Translated by Guy V. Daniels. New York: Alfred A. Knopf, 1975. xvi, 109p. $5.95.
Sakharov is well aware that all the changes, both material and cultural, he spells out for the

peaceful evolution of Soviet society, on the basis of its modified socialist economy, depend as much on the policies of the relatively free nations of the West as on events within the Soviet Union. He is convinced that the political rulers of the Soviet Union are extremely sensitive to public opinion in the West and to the policies of the nations in NATO. He deplores the absence of unity among the Western countries in their attitudes towards the Soviet Union.

RR, 35:4:486-87

232. Sakharov, Vladimir, and Umberto Tosi. **High Treason.** New York: G. P. Putnam's Sons, 1980. 318p. $11.95.

Sakharov writes of his privileged youth among the elite of Soviet Russia, his exclusive education, and his promising career as a Soviet foreign service officer and part-time KGB agent. This autobiography offers a view of the new Communist elite and presents the argument that a principal Soviet goal is to strangle the West by controlling the Middle East and its oil. The book is suitable for the general reader more than for an expert.

LJBR, 1980:125

233. Shatz, Marshall S. **Soviet Dissent in Historical Perspective.** Cambridge: Cambridge University Press, 1980. x, 214p. $19.95.

Against the background of modern Russian history, Shatz uses autobiographical and literary sources to uncover the personal roots of dissent, tracing relations between the Russian state and the educated classes from the tsarist period to the present. Shatz's analysis shows how pre-Stalinist patterns are repeating themselves in the post-Stalin period.

234. Solzhenitsyn, Alexander, et al. **From under the Ruble.** Translated by A. M. Brock. Introduction by Max Hayward. Boston and Toronto: Little, Brown & Company, 1975. xii, 308p. $8.95.

Consciously invoking the spirit of the *Vekhi* group, the essays in this volume are rooted in a nationally Russian and spiritually Christian outlook. They are, primarily, a writ of accusation against the Russian intelligentsia for having deserted its people, their traditions and destiny. The essays, expressing the views of what has emerged as the conservative and nationalist wing of the dissident movement in the USSR, were written between 1971 and 1974, when all the authors were still in Russia.

SR, 35:3:544

235. Tökés, Rudolf L., ed. **Dissent in the USSR: Politics, Ideology, and People.** Baltimore and London: The Johns Hopkins University Press, 1975. xvi, 453p. $15.00.

This book raises some key issues: the political significance of dissent; the range of ideas, beliefs, and convictions that motivate dissident activities; the methods of communication; and what, if anything, is being accomplished through dissent. None of these problems is, or as yet can be, resolved. That the contributors raised these issues is a token of competence and understanding. Most of the names that appear in its role of prominent Soviet dissidents are now living abroad. This book is essential to all who would understand unofficial Russia.

SR, 37:4:683-85

DIPLOMACY AND FOREIGN POLICY

General Works

236. Eran, Oded. **Mezhdunarodniki: An Assessment of Professional Expertise in the Making of Soviet Foreign Policy.** Ramat Gan, Israel: Turtledove Publishing, 1979. 331p. $18.50.

This book traces the development and role of the various Soviet institutes specializing in international relations and area studies. The author focuses primarily on the relationship between the institutes and the party elite, seeking explanation for the frequent organizational and cadre changes and the fluctuations taking place on wider policy debates. The book's value is limited to a source of general information on the Soviet institutes.

237. Schwartz, Morton. **The Foreign Policy of the USSR: Domestic Factors.** Comparative Foreign Relation Series. Encino and Belmont, CA: Dickenson Publishing Company, 1975. ix, 214p. $15.95.

This is a stimulating effort toward explaining Soviet policy as an interplay of domestic and external factors. Schwartz examines environmental, demographic, and economic strengths and weaknesses; Soviet military capabilities; political processes; attitudes and values of leaders regarding the Soviet role in world affairs. This book provides students with a foundation for further reading, helping them to develop an interest in deeper study.

SR, 35:1:138-39

To 1917

238. Bartley, Russell H. **Imperial Russia and the Struggle for Latin American Independence, 1808-1828.** Austin, TX: Institute of Latin American Studies, University of Texas at Austin, 1978. xviii, 236p. $14.95. Distributed by University of Texas Press, Austin, TX.

Bartley views the end of the Napoleonic Wars as auguring a transitional phase in Russian New World policy as Tsar Alexander I moved away "from the pursuit of broad commercial and geopolitical advantages throughout the Western Hemisphere to the defense of a modest presence in California and Brazil." This shift in policy evinced a pragmatic reappraisal and limitation of Russian objectives in North America. Brazil, in particular, became "a key link in the chain of maritime communications" binding the Russian colonies in the Pacific Northwest to St. Petersburg. With its use of Russian, Spanish, and Portuguese archival materials, the study illuminates various aspects of Russian New World policy.

SR, 39:1:116-17

239. Cross, A. G. **By the Banks of the Thames: Russians in Eighteenth Century Britain.** Newtonville, MA: Oriental Research Partners, 1980. viii, 358p. $22.50.

In addition to at least a dozen British manuscript repositories, Cross has worked in four of the main Soviet collections. He has also consulted a wide range of printed sources and secondary works in his search for Russians who spent time in Britain in the eighteenth century, some 512 of whom he has succeeded in identifying. The book deals also with Russian diplomats and chaplains, students of all kinds, and N. M. Karamzin's "Love affair with England"—a case study of the "Anglophilia" of the late eighteenth century that helped give rise to the Russian "Anglomania" of the early nineteenth century. This book is the first of a projected two volumes on eighteenth-century Anglo-Russian relations.

RR, 39:4:495

240. Gillard, David. **The Struggle for Asia, 1828-1914: A Study in British and Russian Imperialism.** London: Methuen, 1977. viii, 214p. £8.95.

This book is an essay on the relations between Britain and Russia in the nineteenth century. It is first-rate, by far the best work on the subject. It can best be appreciated by those who already have a good knowledge of the modern history of Europe and Asia. More than half the book is concerned with the first 30 years, from the Russo-Persian war to the end of the Crimean War. A further 40 pages take the reader to the completion of the Franco-Russian convention, followed by the periods of Anglo-Russian rivalry and the Russo-Japanese war.

SEER, 57:4:602-604

241. Ingle, Harold N. **Nesselrode and the Russian Rapprochement with Britain, 1836-1844.** Berkeley: University of California Press, 1976. xi, 196p. $11.75.

The author treats the events of a crucial period in Russian-European relations in the context of his chief protagonist's convictions and hopes and thereby gives predominant place to the moral questions underlying the hardnosed world of diplomacy. Nesselrode, a German Protestant who entered the tsar's service in 1796, apprenticed at Russian embassies in Western Europe, helped negotiate the settlements after Napoleon's defeat, and in 1816 took charge of the Ministry of Foreign Affairs, a post he kept until 1856. The Straits Convention of 1841, which assured closure of the Dardanelles and Turkish neutrality, marked the triumph of his policies. The book, which is thoroughly researched and carefully argued, successfully portrays Nesselrode as a talented diplomat.

CSP, 19:1:93-94

242. Kennan, George F. **The Decline of Bismarck's European Order: Franco-Russian Relations, 1875-1890.** Princeton, NJ: Princeton University Press, 1979. xii, 466p. $25.00.

Kennan's central interest is Russian foreign policy – the men who made it, the interests it served, the schemers who sought to influence it, and the view of Europe as seen from St. Petersburg. Bismarck is there, of course, looming large in the calculations, and especially the suspicions, of the Russian leaders; and a parade of lesser French characters keeps popping on and off stage. The spotlight, however, remains pretty consistently fixed on Petersburg. Kennan believes, despite the prevailing mood of historians these days, that individuals can and do play important roles in history.

RR, 39:4:499-500

1917 to the Present

243. Debo, Richard K. **Revolution and Survival: The Foreign Policy of Soviet Russia, 1917-18.** Toronto and Buffalo: University of Toronto Press, 1979. xiv, 462p. $25.00.

Debo's Lenin is the theorist-cum-pragmatist who never gave up his dedication to revolution, but who, almost without ever having intended to do so, found himself defending a nation and his right to rule it. Consciously rejecting the Trotskyesque dream of immediate and permanent revolution, Lenin sought realistic ways to maintain Bolshevik power. This book is a valuable addition to our analyses and understanding of Soviet foreign policy.

SR, 39:2:307-308

244. Edmonds, Robin. **Soviet Foreign Policy, 1962-73: The Paradox of Super Power.**
New York: Oxford University Press, 1975. xiv, 197p. $12.00.
The period covered here begins with the nuclear war scare of October 1962 and ends with
the global nuclear alert of October 1973. It is the merit of Edmonds' book that he follows
the decisions of Soviet policy step by step, issue by issue, and year by year, relating them to
each other and to the Soviet internal situation, which was always the leaders' first concern.
During this time, the leadership's decisions were, above all, practical, sometimes dictated
by events, often the result of tentative and uneasy compromises, certainly not the
predetermined results of a fixed long-term strategy or ideology. The author, a senior
British diplomat who was minister in Moscow in 1969 to 1972, describes Soviet policy with
clarity and an economy of words.
RR, 35:2:215-16

245. Griffith, William E., ed. **The Soviet Empire: Expansion and Détente.** Critical
Choices for Americans, vol. 9. Lexington, MA, and Toronto: Lexington Books, D.
C. Heath, 1976. xxii, 421p. Tables. Map. $19.95.
Two features of this volume distinguish it from most edited works on Soviet foreign policy
and make it particularly useful for both specialists and general readers. Several of the
chapters, addressed specifically to analysis of internal developments that may or may not
affect present and future Soviet conduct abroad, make a real contribution toward a
balanced and comprehensive perspective on complex and controversial issues. The Soviet
Union is not seen as an ideologically motivated revolutionary power that places great
reliance on military strength and that will attempt to expand its influence on a global scale.
SR, 37:4:679-80

246. Kohler, Foy D., et al. **Soviet Strategy for the Seventies: From Cold War to Peaceful
Coexistence.** Miami: University of Miami Press, 1977. v, 241p. $7.95.
This is not a new book (it was published eight years earlier and reprinted in 1977), but in
this lies its great advantage—it has withstood the test of time with an almost uncanny
prescience, which only demonstrates the authors' profound understanding of the
immutables in Soviet foreign policy. In the analytical part of the book, the authors trace
the evolution of the concept and policy of "peaceful coexistence" from its initial
formulation by Lenin in 1921 to its role in Soviet foreign policy under Brezhnev.
Considering that the book was written well before active Soviet involvement in the
struggles in Africa and invasion of Afghanistan, it can be regarded as truly prophetic.
CSP, 21:1:116-17

247. Lowenthal, Richard. **Model or Ally?: The Communist Powers and the Developing
Countries.** New York: Oxford University Press, 1977. xii, 400p. $12.95.
Lowenthal's work is devoted to a number of variations of the central theme—"Model or
Ally?" Basically, it is an anthology of articles published by him on previous occasions,
suitably updated and amended. It is a remarkably coherent book and will provide a most
useful and readable text for all students concerned with this aspect of Soviet international
policy.
SR, 36:4:687-89

248. Mastng, Vojtech. **Russia's Road to the Cold War: Diplomacy, Warfare, and the
Politics of Communism, 1941-1945.** New York: Columbia University Press, 1979.
xxii, 409p. $16.95.
This is a book that should be read and pondered by everyone concerned with the foreign
policy of the Soviet Union as it was shaped by the conflicts and alliances of the Second

World War. The two principal reasons for the book's excellence are: 1) the author's mastery of the formidable, diverse, and controversial literature on Soviet actions and interactions in the wartime and early post-war period; and 2) his refreshing lack of inhibitions in candidly stating conclusions, such as the flat judgment that "the evils of the Soviet system were the ultimate course of the Cold War."

SR, 39:1:122-23

249. McCagg, William, Jr. **Stalin Embattled, 1943-1948.** Detroit: Wayne State University Press, 1978. 423p. $18.95.

Other authors who have attempted an analysis of the origins of the Cold War generally restrict their research to the area of foreign policy, but McCagg has attempted a much more ambitious project. Although he has focused on a short span of years, 1943 to 1948, his inquiry into Soviet affairs covers a large slice of Russian life. From his perspective, Soviet foreign policy cannot be grasped unless the hidden domestic issues and struggles are appreciated. The year 1945 represented for Stalin not only victory over Nazi Germany, but a challenge to stop the erosion of his power and, if possible, to regain the absolute control which he had inevitably lost during the war years. McCagg suggests that the Cold War was the result of confusion and misunderstanding. Western leaders simply failed to understand that Stalin was forced to use a revolutionary vocabulary and failed to see that his practical actions were essentially opposed to revolution.

CSP, 22:3:420-21

With the United States

250. Bolkhovitinov, Nikolai N. **The Beginnings of Russian-American Relations, 1775-1815.** Translated by Elena Levin. Cambridge, MA: Harvard University Press, 1975. xx, 484p. $35.00.

This account of early Russian-American relations first appeared in Russian in 1966. This revised and expanded version should prove a classic. Diplomatic and commercial relations, within the general European context, are analyzed. Russian America is examined, as are the impressions of Americans in Russia and Russians in America. The attitudes American leaders have toward Russia — and those of Catherine II, Alexander I, Radishchev, Novikov, Karamzin, and others to America — are discussed. The image of Russia in the American press and vice versa is considered.

CSP, 19:1:92-93

251. Bolkhovitinov, Nikolai N. **Russia and the American Revolution.** Translated and edited by C. Jay Smith. Tallahassee, FL: The Diplomatic Press, 1976. xvi, 277p. $29.70.

Concentrating on a limited part of the period, this volume differs from the original Russian text in the omission of discussions of John Ledyard in Siberia and of John Paul Jones in Russia. The work deals with diplomatic, trade, scientific, and cultural relations between the two countries, and chapters are devoted to the American theme in the Russian press, to Radishchev and America, and to the participation of natives of Russia in the War of Independence. The reports of Russian diplomats on the American Revolution are published for the first time in the appendix. The translator has added helpful, explanatory notes of his own as footnotes.

CSP, 19:1:92-93

252. Cate, Curtis. **The Ides of August: The Berlin Wall Crisis, 1961.** New York: M. Evans & Co., 1978. x, 534p. + 16pp. plates. Maps. $15.00.

Cate has written a very good book about a critical American-Soviet confrontation. In 1961, encouraged by the Bay of Pigs debacle, Khrushchev decided to end the unacceptable drain on East Germany's manpower. By closing the porous East Berlin border, he hoped to strengthen Walter Ulbricht's authority, to end the exodus, and eventually to evict the Western powers from Berlin. While the Berlin Wall was built, Western leaders remained unsure of what to do. Only after a week, when the collapse of public morale in Germany had reached critical proportions, the decision was made to send Vice-President Johnson, aided by Lucius Clay and by the dispatch of a small contingent of troops, to Berlin. The book deserves a wide readership, especially among young Americans who do not know enough about the history of their country.

    SR, 39:2:318-19

253. Dinerstein, Herbert S. **The Making of a Missile Crisis: October 1962.** Baltimore and London: The Johns Hopkins University Press, 1976. xiv, 302p. $14.95.
The Cuban missile crisis of 1962 has been well recorded by historians and dramatists. This highly researched book gives the reader an insight into the causes of that crisis, dating back to when the Soviets first introduced arms into Latin America in Guatemala in 1954 at the peak of the Cold War. According to Dinerstein, faulty perceptions, miscalculations, and varying theories within and among the three involved nations (USSR, Cuba, USA) led to a situation that none of these three desired and all could have avoided. This book should be required reading for the student of world diplomacy and Russian, Latin American, and United States foreign policy.

    SR, 36:1:109-110

254. Eidelberg, Paul. **Beyond Détente: Toward an American Foreign Policy.** La Salle, IL: Sherwood Sugden & Company, 1977. xvi, 255p. $12.95.
The author of this book is convinced that America's drift toward military weakness, when contrasted to the build-up of Soviet power, has destroyed United States will and reduced its interest in confronting the expansion of Soviet influence around the globe. He asserts that détente has destroyed the will of the United States to protect the world against Soviet encroachments.

    SR, 38:2:308-309

255. Friedland, Edward, Paul Seabury, and Aaron Wildavsky. **The Great Détente: Oil and the Decline of American Foreign Policy.** New York: Basic Books, 1975. x, 210p. $7.95.
This is not a scholarly study but a book written by three scholars who are upset about the position of the United States in the world as a result of U.S.-Soviet détente and the oil crisis of 1973-1974. They conclude that the Soviet Union, taking advantage of the West's myopia about détente and inability to define and defend its own vital interests, is making uncontested gains so that the choice must now be made between defense and surrender, between order and disorder.

    SR, 35:3:536-37

256. Gaddis, John Lewis. **Russia, the Soviet Union and the United States: An Interpretive History.** New York, Santa Barbara, CA, Toronto: John Wiley & Sons, 1978. xiii, 309p. £9.20.
This is a well-written and well-informed account of the relations between two powers from the time of the American Revolution. Its two main themes may be stated as follows: 1) that the relations of the powers, whether under the tsars or the Communists, have been far better than is generally believed; and 2) that conflict only arose when an ideological factor

was imposed upon these relations. This is an excellent book for students as well as for those interested in the relations between Russia and America.

SEER, 58:3:450-51

257. Harriman, W. Averell, and Elie Abel. **Special Envoy to Churchill and Stalin, 1941-1946.** New York: Random House, 1975. xii, 595p. + 16pp. photographs. $15.00.

This is a well-written, familiar story of the Big Three relationships during World War II, told from Averell Harriman's angle of vision. What is new in this book is the insight into Harriman's own character and the tart judgments he makes of the men with whom he worked. He presents himself as a vigorous man of action and sound judgment, skilled in diplomacy. If he has changed his mind on anything, he does not mention it. Of Stalin he says: "I found him better informed than Roosevelt, more realistic than Churchill, in some ways the most effective of the war leaders. At the same time he was, of course, a murderous tyrant."

SR, 36:2:307-308

258. Kushner, Howard I. **Conflict on the Northwest Coast: American-Russian Rivalry in the Pacific Northwest, 1790-1867.** Contributions in American History, no. 41. Westport, CT, and London: Greenwood Press, 1975. xii, 228p. $13.95.

This study attributes the purchase of Alaska to constant friction between the United States and Russia, which began with the appearance of American maritime fur traders on the Northwest Coast and lasted until Russia, convinced that she would lose Alaska to an expansionistic America anyway, decided to depart gracefully. There is much evidence to bear out this thesis. There are extensive notes and a lengthy bibliography that will be useful to other researchers.

SR, 35:4:735

259. Larson, Thomas B. **Soviet-American Rivalry.** New York and Toronto: W. W. Norton and George J. McLeod, 1978. xii, 308p. $13.95.

Larson, a veteran State Department official, has written an excellent study of the complex relationship between Moscow and Washington. It is not merely an examination of bilateral relations between the two superpowers, but a sophisticated investigation of their interactions in the economic, ideological, military, political, and diplomatic arenas. In comparing the achievements and failures of the two superpowers, the author has achieved a remarkable degree of objectivity. In addition, the information on a wide range of topics contained in his book will be useful to students, businessmen, and political leaders.

SR, 38:3:497-98

260. Libbey, James K. **Alexander Gumberg and Soviet American Relations, 1917-1933.** Lexington: The University Press of Kentucky, 1977. xii, 229p. $13.50.

This study is based upon apparently exhaustive research in the papers of Alexander S. Gumberg, who was closely associated with the well-known group of colorful Americans in Russia during 1917 to 1918, and also with Americans prominent in business and politics during 1921 to 1933. Libbey has consulted other private papers for further information on the role played by Gumberg, an unofficial agent in the effort to normalize Soviet-American relations, especially during the time of the Harding, Coolidge, and Hoover administrations. He was born in Russia in 1887 and immigrated to the United States in 1902. His two brothers were Bolsheviks and occupied high positions in Soviet Russia.

SR, 37:2:299

261. Maddux, Thomas R. **Years of Estrangement: American Relations with the Soviet Union, 1933-1941.** Tallahassee, FL: University Presses of Florida, 1980. ix, 238p. $15.00.

Maddux's account of U.S.-Soviet relations during the "years of estrangement" effectively captures the conflict between the two governments, along with the inconsistent policies that resulted from the fact that neither country's wartime approach succeeded in fully displacing the other. The result, Maddux concludes, was the worst of both worlds—a set of wartime agreements, concluded by Roosevelt that Moscow would be very unlikely to keep, and an American public so indoctrinated with unrealistic expectations of the future course of Soviet conduct that overreaction, and a consequent plunge into undifferentiated hostility when the postwar conflicts of interest emerged, was inevitable.
    RR, 40:1:65-66

262. Martel, Leon. **Lend-Lease, Loans, and the Coming of the Cold War: A Study of the Implementation of Foreign Policy.** Boulder, CO: Westview Press, 1979. xx, 304p. $24.50.

This is a good book in which the author examines a wide variety of government archives and private papers to present the first proper history of Soviet requests for reconstruction aid after World War II. Martel shows that after the extension of the lending capacity of the Export-Import Bank in July 1945, the State Department deliberately delayed a decision on the proposed loan of one billion dollars because it believed that the money might be used for military purposes and because it wanted concessions from Moscow, such as allowing a wider range of political participation in East European governments.
    SR, 40:1:119-20

263. **National Security and Détente.** Foreword by General Andrew J. Goodpaster. With contributions by faculty members of the U.S. Army War College. New York: Thomas Y. Crowell, 1976. xxiv, 360p. $10.00.

This symposium, in addition to General Goodpaster's thoughtful essay on the ambiguities of the American-Soviet relationship, contains 17 separate contributions by members of the faculty of the Army War College and its subordinate departments. The essays cover a wide range of geographical and functional aspects relating to contemporary international politics. This volume provides a stimulating cross-fertilization with other specialties and disciplines.
    SR, 37:2:303-304

264. Rummel, R. J. **Peace Endangered: The Reality of Détente.** Beverly Hills, CA, and London: Sage, 1976. x, 189p. $10.00.

Rummel's study of U.S.-Soviet relations focuses on the military balance and its effect on American interests and will. For him, a successful deterrent requires the prevention of Soviet first-strike capability, power to cover all danger points, and conventional forces of sufficient strength to deter or win a local, limited war without resorting to nuclear weapons. He believes that détente was based on false assumptions, and it placed the United States in a position of military inferiority.
    SR, 38:2:308-309

265. Schwartz, Morton. **Soviet Perceptions of the United States.** Berkeley: University of California Press, 1978. viii, 216p. $12.50.

In this substantial, occasionally provocative study, Schwarz presents an image of the United States as portrayed in the publications of Moscow's U.S.A. Institute and the 1970 through 1976 issues of the Institute's journal *SShA*. Unfortunately, he has not compared the content of *SShA* with mass media reports or with statements about the United States made by Soviet political leaders. This omission somewhat weakens his argument that Soviet Americanists present an image significantly different from that contained in the mass media. Schwarz characterizes the Soviet Americanists as "scholar-publicists of détente." They have produced well-documented "Marxist" studies on the shaping of American foreign policy. The book offers solid information and informed judgment on a subject of vast importance.

SR, 38:4:685-87

266. Weeks, Albert L. **The Troubled Détente.** Introduction by Gene Sosin. New York: New York University Press, 1976. xxiv, 190p. $10.00.

Weeks approaches détente from the perspective of a Soviet specialist and traces, from Lenin to the mid-1970s, largely familiar aspects of Soviet doctrine on relations with capitalist countries. His emphasis is on continuing, underlying elements, though he notes fluctuations in operational Soviet policies over the decades. Weeks provides a useful, if selective, updating through the Twenty-Fifth Party Congress.

SR, 37:2:303-304

267. Yergin, Daniel. **Shattered Peace: The Origins of the Cold War and the National Security State.** Boston: Houghton Mifflin, 1977. xii, 526p. $15.00.

This book covers the years between the Yalta Conference and the Berlin blockade that marked the end of the wartime alliance. Of all Cold War studies that abound, *Shattered Peace* is probably the most thoroughly researched. The impressive bibliography contains dozens of interviews and unpublished private papers, many of which provide new information. Although his is a revisionist interpretation, Yergin maintains an appropriate distance from other revisionist writings that alternately blame the first atomic bombs on America's economic imperialism, multilateralism, and an alleged anti-Soviet purpose. According to Yergin, the Soviet Union can be seen as a revolutionary state that denies the possibility of coexistence and aims at world mastery.

SR, 38:1:117-18

With Communist Countries

268. **Behind Closed Doors: Secret Papers on the Failure of Romanian-Soviet Negotiations, 1931-1932.** Translated, with an Introductory Essay by Walter M. Bacon, Jr. Stanford: Hoover Institution Press, 1979. xv, 212p. $17.50.

This volume consists of 103 documents (letters, interdepartmental memos, telegrams, reports, drafts, and like material) dealing with the 1931-1932 Rumanian-Soviet secret negotiations for a nonaggression treaty. The evidence comes from the collection of Nicolae Titulescu, Rumanian Minister of Foreign Affairs, which is presently held in the archives at the Hoover Institution. The selections are preceded by the editor's excellent essay, which briefly traces Rumanian-Russian-Soviet relations before 1931, sets the stage for the negotiations, and reviews their progress. The central theme of these documents is the issue of Bessarabia.

RR, 39:1:91-92

269. Ginsburg, George, and Carl F. Pinkele. **The Sino-Soviet Territorial Dispute, 1949-1964.** New York: Praeger Publishers, 1978. viii, 145p. $16.95.

This excellent monograph provides a detailed and fascinating reconstruction of the Sino-Soviet territorial dispute in the 1962 through 1964 period. After reviewing the evidence of possible conflict over border issues in the 1950s, the authors analyze the public exchanges sparked by N. S. Krushchev's taunting criticism of the Chinese Communists' ostensible reluctance to destroy the last enclaves of Western imperialism on Chinese territory, and by the CPC's thinly veiled threat to challenge the legitimacy of the "unequal treaties" that provided the judicial basis of the Sino-Soviet border. It must be emphasized that the authors deal with the numerous *ex post facto* disclosures provided by Soviet and Chinese sources in the post-1964 period with great care and subtlety.

RR, 40:2:206-207

270. Leong, Sow-Theng. **Sino-Soviet Diplomatic Relations, 1917-1926.** Honolulu: The University Press of Hawaii, 1976. 362p. $15.00.

Leong cogently argues that, from the beginning, Soviet diplomacy toward China was motivated by self-interest. Intended for the serious student of Chinese history and of Soviet foreign policy, this work relies extensively on primary source material, published and unpublished, from the Institute of Modern History in Taiwan, Japanese primary source material, and Russian works.

History, 5:7(1977):158

271. Micunovic, Veljko. **Moscow Diary.** London: Chatto & Windus, 1980. xxvi, 474p. £12.50.

This is the English edition of the diaries of the Yugoslav ambassador to Moscow, covering the period from March 1956 to October 1958. Micunovic was the first ambassador from Yugoslavia to Moscow after the resumption of full diplomatic relations, was a personal friend of Tito, and developed particularly close personal contact with Khrushchev. His diaries thus give what is probably the nearest "inside view" of both Soviet-Yugoslav relations specifically and of Soviet domestic and foreign political affairs during that period.

SS, 32:4:613

272. Shanor, Donald R. **The Soviet Triangle: Russia's Relations with China and the West in the 1980s.** New York: St. Martin's Press, 1980. 288p. $13.95.

Shanor's study is a survey of Soviet foreign policy in the 1970s and prospects for the future. Successively treating Soviet relations with the People's Republic of China, the United States, and the European countries, Shanor also focuses on two major elements of détente policies: arms control and trade. He enriches his analysis with summaries of interviews with influential and ordinary citizens, especially in the Soviet Union and Eastern Europe. This volume is recommended for both public and academic collections.

LJBR, 1980:370

273. Wich, Richard. **Sino-Soviet Crisis Politics: A Study of Political Change and Communication.** Cambridge, MA: Council on East Asian Studies, Harvard University, 1980. 313p. $15.00.

This study focuses on the political changes that took place between the Soviet invasion of Czechoslovakia and the opening a year later of Sino-Soviet negotiations over the bitterly disputed border between the Soviet Union and China. The seismic events that followed on the world scene, notably the Sino-American and Sino-Japanese rapproachements, underlined the centrality of China to the major and decisive developments in the global balance of power. Wich's painstaking study will be primarily of interest to specialists.

LJBR, 1980:220

With Western and Third World Countries

274. Albright, David E., ed. **Communism in Africa.** Bloomington and London: Indiana University Press, 1980. vii, 278p. $12.95.
The marked intensification of Moscow's intrusion into Africa during the 1970s has revived academic interest in the role the Soviet Union is playing on that continent. This collection of essays is a product of this renewed concern, representing a significant and timely contribution to the understanding of the issues involved. Most of the authors are Americans and specialists on Communist affairs, rather than being Africans. The focus of the book is on "the dynamics of Soviet-African relations" and particularly on the USSR's priorities, objectives, and strategy in Africa.
     CSP, 23:3:362-63

275. Atkin, Muriel. **Russia and Iran, 1780-1828.** Minneapolis: University of Minnesota Press, 1980. xvi, 216p. Maps. $20.00.
Atkin presents a detailed discussion of Russian policy making and military activities, along with the situation of the Iranian monarchy and the work of British and French military and diplomatic missions in Iran. This work does break new ground as a useful contribution to the history of Russia's frontiers in Asia.
     LJBR, 1980:178

276. Calhoun, Daniel F. **The United Front: The TUC and the Russians 1923-1928.** New York: Cambridge University Press, 1976. xi, 450p. $27.50.
The focus of this study is on the changing relationship during the 1920s between the British Trades Union Congress (TUC) and the Soviet Union as represented by the Russian Communist Party, the Comintern, the Profintern, and the Russian trade union organization. The Comintern, controlled by the Bolsheviks, at the end of 1921 had adopted a united front policy that aspired to rally mass support for their programs through joint efforts with "reformist" elements in the European labor movement. The study makes a major scholarly contribution to the subject discussed.
     CSP, 19:4:512-13

277. Dawisha, Karen. **Soviet Foreign Policy towards Egypt.** London: Macmillan, 1979. 271p. £12.00.
In the course of the nine chapters of this book, the author first describes and then analyzes Soviet-Egyptian relations with painstaking thoroughness; the first section describes relations, while the second analyzes the situations. In the first part of the book, a detailed chronology of Soviet-Egyptian relations presents an accurate account of the arduous course of Soviet foreign policy with respect to Egypt. In the second part, the author analyzes the more often than not enigmatic motivations, intentions, and capabilities of Soviet foreign policy. This work is replete with illuminating tables and figures, well placed to help the reader through the complex economic and military data.
     SS, 32:3:434-35

278. DePorte, A. W. **Europe between the Superpowers: The Enduring Balance.** New Haven and London: Yale University Press, 1979. xvi, 256p. $18.50.
This is an excellent work, tightly argued and spritely written. It provides the best exposition in print of how the Euratlantik system came into being after World War II, why it appears strong, and why it apparently continues to grow and prosper. The book is a welcome and timely contribution to the debate over the Western response to Soviet expansion and turmoil in the Third World. The extension of the Brezhnev Doctrine to Asia and its

rejection of previous doctrines, based on support of national bourgeois regimes, pose new threats to Western cohesion. This is an important book for students and practitioners.

SR, 39:4:688-89

279. Donaldson, Robert H. **Soviet Policy toward India: Ideology and Strategy.** Cambridge, MA: Harvard University Press, 1974. xiv, 338p. $15.00.

Donaldson's study focuses on Soviet efforts to bring about changes in Marxist-Leninist doctrine to suit their changing postures toward India. He believes that considerations of Soviet national interests, rather than those of ideology, have determined Moscow's policy toward India. The author makes careful and judicious use of his sources. The book adds immensely to the understanding of Moscow's efforts to reinterpret Marxism-Leninism in order to justify or support changes in foreign policy.

SR, 36:2:316

280. Freedman, Robert O. **Soviet Policy toward the Middle East since 1970.** (Revised Edition). New York: Praeger Publishers, 1975. xii, 198p. $16.50.

This study deals primarily with Moscow's policy toward Egypt between 1970 and 1974, but with attention also given to Iraq, Syria, the Sudan, and Jordan. The book also contains a very brief introduction, a chapter on the 1945 to 1970 period, and a concluding chapter. There are, however, too many sweeping generalizations.

SR, 35:3:535-36

281. Ginsburgs, George, and Alvin Z. Rubinstein, eds. **Soviet Foreign Policy toward Western Europe.** Praeger Special Studies. New York and London: Praeger Publishers, 1978. viii, 295p. $20.00.

This book is divided into four sections. The first is the editors' introduction. The second section examines the major nations of Western Europe individually and by region in order to assess the extent to which "Finlandization" is appropriate in describing each nation's present and future foreign policy orientation toward the Soviet Union. The third section addresses the basic functional relationship coloring Soviet-West European relations, and the final section addresses the implications for U.S. foreign policy. For the specialist interested in international affairs and international law in general, or Soviet foreign policy in particular, this book (a collection of 13 papers) offers much important information central to the development of current East-West relations in Europe.

SR, 39:4:690-91

282. Glassman, Jon D. **Arms for the Arabs: The Soviet Union and War in the Middle East.** Baltimore and London: The Johns Hopkins University Press, 1975. x, 243p. $12.50.

The author examines the strategy behind, and the motivation for, the Soviet arms shipment to the Middle East. He traces involvement through the Arab-Israeli wars, cataloging all known information on this matter. His comment that "Moscow will continue to play an important political-military role in the region" is a sound one. Despite some errors, the book is interesting and instructive, well worth reading by any student of Middle East and Soviet affairs.

SR, 35:4:739-40

283. Golan, Galia. **Yom Kippur and After: The Soviet Union and the Middle East Crisis.** New York and London: Cambridge University Press, 1977. ix, 350p. $18.95.

Golan has produced a detailed, informative, and interesting survey of many of the factors that contributed to the October 1973 Yom Kippur War and to the continuing series of unexpected post-war developments. She places the Middle East developments in the perspective of Soviet global economic, strategic, ideological, and political interests. In this perspective, she submits that the area ranks no higher than fourth on the Soviet priority scale – behind the United States, Europe, and Asia. Golan does very well in developing the factors that tend to negate Soviet foreign policy objectives in the Middle East. Anyone interested in world events should read her book.

CSP, 20:2:265-66

284. Gorodetsky, Gabriel. **The Precarious Truce: Anglo-Soviet Relations 1924-27.** Soviet and East European Studies series. New York and London: Cambridge University Press, 1977. xiv, 289p. $18.95.

Building skillfully on the solid foundation laid by Richard Ullman in his three-volume study of Anglo-Soviet relations, Gorodetsky has taken up the story and carried it from the advent of the first Labour government to the rupture that followed the Arcos raid. In the process, he shows how fearfully symmetrical this relationship was. The prime value of this exhaustively documented study is that the author makes it clear, for example, that Austen Chamberlain's Locarno policy and his post-Locarno dealings with Moscow were, at worst, no more than passively anti-Soviet. On the Soviet side, Gorodetsky states that the emergence of Stalin caused revolutionary activism to become subordinate to national rehabilitation.

SR, 37:2:296-97

285. Gouré, Leon, and Morris Rothenberg. **Soviet Penetration of Latin America.** Washington, DC: Center for Advanced International Studies, University of Miami, 1975. vii, 204p. $5.50, paper.

According to the authors, the Cuban Revolution and the survival of Fidel Castro's government caused the Soviet Union after 1959 to reexamine the revolutionary potential of, and United States influence in, Latin America and to reconsider its own opportunities and policies in the area. As a result, beginning in the 1960s, the Soviet government increasingly encouraged anti-American nationalism in its political and economic forms and gave varying degrees of support to many radically oriented governments and nonruling parties and movements. Fifteen tables bring together useful information on Soviet-Latin American economic and cultural relations.

RR, 35:2:219-20

286. Jain, R. K. **Soviet South Asian Relations, 1947-1978.** Vol. 1: *The Kashmir Question, 1952-1964. The Kutch Conflict of 1965. Bangladesh Crisis and Indo-Pak War of 1971. India.* Vol. 2: *Pakistan, Bangladesh, Nepal, Sri Lanka.* Atlantic Highlands, NJ, and Boston: Humanities Press, 1979. Vol. 1: xx, 602p. $20.00; Vol. 2: xx, 459p. $20.00.

This is a unique and valuable collection of documents and other data essential to the understanding of recent diplomacy in South Asia. Originally published by Radiant Publishers in India, it is now available in this American edition. Despite the lack of an introduction and editor's explanation as to the selection of documents included, the two-volume work remains a very useful research tool to study Soviet diplomacy in the Third World.

287. Johnston, Robert H. **Tradition versus Revolution: Russia and the Balkans in 1917.** East European Monographs, 28. Boulder, CO: *East European Quarterly*, 1977. viii, 240p. $14.00. Distributed by Columbia University Press, New York.

This is a concise and comprehensive account of all aspects of the foreign policy of the Russian Provisional Government in 1917, both in terms of the role that foreign policy played in bringing on the transition from the February Revolution to the October Revolution and in terms of the Provisional Government's relations with Russia's allies from 1914 to 1917. The author sheds considerable new light on the contents of the available sources through the judicious use of unpublished British, American, German, and Italian World War I documents. The result is a book which should be especially rewarding to those with a special interest either in World War I diplomacy and war aims or in the eight-month rule of the Provisional Government in Russia.

SR, 38:1:113-14

288. Joshi, Nirmala. **Foundations of Indo-Soviet Relations: A Study of Non-Official Attitudes and Contacts, 1917-1947.** Foreword by Y. B. Chavan. New Delhi: Radiant Publishers, 1975. xiv, 204p. Rs.30.

The main value of this work lies in the exposition of the generally positive appraisal of Russia by Indian nationalist leaders. The "Russian menace" was never taken seriously by Indian nationalists who viewed it as a British ploy to preserve hegemony in India. The Indian image of the Soviet Union was not, however, entirely an uncritical one. The major leaders of the Indian Left were democrats who were repelled by the suppression of civil liberties, and they became progressively disillusioned with Soviet foreign policy after the signing of the 1939 Nazi-Soviet pact. Overall, the author has done well in illuminating the wellsprings of the official Indian approach to the Soviet Union.

SR, 36:1:125-26

289. Kass, Ilana. **Soviet Involvement in the Middle East: Policy Formulation, 1966-1973.** Boulder, CO, and Folkestone, England: Westview Press and Wm. Dawson & Sons, 1978. xiv, 273p. $18.25.

This book examines four central organs of the Soviet press from 1967 through 1970 in order to compare their respective perceptions of the Arab-Israeli conflict, domestic Arab politics, and the Soviet role in each. *Pravda* consistently advocated a political settlement of the Arab-Israeli conflict, while *Izvestiia* and *Krasnaia zvezda* both emphasized the value of Soviet assistance in achieving their perceptions of Arab goals. *Trud* "dissented" by arguing indirectly for an overall reduction in Soviet commitments without greater certainty of Soviet benefit.

SR, 39:1:123-24

290. Klinghoffer, Arthur Jay. **The Angolan War: A Study in Soviet Policy in the Third World.** Boulder, CO: Westview Press, 1980. 231p. $23.75.

This first study discusses both the Soviet and the Cuban involvement in Angola and assesses the decisive change in Soviet foreign policy that contributed to the reevaluation of détente by the United States. Klinghoffer addresses key questions in regard to Soviet involvement in Angola and its relationship to U.S. policy in Africa.

291. Maude, George. **The Finnish Dilemma: Neutrality in the Shadow of Power.** Published for the Royal Institute of International Affairs. London: Oxford University Press, 1976. vi, 153p. $13.25.

After the Second World War, the Soviet border on the west was protected by Moscow-controlled states, with the exception of Finland, a free non-Communist country. This well-written and instructive book deals with Finland's intricate connections with her neighbor. Maude presents Finnish neutrality against the background of a brief outline of Finland's modern history and concentrates on Soviet-Finnish relations.

SR, 36:2:304

292.   Morley, James William, ed. **Deterrent Diplomacy: Japan, Germany, and the USSR, 1935-1940.** Selected translation from *Taiheiyō sensō e no Michi: Kaisen Gaikō Shi.* Japan's Road to Pacific War Series, vol. 1. New York: Columbia University Press, 1976. xii, 363p. $17.50.

Three essays by distinguished Japanese scholars are assembled in this study. The essays entitled "The Anti-Comintern Pact, 1935-1939," "The Japanese-Soviet Confrontation, 1935-1939," and "The Tripartite Pact, 1939-1940," are based predominantly on published and unpublished Japanese sources, and their translation makes valuable information available to Western students of this period.

SR, 37:3:501-502

293.   Nir, Yeshayahu. **The Israel-Arab Conflict in Soviet Caricatures, 1967-1973.** A Research Monograph in Visual Communication. Tel Aviv: Tcherikover Publishers, Ltd., 1976. 126p. Illus. Paper.

Nir's book constitutes a valuable visual, as well as documentary, compendium, with very helpful, if brief, commentary. The caricatures speak for themselves and raise another issue to which Nir alludes, but which he does not discuss in detail – namely, to what extent does this material reflect almost obsessive elements in the approach of the Soviet leadership to the "Zionist" issue?

SR, 38:1:119-21

294.   Remnek, Richard B. **Soviet Scholars and Soviet Foreign Policy: A Case Study in Soviet Policy towards India.** Foreword by W. W. Kuslki. Durham, NC: Carolina Academic Press, 1975. xvi, 343p. $11.00.

The Khrushchev-Bulganin visit to India in 1955 signaled the advent of a more pragmatic turn in Soviet foreign policy. Scholars were quick to respond to this development. In many ways, this book is impressive and valuable. The author has exhaustively researched the subject and displays a thorough knowledge of Soviet writings on India. However, the volume is not a study of Soviet foreign policy. It is, instead, an explicit attempt to study the impact of Soviet scholars on the Soviet approach to India.

SR, 36:2:315-16

295.   Ro'i, Yaakov. **From Encroachment to Involvement: A Documentary Study of Soviet Policy in the Middle East, 1945-1973.** New York and Toronto: Halsted Press, a division of John Wiley & Sons. Jerusalem: Israel Universities Press, 1974. xi, 616p. $26.75.

The author has brought together 116 documents, speeches, communiques, and commentaries that touch on all the key crises and developments of the 1945 to 1973 period – the postwar settlement; the Iranian and Palestinian questions; Stalin's tentative thrusts; the evolution of Soviet perceptions of Arab world developments; the crises of 1956, 1958, and 1961; Soviet reactions to Egyptian-Iraqi feuding; the Yemeni civil war; changing Iranian and Turkish policies; and the June 1967 and October 1973 wars. The usefulness of the materials – most of which are Russian and Arabic in origin – is greatly enhanced by Ro'i's background essays.

SR, 35:3:535-36

296. Ro'i, Yaakov. **Soviet Decision Making in Practice: The USSR and Israel, 1947-1954.** New Brunswick, NJ: Transaction Books, 1980. 540p. $22.95.

It is the very sharpness and brief duration of the Soviet-Israel rapprochement that makes it a perfect model for the study of national decision making in practice. This task has been admirably undertaken by Ro'i. Beginning with Moscow's most fleeting interest in the fate of the Palestinian Jews, Ro'i's tightly packed volume chronicles their general coincidence of interest; the early contacts through the United Nations; the enlargement of the relationship into a diplomatic partnership and, via clandestine sources in Czechoslovakia, as a supplier of arms; and, finally, the disintegration of the strange friendship over the issues of Russia's domestic purges, East European anti-Semitism, and the emigration of Soviet Jewry to Israel. In all, this is an important volume and a logical companion to Ro'i's earlier works.

RR, 40:2:205-206

297. Rothenberg, Morris. **The USSR and Africa: New Dimensions of Soviet Global Power.** Monographs in International Affairs. Foreword by Mose L. Harvey. Coral Gables, FL: Advanced International Studies Institute, in association with the University of Miami, 1980. xii, 280p. $12.95.

Soviet advances in Africa, Rothenberg suggests, were instigated originally by Karen Brutents, a member of the CPSU Central Committee. He asserts that "it is a question of carrying on the offensive against imperialism and world capitalism as a whole in order to do away with them." Coupled with growing Soviet logistics capabilities, the availability of large Cuban expeditionary forces gives the USSR a potent new instrumentality for extending its influence in Africa. The Soviet aim is to force Western out of Africa in order to break the back of the world system headed by the United States.

298. Rubinstein, Alvin Z. **Red Star on the Nile: The Soviet-Egyptian Influence Relationship since the June War.** Princeton, NJ: Princeton University Press, 1977. xxiv, 383p. $25.00.

The author set for himself the task of finding from this case study some general laws of behavior governing the relationship of influence between a superpower and any Third World country. The body of the book is written in a lively and engaging style. It traces the ups and downs of the Soviet-Egyptian relationship in an intrigue-by-intrigue account of persistent Soviet attempts at gaining commanding influence over Egypt and of Egypt's largely successful parries to these attempts while making full use of desperately needed Soviet aid and diplomatic support.

CSP, 20:2:264

299. Rubinstein, Alvin Z., ed. **Soviet and Chinese Influence in the Third World.** New York: Praeger Publishers, 1975. xii, 232p. $17.50.

This study encompasses a broad geographical spectrum of such diverse nations as India, Indonesia, Egypt, and Cuba in an attempt to examine Soviet (and to a lesser degree, Chinese) influence in the Third World at large by utilizing the concept of influence within a well-ordered methodological framework. While individual contributors offer numerous insights into events in their areas of specialization, similar depth is lacking in their reviews of trends and developments within the Soviet Union and the People's Republic of China.

SR, 37:1:141-42

300. Solzhenitsyn, Alexander. **Warning to the West.** Introduction by George Meany. New York: Farrar, Straus & Giroux, 1976. viii, 146p. $7.95.

Solzhenitsyn submits that a system (Soviet) so corrupt and abusive to its own people cannot be trusted in its dealings with foreign partners, especially if the latter, spellbound by capitalist greed, pragmatism, and democratic procedures, manifests little stomach for long-term struggle. Apart from some of Solzhenitsyn's exaggerations and oversimplifications, his views deserve attention now more than ever before.

301. Swearingen, Rodger. **The Soviet Union and Postwar Japan: Escalating Challenge and Response.** Stanford: Hoover Institution Press, 1978. xvi, 340p. $14.95.
This volume presents an admirably comprehensive picture of Soviet-Japanese relations since World War II. Its coverage is indeed impressive. Briefly surveying the interests and the images each country had of the other as far back as 1700, the book goes on to discuss the shifts in cultural, diplomatic, and economic relations during the various stages of Japan's post-1945 history, a time that witnessed the rise of the defeated and occupied nation to the status of a leading industrial power. All the major components of the story are covered in skillfully organized and subdivided sections.
RR, 39:1:97-98

302. Vloyantes, John P. **Silk Glove Hegemony: Finnish-Soviet Relations, 1944-1974: A Case Study of the Theory of the Soft Sphere of Influence.** Kent, OH: Kent State University Press, 1975. xiv, 208p. $10.00.
Insofar as the narrative concerns the vicissitudes of Finnish politics, the author presents an informed account that is more than adequate for the general reader. Specialists, however, will be less enthusiastic. There are many errors in the book, including misspelling of Kekkonen's first name. Nonetheless, the book is informative and readable.

303. White, Stephen. **Britain and the Bolshevik Revolution: A Study in the Politics of Diplomacy, 1920-1924.** New York: Holmes & Meier, 1980. xiv, 317p. $32.00.
White has organized this book chronologically to emphasize three themes—part 1 concerns the attempts of the Lloyd George government to "normalize relations with Soviet Russia"; part 2 deals with the confrontationist tactics of Bonar Law's imperial-minded Conservative government in the international scene; part 3 completes the story with the British recognition of the Soviet government by Britain's first Labour government. White argues persuasively that any ideological affinity between the Labour party and the Bolsheviks was secondary to more practical considerations. He has made exhaustive use of British public and private papers and available published Soviet works, writing a solid book on a neglected subject.
SR, 40:3:479-80

304. Wilson, Edward T. **Russia and Black Africa before World War II.** New York and London: Holmes & Meier, 1974. xvi, 397p. $26.00.
The author's main theme is the continuity between tsarist and Soviet motivations for involvement in Africa. In both cases, "calculation of realpolitik had taken precedence over considerations of friendship or ideological affinity" (p. 71), and security considerations were predominant in both cases. With its wealth of hitherto unused sources, this volume provides valuable insight into understanding the genesis of current Soviet involvement in Africa.
SR, 34:4:827-28

HISTORY

Bibliographies, Encyclopedias, Source Materials

305.	Armstrong, Terence, ed. **Yermak's Campaign in Siberia: A Selection of Documents.** Translated by Tatiana Minorsky and David Wileman. London: Hakluyt Society, 1975. x, 315p. $18.00.
This book brings together most of the available information on Yermak's campaign in 1581, which involved merely the Khanate of Sibir, just east of the Urals. In an informative introduction, Armstrong ascribes the beginning of Moscow's eastward march to Ivan III, but the first major stroke—the taking of Kazan—is credited to Ivan IV. Of the several chronicles of these events, all evidently derived in some measure from earlier prototypes now lost, four have been selected for inclusion in this volume—the so-called New chronicle, the Stroganov chronicle, the Remezov chronicle, and the Yesipov chronicle of 1649.
	CSP, 18:4:468-69

306.	Ascher, Abraham, ed. **The Mensheviks in the Russian Revolution: Documents of Revolution.** London: Thames & Hudson, 1976. 147p. £6.00.
The editor has compiled a documentation (resolutions, speeches, articles) presenting the history of the RSDP, the so-called Mensheviks. He knows his sources well and has chosen appropriate texts that adequately acquaint the English reading audience with the Russian Revolution in general and with the Mensheviks in particular. The documentation is divided into six chronological chapters covering the period from 1903 to the early 1920s when the party was banned by Soviet authorities.
	SEER, 55:1:123-24

307.	Bartlett, R. B., and P. H. Clendenning, comps. **Eighteenth Century Russia: A Select Bibliography.** Newtonville, MA: Oriental Research Partners, 1978. 280p. $13.00.
This work is an essential reference tool dealing with eighteenth-century Russian history, culture, society, diplomacy, nationalities, and economics. The book is divided into two parts. Part 1 of each section lists the most important works in English and is primarily for the undergraduate or interested layperson. Part 2 lists appropriate works in Russian, German, and French and is aimed at the graduate and more senior researcher. Each section begins with a brief annotation of some of the included works, with concentration mainly on items dealing with the eighteenth century that have appeared in the most important Soviet and Western journals and yearbooks in the last 10 years, as well as the most important Ph.D. dissertations written in the last 15 years. Over 3,000 items and a 15-page index are provided.

308.	**The Debate on Soviet Power: Minutes of the All-Russian Central Executive Committee of Soviet.** Second Convocation, October 1917-January 1918. Translated and edited by John L. H. Keep. Oxford: Clarendon Press, 1979. xiv, 465p. $39.00.
It is a remarkable commentary on the state of historical scholarship in the Soviet Union that the most comprehensive edition of the minutes of that regime's first legislature should be published in English by a Western historian. In 1918 an incomplete, censored version was published in Moscow, but it is available in only a few Western libraries and is rarely cited by scholars. Keep has provided an excellent introductory essay on the Revolution of 1917 and detailed notes on little-known events and persons mentioned in the discussions. This splendid work enables us to examine once again the performance of the Convocation, not only on a theoretical level, but within the context of concrete historical developments.
	RR, 39:1:83-84

309. Gilbert, Martin. **Soviet History Atlas.** London: Routledge & Kegan Paul, 1979. 69p. £6.75.

The first section of this book, up to the Russian Revolution, contains 10 maps, with the main section, The Soviet Union, having 59 maps. All maps have been specially drawn, incorporating information from a broad range of atlases, maps, books, and articles. The clarity of cartography and printing is excellent.

SS, 31:2:460

310. Kirby, D. G., ed. **Finland and Russia, 1808-1920: From Autonomy to Independence. A Selection of Documents.** Studies in Russian and East European History series. London: Macmillan, 1975. xii, 265p. £10.00.

This work is a collection of documents edited and translated by D. G. Kirby, covering the whole period during which a legal and constitutional connection existed between Finland and Russia to its formal dissolution in the peace treaty of 1920. The documents are introduced and linked by very brief historical surveys that are confined to setting the documents into their immediate historical context. The range of sources used is wide and embraces official documents, extracts from newspapers and journals, and private diary and letter material.

SEER, 55:2:260-61

311. Pierce, Richard A., ed. **Documents on the History of the Russo-American Company.** Translated by Marina Ramsey. Kingston, Ontario: The Limestone Press, 1976. viii, 220p. $9.50.

This collection is a translation of *K istorii Rossiisko-Amerikanskoi Kompanii (Sbornik dokumentalnykh materialov)*, which appeared in 1957. It includes "An Historical Calendar of the Russo-American Company (1817)" and 23 documents relating to the administration of the Company in Alaska, and the voyages and operation of its office in St. Petersburg.

312. **Russia under Catherine the Great.** Vol. 1: *Select Documents on Government and Society.* Translated and with an introduction by Paul Dukes. Newtonville, MA: Oriental Research Partners, 1978. viii, 176p. $12.00.

There are 10 groups of documents in this work – the Table of Ranks of 1722, Tatishchev's treatise of around 1730, the decree on the freedom of the nobility in 1762, Catherine's directions of 1764 to Viazemskii, Desnitskii's governmental proposals of 1768, Polenov's analysis of serfdom, Richkov's model instructions of 1770 to stewards, various documents about the Pugachev Revolt, and the preambles to the Guberniia Reform of 1775 and the Charter of the Nobility of 1785, followed by synopses of those lengthy enactments. A list of select translated terms and a brief bibliography close the slim volume. This book is aimed mainly at advanced undergraduate seminars, where students would have some familiarity with the period and could receive considerable specialized guidance.

SR, 39:3:495

313. Wieczynski, Joseph L., ed. **The Modern Encyclopedia of Russian and Soviet History** (MERSH). Gulf Breeze, FL: Academic International Press, 1976- . Vols. 1-7 in progress. $30.50/each.

This represents an ongoing project that is expected to reach more than 50 volumes before completion, at which time it will be the most comprehensive encyclopedic guide to Russian/Soviet history in the English language and an indispensable source for both the student and specialist.

General Surveys, Readers

314. Auty, Robert, and Dimitry Obolensky, eds., assisted by Anthony Kingsford. **An Introduction to Russian History.** Companion to Russian Studies, vol. 1. Cambridge: Cambridge University Press, 1976. xvi, 403p. Maps. $32.50.

This is the first of three volumes, the other two of which will be devoted to language and literature, and art and architecture. The work includes the following essays: "The Geographical Setting," "Kievan Russia," "Appanage and Moscovite Russia," "Imperial Russia from Peter I to Nicholas I," and "Imperial Russia from Alexander II to 1917." Four other essays treat the Russian Orthodox church, Soviet government and politics, the Soviet economy, and "The Soviet Union and Its Neighbours." The essays are of high quality, almost uniformly so. The volume ought to have a long and useful life as a handbook for students and a reference work for scholars.

  SR, 36:3:494-95

315. Dmytryshyn, Basil. **A History of Russia.** Englewood Cliffs, NJ: Prentice-Hall, 1977. xviii, 645p. Illus. $14.95.

Dmytryshyn's book is well organized, concise, and straightforward. It is divided into five parts (Kievan Rus', Divided Rus', Muscovy, Imperial Russia, and Soviet Russia) and contains 20 chapters. In addition to photographs and illustrations, there are a number of maps, tables, and charts. If this text were to be used effectively in a college course, extensive supplementary readings, discussions, and lectures would be required for more detail and depth.

  SR, 37:2:290

316. Dmytryshyn, Basil. **USSR: A Concise History.** 3rd ed. New York: Charles Scribner's Sons, 1978. xvii, 646p. $17.50.

This is an updated and well-received textbook (1st ed. 1965) of the Soviet Union history. In the third edition, "the basic change is in the material concerned with Khrushchev's and Brezhnev's tenures in power." Teachers of Russian/Soviet history would do well to consider this textbook as the best available.

  NP, 6:2:215-16

317. Dziewanowski, M. K. **A History of Soviet Russia.** Englewood Cliffs, NJ: Prentice-Hall, 1979. x, 406p. $13.95, paper.

Dziewanowski has written a textbook of distinction. Scholarly, witty, well coordinated, up to date, and eminently readable, it offers an attractive alternative to the established entries in the field. The book provides more than lucid descriptions of events — interpretations are given with clarity and confidence. The author finds the Provisional Government of 1917 had nothing to offer a battered and chaotic Russia. But, it is the reviewer's opinion that the November Revolution and the Communist regime to which it gave birth have left more tragedy than accomplishment in their trial.

  RR, 39:1:82-83

318. Hingley, Ronald. **The Russian Mind.** New York: Charles Scribner's Sons, 1977. viii, 307p. $12.50.

This volume is an ambitious attempt to discover the "collective national mind," but just what is "typically Russian" remains less than clear. The book is informative and informed, sophisticated and stimulating, much like a series of "social" conversations — clever, interesting, and aimless.

  SR, 38:1:130-31

319. MacKenzie, David, and Michael W. Curran. **A History of Russia and the Soviet Union.** The Dorsey Series in European History. Homeweed, IL, and Georgetown, Ontario: The Dorsey Press and Irwin-Dorsey Limited, 1977. xvi, 689p. Maps. Illus. $14.95.
This text is divided into three parts (Early Russia to 1689; Early Imperial Russia, 1689-1855; and Modern Russia, 1855 to the Present). There are 40 chapters, a general bibliography, four appendices, and a generous number of maps—38. The text offers a feature that many students will find both useful and stimulating: not only does the author introduce conflicting opinions and interpretations, but he also includes examples at several points in the text. In general, the text, which would seem to be aimed at the upper-level college student, is carefully and thoughtfully written.
     SR, 37:2:290

320. Riasanovsky, Nicholas V. **A History of Russia.** 3rd ed. New York: Oxford University Press, 1977. xx, 762p. Illus. $19.95.
Riasanovsky has not altered his account of imperial Russia, though he has added some new works to his bibliography. It is in the section dealing with post-1968 events that new material will be found, for example, the invasion of Czechoslovakia in 1968 or the talks leading up to SALT II.

321. Westwood, J. N. **Russia since 1917.** London: Bastford, 1980. 219p. £3.95.
This is a revised and updated edition of the book first published in 1966, with a new chapter on the Brezhnev years. It is a concise, wide-ranging survey aimed at undergraduate students, covering political, social, and economic history, thus providing a useful initial introduction.

Historiography and Archeology

322. Black, Joseph L., ed. **Essays on Karamzin: Russian Man-of-Letters, Political Thinker, Historian, 1766-1826.** Slavistic Printings and Reprintings, 309. The Hague and Paris: Mouton, 1975. 232p. Kfl. 62., paper.
Arranged according to the chronology of Karamzin's career, the essays give fairly even representation to Karamzin's biography, his fiction, and his work as a historian. The generally high quality of the contributions to this work and the scope of the volume make it a valuable addition to the ever growing English-language literature on Karamzin.
     SR, 36:3:499-500

323. Enteen, George M. **The Soviet Scholar-Bureaucrat: M. N. Pokrovskii and the Society of Marxist Historians.** University Park and London: Pennsylvania State University Press, 1978. xii, 236p. $15.00.
Enteen's work is not a biography nor a work of historiography, but "comes closer to what is called the sociology of ideas." As such, it successfully sketches the evolution of Pokrovskii's historical thought but fails in convincingly explaining the forces that shaped Pokrovskii's writing of history. The book reminds the reader of the static nature and quality of Soviet historiography and alerts the researcher to the problems of working with Russian-language material published in the USSR since 1917.
     NP, 9:1:146-47

324. Enteen, George M., Tatiana Gorn, and Cheryl Kern. **Soviet Historians and the Study of Russian Imperialism.** Pennsylvania State University Studies, no. 45.

University Park and London: Pennsylvania State University Press, 1979. x, 60p. $3.00, paper.

In this brief monograph, the authors present the major conclusions and some of the determinants of Soviet historical writing on tsarist Russian imperialism, covering works from the 1920s to the 1970s. The study examines how Soviet historians have defined imperialism as a historical stage and how they have determined whether conditions for it existed in late tsarist Russia.

SR, 39:3:490

325. Mazour, Anatole G. **Modern Russian Historiography.** Revised edition. Westport, CT, and London: Greenwood Press, 1975 [1939, under the title *An Outline of Modern Russian Historiography*; 2nd ed., 1958]. xiv, 224p. Illus. $13.95.

The latest edition, the third, includes some new materials on the chronicles and the earliest historians of Russia, but it deletes the previous edition's sections on émigré historians, the Eurasian school, and (because Mazour has recently published a separate volume on Soviet historiography) on scholarship since Pokrovskii (except that Siberian historiography is treated through the 1960s). Advanced students should use more than this book, which was modestly designed by its author "merely as a guide" to the important and complex subject of Russian historiography.

SR, 36:1:122-23

326. Vernadsky, George. **Russian Historiography: A History.** Edited by Sergei Pushkarev. Translated by Nickolas Lupinin. Belmont, MA: Nordland Publishing Company, 1978. x, 575p. $35.00.

At the time of his death, according to the editor, Professor Vernadsky had completed this work except for a chapter on Oriental studies and the history of the church, a chapter completed by Sergei Pushkarev. Though Vernadsky surveys the whole of Russia's history, emphasis in the work is on the late nineteenth and early twentieth centuries. The work is thin on historiography outside of Russia and on historians of the Soviet period. The book is basically organized chronologically and by specific historians, and the larger schools of historiography are treated as aggregates. This volume also contains four appendices, an essay bibliography of Vernadsky's works, and bibliographies on the Russian Church and schism of the Old Believers.

NP, 9:1:161

Pre-Petrine Muscovy/Russia

327. Baron, Samuel H. **Muscovite Russia. Collected Essays.** London: Variorum Reprints, 1980. 362p. Tables. £22.00.

Of the 14 papers in this book, eight are devoted to economic and social history; three to the impact on Russia of the West; and three to historiography and sources. Russian merchants and English trade are major preoccupations, involving the author with many a knotty problem: Who were the *gosti*? Patiently, Baron tugs and teases away at his knots. With similar meticulousness he sorts out the materials in British archives bearing on sixteenth-century Anglo-Russian relations. The collection is as much welcome as an exemplar of historical method and elegance of exposition as for the undoubted value of the material it contains.

SEER, 59:3:435-36

328. Payne, Robert, and Nikita Romanoff. **Ivan the Terrible.** New York: Thomas Y. Crowell, 1975. x, 502p. $12.95.

This text is based upon a wide range of contemporary narrative sources and is accompanied by well-chosen illustrations, maps, plans of the Kremlin, a glossary, and an index. The bibliography includes all the major works in Russian, English, and German, along with some esoterica. The book concentrates on military campaigns, diplomatic negotiations, and the horrors of the *oprichnina*. And, yet, in this book, the Ivan that emerges is an Ivan that never existed.

SR, 35:4:730

329. Presniakov, Alexander E. **The Tsardom of Muscovy.** Edited and translated by Robert F. Price. "Master and Man in Muscovy" by Charles J. Halperin. Gulf Breeze, FL: Academic International Press, 1978. xxii, 157p. $12.50.

This classic essay, first published in Petrograd in 1918, delineates in compressed fashion the major factors in the development of the Muscovite autocracy through the seventeenth century. Although Presniakov touches upon a variety of aspects of Muscovite life and society—such as colonization, provincial administration, the peasantry, and the church—he focuses upon the consolidation of central authority, which, for Presniakov, had become a political necessity. This study should be required reading for all students of Russian history.

SR, 39:1:113-14

330. Soloview, Sergei M. **History of Russia.** Vol. 9: *The Age of Vasily II.* Translated and with an introduction by Hugh F. Graham. Gulf Breeze, FL: Academic International Press, 1976. 273p.

Graham's translation of Soloview's work is thoroughly competent, and his introduction and very careful, complete footnotes make this volume a welcome window into sixteenth-century Russian life as well as into the rough-and-tumble of international politics in eastern Europe in the time of such vivid actors as Selim the Grim and Suleiman the Magnificent, Pope Leo X, and Emperor Maximilian I.

SR, 36:3:498-99

331. Szeftel, Marc. **Russian Institutions and Culture up to Peter the Great.** Preface by Donald W. Treadgold. London: Variorum Reprints, 1975. 374p. $37.45.

This is a collection of 13 of Professor Szeftel's republished journal articles and other studies. The pieces span a quarter of a century, from 1949 to 1973. His work is characterized by remarkable expertness, clarity, and precision. The contributions are in three languages—English, Russian, and French.

SR, 36:2:292

Imperial Russia

332. Alexander, John T. **Bubonic Plague in Early Modern Russia: Public Health and Urban Disaster.** Baltimore: Johns Hopkins University Press, 1980. xvii, 385p. $30.00.

In this study of the background and onslaught of the bubonic plague that swept through Russia in the early 1770s, Alexander vividly and aptly describes how various levels of society, especially Muscovite, reacted to the plague's effects. Almost all of the estimated 120,000 victims were from the lower orders, as most of the nobles and high-ranking clergy, merchants, and officials had already fled the city at the first sign of the oncoming catastrophe. Perhaps the most intriguing part of the story is the courageous role played by

the small group of foreign and Russian doctors. Alexander has written a most valuable book, one which can be read with profit by both scientific and social historians.
RR, 40:2:185-86

333. Balmuth, Daniel. **Censorship in Russia, 1865-1905.** Washington, DC: University Press of America, 1979. 249p. $9.75.
In the first two chapters of this book, Balmuth surveys Russian press law to 1865 and, in the next two chapters, he examines Alexander II's press policies. Subsequent chapters cover related conditions under Alexander III and Nicholas II. According to Russian sources, over 125 million items entered Russia between 1901 and 1905; of these, the censors examined only 4,400. In comparison with Soviet censorship, one can appreciate how modern Soviet Russian censors have improved over their tsarist ancestors. This study is the only work in English. It is for graduate students and a welcome contribution to historical literature.

334. Bartlett, Roger P. **Human Capital: The Settlement of Foreigners in Russia, 1762-1804.** Cambridge and New York: Cambridge University Press, 1980. xviii, 358p. Maps. $45.00.
This study not only explores the settlement of foreigners in Russia in the second half of the eighteenth century, but also contributes to the understanding of wider social and economic issues, as well as government policy. This book is based on a variety of sources, and the archival material includes Senate papers, reports from officials from the colonies, and the records of the Board of State Economy, which was the institution set up to manage foreigners' affairs. The process of colonization is examined from many angles. This book is a well-balanced and entertaining account and adds considerably to the knowledge of this aspect of eighteenth-century Russia.
SEER, 59:1:102-103

335. Barratt, Glynn. **The Rebel on the Bridge: A Life of the Decembrist Baron Andrey Rozen (1800-84).** Athens: Ohio University Press, 1975. xviii, 310p. + 8pp. plates. Maps. $19.00.
Born in 1800 into a German aristocratic family in Estonia where his family had held land for centuries, Rosen served as an officer in the Russian army. He joined the Decembrists only in the final day before the uprising of December 14, 1825, and, at the decisive moment, he kept his regiment on St. Isaac's Bridge, neither coming to the aid of the rebels nor assisting tsarist forces. This ambivalent behavior earned Rozen deprivation of his title and rights, 10 years of hard labor, and perpetual exile in Siberia. Rozen is of interest to the historian primarily on account of his utterly divided loyalties on December 14. Barrat argues that his memoirs are the most trustworthy of all the Decembrists' recollections.
SR, 39:1:117

336. Brekke, B. F. **The Copper Coinage of Imperial Russia, 1700-1917.** Malmo, Sweden: Forlangshuset Norden AB, 1977. 296p. $50.00.
Brekke, a professional numismatist in Denmark, carefully points out that copper coins, compared to gold and silver coins, provided for the overwhelming part of the money in circulation for the average Russian during the imperial period. Through the study of copper coinage, Russian history emerges — the student can follow the country's expansion into new territories, such as the Crimea, Georgia, Moldavia and Wallachia, Poland, Finland, the Ionian Isles, and parts of Central Asia. At the back of the book, Brekke furnishes a compendious price list in United States dollars for all copper coinage of

imperial Russia 1700-1917. This catalog is of indispensable value to those interested in Russian economic and political history.

RR, 39:1:74-75

337. Curtiss, John Shelton. **Russia's Crimean War.** Durham, NC: Duke University Press, 1979. xi, 597p. $29.75.
The causes and effects of the Crimean War have been repeatedly examined by Western scholars but until now with an emphasis on the Allies – Britain, France, and the Ottoman Empire. Curtiss provides the first full treatment in English of the Russian side of the war. While the British public pushed the government into war, Napoleon drew the French along behind him. In Russia, "War feelings were strong in all classes; Nesselrode seemed to be the only sane person in sight." This book provides a fresh, new look at a vitally important subject and a clear perception of its impact on Russia and the world.

RR, 39:1:240-41

338. Field, Daniel. **The End of Serfdom: Nobility and Bureaucracy in Russia, 1855-1861.** Russian Research Center Studies, 75. Cambridge, MA, and London: Harvard University Press, 1976. xvi, 472p. $17.50.
Field views the emancipation debates among educated society, the nobility, the higher bureaucracy, and the Imperial Court as the end of an important era in Russia's history. He constructs his narrative in a way which takes the reader step by step, with each step meticulously reconstructed, through the emancipation debates as they evolved during the first half-decade of Alexander II's reign. This is the most thorough and detailed account yet written about the political processes that produced the emancipation of the Russian serfs on February 19, 1861.

SR, 36:2:294-95

339. Field, Daniel. **Rebels in the Name of the Tsar.** Boston: Houghton Mifflin, 1976. xvi, 220p. $9.95.
Field offers well-chosen documents and intelligent, balanced commentary concerning two famous cases of Russian "naive-monarchism" – the Bezdna peasant demonstration and massacre of 1861 and the so-called "Chigirin affair" of 1877. At both Bezdna and Chigirin, Russian and Ukrainian peasants invoked the name of the tsar-*batiushka*, their benevolent ruler and protector, when they claimed to carry out his will in refusing to obey the order of officials and soldiers, who actually were the approved local representatives of the tsar.

SR, 36:1:115-16

340. Healy, Ann Erickson. **The Russian Autocracy in Crisis, 1905-1907.** Hamden, CT: Archon Books, 1976. 328p. $15.00.
This study focuses on the hopes, achievements, and failures of the First Duma, which was convened in St. Petersburg on May 10, 1906. Constitutional developments in Russia during the reign of Nicholas II have become the subject of special interest. Healy's volume is one of a growing number of monographs published in recent years that deal with the Russian experiment, and it is an interesting and important work.

CSP, 19:2:226-27

341. Hennessy, Richard. **The Agrarian Question in Russia, 1905-1907: The Inception of the Stolypin Reform.** Marburger Abhandlungen zur Geschichte und Kultur Osteuropas, Band 16. Giesen: Wilhelm Schmitz Verlag, 1977. 203p. DM 38.00.
This book examines the inception of the reforms. It is less about the agrarian question than about the evolution of the government's understanding and treatment of the issue. The

nature of the agrarian question is assumed rather than defined, and the basic assumption is that the peasants wanted more land, especially land that remained in gentry estates. What this book demonstrates is the inconsistency of policies in the early twentieth century. There is no question of the reform being a continuity from emancipation. Stolypin's reform also clearly shows the remoteness from the peasantry of the government.

    SEER, 57:2:301-302

342.   Jewsbury, George F. **The Russian Annexation of Bessarabia: 1774-1828: A Study of Imperial Expansion.** East European Monographs, 15. Boulder, CO: *East European Quarterly*, 1976. vi, 199p. $12.00. Distributed by Columbia University Press, New York.

This book deals with Russian administrative policies within the new *oblast* of Bessarabia and the successively attempted solutions to the problem of integrating the province into the structure of the empire upon its annexation in 1812. The author concludes by assessing the resort to a centralist solution as indicative of the failure to successfully integrate the province into the empire. Although based on published source material, this book represents a welcome contribution to the extremely scarce English-language literature on the subject.

    SR, 36:2:293

343.   Josselson, Michael, and Diana Josselson. **The Commander: A Life of Barclay de Tolly.** Oxford, New York, Toronto, Melbourne: Oxford University Press, 1980. ix, 275p. Plates. £12.95.

Michael Barclay de Tolly was born to a Scots family long settled in Livonia. He was, first of all, representative of the Germanic upper classes of the Baltic province. His reserved and taciturn nature was to hold him at one remove from the ordinary Russian soldiers, to the welfare of whom he was passionately devoted. Rising entirely through his own merits, Barclay first commended himself to his superiors for his part in the bloody storm of Ochakov in 1788. He was a major general by the end of the century. He actively participated in the war in Finland in 1808 and against Napoleon in 1812, as commander-in-chief. This work represents a major contribution to the history of the Napoleonic Wars and the Russian army.

    SEER, 59:1:104-106

344.   Kochan, Miriam. **The Last Days of Imperial Russia, 1910-1917.** New York: Macmillan, 1976. 224p. Illus. $15.95.

Kochan's book on the last days of imperial Russia is a handsomely illustrated volume intended for the general reader. Its primary aim is to convey some notion of the way people in various classes of society lived, combined with a description of the growing atmosphere of political apocalypse. The author has relied chiefly on memoirs, either those of foreigners who were present or of Russians whose memoirs have been translated into English. Kochan has found a number of excellent old photographs with which to illustrate her story, many of them unfamiliar.

    SR, 36:2:300

345.   Lincoln, W. Bruce. **Nicholas I: Emperor and Autocrat of All the Russias.** Bloomington and London: Indiana University Press, 1978. 424p. $15.95.

The goal of this study is to review the negative picture of Nicholas I presented in most accounts, not by way of "apology" but to "place [Nicholas] and his policies in a more balanced historical perspective." Lincoln concludes that Nicholas "sought to create the epitome of an eighteenth-century West European police state ... in the manner of an enlightened despot." Nicholas failed at his task, however, because it was "utterly impossible" to govern "vast and diverse" Russia with programs designed for homogeneous states. This study provides the best-informed short discussion of any book available — whether based on archival work or secondary sources — on numerous topics.

SR, 38:1:109-110

346. Lincoln, W. Bruce. **Nikolai Miliutin: An Enlightened Russian Bureaucrat of the 19th Century.** Newtonville, MA: Oriental Research Partners, 1977. 130p. $9.00.
This is the first study of Miliutin printed in the English language. The work is documented from Western and Soviet archives. Miliutin's experience as a reformer in the period of Nicholas I, which prepared him for his later work in the Editing Commission, and the strengths and weaknesses of the enlightened bureaucrat are traced well in this book. Lincoln excels in explaining Miliutin's opposition to serfdom because of that institution's negative effect on the state itself, rather than as a result of a strictly humanitarian concern.

CSP, 20:4:568-69

347. Nikitenko, Aleksandr. **The Diary of a Russian Censor: Aleksandr Nikitenko.** Abridged, edited, and translated by Helen Saltz Jacobson. Amherst: University of Massachusetts Press, 1975. xxii, 397p. $20.00.
A. V. Nikitenko (1804-1877) occupied a central position in Russian intellectual, literary, and political history during the years covered by his *Diary*, 1826 to 1877. Nikitenko was born a serf in Ukraine. Jacobson's abridged edition of Nikitenko's *Dairy* is based on the Soviet three-volume edition published during 1955 to 1956. She selected with judicious care those entries having observations on the more important literary and political episodes of the time. Nikitenko was considered by many writers and public figures as a moderate and humane censor, and the entries included certainly testify to this appraisal. The work is a valuable contribution to intellectual and political history of Russia.

CSP, 18:3:358-59

348. Palmer, Alan. **Alexander I: Tsar of War and Peace.** New York: Harper & Row, 1974. xviii, 487p. $15.00.
Palmer is one of the most popular writers on the Napoleonic period. After his *Napoleon in Russia* and *Metternich*, his biography of Alexander I shows a comprehensive acquaintance with the memoir literature. Alexander is portrayed as vaguely liberal but weak, emotional, mystical, and messianic — nothing more. His internal policies receive little attention.

SR, 34:4:814-16

349. Pearson, Raymond. **The Russian Moderates and the Crisis of Tsarism, 1914-1917.** New York: Barnes & Noble, 1977. x, 208p. $22.50.
In this monograph, Pearson provides the details of a story whose main features are known to students of modern Russia — the conflicts between the moderates in the Duma (the Progressists, Constitutional Democrats, and Octobrists) and the tsarist government in the years 1914 to 1917. In addition to consulting the usual sources, Pearson had access to a fair amount of archival material in Moscow and Leningrad. He has made especially good use of the files of the *Okhrana*, which contain "a chronologically complete account of the moderates, frequently at variance with that offered in published memoirs." This study constitutes the most complete account of the political attitudes, maneuvers, and intrigues both of government leaders and the moderate parties during the critical wartime years.

RR, 39:1:79-80

350. Ragsdale, Hugh. **Détente in the Napoleonic Era: Bonaparte and the Russians.** Lawrence: The Regents of Kansas, 1980. xii, 183p. $17.50.
This short book is really an essay based on considerable archival research. The point of the essay is to interpret Napoleon's foreign policy as a repeated effort to divide Europe, and especially the Ottoman Empire, with Russia by peaceful or military means. The volume is clearly written, well proofread, and attractively presented.
    RR, 40:2:186-87

351. Ragsdale, Hugh, ed. **Paul I: A Reassessment of His Life and Reign.** Series in Russian and East European Studies, no. 2. Pittsburgh, PA: University Center for International Studies, 1979. xxiii, 188p. $15.00.
This collection of essays is the first major English-language work on Paul since the English translation of Waliszewski's biography in 1913. The book does two jobs particularly well—first, it will be an essential starting point for future research on the reign as it includes a valuable historiographical survey and an extremely useful essay on research materials, particularly memoir literature; second, it gives a good impression of the "state of play" of research on Paul I and his reign. It may be that this useful and interesting collection will stimulate exactly the research needed.
    RR, 40:1:61-62

352. Riasanovsky, Nicholas V. **A Parting of Ways: Government and the Educated Public in Russia, 1801-1855.** Oxford: Clarendon Press, 1976. x, 323p. $25.25.
Riasanovsky's work provides a comprehensive survey of political, social, and cultural developments, as well as of changing fashions in thought, from Catherine II's accession to the Crimean War. The main theme is the breakdown of that tacit understanding which, the author convincingly shows, existed between the government and educated society during the eighteenth century. The reasons for the breach lie in "the evolving structure of intellectual life"—in the growth of the universities and of journalistic enterprise, which encouraged a mature professional spirit to develop among Russian writers.
    SR, 37:1:124-25

353. Robbins, Richard G., Jr. **Famine in Russia 1891-1892.** New York and London: Columbia University Press, 1975. 262p. $12.50.
This is a history and an assessment of the functioning of the various echelons of tsarist Russian government during the period when famine became increasingly acute. This is a well-written and thoroughly researched and documented piece of work. With the insights that Robbins provides on the functioning of the government and its relation to society, the events of the succeeding turbulent decades seem somehow less shocking.
    SR, 34:4:816-17

354. Stone, Norman. **The Eastern Front, 1914-1917.** New York: Charles Scribner's Sons, 1975. 348p. Maps. $15.00.
Stone has given much valuable information and analysis in this book but is unable to do full justice to this significant and neglected subject. Especially valuable are Stone's clear and sensible discussions of the fundamental strategies, often based on misconceptions, that both sides pursued. Despite all of its drawbacks, this study contains much new and fascinating material.
    SR, 36:2:301-302

355. Tikhmenev, P. A. **A History of the Russian-American Company.** Translated and edited by Richard A. Pierce and Alton S. Donnelly. Seattle and London: University of Washington Press, 1978. xiv, 522p. Illus. $35.00.

In 1857, a young Russian naval lieutenant named P. A. Tikhmenev was hired by the Russian-American Company to write the company's history. He labored diligently in the company's archives, and, from 1861 to 1863, he published two large volumes, which combined a detailed history and a compilation of documents long acknowledged as a major source for the study of Russian activities in Alaska. Tikhmenev's narrative in this excellent new translation will be of particular interest to specialists in both Russian and American history, as will be his documentary appendices, which will be published separately by Limestone Press of Kingston, Ontario.

SR, 38:2:299

356. Zaionchkovsky, Peter A. **The Abolition of Serfdom in Russia.** Edited and translated by Susan Wobst. Introduction by Terence Emmons. The Russian Series, vol. 20. Gulf Breeze, FL: Academic International Press, 1978. [Moscow, 1968]. xvi, 250p. $19.50.

This is a translation of the third edition of a work that has long been regarded as the most lucid and thorough explanation of the drafting, implementation, and reception of legislation emancipating the serfs. The book provides unusual insights into the complex relationship among the state bureaucracy, local landowners, and the peasantry at every level of their interaction. This book remains one of the best examples of empirical research in Soviet historical literature. It provides a wealth of material not available to non-Russian readers, and it incorporates the latest research, including that of American scholars. Regrettably, the translation suffers from a number of serious shortcomings.

SR, 39:4:601-602

357. Zaionchkovsky, Peter A. **The Russian Autocracy in Crisis, 1878-1882.** Edited and translated by Gary M. Hamburg. The Russian Series, vol. 33. Gulf Breeze, FL: Academic International Press, 1979 [Moscow, 1964]. xvi, 375p. $26.00.

This book is an important collection of paraphrased or directly quoted excerpts from diaries, memoirs, letters, government reform proposals, drafts of legislation, and so forth, all garnered from Soviet archives, with much of the material unavailable in published form. It gives a vivid picture of the pressure groups and individuals who attempted to influence politics during this crucial time. The author's commentary amounts to a reiteration that the autocracy was in crisis because it could no longer govern by traditional means.

SR, 39:4:680-81

358. Zaionchkovsky, Peter A. **The Russian Autocracy under Alexander III.** Edited and translated by David R. Jones. The Russian Series, vol. 22. Gulf Breeze, FL: Academic International Press, 1976 [Moscow, 1970]. xiv, 308p. $19.50.

Zaionchkovsky's approach in this book is to avoid broad, simplistic characterizations and to focus upon specific interactions and clashes taking place within the Russian state under Alexander III. For this purpose, he has marshaled great amounts of unpublished material and is thus able to reveal what was happening behind the scenes during this time. His book shows how state policy evolved in the midst of the fear, confusion, and corruption of the late nineteenth-century bureaucracy.

SR, 37:1:127

Revolution and Civil War

359. Elwood, Ralph Carter. **Roman Malinovsky: A Life without a Cause.** Newtonville, MA: Oriental Research Partners, 1977. 107p. $8.00.
The author's colorful account in this book of Roman Malinovsky thoroughly informs us of the enormous range of activities and the great energy of this figure, drawing this tragic and enigmatic man fully into the light of day. Malinovsky was the leader and outstanding orator of the Bolshevik Duma contingent, Lenin's closest link to the Russian Bureau of the Bolshevik Central Committee, and also an Okhrana agent before 1917. Penetrating a thick fog, Elwood, by adding meticulous research to commonsense thinking, has finally made sense out of the worst scandal involving Lenin.
CSP, 21:1:112-13

360. Elwood, Ralph C., ed. **Reconsiderations on the Russian Revolution.** Cambridge, MA: Slavica Publishers Inc., 1976. x, 278p. $14.95.
This volume consists of papers, some of which are substantive pieces of research, originally delivered at the Banff International Conference in 1974. What emerges from the 12 papers is that the history of the October Revolution has not yet been written and will not be written in the near future. Several of the contributors pose more questions than they answer. The main virtue of this volume is to make the student aware that many received opinions, from East and West, should be looked at again with a critical eye.
SEER, 57:2:304-306

361. Farnsworth, Beatrice. **Aleksandra Kollantai: Socialism, Feminism, and the Bolshevik Revolution.** Stanford: Stanford University Press, 1980. xiv, 432p. $28.50.
Kollontai is being discussed here as revolutionist, opposition leader, highest-ranking woman member of the Soviet regime, and, finally, diplomat in virtual exile. Her successes and failures illuminate the often harsh realities of Communist political life from the pre-revolutionary years through the Stalinist era, showing how the Party treated women in its ranks. The work, clearly written and well documented, is an important contribution to the subject of women and revolution.

362. Fic, Victor M. **The Bolsheviks and the Czechoslovak Legion: The Origins of Their Conflict, March-May 1918.** New Delhi: Albhinav Publications, 1978. xix, 495p. $19.00.
This is the second volume of Fic's trilogy. He supplies valuable information on the strength of the Bolshevik armed forces, the number and significance of German prisoners of war, Lenin's cooperation with Germany's General Staff, and Wilson's refusal to send American troops into Siberia.
NP, 6:2:226-27

363. Fic, Victor M. **Revolutionary War for Independence and the Russian Question: Czechoslovak Army in Russia, 1914-1918.** New Delhi: Albhinav Publications, 1977. 270p. $12.00.
This book's theme is almost entirely focused on the policies and strategies vis-à-vis the relations of the seceding Czechs and Slovaks, first with tsarist Russia and then with the regime of Lenin during the formative period of the Soviet government and the Czechoslovak Legions in Russia. The author has drawn upon Czech, Slovak, Russian, and German sources. In fact, Fic's contribution is a most definite and able presentation of this controversial period of Czechoslovak-Russian relations.
NP, 6:1:89

364. Gill, Graeme J. **Peasants and Government in the Russian Revolution.** New York: Barnes & Noble, Harper & Row, 1979. xiv, 233p. $22.50.

Gill describes the attitudes and behavior of Russian peasants from March to October 1917 and details the programs and actions of successive governments toward the peasants during this period. The focus of the narrative is on the hierarchical systems of land and food (supply) committees set up by the government, their overlapping competence and incompetence, and peasant participation in or rejection of them. The book contains useful passages about the seasonability of peasant life and its effects on peasant behavior.

SR, 39:2:304-305

365. Goldhurst, Richard. **The Midnight War: The American Intervention in Russia, 1918-1920.** New York: McGraw-Hill, 1978. xvi, 288p. + 16pp. photographs. Maps. $14.95.

The strength of this book, especially for aficionados of military history, is the great detail it provides on a number of individual military engagements. The tactics of American and other leaders of the intervention are subjected to microscopic investigation. The fate of the Czechs, hopelessly caught in the quagmire of advancing Bolshevik armies, the ineptitude of the Whites, and the confusion of the Allies, serve as the main backdrop for the account. The Czechs are portrayed as the only effective fighting force, deprived of any real impact by the political situation.

SR, 39:4:486-87

366. Keep, John L. **The Russian Revolution: A Study in Mass Mobilization.** Revolutions in the Modern World Series. New York: W. W. Norton, 1976. xvii, 614p. $19.50.

The author of this book has done much research, amassing a rich store of facts, which form intricate patterns of meaning and provide a solid base for interpretation. The facts confirm the author's claim that the peasants were at least as important as the workers in making the Russian Revolution possible. They also confirm the impression obtained from what has been published before – that the workers, soldiers, and sailors provided the cadre without whom the Revolution could not have triumphed. This detailed account of political activity and economic conditions in the two capitals and in the provinces shows that the Bolsheviks did not unleash the forces that contended for power in 1917. However, late in 1917 and in 1918, they succeeded in absorbing some of the revolutionary forces, neutralizing others, and crushing the rest. This is a careful, original, and thoughtful study.

SR, 37:4:668-69

367. Kenez, Peter. **Civil War in South Russia, 1919-1920: The Defeat of the Whites.** Berkeley: University of California Press, 1977. xviii, 348p. Illus. Maps. $17.50.

This book is not a real history of the civil war but an examination of the political and social causes behind the defeat of the Whites. Kenez attributes the Whites' failure only to an ill-defined and unarticulated ideology and to the inability to develop a "functioning administration." He does not mention the treatment of the non-Russian peoples and the policy of Russification; hence, his attempt to explain the failure of the Whites remains incomplete and partial.

SR, 38:2:301-303

368. Mawdsley, Evan. **The Russian Revolution and the Baltic Fleet.** London: Macmillan; New York: Barnes & Noble, 1978. xv, 213p. $23.50.

This book is a narrative covering the life of the Baltic squadron from the eve of the February revolution up to its virtual dissolution in spring 1918. Naturally, the transformation of the sailors from a discontented but unpoliticized community, whose first

demands included the right to wear galoshes, into a key element of the Bolsheviks' power is a major theme of the book. The success of the Bolsheviks in making good use of the sailors at the critical time is ascribed to superior organization. There is nothing new in this material, but the author provides new flesh for old arguments. Despite the highly factual content, the authors has constructed a readable narrative, supported by apt quotations.
SEER, 57:4:610-11

369. Medvedev, Roy A. **The October Revolution.** Translated by George Saunders. New York: Columbia University Press, 1979. xix, 240p. $14.95.
A remarkable synthesis of recently advanced new considerations about the nature and development of the Bolshevik revolution has now come from within the Soviet Union itself, in the work of the renowned Marxist dissident Roy Medvedev. Following his work on Stalinism and the Soviet Union's current political prospects (*Let History Judge: The Origin and Consequences of Stalinism* [New York, 1971]; *On Socialist Democracy* [New York, 1975]), Medvedev has turned back to the period of the Revolution to look for the sources of despotic degeneration in Soviet socialism. Central to Medvedev's argument is the question whether, on the Marxian line of development toward socialism, the October Revolution was "premature."
RR, 39:3:370-72

370. Miliukov, Paul. **The Russian Revolution.** Vol. 1: *The Revolution Divided: Spring, 1917.* Edited by Richard Stites. Translated by Tatyana Stites and Richard Stites. The Russian Series, vol. 44/1. Gulf Breeze, FL: Academic International Press [1921, under the title *Istoriia vtoroi russkoi revoliutsii*, vol. 1, part 1]. xxviii, 227p. $19.50.
Miliukov, as a trained historian, consciously attempted to bring the historian's analysis to bear, and thus this book is an explanation, a theory of the Revolution, and a memoir of his activities. Though few would agree with all of Miliukov's arguments and analyses, it is testimony to the power of his intellect that many of his judgments still carry great weight and must be considered by any historian. Stites provides a brief but excellent preface. Especially good is the discussion of the notion of *gosudarstvennost'* and how that shaped Miliukov's actions and perceptions, giving them a unifying purpose.
SR, 39:3:497-98

371. Nabokov, Vladimir D. **V. D. Nabokov and the Russian Provisional Government, 1917.** Edited by Virgil D. Medlin and Steven L. Parsons. Introduction by Robert O. Browder. New Haven and London: Yale University Press, 1976. viii, 188p. $12.50.
V. D. Nabokov was an eminent Russian liberal and Kadet who, during the February Revolution, became head of the new Provisional Government's chancellery. From that position he was able to observe, and even participate in, the inner circle of the government during the critical first two months of the Revolution, and he remained active in the Revolution as a Kadet leader even after leaving the chancellery. These two vantage points, plus his own acumen, make his memoir one of the most valuable sources on the Russian Revolution.
SR, 37:2:295-96

372. Porter, Cathy. **Fathers and Daughters: Russian Women in Revolution.** London: Virago, 1976. 309p. £5.95.
Porter's book can be divided into two parts. The first, the more general and the less successful, is a brief history of Russian women through the ages, up to the beginnings of emancipation in the 1850s. Then the author discusses the emergence of feminism in the 1850s and 1860s, when young women from the educated and gentry classes began to revolt

against the roles that they were expected to perform. It is on such women that Porter has chosen to concentrate, those who joined the terrorism of *Narodnaya volya*.
SEER, 55:1:122-23

373. Rabinowitch, Alexander. **The Bolsheviks Come to Power: The Revolution of 1917 in Petrograd.** New York: W. W. Norton, 1976. xxxvi, 393p. Illus. $14.95.
The author's primary aim in this book is "to reconstruct as fully and accurately as possible, the development of the 'revolution from below.' " In so doing, he comes to several conclusions: First, the Bolshevik program of land, peace, and bread had widespread support among the masses. Second, the Bolshevik program achieved this popularity precisely because of the inability — or lack of desire — of other political parties to respond to these demands. Third, moderate socialist parties' continued support of the Provisional Government undermined their credibility in the eyes of the masses. And fourth, in Petrograd in 1917 the Bolshevik Party was successful precisely because it was flexible and responsive to the moods of the populace, in striking contrast to the traditional Leninist model. The footnoting of this book is thorough, and there is a comprehensive bibliography. This book is indispensable reading for the student of Soviet history.
SR, 37:4:669-70

374. Radkey, Oliver H. **The Unknown Civil War in Soviet Russia: A Study of the Green Movement in the Tambov Region 1920-1921.** Stanford: Hoover Institution Press, Stanford University, 1976. xiv, 456p. $12.95.
The author of this book focuses on one particularly tenacious and well-organized uprising against Soviet Russia that took place mainly in 1921 in a few *uezdy* of the Tambov region and lasted for about nine months. Once the regime introduced the NEP, the peasants' discontent subsided and their support for the uprisings dried out.
SR, 36:4:682-83

375. Roobol, W. H. **Tsereteli — A Democrat in the Russian Revolution.** The Hague: Martinus Nijhoff, 1976. xi, 273p. Dfl. 80.
Irakli Tsereteli was a historical figure of the second order. Born in 1881 the son of a noble Georgian landowner, he had an early career typical of those of upper-class revolutionaries of his generation — radical student politics, some journalism, the obligatory short spell in prison. As a key "link-man" between the Soviet majority and the Provisional Government, he reluctantly joined the first Kerensky coalition (as a Menshevik) as Minister of Posts and Telegraphs. His political career ended in failure, exile, and eventual resignation. Roobol's examination of the career of Tsereteli helps in understanding his failure. In this respect, it is a useful contribution to the historiography of the year 1917 in Russia.
SEER, 57:1:135-36

376. Saul, Norman E. **Sailors in Revolt: The Russian Baltic Fleet in 1917.** Lawrence: The Regents Press of Kansas, 1978. xiv, 312p. + 8pp. plates. $17.50.
In attempting to determine why the sailors of the Baltic Fleet constituted one of the most radical segments of the Russian population in 1917, Saul explores the relationship between the war and the Revolution, the nature of organizations and leadership at various levels within the fleet, and the influence of party programs on rank-and-file sailors, while noting the importance of factors peculiar to the fleet. Saul has used Finnish archives containing many original naval documents of the period and has carefully employed Soviet documentary collections, monographs, and articles, as well as Soviet and émigré memoirs.
SR, 38:4:674-75

377.   Smith, Canfield F. **Vladivostok under Red and White Rule: Revolution and Coun-terrevolution in the Russian Far East, 1920-1922.** Seattle and London: University of Washington Press, 1975. xvi, 304p. $11.00.

Focusing his attention on Vladivostok because of its strategic location and its political, economic, and diplomatic importance, Smith analyses the changes in political power in Vladivostok from January 1920 to October 1922. He demonstrates graphically how the lack of discipline among the Whites and the brutality of their rule drove the population into the hands of the Communists. This study is impressively documented with a wide range of Russian and Western official and private sources. The bibliography is extensive and critically annotated.

   SR, 36:1:121

378.   Snow, Russell E. **The Bolsheviks in Siberia, 1917-1918.** Madison, NJ: Fairleigh Dickinson University Press, 1977. 269p. $13.50.

Snow has broadened the geographical scope of the 1917 Russian Revolution with this study, and informed us about the Bolshevik activities and organization in the vast region of Siberia. He finds that Bolsheviks showed considerable strength there from the very beginning of the Revolution, and one of his important conclusions is that the Bolshevik leadership was mostly locally generated, having little connection with Lenin in Petrograd.

   NP, 7:2:237

379.   Starikov, Sergei, and Roy Medvedev. **Philip Mironov and the Russian Civil War.** Translated by Guy Daniels. New York: Alfred A. Knopf, 1978. xvi, 267p. $15.00.

The authors of this work set out to rehabilitate one of the genuine military heroes of the Revolution and civil war — the Don Cossack general, Philip Mironov. Through impressive research in Soviet archives, the authors have recreated the career of Mironov and, in doing so, they have provided a vivid picture of the chaos and violence that ravaged the Cossack lands in the post-Revolutionary period. Mironov was executed in the courtyard of the prison in Moscow. His rehabilitation by a military collegium in 1960 was not followed by a posthumous recognition of his military and political accomplishments.

   SR, 38:4:675-76

380.   Wildman, Allan K. **The End of the Russian Imperial Army: The Old Army and the Soldiers' Revolt, March-April 1917.** Princeton, NJ: Princeton University Press, 1980. 402p. $25.00.

This is the first volume of a two-part study of the army in the Russian Revolution. While this volume analyzes the role of the soldiers in bringing down the monarchy, its sequel will discuss the participation of the soldiers in the establishment of the Soviet regime. Wildman wrote this book from the point of view of passionate commitment to the cause of simple soldiers. His ability to penetrate to the lowest levels of society gives the book a unique value. But, his reconstruction of soldiers' opinions is not convincing. He sees a consistency in the soldiers' attitude to the Revolution and rejection of the war which was, perhaps, not there. The book is one of the few recent major contributions to the study of the Russian Revolution.

   RR, 39:4:501-502

RSFSR and USSR

381.   Lyons, Graham, ed. **The Russian Version of the Second World War: The History of the War as Taught to Soviet Schoolchildren.** Hamden, CT: Archon Books, Shoe String Press, 1976. xviii, 142p. Plates. $10.00.

This is actually two books under one cover. The first and main portion of the volume consists of passages selected and translated from two Soviet modern history texts assigned to tenth-grade students. The second portion, the Appendix, is a set of selected excerpts from popular histories and memoirs for Soviet adult general readers, dealing with the Stalin-Hitler Pact of 1939; the Russo-Finnish War, 1940-41; and the Russian refusal to help the insurgents in the Warsaw Uprising of 1944. This book should be of genuine value to anyone concerned with questions of political socialization and the sociopolitical aspects of historiography, as well as to historians.

SR, 36:3:503-504

382.   Tucker, Robert C., ed. **Stalinism: Essays in Historical Interpretation.** New York: W. W. Norton, 1977. xx, 332p. $19.95.

This symposium contains a number of exceedingly valuable papers that must figure in any bibliography of essential reading on the subject. There are 13 contributors. Not only has Tucker written an introduction and "some conclusions for a scholarly agenda," but also an intellectually challenging paper, "Stalinism as Revolution from Above," in which he stresses the traditional Russian despotic elements. He summarizes the conclusions by stating that Stalinism was, in some sense, an offspring of classical Marxism. "What one views as a legitimate child, the other sees as a bastard," he states.

SR, 37:1:128-30

Special Studies — Society, Women, Urban History

383.   Black, J. L. **Nicholas Karamzin and Russian Society in the Nineteenth Century: A Study in Russian Political and Historical Thought.** Toronto and Buffalo: University of Toronto Press, 1975. xvi, 264p. $17.50.

The significance of Karamzin's political and historical thought still needs attention. For this reason, this book is a most welcome contribution to the available literature, providing a judicious study of Karamzin's considerable impact on Russian society. The study focuses exclusively on Karamzin's political and social thought, rather than attempting to survey Karamzin's total achievements in all fields.

SR, 36:1:116

384.   Broido, Vera. **Apostles into Terrorists: Women and the Revolutionary Movement in the Russia of Alexander II.** New York: The Viking Press, 1977. xii, 238p. Illus. $15.00.

Vera Broido, daughter of the Menshevik leaders, Eva and Mark Broido, offers in this book an account of the "nihilist," Populist, and terrorist women of the Russian radical movement in the years 1855 to 1881, an eminently sensible unit of study. The book is not a "definitive scholarly work" as claimed by the publisher, yet it is a pleasure to read, an eye-opener for the novice, and a needed corrective to standard accounts of the Populist movement.

SR, 37:3:497-98

385.   Clements, Barbara Evans. **Bolshevik Feminist: The Life of Aleksandra Kollontai.** Bloomington and London: Indiana University Press, 1979. xxvi, 352p. Photographs. $15.00.

This book is clear in its purpose, cogent in its analysis, and pervaded by an intuitive sense of the psychology of its subject. The author is at her best when she correlates Kollontai's ideas on politics and sex with formative failings in society. Clements explores Kollontai's contention that women are the agents, as well as the beneficiaries, of their own emancipation. The footnotes and bibliography are exemplary and constitute an excellent source for scholars who wish to investigate further the many facets of Alexandra Kollontai's career.

SR, 39:2:306-307

386. Fedor, Thomas Stanley. **Patterns of Urban Growth in the Russian Empire during the Nineteenth Century.** Research Paper no. 163. Chicago: University of Chicago, Department of Geography, 1975. xxvi, 245p. Tables. Illus. $6.00, paper.

This is a realistic study of urban growth in the Russian Empire during the nineteenth century. The author attempts to evaluate the urban data from the *revizii* and other civil administrative authorities, as well as to investigate the problems of delimiting urban settlements, and displays appropriate skepticism about the accuracy of the data. This significant study should be of interest not only to students of nineteenth-century Russia but also to those concerned with early urban development.

SR, 36:1:112

387. Hamm, Michael F., ed. **The City in Russian History.** Lexington: The University Press of Kentucky, 1976. x, 350p. Maps. $15.00.

Urban history has often been neglected by Western students of Russia. This collection is meant as "the first attempt outside the Soviet Union to examine the character of the town ... from the medieval period to the present." The compendium should interest both students of urbanism and students of Russia, providing an impetus for further research.

SR, 36:1:110-12

388. Hittle, J. Michael. **The Service City: State and Townsmen in Russia, 1600-1800.** Cambridge, MA: Harvard University Press, 1979. viii, 297p. $20.00.

By the term "service city" Hittle refers to the early modern Russian town not asa a geographic concept but as an expression of the *posad* commune with its various administrative and tax obligations. For primary materials, Hittle draws on the collection of Russian laws and the town *nakazy* presented to Catherine II's Commission on Law (1767 to 1768). His contribution lies in a fresh and persuasive synthesis of known facts, adding to the understanding of the place of cities in the context of Russian state building.

RR, 39:3:359-61

389. Johnson, Robert Eugene. **Peasant and Proletarian: The Working Class of Moscow in the Late Nineteenth Century.** New Brunswick, NJ: Rutgers University Press, 1979. xii, 225p. $17.50.

The concentration of heavy industry into large units did not take place primarily in Moscow but in industrial settlements scattered across the countryside, which maintained patriarchal relations not unlike over-growth villages. Smaller units for dyeing and weaving were often maintained, rather than driven out, as necessary adjuncts to the larger enterprises. Mechanization and concentration did not, therefore, lead to an ever increasing sense of class identity. Although year-round labor and long-term residence became a firm pattern in the Moscow textile industry quite early, it had little impact on the family cycle characteristics of all peasant *otkhodniki*. Workers in large enterprises who remained at the same factory for many years retained their allotments, left their families behind in parent households, and in their mid-forties returned to their villages to assume their roles as the *bolshak*.

RR, 40:1:63-65

390. Ransel, David L., ed. **The Family in Imperial Russia: New Lines of Historical Research.** Urbana, Chicago, and London: University of Illinois Press, 1978. x, 342p. $16.50.

This interesting and imaginative volume dealing with the daily life of broad masses of people makes a good start for Russia along lines that have been better developed for Europe and America and makes something like beginning comparisons possible. The most interesting and informative essay is on the Russian clerical family and the clerisy reforms of the late 1860s. Other essays deal with the peasant family, family relations and the urban-rural nexus, fosterage of unwanted children, medical care, and the training of midwives. It is a book that should absorb many and prompt some to forge ahead on the paths begun here.

SR, 39:1:115-16

391. Rozman, Gilbert. **Urban Networks in Russia, 1750-1800, and Premodern Periodization.** Princeton, NJ: Princeton University Press, 1976. x, 337p. Tables. Graphs. Maps. $16.50.

An explicit concern of this work is: In what sense was Russia backward? Once urban development began in Russia at the end of the eighteenth century, it progressed at a faster rate than in any other society examined by the author. The lack of self-government in Russian cities is shown to be a result of early centralization of control rather than of "backwardness" in a meaningful sense. This centralization probably facilitated urban development in general.

SR, 36:1:113-14

392. Stites, Richard. **The Women's Liberation Movement in Russia: Feminism, Nihilism, and Bolshevism, 1860-1930.** Princeton, NJ: Princeton University Press, 1978. xx, 464p. Illus. $37.50.

Despite the large scope of his study, Stites shows excellent command of literature, including newspapers, journals, political literature, police reports, and minutes of professional congresses. He has also consulted much literature on the women's movement from elsewhere, never losing sight of the strong influence that the West was exerting on Russian events. Stites liberally seasons his discussion with statistical data and survey results. This important addition to the history of modern Russia will be much read and much discussed.

SR, 37:3:498-500

MILITARY AFFAIRS

Handbooks, Encyclopedias

393. Jones, David R., ed. **The Military-Naval Encyclopedia of Russia and the Soviet Union.** Vol. 1: *"A" (Gliders)-Administration, Military.* Vol. 2: *Administration, Military, Science of—Admiral Makarov (ship).* Gulf Breeze, FL: Academic International Press, 1978. viii, 247p. $29.50; vol. 2: 1980. vi, 245p. Figures. Tables. $31.00.

This ambitious project should earn a solid place in the field of reference works on military history and Soviet/Russian studies. The volume, the first of a series which is likely to run to between 40 and 50 volumes, lives up to its editor's claim that "almost half of the contents ... concern items never recorded previously in other standard reference works," that it will be a "helpful bibliographic tool for all those interested in Russia's military history," and "if a

topic might interest any general or specialist reader, or any student or teacher, it has been included."
SR, 39:3:505-506

394. Norby, M. O. **Soviet-Aerospace Handbook.** Washington, DC: U.S. Government Printing Office, 1978. 223p.
This military manual provides information on the following: general administration, branches (air force, strategic missile forces, air defense, naval aviation, the space program, research and development), doctrine, manpower and finance, service conditions, biographies of 21 key figures, Russian and Western bibliography. The handbook is well illustrated, including some 70 pictures of aircraft and missiles and 18 pages in color of uniforms, insignia, and medals.

To 1917

395. McCully, Newton A., Lt. Commander, U.S. Navy. **The McCully Report: The Russo-Japanese War, 1904-05.** Edited by Richard A. von Doenhoff. Annapolis, MD: Naval Institute Press, 1977. xiv, 338p. Illus. $14.95.
McCully was an American naval officer who received orders on February 12, 1904 to proceed from St. Petersburg as assistant naval attaché to act as an observer with the Russian forces at the front during the Russo-Japanese War. He was able, in spite of important restrictions, to see and report a great deal pertaining to Russia's military forces, its transportation system, and the conduct of the war. He traveled by train and recorded accurately everything he observed in Siberia, Manchuria, and about Port Arthur. The editor has done a valuable service in making public this recently declassified document. The book includes 11 appendices, giving information on the military forces, the defense of Port Arthur and of Vladivostok, and other pertinent matters.
SR, 39:1:119

1917 to the Present

396. Adelman, Jonathan R. **The Revolutionary Armies: The Historical Development of the Soviet and the Chinese People's Liberation Armies.** Westport, CT: Greenwood Press, 1980. 232p. $22.50.
The parallels between the Soviet and Chinese armies are obvious, according to this book. Each country fought a victorious civil war; each was subsequently maintained as a multi-million-man force, largely of peasants, to preserve the gains of the revolutions. Yet, the similarities, according to Adelman, end there. The Soviet army remained without political or social role for decades; it became exclusively a militaristic entity serving the Party and the State. This study, based on Soviet sources, offers an important contribution to the study of comparative Communism.

397. Boyd, Alexander. **The Soviet Air Force since 1918.** Foreword by John Erickson. New York: Stein & Day, 1977. xx, 259p. + 12pp. photographs. $10.00.
Boyd's study is an important contribution to Soviet military history. Using a large number of Soviet and Western sources, Boyd has done a remarkable job of writing a detailed history of the Soviet air force, covering such fascinating subjects as the Russo-German cooperation in the twenties; early Soviet theories about the deployment of air powers; employment of imprisoned designers by the NKVD; the failures in the first two years of the Great Patriotic War; and, finally, victory and postwar rebirth.
SR, 37:1:138

398. Erickson, John. **The Road to Stalingrad: Stalin's War with Germany.** vol. 1. New York: Harper & Row, 1975. x, 594p. + 8pp. photographs. $25.00.
Erickson, the noted British military historian and writer, is one of the most knowledgeable observers of Soviet military affairs, and this book is probably the best account to date of the first 18 months of the Russo-German conflict of the Second World War. The work suffers from the inadequacies of official Soviet records that still remain unavailable to Western historians. The first volume is divided into three general parts. Book one is an account of the rebuilding of the Red Army after the Finnish Campaign, while book two covers the period from the German attack through mid-November 1942, ending with the Soviet encirclement of Paulus' forces in Stalingrad. The remainder of the volume—almost 100 pages—contains the third part, "Sources and References," which presents a great deal of data and constitutes a most valuable resource.
      SR, 35:2:337-38

399. Erickson, John, and E. J. Feuchtwanger, eds. **Soviet Military Power and Performance.** Hamden, CT: Shoe String Press, 1979. xiii, 219p. $25.00.
This is a collection of papers presented by experts at a conference in 1977. Despite an obvious unevenness in the contributions, the editors have provided a useful, often stimulating but sometimes irritatingly pedestrian, contribution to the literature on contemporary Soviet military affairs.
      RR, 39:2:260-61

400. Jones, David R., ed. **Soviet Armed Forces Review Annual.** Gulf Breeze, FL: Academic International Press. Vol. 1: 1977, x, 277p. $29.50; Vol. 2: 1978. 372p. $35.00; Vol. 3: 1979. ix, 364p. $36.00.
This publication provides an up-to-date forum for the discussion of Soviet military affairs. Volume one includes 20 articles on a wide variety of topics. The book also includes bibliographic articles on the Soviet military. These articles should prove to be a valuable source for both specialists and students. The yearbook represents an important contribution to the field of Soviet military studies.
      SR, 37:1:134-35; SEER, 59:1:150-51

401. Pipes, Richard, ed. **Soviet Strategy in Europe.** New York: Crane, Russak & Co., 1976. 316p. $14.50.
This work is concerned with Soviet strategy in Europe in the sense of a unified application of all means of state power in the service of foreign policy objectives. The first four papers address the political dimension of the problem. The next two papers focus on the military dimension of the issues, and the final two papers, under the heading of the economic dimension, probe the question of the degree of mutual economic dependence or the relative lack of it. The quality of the papers is exceptionally high.
      SS, 31:4:586

402. Scott, Harriet Fast, and William F. Scott. **The Armed Forces of the USSR.** Boulder, CO: Westview Press, 1979. xvi, 439p. Illus. $24.00.
The authors have used an impressive range of sources in this book, including the leading Soviet military periodicals and the volumes published by *Voenizdat*. Their familiarity with the Soviet defense establishment and the evolution of Soviet military doctrine, as well as their attention to the institutional and ideological aspects of Soviet decision making, contribute to an informative volume. The Scotts have divided their study into a historical prologue and three sections dealing with military doctrine and strategy, the contemporary

structure of Soviet armed forces, and the integration of those forces into Soviet national life.
SR, 39:3:504-505

403. Scott, William F. **Soviet Sources of Military Doctrine and Strategy**. New York: Crane, Russak & Co., 1975. viii, 72p. $2.75.
This is an invaluable reference book for anyone interested in Soviet military affairs. After a brief but relevant introduction, the book begins with a chapter on Soviet political-military spokesmen; this is followed by a discussion on basic sources, which evaluates and describes the function of the major Soviet newspapers and journals that deal with military affairs. The bulk of the book is devoted to a critical examination of the most important Soviet works on military affairs that have been published between 1960 and 1974. Colonel Scott's book ends with a list of English translations of Soviet military books.
SEER, 55:2:273-74

Navy

404. Dismukes, Bradford, and James M. McConnell, eds. **Soviet Naval Diplomacy**. New York: Pergamon Press, 1979. xvii, 409p. $25.00.
This detailed study of the Soviet navy's peacetime role contains selections by a number of authors with the Center for Naval Analyses, an affiliate of the University of Rochester. The unifying theme is that the Soviet ambition to Communize the world has been constant, although the doctrine of inevitable war with the capitalist West that prevailed in the Stalinist era has been changed to one of "peaceful coexistence" to attain the ultimate goal. This alteration in grand strategy emphasizes the exploitation of less developed countries, bringing a modification in naval policy to provide for, in Admiral Sergei Gorshkov's words, "a balanced fleet."
RR, 39:2:257

405. MacGwire, Michael, Ken Booth, and John McDonnell, eds. and comps. **Soviet Naval Policy: Objectives and Constraints**. Published for the Centre for Foreign Policy Studies, Department of Political Science, Dalhousie University. New York: Praeger Publishers, 1975. xxvi, 663p. $32.50.
Twenty-seven British, Canadian, Australian, and American authors, contributors to the Seminar on Soviet Naval Developments at the Second Dalhousie University Conference (Halifax, N.S.), offer in this book informed analysis and debate on the Soviet naval policy. This volume is the second of a trilogy stemming from the conferences held in 1972, 1973, and 1974. The first volume, *Soviet Naval Developments: Capacity and Context*, and the just-published *Soviet Naval Influence: Domestic and Foreign Dimensions* (1976), provide a unique source of the latest developments concerning the Soviet navy.
SR, 35:4:740-41

406. MacGwire, Michael, and John McDonnell, eds. **Soviet Naval Influence: Domestic and Foreign Dimensions**. Published for the Centre for Foreign Policy Studies, Department of Political Science, Dalhousie University, Halifax, Nova Scotia. New York and London: Praeger Publishers, 1977. xxxvi, 660p. $27.50.
The contributions of 28 members of the third seminar that met in September 1974 at Dalhousie University are arranged under eight headings: aspects of Soviet foreign policy, the place of the navy in the policy processes, war fighting capability, projection capability,

some analytical material, East-West naval interaction, the Soviet navy and the Third World influence building, and future prospects. This book has value in providing additional details in convenient form and in recording the Western perception of Soviet naval intentions in a particular time frame.

SR, 37:1:138-40

407. Moore, John E. **The Soviet Navy Today.** Introduction by John Erickson. New York: Stein & Day, 1976. 255p. Photographs. $15.95.

This book is divided by ship types, each section introduced by a short historical narrative and each ship class replete with vital statistics, a silhouette, and one representative photograph. Since statistics alone do not tell a story, Moore does, using the historical development of the post-World War II navy as his vehicle. He focuses on serious qualitative handicaps in the Soviet navy, such as lack of experience in global naval operations, poor relations between the navy and the political commissars, and other problems.

SR, 36:2:319-20

408. Morris, Eric. **The Russian Navy: Myth and Reality.** New York: Stein & Day, 1977. 150p. $9.95.

This book contains much that the scholar needs to know in order to gain some appreciation of the complex factors affecting the development of contemporary Soviet naval power. Morris presents a balanced picture of checkered Russian maritime history. He makes clear that a coherent Soviet naval policy did not emerge quickly, even under the Bolsheviks. The development of the contemporary Soviet navy is described in a less disciplined, but quite readable, manner.

SR, 37:3:506-507

409. Murphy, Paul J., ed. **Naval Power in Soviet Policy.** Studies in Communist Affairs, vol. 2. Published under the auspices of the United States Air Force. Washington, DC: U.S. Government Printing Office, 1978. xiv, 341p. $5.25, paper.

Most of the 16 contributors to this volume are well-known specialists. Some are former United States naval officers whose careers included service directly concerned with the analysis of Soviet naval affairs. Divided into several principal parts, the volume begins with four essays that focus on the origins of Soviet naval policy. The second part, containing eight articles, is devoted to an assessment of Soviet naval combat characteristics. The third section provides two essays on Soviet initiatives for naval arms limitation, and the final portion features two historical pieces on Soviet naval deployment in the Mediterranean Sea and Indian Ocean. The book should certainly be required reading for anyone interested in contemporary international security affairs.

SR, 39:2:316-17

410. Ruge, Friedrich. **The Soviets as Naval Opponents, 1941-1945.** Annapolis, MD: Naval Institute Press, 1979. viii, 210p. $16.95.

Friedrich Ruge served in the German High Seas Fleet in World War I and held various responsible posts in the *Kriegsmarine* during World War II, along with occupying high positions in the Federal German Navy. His book is not a memoir but a well-considered narrative based on German war diaries, Soviet publications, and works by Western scholars. The work contains no surprising revelations, although many readers will be surprised to learn that the Russo-German naval war was waged primarily with small numbers of ships of comparatively small size. Motortorpedo boats, mine vessels, and submarines predominated, with Soviet naval air acquiring increased importance as the war progressed.

RR, 39:2:257-59

411. Wegener, Edward. **The Soviet Naval Offensive: An Examination of the Strategic Role of Soviet Naval Forces in the East-West Conflict.** Translated from the German by Henning Wegener. Annapolis, MD: Naval Institute Press, 1975 [1972, 1974]. x, 135p. $11.00.

Wegener, a retired German naval officer who served both during World War II and in NATO Command, has written an important book not only for strategists but for all persons seriously concerned with Soviet foreign policy. He provides a plausible strategic doctrine for evaluating Soviet and Western naval postures.

SR, 35:4:742

Special Studies

412. Colton, Timothy J. **Commissars, Commanders, and Civilian Authority: The Structure of Soviet Military Politics.** Cambridge, MA, and London: Harvard University Press, 1979. xii, 365p. Tables. $25.00.

Colton challenges the specific conclusion that the CPSU leadership uses the military's *Glavnoe Politicheskoe Upravlenie* (Glavpu) and its network of political officers to monitor and control the professional military men subordinate to the Minister of Defense, as well as the general interpretation that the Soviet military leadership is locked in a zero-sum struggle for influence with the Soviet political leadership. Colton demonstrates that the Glavpu is not an instrument of control by examining its behavior in the light of Western definitions of an effective monitoring agency.

SR, 40:1:123-24

413. Deane, Michael J. **Political Control of the Soviet Armed Forces.** New York: Crane, Russak & Co., 1977. xi, 297p. $17.50.

The purpose of Deane's book is to "define types of interest groups represented by the MPA, the Party and the professional military." Providing a historical overview of party-army relations from 1917 to Ustinov's promotion to defense minister in 1976, Deane concludes that civilian party leaders experience continuing problems in their efforts to control the MPA and the professional military. Unfortunately, the author fails to define interest groups properly and the meaning of political work by the MPA, and he relies too much on secondary sources for the pre-Khrushchev period.

SR, 37:1:134-35

414. Gabriel, Richard A. **The New Red Legions.** Vol. 1: *An Attitudinal Portrait of the Soviet Soldier.* Vol. 2: *A Survey Data Source Book.* Westport, CT: Greenwood Press, 1980. Vol. 1: 312p. $22.50; Vol. 2: 280p. $40.00.

This is the first study of the Red Army based on concrete empirical data. Gabriel conducted a comprehensive survey of recent emigres from the Soviet Union, men who had served in the Soviet Army at various times over a 40-year period. The study profiles Soviet soldiers of every rank — new conscripts, NCOs, and officers — and analyzes their leadership qualities, combat abilities, and relations with other ranks. Every aspect of daily army life — food, pay, housing, leaves and furloughs — is discussed. The morale and fighting spirit and the combat effectiveness of the army as a whole are also considered in detail. This is the most thoroughly researched work yet produced on the Soviet soldier.

415. Goldhamer, Herbert. **The Soviet Soldier: Soviet Military Management at the Troop Level.** New York and London: Crane, Russak & Co., and Leo Cooper Ltd., 1975. xvi, 352p. $17.00.

The author of this book has put together a rather remarkable account of the life and times of the Soviet soldier and lower grade officer. He has made good use of the resources available, and shows that data exist upon which some critical judgments may be made. The book is a valuable addition to the knowledge of the adversary and will serve students of the Soviet military.

    SR, 36:1:131-32

416. Goure, Leon. **War Survival in Soviet Strategy: USSR Civil Defense.** Foreword by Ambassador Foy D. Kohler. Monographs in International Affairs. Miami, FL: Center for Advanced International Studies, University of Miami, 1976. xxiv, 218p. $11.95, paper.

The author addresses the subject from the standpoint of his — and the Miami Center's — broad concerns over Soviet political-military intentions and capabilities. The book includes an extensive review of the copious and detailed Soviet open literature on civil defense. The availability, in an analytic summary, of this information to a readership of Soviet affairs specialists and, more broadly, of interested citizens is all to the good. The study makes a useful — if flawed — contribution to a subject that indeed deserves attention.

    SR, 36:2:318-19

417. Higham, Robin, and Jacob W. Kipp, eds. **Soviet Aviation and Air Power: A Historical View.** Boulder, CO: Westview Press, 1977. London: Brassey's, 1978. xii, 328p. Illus. $25.00.

The 11 essays in this book investigate the evolution of Soviet air power from its feeble prerevolutionary origins through the perilous years of World War II to its present position of impressive strength, vitality, and leadership. A number of essays are devoted to topical subjects, including the development of the naval air arm, civil aviation, the strategic air force, civil defense, lessons of World War II, strategic missile forces, cosmic research, and patterns of Soviet aircraft development. Unlike most of the more technical works on the Soviet air forces, these essays do a good job of linking politics and leaders to both technical and organizational development. This is a good and important book that displays balance and crispness and offers carefully drawn conclusions.

    SR, 38:3:496-97

418. Holzman, Franklyn D. **Financial Checks on Soviet Defense Expenditures.** Lexington, MA: Lexington Books, D. C. Heath, 1975. xvi, 103p. Tables. $11.50.

This book is based on the author's 1965 report prepared for the United States Arms Control and Disarmament Agency, but it includes some revisions and updated material. It is clear from Holzman's investigation, as has been noted by other specialists, that, given the state of our information on Soviet finances, the concealment problem is indeed significant. Holzman proceeds to examine methods of financial verification that take the concealment problem into account.

    SR, 35:3:537-39

419. Jacobsen, C. G. **Soviet Strategic Initiatives: Challenge and Response.** Praeger Special Studies. New York: Holt, Rinehart & Winston, 1979. xiv, 168p. $19.95.

Jacobsen has thoroughly searched the Russian-language sources in his analysis of selective Soviet strategic undertakings. This volume is a collection of specialized essays that make important contributions to their respective fields — maritime law, arctic political and strategic developments, and Soviet force projection potential. The author has provided valuable details on the extensive Soviet-Norwegian discussions about fishing rights and territorial waters, as well as cartographic and oceanographic problems related to the Canadian arctic region. This book provides a valuable and very worthwhile contribution by identifying trends and persistent problems faced by Soviet planners.

SS, 32:4:596-97

420. Shtemenko, S. M. **The Last Six Months: Russia's Final Battles with Hitler's Armies in World War II.** Translated by Guy Daniels. Garden City, NY: Doubleday, 1977. xvi, 436p. Illus. $10.00.

The considerable value of the first volume of General Shtemenko's memoirs, published in Moscow in 1968 under the title *General'nyi shtab v gody voiny*, was that it gave insight into the actual working of the General Staff during World War II. The second volume, presented in a serviceable English translation by Daniels, is of considerably less value. Not only has Shtemenko covered the major developments of the war in the first volume but, in the second, the propaganda content is substantially higher and the informational yield correspondingly lower. This volume deals basically with the last few months of the war and provides some interesting information about Stalin's behavior at that time.

SR, 37:1:131-32

421. Spielmann, Karl F. **Analyzing Soviet Strategic Arms Decisions.** Boulder, CO: Westview Press, 1978. xvi, 184p. $16.00.

In this book, Spielmann considers "strategic [rational] factor" and pluralistic (bureaucratic interest) decision-making models and then proposes an additional variant of both, which he calls a "national leadership decision-making" approach. But his main theme and contribution is to argue for applying multiple approaches to the study of this (and other) decision-making problems. The author presents an interesting "case study" of the deployment decision for the first Soviet ICBM system, the SS-6. The book should prove useful to those with particular interest in Soviet political-military affairs.

RUSSIAN LANGUAGE

Bibliographies

422. Worth, Dean S. **A Bibliography of Russian Word-Formation.** Columbus, OH: Slavica Publishers, 1977. xliv, 317p. $11.95.

Worth's book contains 3,500 citations to books, contributions to *sborniki*, and journal articles treating word formation in Russian. The bibliography is arranged by specific subject or format and includes an author index.

SR, 37:5:552

Dictionaries and Glossaries

423. Borkowski, Piotr. **The Great Russian-English Dictionary of Idioms and Set Expressions: Over 8,600 Russian Entries.** London: Piotr Borkowski, 1973. xx, 384p. £5.00.

This book gives good English equivalents for the Russian entries, all of which are accented and labeled to indicate stylistic levels and usage. The work is arranged so that it is almost always easy to find the expression that one is looking for. In many cases, the Russian expressions are first translated by an English expression of the same stylistic level, which is then followed by a more literal and stylistically neutral translation, making it more comprehensive.

SR, 35:4:780-81

History and Linguistics

424. Comrie, Bernard, and Gerald Stone. **The Russian Language since the Revolution.** Oxford: Clarendon Press, 1978. xii, 258p. $24.95.

This work is a sociolinguistic compendium of the Soviet Russian language. It illustrates language change in progress and the divergence between prescriptive norms and actual usage. Best documented are the chapters on more traditional linguistic topics. The book should be read by all who have an interest in contemporary Russian language and society. It offers nonspecialists crucial yet little-known information on speakers of Russian.

SR, 38:3:538-39

425. Hill, Steven P. **The N-Factor and Russian Prepositions: Their Development in Eleventh-Twentieth Century Texts.** The Hague, Paris, and New York: Mouton Publishers, 1977. 365p. DM 98.00. Distributed by Walter DeGruyter, New York and Berlin.

The author traces the entire history of prepositions in Russian, from the earliest eleventh-century texts up to ones from the mid-twentieth century. The book has five parts and closes with appendices containing source lists, reference lists, and indexes of authors and of prepositions. It is the most important work in existence in its field and will be recognized as one of the standard works on Russian language history.

SR, 39:1:163-64

Textbooks and Grammars

426. Corbett, G. G. **Predicate Agreement in Russian.** Birmingham Slavonic Monographs, No. 7. Birmingham, England: Department of Russian Language and Literature, University of Birmingham, 1979. xii, 111p. £2.80.

Corbett's monograph makes a substantial contribution to the debate on predicate agreement in Russian. The approach used here is to take Russian language samples that exhibit actual usage and that, together, form the corpus to be investigated. The particular focus involved is the behavior of predicates following unspecified and incomplete specified subjects. Corbett has written a very useful monograph that is commended both to students of Russian and to students of general linguistics.

SEER, 59:2:284-86

427. Crockett, Dina B. **Agreement in Contemporary Standard Russian.** Cambridge, MA: Slavica Publishers, 1976. iv, 456p. $10.95, paper.

Although this is an exhaustive treatment of grammatical agreement in Russian, it is not a mere compendium of variations or exceptions to the straightforward agreement conventions of Russian. On the contrary, at every point the attempt is made to provide an adequate linguistic explanation. This is the best book available on agreement in Russian. It is outstanding for its breadth of coverage, illustrative material, reference to scholarly literature, and firm theoretical foundation.

SR, 37:2:362-63

428. Derwing, Bruce L., and Tom M. S. Priestly. **Reading Rules for Russian: A Systematic Approach to Russian Spelling and Pronunciation.** With Notes on

Dialectal and Stylistic Variation. Columbus, OH: Slavica Publishers, 1980. vi, 247p. $10.95, paper.

Advanced undergraduate students, graduate students, and specialists in Russian linguistics will find much in this book that is useful and informative. In developing their rules, the authors provide a great deal of essential information about the phonological processes of Russian in a manner that is clear, concise, complete, and systematic enough for the student to grasp. At the same time, the specialist will find ample stimulation in the comprehensive notes and up-to-date bibliography.

SR, 40:3:510

429. Gustavsson, Sven. **Predicative Adjectives with the Copula byt' in Modern Russian.** Stockholm: Almqvist & Wiksell, 1976. 399p. Kr. 94.00.

This book attempts to establish rules determining the choice between the short form (SF), long form (LF), and instrumental form (IF) of adjectives used predicatively with the copula *byt'* expressed, and between the SF and LF where the copula is not expressed. All who have ever learned or taught Russian as a foreign language will readily appreciate the thorniness of this problem. It is to be hoped that teachers of Russian will profit from the rich collection of examples provided.

CSP, 19:4:541-42

430. Hamilton, William S. **Introduction to Russian Phonology and Word Structure.** Columbus, OH: Slavica Publishers, 1980. iv, 187p. $8.95, paper.

Hamilton's book consists of 21 chapters that are grouped to form sections on phonetics, phonemics, and morphophonemics. In addition, there are several appendices, two of which carry a summary of the mechanics of fleeting vowels and of prefix/suffic morphemes. This book pursues pedagogical aims, with the material therefore being carefully sequenced and supported by sets of exercises—the solutions to which are given in full. The book is a useful addition to the sparse literature in English on the phonology of Russian word structure. It may help to raise the level of undergraduate enthusiasm for its theme.

SEER, 59:2:282-83

431. Levin, Jules F., and Peter D. Haikalis, with Anatole A. Forostenko. **Reading Modern Russian.** Columbus, OH: Slavica Publishers, 1979. viii, 321p. $10.95, paper.

The stated aim of this book is to teach "the comprehension of Russian expository prose" to students with no prior knowledge of the language. The book is composed of 31 chapters, four appendices, a vocabulary list, and a brief subject index. Each chapter begins with a vocabulary, followed by explanations of grammar and usage and lists of sample sentences in Russian. On the whole, with only occasional lapses, this book is reasonably well done.

SR, 39:4:722-23

432. Nakhimovsky, Alexander, and Richard Leed. **Advanced Russian.** Columbus, OH: Slavica Publishers, 1980. 380p. $11.95, paper.

This book represents a significant contribution to Russian textbook publishing. Being solidly based on original scholarly research, the volume goes considerably beyond previous textbooks in its treatment of certain grammatical problems that have thus far eluded satisfactory explanation. For this reason, the text will not only be of great benefit to advanced language students but will undoubtedly be greeted enthusiastically by teachers in the profession.

SEEJ, 25:1:128-30

433. Schooneveld, C. H., van. **Semantic Transmutations: Prolegomena to a Calculus of Meaning.** Vol. 1: *The Cardinal Semantic Structure of Prepositions, Cases, and Paratactic Conjunctions in Contemporary Standard Russian.* Bloomington, IN: Physsardt, 1978. 251p. $10.00, paper.

The present volume is the first of a projected series of studies that will deal with the lexical meaning of the verb, the adjective-adverb, and the substantive, as well as with the verbal aspect, deixis, parataxis, hypotaxis, and the whole question of grammatical meaning. The first volume discusses the semantic of verbal prefixes, prefixes, prepositions, paratactic, and the case system of Russian.

     SR, 39:2:358-59

434. Svedstedt, Dag. **Position of Objective Personal Pronouns: A Study of Word Order in Modern Russian.** Stockholm: Almqvist & Wiksell International, 1976. iv, 191p. SwKr. 49.50, paper.

In his attempt to account for the varying position of objective personal pronouns, both direct and indirect, Svedstedt applies "actual bipartition" (AB) theory (also known as "functional sentence perspective"). This theory divides the clause into the *base* (the basic information; i.e., what is understood as given) and the *nucleus* (the actual or new information). This study fills a gap in the literature and is recommended to all linguists who have the patience to endure the monotonous exposition and awkward style.

     CSP, 20:2:282-83

Semiotics

435. Baran, Henryk, ed. **Semiotics and Structuralism: Readings from the Soviet Union.** White Plains, NY: International Arts and Sciences Press, 1976. xxvi, 369p. $15.00.

This welcome book brings together 15 essays in English translations that first appeared between 1974 and 1977 in the journal *Soviet Studies in Literature.* It is to be hoped that this book will come to the attention of a wide scholarly public outside the Slavonic field.

     SEER, 56:4:632-33

436. Eimermacher, Karl, and Serge Shishkoff. **Subject Bibliography of Soviet Semiotics: The Moscow-Tartu School.** Bibliographic Series, 3. Ann Arbor: Michigan Slavic Publications, 1977. xv, 153p. $5.00, paper.

This new and very well-organized bibliography meets an urgent need. It has seven major divisions: Semiotics, Linguistics, Text, Literature, Non-Verbal Arts, Folklore and Culture, most of which are helpfully subdivided. The author's classification is both sound and helpful.

     SEER, 56:4:616-17

437. Lotman, Jurij. **The Structure of the Artistic Text.** Translated from the Russian by Ronald Vroon. Michigan Slavic Contributions, no. 7. Ann Arbor: University of Michigan, Department of Slavic Languages and Literature, 1977. xiii, 300p. $6.00, paper.

Lotman's book, which came out in Russian in 1970, was the culmination of the first period of his development as a semiotic thinker; this was the period when the natural inclination of his mind to historicism was overshadowed by the essentially synchronic and more abstract structuralist-semiotic approach. His work is rich in insights, contains some of the finest analyses of poetry, and its references range over the whole course of Russian literature in illustration of theoretical points.

     SEER, 57:1:115-17

438. Lucid, Daniel P., ed. and trans. **Soviet Semiotics: An Anthology.** Baltimore and London: The Johns Hopkins University Press, 1977. x, 259p. $16.00.

Lucid presents in this volume a very good and varied selection of writings by the older generation of Soviet semioticians, especially of the members of those narrow core units that developed in the 1960s. This volume presents the flowering of the movement with its defined lines of interest, as reflected in the topical groupings: general concepts, modeling systems, communication studies, text analysis, art and literature, and typology of culture. The short selective bibliography at the end will be helpful to the uninitiated. This is a valuable volume for both the specialist and the nonspecialist.

SR, 39:3:533-34

439. Shukman, Ann. **Literature and Semiotics: A Study of the Writings of Yu. M. Lotman.** Meaning and Art, 1. North Holland, Amsterdam, New York, and Oxford, 1977. 239p. $34.75.

Shukman's pioneering book appears at a time when Soviet literary semiotics is still a living force and when its leader and inspiration, Professor Lotman, is in the prime of his creative life. The author devotes the bulk of her text to careful summarizing of the writings within her purview. This is no mechanical task; it is not only Lotman's own writings that teem with neologisms, barbarism, hideously complex syntax, the ever-present feel for those brought up on traditional Russian literary criticism that the language is being made to cope with thought-patterns foreign to it. The author interposes in her text some brief critical discussions of the material.

SEER, 57:1:117-19

RUSSIAN LITERATURE

Bibliographies, Biographies, Encyclopedias

440. Berry, Thomas E. **Plots and Characters in Major Russian Fiction: Vol. 1: Pushkin, Lermontov, Turgenev, Tolstoi.** The Plots and Character Series. Hamden, CT: Archon Books, Shoe String Press; Folkestone, England: Wm. Dawson & Sons, Cannon House, 1977. xiv, 226p. $15.00.

Although Berry states that his work "is designed to help and encourage the reading of Russian literature," its appeal will certainly be to the serious student and reference librarian. This reference aid is divided into two parts: plots (with character lists) and characters. The section on plots consists of short summaries of selected works of the authors covered and a list of the characters in each work. The section on characters is arranged alphabetically and contains short annotations that identify the characters and the work in which they appear. Library of Congress transliteration is used, and some cross-references are provided for names that may cause confusion.

SR, 37:3:550

441. Egan, David R., and Melinda A. Egan, comps. **An Annotated Bibliography of English-Language Sources to 1978.** Scarecrow Author Bibliographies, no. 44. Metuchen, NJ: Scarecrow Press, 1979. xxxv, 267p. $15.00.

Listing 2,054 citations gathered from a wide range of scholarly and popular journals, anthologies, bibliographies, and other reference sources, this bibliography is an effective guide to a large body of Western scholarship on Tolstoy. Annotations of each book, essay, and chapter available for examination discuss the scope of the work and its main theses.

Periodical articles are briefly annotated. The bibliography also includes reviews of cited works. Arranged in broad subject categories with many cross-references and detailed author and subject indexes, the format provides convenient and thorough access and helps make the work an extremely useful reference source.

SR, 39:3:539

442. Hingley, Ronald. **Dostoyevsky: His Life and Work.** New York: Charles Scribner's Sons, 1978. 222p. Illus. $14.95.

The strongest feature of this biography is its methodical sequentiality. No gaps or fluffy generalizations are evident. Liberal evidence from his correspondence with friends and family, government records, and memoirs are filtered through Hingley's judicious inspection. Just as helpful is Hingley's knowledgeable sense of the social and political climate in which Dostoyevsky lived and worked. The clear sense of periodization in the book elucidates the liberalized censorship of Alexander II around the time of Dostoyevsky's first periodical, *Vremia*, in 1861. The author includes a number of interesting plates of Dostoyevsky at different ages, important people in his life, and representative scenes from Russian contemporary life. It is the nonspecialist who is best served by this book.

SR, 39:1:156-57

443. Ivinskaya, Olga. **A Captive of Time.** Translated and with an introduction by Max Hayward. Garden City, NY: Doubleday, 1978. xxxii, 462p. + 28pp. photographs. $12.50.

Ivinskaya claims to have been Pasternak's "right hand," aware of his thoughts, deeds, and plans. She painstakingly collates information from every source available to her and provides a narrative of key episodes in Pasternak's life. Ivinskaya portrays Pasternak as a generous and unworldly figure who has the courage of his convictions and who willingly delegates to her tasks too odious for his noble nature to bear. Her book is a web of contradictions and she idealizes her relationship with the poet. This English-language version has been edited by the late Max Hayward with the same meticulous care for which his other work is noted.

SR, 38:4:716-17

444. Laffitte, Sophie. **Chekhov: 1860-1904.** Translated by Moura Budberg and Gordon Latta. New York: Charles Scribner's Sons, 1975 [1971, 1973]. viii, 246p. + 8pp. photographs. $8.95.

The author presupposes a minimal acquaintance with Chekhov's life and works, and, while essentially covering the same well-known facts available in scores of other biographies, she presents them in a fresh, concise way that makes this book a fine introduction to Chekhov. The book is divided thematically, rather than strictly chronologically, and several of the chapters stress areas of his life that are not usually emphasized in brief biographies.

SR, 35:3:578-79

445. Lehrman, Edgar H. **A Guide to the Russian Text of Tolstoy's War and Peace.** Ann Arbor, MI: Ardis, 1980. xiv, 225p. $15.00.

This guide is the second in a series of handbooks prepared by Lehrman. The first was entitled *Handbook to the Russian Text of Crime and Punishment* (The Hague: Walter deGruyter, 1977). The object of the *Guide* is to help the advanced student of Russian to read the original text of *War and Peace* "with both pleasure and understanding." It has been designed for those who have had at least three years of college Russian or the equivalent. This book has glossers, instructions on how to use them, notes on language, and seven appendices.

RR, 39:4:517-18

446. Leighton, Lauren G. **Alexander Bestuzhev-Marlinsky.** Twayne's World Author Series, no. 344. Boston: Twayne Publishers, 1975. 161p. $7.50.
In five major chapters we learn of A. Bestuzhev's biography, his activity as a critic, his pre-Decembrist prose tales (1820-1825), his contribution after 1830, and about Bestuzhev as poet. The book includes a selected bibliography, along with a list in English and Russian of his titles, arranged according to cycles and/or genres. In treatment and tone, Leighton's study provides a suitable emulative model for a larger series of monographs in English on Russian romantic fictionists.

SR, 35:1:176-77

447. Luker, Nicholas J. L. **Alexander Kuprin.** Twayne's World Author Series. Boston: Twayne Publishers, G. K. Hall, 1978. 171p. $10.95.
Although Kuprin's special renown did not long survive the success of his accusatory novel *Duel* (1905), his numerous short stories and the several novels written between 1896 and 1937 continue to claim their audience, as Luker's circumstantial account of his life and works (the first monograph in English) shows. A Realist, Kuprin exemplified Russian literature's endemic quest for a connecting link between social engagement and personal fulfillment, a tradition which Turgenev and Chekhov also represented but more certainly transcended. This book is well researched and includes a succinctly annotated bibliography.

SR, 39:1:161-62

448. McLean, Hugh. **Nikolai Leskov: The Man and His Art.** Cambridge, MA: Harvard University Press, 1977. xvi, 780p. $30.00.
Leskov is the most Russian or Russian writers, making the appearance of this massive critical and biographical study indeed welcome. McLean charts the course of Leskov's stormy life in detail, piecing together an impressive portrait of this irascible and fascinating personality. The discussions of Leskov's writings are set firmly in the context of his life experiences. Such an approach is particularly appropriate for Leskov, whose art and life are so closely intertwined. As the most comprehensive study of a major Russian writer, it should be on the shelves of every student of Russian literature.

CSP, 21:1:124

449. McVay, Gordon. **Esenin: A Life.** Ann Arbor, MI: Ardis, 1976. 352p. Photographs. $10.00.
Through his exhaustive biographical resources, McVay tries to unravel the clues to Esenin's complex personality—the peasant poet of the village, the problems with religion and the Revolution, the drunken brawls and confused love life, the all-too-familiar years with Isadora Duncan, and Esenin's literary cricle (an area McVay treats particularly well). The book includes an excellent set of photographs, a very useful select bibliography, and notes.

SR, 36:3:538-39

450. Mochulsky, Konstantin. **Andrei Bely: His Life and Works.** Translated by Nora Szalavitz. Ann Arbor, MI: Ardis, 1977. 230p. $13.95, paper.
The original book was published in 1955, after Mochulsky's death by YMCA-Press (Paris) from unfinished manuscripts. The translator of the present book has minimized the organizational problems of the original by moving the several appendices of the Russian

edition to their proper chronological positions in the text and by moving the dislocated pages (pp. 45-46) to their correct place. A few additional notes have been supplied to aid the English reader, as has a brief introduction that includes a biographical sketch of Mochulsky's life. The translation itself is reasonably good. This book remains the most complete analytical survey of Bely's works yet to appear.

451.   Moody, Fred, ed. **The Bibliographies of Twentieth Century Russian Literature.** Ann Arbor, MI: Ardis, 1977. 175p. $14.95.
The subjects of the bibliographies listed in this book are Kuprin, Annenskii, Blok (*The Twelve* only), Evreinov, Mayakovsky (1912-1930), Grin (1880-1932), Aksenov, Soviet publications of Russian versification (1958-1972 only), Akhmadulina, and Brodsky. The Evreinov and Kuprin bibliographies are new; the others were published previously in *Russian Literature Triquarterly.* Some of the bibliographies include introductory notes, some have indexes, some are in Cyrillic, some are transliterated; most are complete through 1971. They are all arranged differently: some by year of publication, others by broad categories of publications by and about these authors, and the rest by other arrangements. It is gratifying to see increased interest in bibliography by American literary scholars, but the usefulness of republishing the bibliographies is questionable.
   SR, 38:3:546

452.   Proffer, Carl R., and Fred Moody, comps. **Index to Russian Literature Triquarterly, 1971-1976.** Ann Arbor, MI: Ardis, 1978. 64p. $5.00, paper.
Complete index to articles, documents, texts, translations, reviews, bibliographies, and the like in the first five years of RLT, the English-speaking world's only journal of Russian literature.

453.   Proffer, Ellendea, comp. **An International Bibliography of Works by and about Mikhail Bulgakov.** Ann Arbor, MI: Ardis, 1976. 133p. $15.00.
This first bibliography of Bulgakov is divided into sections containing his works in Russian, critical works about him in Russian publications in English, translations into other languages, and critical works in other languages.

454.   Pyman, Avril. **The Life of Aleksander Blok.** Vol. 1: *The Distant Thunder, 1880-1908.* Oxford and New York: Oxford University Press, 1979. xvi, 359p. + 16pp. plates. $19.95. Vol. 2: *The Release of Harmony, 1908-1921.* Oxford: Oxford University Press, 1980. viii, 421p. $48.00.
Pyman's intention was to write a biography of Blok; hence, she eschews intensive literary or other analyses of his works. His family background, childhood, and youth are portrayed in great detail. Placing particular emphasis on the trauma associated with Blok's "fall from innocence" (his contraction of venereal disease while still a teenager), Pyman maintains that "this problem of paradise lost and redemption is at the root of all Blok's preoccupation with Christianity, as it is the root of his lifelong demonism, of resentment against the Author of perfection who had permitted him to be deprived of wholeness." Pyman's biography is the most complete in English, filling important gaps in our knowledge of the young Blok.
   SR, 39:3:528-29; RR, 40:3:354-56

455.   Schapiro, Leonard. **Turgenev: His Life and Times.** New York: Random House, 1978. xvi, 382p. + 16pp. plates. $15.95.
The author gives in this biography a meticulous account of Turgenev's comings and goings, his letters to Pauline Viardot and others, his financial affairs, the genesis of his works,

relationships with critics and writers, and various marginalia that have come to light since Avram Yarmonlinsky's biography of Turgenev, published in 1959. All this is of service to scholars. The author's comments on Turgenev's works are sufficiently devoid of interpretation to make them seem relatively uninteresting.

SR, 39:2:351

456. Weber, Harry B., ed. **The Modern Encyclopedia of Russian and Soviet Literatures (Including Non-Russian and Emigre Literatures).** Gulf Breeze, FL: Academic International Press, 1977- . Vols. 1-2 in print. $28.50/each.

The encyclopedia, the first of its kind, is planned in some 50 volumes. As of 1981 four volumes (Chakhrukhadze, Grigol—Cosmism) have been published. This unique reference source will for decades to come remain the basic tool to be available in university as well as public libraries.

457. Wright, A. Colin. **Mikhail Bulgakov: Life and Interpretations.** Toronto and Buffalo: University of Toronto Press, 1978. viii, 324p. $25.00.

This is a full-length biography of Mikhail Bulgakov and a comprehensive critical account of his works. Wright exhibits the courage and perception essential to the critic. He recognizes in *The Master and Margarita* "an optimistic insistence on the power of the spiritual in human life and on the individuality of man," and he sees the novel's uniqueness in its comic form. Wright does not go beyond his apt perceptions in explaining the novel's tremendous impact in the Soviet Union. The bibliography is excessively complete—almost half of the references are to periodicals difficult to obtain outside the USSR.

SR, 39:1:160-61

General Surveys and Histories

458. Auty, Robert, and Dimitri Obolesky, eds., assisted by Anthony Kingsford. **An Introduction to Russian Language and Literature.** Companion to Russian Studies, vol. 2. New York and London: Cambridge University Press, 1977. xiv, 300p. $24.50.

This volume contains ten essays, nine of which were written by British academics; the tenth, on Russian literature from 1820 to 1917, is by Vsevolod Setchkarev of Harvard University. The studies include a linguistic treatment of the development of Russian, Russian writing and printing, and Russian literature from its beginnings to 1975; the five essays on literature form the bulk of the book. There are also three sketches on the Russian theater. Each chapter closes with a minibibliography entitled "Guide to Further Reading." The true audience of this book would range from graduate students firmly committed to Russian to full professors who wish to be shaken up by informed but differing viewpoints.

459. Brown, Deming. **Soviet Russian Literature since Stalin.** New York and London: Cambridge University Press, 1978. vi, 394p. $24.95.

This excellent survey of recent Soviet Russian literature is organized not chronologically as a history but in an eclectic fashion—by genres, topics, and individual authors. There are four chapters on poets and three chapters on prose, which are divided according to theme. In addition, two chapters deal with special concerns (the past and the present), two separate chapters treat Solzhenitsyn and Siniavsky, and one chapter is allotted to underground literature. Within these divisions, Brown's discussions are sober, judicious, imaginative, and incisive, with a major portion necessarily going to biographical sketches and plot summaries. This is an important book, and it fills an existing void.

SR, 37:4:716-17

460. Cross, A. G., ed. **Russian Literature in the Age of Catherine the Great—A Collection of Essays.** Oxford: Willem A. Meeuws, 1976. 229p. $4.50, paper.
The seven essays that form the core of this book span literary criticism and the history of ideas. Essays are accompanied by two valuable study aids: synchronic tables setting out the salient events in Russia's literary history in parallel tables for each year between 1762-1796 and a bibliography of works on eighteenth-century Russian literature, thought, and culture published in English from 1900 to 1974. The whole volume is scrupulously annotated.
SEER, 59:1:155-56

461. Drage, C. L. **Russian Literature in the Eighteenth Century: The Solemn Ode. The Epic. Other Poetic Genres. The Story. The Novel. Drama. An Introduction for University Courses.** London: Author's Publication, 1978. 281p. £5.00. Copies available from 94 Inverness Terrace, London W2, England.
The principal merit of this book is that it concerns itself undeviatingly with literature as a body of written texts; the author has obviously made a detailed first-hand study of all the texts he discusses. No space is given to biographical, sociological, or political data. The finely detailed list of contents and the index will facilitate the use of the book as a work of reference. The book will be an indispensable guide for the readership the author is aiming at, but it will also be of great value to specialists as a work of stocktaking and reference.
SEER, 59:2:287-88

462. Freeborn, Richard, Georgette Donchin, and N. J. Anning. **Russian Literary Attitudes from Pushkin to Solzhenitsyn.** Edited by Richard Freeborn. London: Macmillan; New York: Barnes & Noble, Harper & Row, 1976. viii, 158p. $22.50.
This is a collection of essays on the total literary careers of six authors (chronologically presented): Pushkin, Dostoyevsky, Tolstoy, Gorky, Pasternak, and Solzhenitsyn. The work is aimed at the serious student of Russian literature. A select annotated bibliography of important works in English and Russian increases the value of this work for the student.
SR, 36:2:345-46

463. Hosking, Geoffrey. **Beyond Socialist Realism: Soviet Fiction since Ivan Denisovich.** New York: Holmes & Meier, 1980. x, 260p. $27.50.
Hosking's book is an intelligent effort to reevaluate what he calls the "socialist realist tradition," and he discovers in recent Soviet literature evidence not only of departures from that tradition but also of its persistence, even in certain dissident and emigré writers. In the course of developing his ideas, the author has surveyed and analyzed a representative sample of contemporary Russian writing, and his book is necessary reading for anyone concerned with that subject.
RR, 39:4:520-22

464. Katz, Michael R. **The Literary Ballad in Early Nineteenth-Century Russian Literature.** London: Oxford University Press, 1976. xiv, 248p. $22.00.
The title of this book does not do it justice; in addition to a thorough investigation of the Russian ballad in the early nineteenth century, the book contains an extensive survey of the history of the genre of the ballad in Western Europe (England, Germany, and France), as well as a short history of the Russian literary epithet in the eighteenth and early nineteenth centuries. The author also includes theoretical discussion dealing with the concepts of "ballad" and "epithet" and provides statistical data on the types and frequency of epithets in Russian and Western folk ballads. The book is recommended to students of Russian poetry.
SR, 37:2:341-43

465. Segel, Harold B. **Twentieth-Century Russian Drama: From Gorky to the Present.** New York: Columbia University Press, 1979. xviii, 502p. Photographs. $27.50.
At long last we have a scholarly, well-written, and richly illustrated history of Russian drama since Chekhov. This is indeed a pioneering work that succeeds in an ambitious task. Segel's book is a major contribution to the study of modern Russian literature and of drama generally.
> SR, 40:1:145-47

Critical Studies

466. Baines, Jennifer. **Mandelstam: The Later Poetry.** Cambridge: Cambridge University Press, 1976. 253p. £8.00.
This book deserves attention as practically the first serious attempt to discuss Mandelstam's later poetry of the 1930s. Baines was fortunate to have had at her disposal the personal typescript copy of Mandelstam's later poems belonging to the poet's widow, along with her commentaries on them. This new material represents the most interesting and valuable feature of the book. Her book will prove indispensable to the specialist, if only for Nadezhda Mandelstam's commentaries.
> SEER, 58:4:588-90

467. Barooshian, Vahan D. **Brik and Mayakovsky.** Slavistic Printings and Reprintings, 301. The Hague: Mouton, 1978. x, 157p. DM 48.00.
Osip Brik was not just a devoted friend of Mayakovsky but a substantial figure in his own right, a founder-member of *Opoyaz* and one of the leading spirits behind *Iskusstvo kommuny* and later LEF. The author's method in this book is basically chronological and biographical. There is an impressive bibliography of Brik's publications, some 160 items in all. The value of the book is increased by copious quotations from unpublished sources. The book is undoubtedly valuable in many respects—the detailed accounts of Mayakovsky's last days and of the campaign for his rehabilitation in 1934-1935 are fuller than any yet published.
> SEER, 58:2:285-86

468. Berry, Thomas E. **Plots and Characters in Major Russian Fiction.** Vol. 2: *Gogol, Goncharov, Dostoevskii.* The Plots and Characters Series. Hamden, CT: Archon Books, Shoe String Press. Folkestone, England: Wm. Dawson & Sons, 1978. xii, 265p. $17.50.
In volume 1, Berry summarized the plots of the major works of Pushkin, Lermontov, Turgenev, and Tolstoy. He devotes the present volume to plots and characters in the fiction of Gogol, Goncharov, and Dostoyevsky. Berry's work is one of a larger series of plot and character studies in American and European fiction that is edited by Robert L. Gale. The most valuable part of Berry's book is the extensive list of characters that follows the plot section of the work. In fact, two-thirds of the volume is devoted to characters. The serious student who is already well versed in the subject may find this work useful.
> SR, 39:1:157-58

469. Bilokur, Borys. **A Concordance to the Russian Poetry of Fedor I. Tiutchev.** Providence, RI: Brown University Press, 1975. xiv, 343p. $20.00.
Tiutchev's importance as a poet, and especially the change in the way he used words during his career, makes a concordance to his poetry particularly welcome. This study is much more than a concordance and also much less—more, because under the head "words" it gives definitions together with examples in context; less, because the use listings are only

locational. The appearance of the Tiutchev concordance, along with others, makes possible a new stage in the study of Russian poetry.
SR, 35:4:779-80

470. Broyde, Steven. **Osip Mandel'štam and His Age: A Commentary on the Themes of War and Revolution in the Poetry 1913-1923.** Harvard Slavic Monographs, vol. 1. Cambridge, MA; and London: Harvard University Press, 1975. xiv, 245p. $8.00.
The author presents a close analysis of about 12 poems written between 1913 and 1923 that deal with the themes of war and revolution. Broyde's objective is to demolish the popular fallacy that Mandelstam was indifferent to the social developments of his time. It is the author's achievement that his systematic demonstration of Mandelstam's varied reactions to the historical events of his time should lay to rest once and for all such simplistic views of Mandelstam as an aloof Parnassian.
SR, 35:2:386-87

471. Cain, T. G. S. **Tolstoy.** London: Paul Elek, 1977. xiii, 200p. £5.95.
The appeal of this short introduction to Tolstoy's fiction must be to the general reader rather than the scholar. Cain makes it his task to trace Tolstoy's evolution as a novelist by taking his most important works of fiction in chronological order, prefacing his examination of them by a general chapter on Tolstoy and his world. This book is well written, lucid, and economical. If it does not break any new ground, it achieves what it sets out to do in a sensible and agreeable manner.
SEER, 55:4:534-35

472. Černy, Václav. **Dostoevsky and His Devils.** Translated by F. W. Galan. Ardis Essay Series, no. 3. Ann Arbor, MI: Ardis, 1975. 77p. $2.50, paper.
Černy is a Czech critic and scholar. His fierce independence of mind and his outspoken participation in the ideological battles of his time have earned him the enmity of the dictatorship that plagued Czechoslovakia. The essay contains not only a rejection of the orthodox Marxist interpretation of Dostoyevsky as a realist but also a ringing denunciation of Marxist ideology and its justification of any lie, even murder, for the end of a future Utopia of universal justice — a message Černy appropriately finds in the text of *The Devils*.
SR, 35:2:384-85

473. Chances, Ellen B. **Conformity's Children: An Approach to the Superfluous Man in Russian Literature.** Columbus, OH: Slavica Publishers, 1978. x, 210p. $9.95, paper.
This study seeks "to redefine the superfluous man and to examine him from the perspective of certain conclusions." In the process, Chances reexamines over 20 of the most famous works in Russian literature. This work is well researched and well written, although the increase of social pressures to conform in Russia since 1917 should have been better indicated.
SR, 39:3:526

474. Charters, Ann, and Samuel. **I Love: The Story of Vladimir Mayakovsky and Lili Brik.** London: André Deutsch, 1979. xvi, 398p. £8.95.
Mr. and Mrs. Charters have given us a conscientious and readable account of the relationship between Mayakovsky and Lili Brik. It does, however, rely heavily (and explicitly) on published sources, the memoirs of persons who knew Mayakovsky and Brik. The authors admittedly had the additional benefit of conversations with women who half a century before played key roles in the drama — Lili Brik, Tatyana Yakovleva, and Rita

Rait. The book contains a useful bibliography, source references, and a number of handsome photographs.
SEER, 59:1:86-87

475. Dunham, Vera S. **In Stalin's Time: Middleclass Values in Soviet Fiction.** Introduction by Jerry F. Hough. Cambridge: Cambridge University Press, 1976. xvi, 283p. $16.95.
In some 100 works of fiction, poetry, and drama, Dunham reveals a pattern of relationships—the "Big Deal"—between the regime and the class of bureaucrats and technicians that supports the regime. She chooses to concentrate on works written after the war, during a period in which the Big Deal seemed most firmly established and the regime most generous in its rewards to those who moved to responsible administrative positions.
SR, 36:1:155-56

476. Ehre, Milton, ed. **The Theater of Nikolay Gogol: Plays and Selected Writings.** Translated by Milton Ehre and Fruma Gottschalk. Chicago and London: University of Chicago Press, 1980. xxvi, 205p. $18.50.
This volume includes translations of Gogol's three completed plays (*Marriage, The Government Inspector, The Gamblers*), an introduction, notes, a bibliography, and an appendix consisting of Gogol's statements about *Revizor* culled from letters, *Rozviazka Revizora*, and so forth. The non-Russian-speaking readers for whom this collection is designed will appreciate this attempt to convey a sense of the original Russian and to provide materials for an interpretation of the plays. In his introduction, Ehre situates Gogol's plays in their literary historical context and carefully provides Gogol's own views on how *Revizor*, in particular, should be produced.
SR, 40:3:503-504

477. Erlich, Victor, ed. **Pasternak: A Collection of Critical Essays.** Twentieth Century Views. Englewood Cliffs, NJ: Prentice-Hall, 1978. xii, 192p. Chronology. $3.45, paper.
The reader will find this volume a valuable and convenient presentation of 14 of the most significant contributions to Pasternak criticism. Some of the items have been happily rescued from the obscurity of various journals, some appear here for the first time in English, and the editor's introductory essay with its perceptive reflections on Pasternak's "Marburg" has not been printed before. A select bibliography of materials in English is included.
SEER, 58:2:286-87

478. Fanger, Donald. **The Creation of Nikolai Gogol.** Cambridge, MA: The Belknap Press of Harvard University Press, 1979. xi, 300p. $16.50.
This splendid work essays a necessary and fundamentally new project—to determine how the Gogolian text has produced the wealth of disparate readings that constitute Gogol scholarship and how it continues to do so. Fanger undertakes this with a "plural" perspectivist approach, not directed by a single discipline or method, not shaped into a formalistic cataloguinst of devices. The book, which has drawn upon several trends in modern criticism, is of exceptional freshness, a model study in critical illumination, and a joy to read.
RR, 49:3:3887-89

479. Feuer, Kathryn, ed. **Solzhenitsyn: A Collection of Critical Essays.** Englewood Cliffs, NJ: Prentice-Hall, 1976. xv, 144p. $7.95.

Feuer has collected 12 essays on the artistic qualities of Solzhenitsyn's prose and has contributed an introduction that places Solzhenitsyn squarely in Russian literary tradition. All but the essays by Jackson, Blake, Gibian, and Kaufman have been previously published. A map locating the forced labor camps in the USSR compiled by Isaac Don Levine in 1951, a chronology of important dates, notes on contributors, and a selected bibliography also appear.

CSP, 18:4:498-99

480. Forsyth, James. **Listening to the Wind: An Introduction to Alexander Blok.** Oxford: Willem A. Meeuws, 1977. 134p. £2.25.

In this narrative of Blok's life and works, we are introduced to the poet's family, to the writers who influenced him, to his friends and colleagues, to the women with whom he was amorously involved.

SEER, 57:3:435-36

481. France, Anna Kay. **Boris Pasternak's Translation of Shakespeare.** Berkeley, Los Angeles, London: University of California Press, 1978. x, 277p. £10.50.

Since this book is intended for general readers and students of Shakespeare as well as Russian specialists, France includes literal translations of Pasternak's Russian, and these are generally excellent. To attempt a definitive treatment of Pasternak's Shakespeare translations would be a vast undertaking; France provides a series of illuminating perspectives in this well-conceived, carefully researched, and stimulating study.

SEER, 58:3:443-44

482. Frank, Joseph. **Dostoevsky: The Seeds of Revolt, 1821-1849.** Princeton, NJ: Princeton University Press, 1976. xvi, 401p. Illus. $16.50.

Frank's book is essentially an intellectual biography of Dostoyevsky's early years. He has weighed up sanely and presented comprehensively and clearly the sum of scholarship on the early stages of Dostoyevsky's life and career as a writer and has reexamined their most controversial and most obscure areas with commendable diligence, care, and good sense. The author's distinctive approach to the literary works pays huge dividends, and all students of Dostoyevsky and Russian intellectual history will look forward to the publication of the remaining three volumes.

SEER, 56:1:121-22

483. Friedberg, Maurice. **A Decade of Euphobia: Western Literature in Post-Stalin Russia, 1954-64.** Bloomington and London: Indiana University Press, 1977. xii, 371p. $17.50.

Friedberg has assembled rich and varied material on the publication, dissemination, and reception of Western literature, both past and present, in the Soviet Union in the first decade after Stalin's death. He provides information about the publication and reception of major nineteenth-century novelists, such as Dickens, Balzac, Zola, as well as those who are nearer to us in time (Thomas Hardy, Oscar Wilde, Galsworthy) and some of our contemporaries, including Americans (Arthur Miller, Saroyan, Salinger), not omitting many little-known writers of various nationalities. It is often the portrayal of the "evils of capitalism" that is particularly brought to the fore and stressed in their works.

SR, 36:4:717-19

484. Gasiorowska, Xenia. **The Image of Peter the Great in Russian Fiction.** Madison: University of Wisconsin Press, 1979. xiii, 199p. $27.50.

Gasiorowska has read her determined way through the vast body of literature concerning Peter produced during the past two centuries. Even among Petrine novelists there are vast differences, not only of talent and artistic method but of attitude and ideology. For Tsar Peter has never ceased to inspire intense emotion, both political and personal, in all who contemplated him. Not much of the Petrine fiction is really first-rate literature; the obvious exceptions are Pushkin's unfinished *Blackamoor of Peter the Great* and, not mentioned by the author, his *The Mazepa Legend*, glorifying Peter's victory at Poltava.

RR, 39:1:110-11

485. Gifford, Henry. **Pasternak, A Critical Study.** New York: Cambridge University Press, 1977. xiii, 280p. $18.95.
The author presents Pasternak as an artist in his earliest environment and his intellectual and artistic development, as well as his various intellectual aspirations—music and Skriabin's role in Pasternak's early life, his study of philosophy, and, finally, the role of symbolist poetry and Blok's lasting influence upon him. This study very sensitively and sensibly presents Pasternak's tribute to Modernism and Futurism, his participation in "Centrifuge," and, most important, his friendship with and later alienation from Maiakovskii. In spite of certain avoidable deficiencies, this critical study will be useful to both specialists and laypersons.

CSP, 20:2:281-82

486. Gumilev, Nikolai. **On Russian Poetry.** Edited and translated by David Lapeza. Ann Arbor, MI: Ardis, 1977. 192p. $15.00.
This book makes available in English the 5 essays, 36 reviews, and several miscellaneous pronouncements that constitute Gumilev's theoretical and critical writings. The originals appeared between 1908 and 1923, for the most part, in the journal *Apollon*. The present volume is well annotated but contains many typographical errors.

SR, 37:1:170

487. Hackel, Sergei. **The Poet and the Revolution: Aleksandr Blok's "The Twelve."** Oxford: Clarendon Press, 1975. xv, 254p. £10.50.
In this study, Hackel's attention is above all directed to the *realiara*, that is, the religious and symbolic aspects of the poem. The important parallel between "The Twelve" and the Apocalypse has never before been so clearly described. The exemplary scrupulosity of the study is perhaps best illustrated by the author's attempt to interpret even the underscorings and marginalia in Blok's books. The final chapter briefly accounts for Blok's last years after "The Twelve."

CSP, 18:4:481-82

488. Hahn, Beverly. **Chekhov: A Study of the Major Stories and Plays.** Major European Authors Series. New York and London: Cambridge University Press, 1977. xiv, 351p. $19.95.
This book repeats a great deal of facts and views that interested readers know only too well, but it also contains lucid insights and analytic comments that secure it a specific place in the extensive and expanding library of Chekhov criticism.

SR, 38:3:527-28

489. Haight, Amanda. **Anna Akhmatova: A Poetic Pilgrimage.** New York and London: Oxford University Press, 1976. x, 213p. Illus. $10.00.
This biography of Anna Akhmatova, the first in either English or Russian, is a major contribution. In a sense, this is almost an authorized biography that shows Akhmatova's

life much as she might have liked us to see it. It contains much new information about Akhmatova's disastrous marriage to Gumilev, her subsequent marriages, and her life during the silent years of the 1920s, 1930s, and 1940s. All this information sheds important light on her poetry.

SR, 36:3:536-37

490. Hart, Pierr R. G. R. **Derzhavin: A Poet's Progress.** Columbus, OH: Slavica Publishers, 1978. iv, 164p. $8.95.

Hart's work is the first publication in English to trace the path of Derzhavin's creative development. In this sense, his book is certainly an important contribution in this field. It will be useful to those who have only a basic introduction to his poetry and to eighteenth-century Russian literature in general but who wish to become acquainted with these areas in more detail. There is a selected and annotated bibliography of Derzhavin's major publications as well as literature about him.

RR, 40:2:216-18

491. Hingley, Ronald. **A New Life of Anton Chekhov.** New York: Alfred A. Knopf, 1976. xxii, 352p. Index. Illus. $12.50.

Professor Hingley has translated all seven volumes of *The Oxford Chekhov* published thus far and is working on subsequent volumes, so his intimate relationship with this writer is of long standing. Most of the material collected and displayed in this book was known and used by numerous other biographers, but it is all viewed through Hingley's prism – in the way he arranges, illuminates, and interprets the material, which he does in a fascinating and credible way, making Hingley's Chekhov very much alive.

SR, 36:3:533-35

492. Hodgson, Peter. **From Gogol to Dostoevsky: Jakov Butkov, A Reluctant Naturalist in the 1840's.** Munich: Wilhelm Fink Verlag, 1976. x, 190p. DM 28.00, paper.

The focal notion in this study is "reluctant naturalism," seen as "the middle ground between the frivolous subculture and the stylization practiced by Gogol and Dostoevsky." Hodgson's emphasis is on what he terms "the native subculture," i.e., pulp literature, feuilleton, adventure stories, and other forms of popular entertainment. This is a solid piece of scholarship.

SR, 37:2:343-44

493. Hughes, Olga R. **The Poetic World of Boris Pasternak.** Princeton Essays in European and Comparative Literature. Princeton, NJ, and London: Princeton University Press, 1974. xvi, 192p. $9.00.

The author offers a fascinating attempt at interpreting Pasternak's poetic world as a whole, including his prose of various periods. Key passages of this poetry are quoted both in translation and in the original. The book is geared to the sophisticated reader rather than the uninitiated.

SR, 34:4:866-67

494. Jensen, Peter Alberg. **Nature as Code: The Achievement of Boris Pilnjak, 1915-1924.** Copenhagen: Rosenkilde & Bagger, 1979. 360p. D.Kr. 115.00.

Jensen divides his study of Pilnjak's early works into three parts: first, a biography; second, a discussion of the texts; and, finally, a justification of Pilnjak's much maligned style. Each of the three parts leads up to *Mashiny i volki*, the culmination of the first period of his work. This study is one of the most informative and stimulating books on twentieth-century Russian literature to appear so far.

SEER, 59:1:87-89

495. Jones, Malcolm V. **Dostoyevsky: The Novel of Discord.** London: Paul Elek; New York: Barnes & Noble, 1976. 236p. $18.50.

The author's aim is to explore the texture and structure of Dostoyevsky's fictional world, including "some aspects of the technique which created it," and to identify and reformulate "chief problems." Jones perceptive discussion of various aspects of Dostoyevsky's major novels should be of interest to the specialist.

        SEER, 57:3:429-31

496. Jones, Malcolm V., ed. **New Essays on Tolstoy.** Cambridge, London, New York, and Melbourne: Cambridge University Press, 1978. xi, 253p. £10.50.

This collection of essays by English Russianists in honor of the 150th anniversary of Tolstoy's birth is necessarily rather motley but is generally of a high scholarly standard and, in some respects, vigorously original and refreshing. The essays are roughly divided into two parts: those devoted principally to appraisals of Tolstoy's literary heritage and those devoted to his ideas and their influence.

        SEER, 57:3:428-29

497. Kabat, Geoffrey C. **Ideology and Imagination: The Image of Society in Dostoevsky.** New York: Columbia University Press, 1978. xiv, 201p. $15.00.

The author of this book is concerned with the relationship between Dostoyevsky's journalism and his great novels. He argues that all of Dostoyevsky's journalistic works from 1861 onward, as well as the heroes of his major novels, share a consistent point of view about society. Dostoyevsky is alarmed at the inroads of capitalism, the democratization of the *narod* and the gentry after 1861, and the historical gulf between the *narod* and the intelligentsia. In both his journalism and his major novels, Dostoyevsky searches for signs of a more hopeful future—of an organic communal society and an independent Russian identity. This is an intelligent, well-written, and well-documented book.

498. Kagan-Kaus, Eva. **Hamlet and Don Quixote: Turgenev's Ambivalent Vision.** The Hague, Paris: Mouton, 1975. 161p. Dfl. 40.00.

This study attempts to answer such questions as: Where does Turgenev's philosophy originate, and what is the relationship between it and his art? In the course of answering, it provides observations of value and insights of interest, but ends by suggesting that "Turgenev's constant vacillation between faith and doubt, between affirmation and refutation, makes a definitive assessment of his views of the world extremely difficult." This is a very informative, erudite work, invaluable to the specialist and of interest to students.

        SEER, 55:2:241-42

499. Karlinsky, Simon. **The Sexual Labyrinth of Nikolai Gogol.** Cambridge, MA, and London: Harvard University Press, 1976. xii, 333p. Illus. $14.00.

Karlinsky's book is devoted to a close examination of Gogol's sexuality and its reflection in his artistic work. His thesis is that the conflict between Gogol's homosexual desires, on one hand, and his dislike of women and revulsion of marriage, on the other, were at "the nerve center of Gogol's biography and of much of his creative achievement" (p. 6). The biographical facts that the author sheds on Gogol's sexual orientation are carefully and convincingly presented. Whether one chooses to agree with all of the author's conclusions or not, this book is a landmark in Russian literary criticism and is indispensable to any serious and scholarly study of Gogol.

        SR, 36:3:531-32

500. Kodjak, Andrej. **Pushkin's I. P. Belkin.** Columbus, OH: Slavica Publishers, 1979. 112p. $6.95.

This book deals with a very interesting problem, one which has been the subject of debate for over 100 years, namely, the function of the preface to *The Belkin Tales.* Kodjak argues that Pushkin used a code in the preface to fool the censor but that in prison in Siberia "the Decembrists read *The Tales of Belkin* and understood them fully." The author then turns to an analysis of the tales themselves, insisting that they bear the strong imprint of Belkin.

  RR, 39:1:112-14

501. Kodjak, Andrej, and Kiril Taranovsky, eds. **Alexander Pushkin: A Symposium on the One Hundred Seventy-Fifth Anniversary of His Birth.** New York University Slavic Papers, vol. 1. New York: New York University Press, 1976. viii, 220p. $19.50.

The essays published in this collection, which were delivered at the 1974 symposium on Pushkin held at New York University, are divided into three groups: Pushkin's poetry, his prose, and his narrative poetry and drama. While each section contains interesting articles, the essays in the last section seem to be the best because they attempt to relate individual theses to larger ideas or contexts.

  SR, 39:2:349-50

502. Krag, Erik. **Dostoevsky the Literary Artist.** Oslo: Universitetsforlaget; New York: Humanities Press, 1976. 317p. $18.00.

Krag's book first appeared in the original Norwegian in 1962. Its translation into English is belated but nevertheless welcome. The strength of this study lies in its broad, comprehensive approach and the steadiness of the viewpoint firmly fixed on the central theme of Dostoyevsky the literary artist. The texts themselves are analyzed, and the impact of Dostoyevsky's works on contemporary critics is discussed and placed in the context of views expressed by later scholars and writers. This study is further enriched by a comparative approach.

  SEER, 55:4:535-36

503. Krasnov, Vladislav. **Solzhenitsyn and Dostoevsky: A Study in the Polyphonic Novel.** Athens: University of Georgia Press, 1980. 226p. $17.50.

This is a book not about Dostoyevsky but about Solzhenitsyn. Krasnov is firm in his overriding thesis—Solzhenitsyn's novels have close affinities with Dostoyevsky's. Certainly, Solzhenitsyn's nationalism and his Christianity, essentially spiritual and thus hostile to Tolstoy's rationalization of faith, mark his kinship to Dostoyevsky. Students of Solzhenitsyn will find this book useful. Its rigorous focus on a single thesis may make it less appealing to the general reader or to specialists in Russian literature whose interest in Solzhenitsyn is only incidental.

  RR, 39:4:519-20

504. Lantz, Kenneth A. **Nikolay Leskov.** Boston: Twayne Publishers, 1979. 165p. $11.50.

Lantz's book is addressed primarily to the general reader rather than to the scholar, but his *Leskov* will nevertheless be useful to scholars as well, not only as a succinct and dependable summary of information, research, and opinion about Leskov but as a source of original literary insights. In the literary part of the book, Lantz proceeds chronologically through Leskov's entire oeuvre, with the chronological principle modified only to group together some works in the same genre. The book has a selected bibliography, supplemented in the brief annotations to the text. Most essential Leskov research is mentioned.

CSP, 22:3:427-29

505. Linnér, Sven. **Starets Zosima in the Brothers Karamazov: A Study in the Mimesis of Virtue.** Stockholm Studies in Russian Literature, 4. Stockholm: Almqvist & Wiksell International, 1975. 237p. $14.75, paper. Distributed by Humanities Press, Atlantic Highlands, NJ 07716.

Linnér's new book is as stimulating as his previous work, *Dostoevsky on Realism.* Half of the present work deals with the problem of why Dostoyevsky did not depict Zosima realistically even though that was his intention. The second half of the book is devoted to Fedorov's limited influence on Dostoyevsky and to a fascinating study of "life versus the meaning of life" which, according to the author, is more fundamental to *The Brothers Karamazov* than God, *narod*, or church. This book — honest, thoughtful, original — deserves the attention of everyone interested in *The Brothers Karamazov.*

SR, 36:4:714

506. Lotman, Yury (Jurij). **Analysis of the Poetic Text.** Edited and translated by D. Barton Johnson. Ann Arbor, MI: Ardis, 1976. xxx, 309p. $16.95.

This book sums up and, in some cases, repeats the basic lessons Lotman has learned since he began lecturing on Structuralist poetics in 1958. It is divided into two equally divided parts, a series of theoretical propositions and a number of readings of particular poems from Batiushkov to Zabolotskii that illustrate the utility of the theory. This work is of fundamental importance and the translation is competent.

RR, 36:2:240-42

507. Lourie, Richard. **Letters to the Future: An Approach to Sinyavsky-Tertz.** Ithaca, NY: Cornell University Press, 1975. 221p. $8.95.

This book treats all the works, both fiction and criticism, that Sinyavsky published before his arrest in November 1965. A merit of the book is that it tries to see Sinyavsky as a whole, for it is not easy to see how even the best of his critical and historical works published in the official Soviet press, such as the long article on Pasternak, can be related to either his fiction or to *Chto takoe sotsiialisticheskii realizm*? Lourie's answer is to treat the fiction as self-therapy, enabling Sinyavsky, through the creation of Tertz, to come to terms with the trauma of his loss of faith in Soviet Communism.

SEER, 55:2:249

508. Luker, Nicholas J. L. **Aleksandr Grin: The Forgotten Visionary.** Newtonville, MA: Oriental Research Partners, 1980. xii, 93p. $9.50.

The recent centenary of Aleksandr Grin (1880-1932) was marked in the Soviet Union by widespread notices in the press and by several publications of his works. In the West, however, Grin's works are still largely unknown. Luker, who had already done more than anybody else to acquaint the English-speaking world with Grin's achievement, has written a most informative book that is a useful and reliable guide.

RR, 40:2:222-23

509. Maguire, Robert A., ed. and trans. **Gogol from the Twentieth Century: Eleven Essays.** Princeton, NJ: Princeton University Press, 1975. xi, 415p. $17.50.

Maguire introduces his collection of modern critical essays on Gogol with a substantial historical survey of Gogol criticism in Russian, demonstrating how the twentieth-century critics reflect and deviate from their predecessors. The modern critics mirror the past when

they grapple with the issues of the "realism" of Gogol's prose and drama, his humor, and the bond between his literary and nonliterary works. Of greater significance, however, are the innovations−the isolation and productive analysis of the basic stylistic, structural, and thematic components of Gogol's writings by Symbolist writers, Formalist critics, and free-lance academics; the metaphysical commitments equal Gogol's in integrity if not intensity.
CSP, 19:1:101-102

510. Mathewson, Rufus W., Jr. **The Positive Hero in Russian Literature.** 2nd ed. Stanford: Stanford University Press, 1975 [1958]. xxii, 369p. $14.95.
This is a second revised and much improved edition and is being recognized as one of the most important studies produced by a Slavist in the United States. It is primarily a discussion of the long conflict between partisans of literature's autonomy and those predicating its legitimacy on such "useful" functions as creation of literary models for readers to emulate. In a series of five new chapters devoted to Pasternak, Solzhenitsyn, and Sinyavsky, Mathewson discerns a new kind of hero, not a "positive" one nor a Western-type "anti-hero" but a "battered survivor."
SR, 35:3:574

511. Medvedev, P. N., and M. M. Bakhtin. **The Formal Method in Literary Scholarship: A Critical Introduction to Sociological Poetics.** Translated by Albert J. Wehrle. Baltimore and London: The Johns Hopkins University Press, 1978. [Leningrad: "Priboi," 1928]. xxvi, 191p. $12.50.
This treatise has long been recognized as the most sustained and serious critique of Russian Formalism from an ostensibly Marxist perspective. It was first published in 1928 under the name of P. M. Medvedev. Wehrle's translation is generally careful and workmanlike. His introduction, especially as it bears on the intricacies of the Bakhtin circle, is eminently helpful, but it is marred occasionally by a modish lingo and farfetched analogies.
SR, 38:1:154-55

512. Medvedev, Roy A. **Problems in the Literary Biography of Mikhail Sholokhov.** Translated by A. D. P. Briggs. New York and London: Cambridge University Press, 1977 [1975]. viii, 227p. $14.95.
Medvedev's book, originally published in French in 1975, deals with the issue of the authorship of *The Quiet Don.* It includes a detailed analysis of the book written by "D." He agrees with "D" that *The Quiet Don* is the work of two writers−Sholokhov and someone else, probably Fedor Kriukov−but he challenges much of the analysis and information reported by "D," a Soviet scholar and author of *Stremia Tikhoga Dona: Zagadki romana.* In any case, the mystery remains; the rumors persist. And Sholokhov shows no signs of willingness to provide information that might settle the matter once and for all.
SR, 38:2:351-52

513. Milne, Lesley. **The Master and Margarita: A Comedy of Victory.** Birmingham Slavonic Monographs, no. 3. Birmingham, England: University of Birmingham, 1977. iv, 55p.
The special blend of narrative elements in the novel has, Milne suggests, close similarities with the form of the medieval mystery play. Bulgakov can be presumed to have been familiar with this tradition where the sacred mixes freely with the profane, rough humor combines with sublime mystery. A special plea is made for the relevance of the medieval concept of *figura* to appreciate Bulgakov's art in weaving connections between characters and incidents that always elude the rigidity of allegory and complete, one-to-one

equivalence. This short study makes a very real contribution to an understanding of the mechanism of this brave and complex book.

SEER, 57:1:114-15

514.   Moser, Charles A. **Denis Fonvizin.** Boston: Twayne Publishers, 1979. 151p. $13.50.
Moser provides a thoughtful introduction to the sole eighteenth-century Russian writer still read for pleasure. Fonvizin is best known for his plays and travel letters, and the heart of this book is devoted to analysis of these works. Moser dissects them for literary value, social comment, and place in the development of the modern Russian literary language. The book is written with charm and will serve as an excellent introduction for the student and nonspecialist.

RR, 39:2:264-65

515.   Muckle, James Y. **Nikolai Leskov and the "Spirit of Protestantism."** Birmingham Slavonic Monographs, no. 4. Birmingham, England: Department of Russian Language and Literature, University of Birmingham, 1978. viii, 171p. £3.00, paper.
By the end of his career, Leskov was to declare that Christianity and Orthodoxy had nothing in common. Although this later position coincided with Tolstoy's, Leskov had reached it earlier and by a different road. The route traversed by that "different road," however, has never been thoroughly explored in Leskov scholarship, and it is this important task that Muckle has undertaken. He has performed his task with admirable fairness and balance. He begins with an outline of Protestantism as a whole, especially as it appeared in the nineteenth century, and of its basic departure from Orthodoxy. He then analyzes several religious themes in Leskov's writings, carefully tracing the influences that led to this peripeteia.

SR, 39:2:352-54

516.   Oulanoff, Hongor. **The Prose Fiction of Veniamin A. Kaverin.** Cambridge, MA: Slavica Publishers, 1976. vi, 203p. $6.95, paper.
Veniamin Kaverin is best known in the West for his two novels, *Skandalist* (1928) and *Khudozhnik neizvesten* (1931), which were the subjects of an important book by D. G. B. Piper in 1970. Oulanoff treats his material roughly in chronological order. In the first chapter, he looks at the stories of the early 1920s; then he goes on to examine Kaverin's development in the later 1920s into an independent writer. The third chapter deals with Kaverin's major novels. It must be admitted that the book is poorly written.

SR, 29:2:254-55

517.   Peterson, Dale E. **The Clement Vision: Poetic Realism in Turgenev and James.** National University Publications, Literary Criticism Series. Port Washington, NY, and London: Kennikat Press, 1975. x, 157p. $9.95.
This book contains interesting observations on both writers, coordinated by an effort to demonstrate not only instances of direct influence but also of various kinds of convergence and affinity. The convergences between Turgenev and James are obvious. Peterson's study is well informed, competent, and intelligent.

SR, 35:4:772-73

518.   Pitcher, Harvey. **Chekhov's Leading Lady: A Portrait of the Actress Olga Knipper.** London: John Murray; New York and London: Franklin Watts, 1980. 288p. $12.50.

This book makes fascinating reading for it is well written and abounds in interesting first-hand information. The actress, Olga Knipper, who survived her famous husband, the writer Anton Chekhov, by 45 years and died at the age of 90, looks back on her brief marriage to him as the most important period in her life. Pitcher makes available, for the first time, extensive excerpts from the actress' letters to her husband, including those remarkable meditations written after his death that were published in the Soviet Union in 1972 and have been, until now, unknown to English readers. The exposition of the material is followed by extensive notes and references, a Bibliography of Source Material, and an index.

RR, 39:3:369-70

519.   Proffer, Carl R., ed. **Modern Russian Poets on Poetry.** Selected and with an intro-
       duction by Joseph Brodsky. Ann Arbor, MI: Ardis, 1976. 203p. $3.45, paper.
The selection of poets made here is unbiased—all the major poets of a certain generation (all, except Blok, are post-Symbolists) who made significant statements about the nature of poetry have been included. The younger poets appear to be the neo-Romantic heirs of Symbolism. The articles are fully annotated at the back of the book. These notes are useful, but they are blemished by a certain amount of editorial neglect.

SR, 34:4:721

520.   Rabinowitz, Stanley J. **Sologub's Literary Children: Keys to a Symbolist's Prose.**
       Columbus, OH: Slavica Publishers, 1980. 176p. $9.95.
The author introduces the reader to the central concerns and patterns of the literary prose of Fedor Sologub by examining the crucial role that children played in the writer's fictive universe. Treated here are many of the best stories, the fairy tales, and most of the novels that this leading decadent-Symbolist author wrote between 1894 and 1914. The arrangement of chapters according to genre—stories, novels, fairy tales—demonstrates how differently the child functions in each, suggesting Sologub's unique understanding of the limits and special qualities of these genres.

521.   Rayfield, Donald. **Chekhov: The Evolution of His Art.** New York: Barnes & Noble,
       Harper & Row, 1975. vi, 266p. $17.50.
This study uses a "life and works" approach, integrating the writings into the chronological framework of Chekhov's life and career, but the emphasis is much more on the writings, the tone is less narrative and more polemical, the style is more compact, and the statements are sometimes provocative. This quality attests to the author's thorough knowledge of and lucid insight into Chekhov's works.

SR, 36:3:533-35

522.   Reck, Vera T. **Boris Pil'niak: A Soviet Writer in Conflict with the State.** Montreal
       and London: McGill-Queen's University Press, 1975. xii, 243p. $12.50.
Reck's book is political and historical in emphasis rather than biographical or literary; it is a meticulous, carefully documented study of the two major official assaults on Pil'niak, in 1926 and 1929. The book provides a wealth of interesting detail and judicious assessment of the sometimes clumsily orchestrated campaign and the policies and decisions that shaped it. It draws new attention to a writer who deserves still more.

SR, 36:4:716

523.   Rice, Martin P. **Valery Briusov and the Rise of Russian Symbolism.** Ann Arbor, MI:
       Ardis, 1975. iv, 155p. $8.95.

This is an appraisal of Briusov's role as a literary organizer and editor who mobilized the various forces that loosely constituted the Symbolist movement in Russia. The work is well organized and well researched, despite the initial impression that may be given by an introduction that relies a little too much on secondhand generalizations.

SR, 36:2:349-50

524.   Richards, D. J., and C. R. S. Cockrell, eds. and trans. **Russian Views of Pushkin.** Oxford: Willem A. Meeuws, 1976. xxvi, 263p. £8.50.

The 26 essays included were written by Gogol, Belinskii, Herzen, Annenkov, Dobroliubov, Grigoriev, Pisarev, Turgenev, Dostoyevsky, Mereshkovsky, Solov'ev, Gershenzon, Vinogradov, Vinokur, Stepanov, Slonimskii, and a few others. This is a representative group of distinguished men of letters. On the whole (despite the difficulty for the uninitiated created by some of the abridgments), the editors have succeeded in assembling in one volume a representative and interesting body of material.

SR, 36:3:532-33

525.   Ripp, Victor. **Turgenev's Russia.** From **Notes of a Hunter to a Hunter to Fathers and Sons.** Ithaca, NY: Cornell University Press, 1980. 218p. $14.50.

Ripp is concerned with the Russian background out of which Turgenev's novels arose. The first four novels and such earlier works as *Notes of a Hunter* serve as convenient foci for studying Russian educated society's opinions on such issues as serfdom, education, love, and work. As a result, the book is something of a halfbreed — not wuite literary criticism nor yet cultural history. The thrust of his work underlines the prevailing critical opinion of Turgenev as a writer whose novels raised more questions than they answered, mirroring as they did on a society that was groping for understanding and self-definition.

LJBR, 1980:288

526.   Rosenthal, B. G. **D. S. Merezhkovsky and the Silver Age: The Development of a Revolutionary Mentality.** The Hague: Martinus Nijhoff, 1975. vii, 248p. Dfl. 52.25.

Rosenthal examines the development of Dmitrii Merezhkovsky's "revolutionary mentality" and his contributions to both Russian Symbolism and the Bolshevik Revolution in the era 1890-1919. Concentrating on an intellectual rather than literary study of Merezhkovsky, the author shows both the strengths and weaknesses of this remarkable and indefatigable Russian who was so adept at reviewing the concerns and synthesizing the ideas animating many members of the Russian intelligentsia, yet who was so often guilty of fitting the evidence to his preconceived schemes.

CSP, 18:4:482-83

527.   Rowe, William Woodin. **Through Gogol's Looking Glass: Reverse Vision, False Focus, and Precarious Logic.** New York: New York University Press, 1976. x, 201p. Illus. $12.50.

Rowe's book is a reflection of a reflection and bears the character of a pedagogical exercise. He has gone through the major Gogolian texts — from *Evenings on a Farm, Near Dikanka* to *Dead Souls* — identifying and dismantling for our inspection a quantity of examples of stylistic devices that have been discussed by the Formalist school of Gogol criticism. While this book will undoubtedly become a useful mine for students writing papers, it does not contribute any major insights into Gogol's work that will shift our thinking about this anxiety-producing author.

SR, 36:2:346-47

528. Sampson, Earl D. **Nikolay Gumilev.** Twayne's World Authors Series, 500: Russia. Boston: Twayne Publishers, G. K. Hall, 1978. 192p. $12.95.

This is the first monograph on Gumilev to appear in English, and it is therefore primarily introductory in character. After a 30-page biography, three chapters on his lyric poetry follow as does information about the Acmeist Period and the Mature Period (1913-1921). A final chapter deals with Gumilev's narrative and dramatic poetry. His prose and critical writings are mentioned but not discussed in any detail. Sampson interprets Gumilev as a "Romantic Idealist," for whom Acmeist theory was a useful discipline, but no more. He offers a sound introduction that should encourage the reader to go on and read Gumilev for himself.

SEER, 59:2:293-94

529. Seduro, Vladimir. **Dostoesvski's Image in Russia Today.** Belmont, MA: Nordland Publishing Company, 1975. xvi, 508p. $18.50. Appendix, "Dostoevski in Russian Émigré Criticism."

This book is a continuation of Seduro's study, *Dostoyevski in Russian Literary Criticism: 1846-1956* (1957). The book provides a wealth of information, and it will be of particular interest to the Western student of Dostoyevsky who lacks facility in Russian language. It is a serious contribution to Dostoyevsky scholarship in the West that will introduce the reader to a variety of new interpretations and will stimulate his interest in the new, as yet untranslated, studies of Dostoyevsky, the man and the artist.

SR, 35:1:177-78

530. Semenko, Irina M. **Vasily Zhukovsky.** Twayne's World Author Series, 271. Boston: Twayne Publishers, 1976. 167p. $7.95.

Semenko believes that "the integrity of Zhukovsky's poetic emotion and the concentrated intensity of his lyricism still make a deep impression upon his reader." The author proves a worthy champion in the present study, which as the first of its kind in English, should introduce a new audience to the real merits of Zhukovsky's verse and help to overcome his largely unfounded, but nonetheless widespread, image of insipid sentimentality. The book contains, in addition to a preface, chronology, and conclusion, seven chapters devoted to his life and work; the lyric; the lyric and history; the ballad and Russia; the medieval ballad; and epic, drama, and tales. The selected bibliography is adequate.

SEER, 55:2:236-37

531. Shaw, Thomas J. **Baratynskii: A Dictionary of the Rhymes and a Concordance to the Poetry.** Wisconsin Slavic Publications, 3. Madison: University of Wisconsin Press, 1975. xxxii, 434p. $36.95.

532. Shaw, Thomas J. **Batiushkov: A Dictionary of the Rhymes and a Concordance to the Poetry.** Wisconsin Slavic Publications, 2. Madison: University of Wisconsin Press, 1975. xxxii, 358p. $31.95.

While engaged in the project that led to *Pushkin's Rhymes: A Dictionary* (1974), Shaw decided to obtain comparative data by also investigating the rhymes of Batiushkov and Baratynskii. Each rhyme dictionary actually consists of two parts: a lexicon of endwords and a concordance of rhymes. Since the methodology is the same, the strengths and weaknesses of the Batiushkov and the Baratynskii volumes are the same as for the Pushkin dictionary. The lexicon offers grammatical information about each endword and shows the frequency of its occurrence. The concordance not only lists each of the rhymes—arranged alphabetically by rhyming segments—but also manages to describe in detail the grammatical and syntactic characteristics of each endword.

SR, 36:2:350-51

533. Shneidman, N. Norman. **Soviet Literature in the 1970s: Artistic Diversity and Ideological Conformity.** Toronto: University of Toronto Press, 1979. xiii, 128p. $15.00.

The author of this book chooses to discuss only six writers whose works, while publishable and published in the Soviet Union, manage to bypass the strictures of socialist realism in that they convey their perception of Soviet reality in its authenticity and not, as is mandatory, in "its revolutionary development." These authors are: Chingiz Aitmatov, Vasyl Bykov, Iurii Bondarev, Valentin Rasputin, Sergei Zalygin, and Iurii Trifonov. Also several non-Russian Soviet writers are considered. The book is well researched, informative, and reads well.

RR, 39:4:522-23

534. Sorokin, Boris. **Tolstoy in Prerevolutionary Russian Criticism.** Columbus, OH: Ohio State University Press for Miami University, 1979. xii, 328p. $25.00.

This book presents the historical and intellectual context that underlies Russian critical schools and outlines their main trends and positions. It suggests a view of Tolstoy's development as writer and thinker and as investigator of psychological and moral phenomena that makes possible an evaluation of critical opinion, making the book more than a mere catalog. The book provides, in excellent and spirited translations materials hitherto unavailable in English and frequently slighted or ignored in Russian. It is the most useful and substantial contribution to Tolstoy scholarship to appear in several years.

SR, 39:3:526-27

535. Stowell, H. Peter. **Literary Impressionism: James and Chekhov.** Athens: University of Georgia Press, 1980. x, 277p. $17.00.

In literature, impressionism is problematically temporal, and Stowell brings out provocative points—characters rue occasions in which they judge before they see (thus being schooled, as it were, in impressionist ideology); they find impressionistic perceptions to be active (not passive) yet uncontrollable in results, effecting thereby an "arbitrary and inconclusive ambiguity." But, instead of exploring more fully such paradoxes, Stowell moves away from them.

LJBR, 1980:292

536. Taranovsky, Kiril. **Essays on Mandel'stam.** Harvard Slavic Studies, vol. 6. Cambridge, MA: Harvard University Press, 1976. xii, 180p. $19.00.

Taranovsky bases his critical method on a literal interpretation of Mandelstam's text. He does not disallow more impressionistic approaches to Mandelstam's work, but he does favor the most systematic methods possible and tries to define and characterize his own approach. He assumes that everything Mandelstam wrote has a source that can be found and illuminated. Taranovsky's book appears to be leading to ultimate revelation of Mandelstam's artistic system.

SR, 36:2:353-54

537. Thomson, Boris. **Lot's Wife and the Venus of Milo: Conflicting Attitudes to the Cultural Heritage in Modern Russia.** New York and London: Cambridge University Press, 1978. vi, 171p. $14.95.

The author attempts to cover the Marxist attitude toward the art of the past, ideas and practices worked out in the Soviet Union during the 1920s, and the position in the controversy of a great variety of literary and political figures.

SR, 39:4:715-17

538. Todd III, William Mills. **The Familiar Letters as a Literary Genre in the Age of Pushkin.** Princeton, NJ: Princeton University Press, 1976. xii, 230p. $15.00.
This study is divided into an introduction, six chapters that treat the epistolary tradition and its reception in Russia in the period under discussion, a conclusion, an afterword, two appendices (the first consisting of thumbnail biographies of the Arzamasians, the second being N. I. Grech's essay on letter writings in English translations) followed by a bibliography and index. Todd provides a thoughtful and readable account of one of the lesser-known and -researched aspects of Russian literature of the early nineteenth century — the familiar letter as it flourished among the Arzamasians. The book recommends itself to the student of the Arzamas period as a useful initiation to the issues posed by this curious genre.
    CSP, 19:4:540-41

539. Tulloch, John. **Chekhov: A Structuralist Study.** Totowa, NJ: Barnes & Noble, 1980. xii, 225p. $27.50.
Tulloch follows the genetic structuralism of Lucien Goldmann and also adopts some semiotic jargon from R. Barthès. He rejects "a disparate body of Chekhovian criticism" on the grounds that it has been committed to the immanent analysis of texts as determined by the values of New Criticism. He claims to have introduced, for the first time, the genuine key to understanding Chekhov's works by placing the writer in his social context. This climax of the author's theoretical thought is followed by a rather anticlimactic application to specific works. This book will surely find its audience among those interested in sociology of literature. It is a pity that they will be misled on the way to the meaning of Chekhov's works.
    RR, 40:4:353-54

540. Wasiolek, Edward. **Tolstoy's Major Fiction.** Chicago: University of Chicago Press, 1978. 254p. $16.00.
This study of Tolstoy is particularly valuable for its bibliography which, if not comprehensive, provides intelligent and informed comment on recent Tolstoy criticism available in English. This study of Tolstoy is not prophetic, prickly though it may be, yet it is justifiably provocative in its search for a new meaning in Tolstoy's work; there is no better criticism than that.
    SEER, 57:3:425-28

541. Woodward, James B. **Gogol's Dead Souls.** Princeton, NJ: Princeton University Press, 1978. xvii, 276p. $22.00.
Gogol's *Dead Souls* is seen here as an intricate allegory, a salad of symbols, in which the "perfect oval of the egg is stretched and bent into the elongated contours of a cucumber." The close reading of Woodward's study is strangely linked to distanced, unfocused interpretation — the commentary soars above the text on a would-be metaphysical plane of its own. Sexuality plays a key interpretative role, but such concepts as "defeminized peasants" and "masculinized femininity" must not be taken in any sense, and we are warned against the Freudian view.
    SEER, 58:4:580-83

542. Woodward, James B. **Ivan Bunin: A Study of His Fiction.** Chapel Hill: University of North Carolina Press, 1980. xii, 275p. $17.50.
Woodward's strongest contributions in this study lie in his insights into Bunin's narrative method and the composition of his stories. Especially well done is the treatment of the inadequacies of Bunin's fragmentary composition in the early stories and of narrative

retardation in the *Dark Alleys* collection. Woodward's excellent bibliography includes most of the important articles and books on Bunin in Russian and English.

543. Zeldin, Jesse. **Nikolai Gogol's Quest for Beauty: An Exploration into His Works.** Lawrence: The Regents Press of Kansas, 1978. x, 244p. $13.50.
Zeldin's thesis is that Gogol "had a vision before him that he was never to lose, a vision of a harmoniously created universe—that is, of beauty itself—that he believed to be real, even though material phenomena seemed to deny it," and that he spent all his life in futile quest for a full and perfect embodiment of that beauty. Zeldin revives the unfashionable distinction between form and content and in general makes it serve him well. He also sets us to thinking in fresh ways and, most important, creates a picture of a whole and integral Gogol, free of many of those stubborn contradictions that have bemused readers for over a century.
SR, 39:1:155-56

544. Zlobin, Vladimir. **A Difficult Soul: Zinaida Gippius.** Edited, annotated and with an introductory essay by Simon Karlinsky. Berkeley: University of California Press, 1980. 197p. $14.50.
The appearance of Zlobin's *A Heavy Soul* in English translation provides the English reader with an important biographical source on Zinaida Gippius, one of Russia's most important women writers and a leading figure in the Symbolist movement and spirited revival of the turn of the century. In his excellent introductory essay, Simon Karlinsky refers to Gippius as the Dostoyevsky of Russian poetry and her themes as central to Russian Symbolism. The translation is accurate, reads well, and is a welcome addition to the slowly accumulating Gippiusiana of the last decade.
RR, 40:2:224-25

Anthologies

545. Erlich, Victor, ed. **Twentieth-Century Russian Literary Criticism.** New Haven: Yale University Press, 1975. ix, 317p. $15.00.
Erlich attempts to provide the nonspecialist with a selection of the best Russian literary criticism of this century. The result is a collection of 17 essays divided into five unequal parts: the symbolists (2 essays), formalists and near-formalists (7), early Soviet Marxists (2), émigré critics (3), and the recent scene (3). In the preface, the editor discusses the criteria of selection, and the introduction gives a brief though judicious sketch of the highlights of Russian twentieth-century criticism. This anthology is a welcome addition to the body of Russian literary criticism available in English and an especially useful introduction to the subject for the nonspecialist.
CSP, 19:3:390-91

546. Glad, John, and Daniel Weissbort, eds. **Russian Poetry: The Modern Period.** Iowa Translations. Iowa City: University of Iowa Press, 1978. lxii, 356p. $9.95.
Seventy poets are presented in this anthology in six chronological groupings, three covering Soviet Russia and three dealing with the emigration. The scope of the collection is ambitious, and many of the translations, by experienced hands, have appeared previously in American and English journals.
SEER, 58:3:473-74

547. Karlinsky, Simon, and Alfred Appel, Jr., eds. **The Bitter Air of Exile: Russian Writers in the West, 1922-1972.** Berkeley: University of California Press, 1977 [1973]. iv, 475p. Illus. $18.75.

This volume is one of the few pioneering endeavors to attract the attention of the English reading public to a brilliant, but so far nearly closed, section of Russian literary art. The first part, Six Major Émigré Writers, includes six authors; the second part, Some Émigré Poetry, includes four poets; and the third part, Selections of Émigré Prose, contains excerpts from writings of eight authors. All translations are correct, and, in most cases, they are artistically done. The commentaries are concise and reliable.

SR, 37:4:715-16

548. Kern, Gary, and Christopher Collins, eds. **The Serapion Brothers: A Critical Anthology.** Ann Arbor, MI: Ardis, 1975. xxxviii, 178p. $3.45, paper.

The editors have provided a nicely packaged and very useful critical anthology that contains one story apiece by Kaverin, Lunts, Shklovskii, Nikitin, Vsevolod Ivanov, Fedin, and Slonimskii; two stories for Zoshchenko; and the essential polemical writings by Lunts, Gruzdev, and others that defined the position and principles of the brotherhood. The Serapions have always been praised for the aesthetic sophistication evident in their critical writings and for their artistic promise. Thanks to Kern and Collins, it is now possible to read the Serapions. They deserve to be read.

RR, 35:2:227-28

549. Kuzminsky, Konstantin K., and Gregory L. Kovalev. **The Blue Lagoon: Anthology of Modern Russian Poetry.** Vol. I. Newtonville, MA: Oriental Research Partners, 1980. 606p. $28.00.

This first of a projected series of five volumes includes 40 poets, 60 articles, and 97 photographs. The anthology draws upon almost exclusively unpublished archival materials from Moscow and Leningrad. Forthcoming volumes, all with rare illustrations smuggled out of the USSR, will be published soon.

550. Neuhäuser, Rudolf. **The Romantic Age in Russian Literature: Poetic and Esthetic Norms – An Anthology of Original Texts (1800-1850).** Slavistische Beiträge, no. 92. Munich: Verlag Otto Sagner, 1975. 300p. DM 35.00.

This collection consists of excerpts from the original Russian texts, untranslated, arranged in four parts entitled, respectively, Problems of Literary Evolution, Interpretations I – Literary Trends, Interpretations II – Poetics, and Interpretations III – Style and Genres. Over 70 different authors and critics are quoted in all. Each part opens with an introduction, and the quotations themselves are accompanied by useful explanatory and amplifying notes. The select bibliography is divided into four parts: Primary Sources, Reference Works, Histories of Russian Literature and Criticism, and Studies of Russian Romantic Literature.

CSP, 18:4:498

551. Pachmuss, Temira, ed. and trans. **Women Writers in Russian Modernism: An Anthology.** Chicago and London: University of Illinois Press, 1978. xvi, 340p. $17.50.

This anthology fascinates and intrigues the reader by its novelty – it introduces new facts, faces, and unfamiliar personalities demanding further investigation. Its selection is varied and inherently interesting. Although it serves to stimulate the reader's interest, the translations are somewhat awkward, sometimes severely distorting the originals. The book can be recommended to readers seeking to gain greater familiarity with the variety of literary experiences comprising the Silver Age. Pachmuss provides basic data about each author, her publications, value system, literary techniques, and critical acceptance at the time of publication.

SR, 39:1:162

552. Proffer, Carl, and Ellendea Proffer, eds. **The Ardis Anthology of Recent Russian Literature.** Ann Arbor, MI: Ardis, 1975. xvi, 420p. Illus. $5.00, paper.

The emphasis of this volume is on poetry. A fourth of the volume is devoted to translations of poems, with 29 poets represented. It includes Akhmatova, Mandelstam, Pasternak, Mayakovsky, and Tsvetaeva as well as several émigré poets. The anthology is a useful compilation, although it falls short of the excellence that would make it an enduring classic.

SR, 36:1:157-60

553. Proffer, Carl, and Ellendea Proffer, eds. **The Silver Age of Russian Culture: An Anthology.** Ann Arbor, MI: Ardis, 1975. xv, 454p. Illus. $15.00.

This volume contains four sections: Criticism, Poetry, Prose, and Articles. Represented are the following poets and writers: A. Block, V. Akhmatova, A. Belyi, V. Soloviev, V. Ivanov, I. Annenskii, N. Gumilev, and V. Zhirmunskii. The best items in the anthology are 21 excellent translations of Akhmatova's poems by Walter Arndt, instructive articles written by Denis Mickiewicz, and John E. Bowlt's essay ("The World of Art"). The quality of the anthology is marred by abundant typographical errors.

SR, 3:4:776-77

Individual Authors

554. Akhmatova, Anna. (pseud. of Anna A. Gorenko). **Selected Poems.** Edited and translated by Walter Arndt. With "Requiem," translated by Robin Kemmball, and "A Poem without a Hero," translated and annotated by Carl R. Proffer. Ann Arbor, MI: Ardis, 1976. xxxvi, 202p. Illus. $10.95.

555. Akhmatova, Anna. **Requiem and Poem without a Hero.** Translated by D. M. Thomas. Athens, OH: Ohio University Press, 1976. 78p. $8.00.

Two new collections of Akhmatova's poetry in translation bring to four the number available in English. The Ardis volume provides a wealth of photographs, many of them little known or previously unpublished. But the translations themselves are, quite frankly, a disappointment. Thomas' *Poem without a Hero* is indeed the only complete "poetic" translation, although there are now at least six of *Requiem*. His *Requiem* is certainly among the best.

SR, 36:3:536-37

556. Bedford, Harold C. **The Seeker: D. S. Merezhkovskiy.** Lawrence: The University Press of Kansas, 1975. x, 222p. $12.50.

Bedford's study gives the reader insight into Merezhkovskiy's childhood and family background and deals with his conversion from populism (with its attachment to poets such as Nekrasov and Nadson) to symbolism (under the impact of classical antiquity, Bauldelaire, and Nietzsche). A painstakingly compiled bibliography adds to the value of this highly commendable study.

SR, 35:4:774-75

557. Bely, Andrey. **The First Encounter.** Translated and introduced by Gerald Janeček. Notes and Comments by Nina Berberova. Princeton, NJ: Princeton University Press, 1979. 133p. $10.00.

Bely's autobiographical poem, reconstructing atmospheres and epiphanies of the turn of the century, was written in Petrograd during May and June, 1921. The editorial prefaces by Janeček and Berberova focus upon technical aspects of versification and the history of Russian verse declamation, usefully but rather to the neglect of the poem's place in the author's biography.

RR, 39:2:266-67

558. Bely, Andrei. **Petersburg.** Translated, annotated, and with an introduction by Robert A. Maguire and John E. Malmstad. Bloomington and London: Indiana University Press, 1978. xxviii, 356p. $17.50.

The appearance of this excellently translated and annotated edition of Bely's famous novel means that it is now at last possible for readers without a knowledge of Russian to penetrate that mysterious and immensely influential work. Despite deliberate displacement of time and space, the events of that turbulent autumn of 1905 are more vivid in this novel than in many a sober chronicle.

SR, 39:1:159-60

559. Dostoevsky, Anna. **Dostoevsky: Reminiscences.** Translated and edited by Beatrice Stillman. Introduction by Helen Muchnic. New York: Liveright, W. W. Norton, 1975. xxxiv, 448p. $12.50.

Unlike Dostoyevsky's own works, the memoirs of his wife are filled with objects — that is, the cumbersome and comforting paraphernalia of domesticity. Included in the book, of course, are the famous anecdotes about Dostoyevsky's courtship of the young stenographer, his visits to the gambling tables, and his reestablishment of relations with Nekrasov. But the real impact of the *Reminiscences* comes from the accumulation of observed detail, from the passing scene which grips the reader unaware. Stillman has provided a proficient translation, has revised the notes to suit the needs of a non-Russian reading audience, and has included a useful biographical glossary.

SR, 36:1:153-54

560. Dostoevsky, Feodor. **Crime and Punishment.** Revised Edition. Edited by George Gibian. Translated by Jessie Coulson. A Norton Critical Edition. New York: W. W. Norton, 1975 [1964]. xii, 670p. $15.00.

This revised edition provides an improved format for the novel, more explanatory notes, a passage from an early draft in which Roskolnikov is the first-person narrator, an updated bibliography, and six new critical selections.

SR, 35:2:386

561. Dostoevsky, Feodor M. **The Diary of a Writer.** Translated by Boris Brosol. Introduction by Joseph Frank. Santa Barbara, CA, and Salt Lake City: Peregrin Smith, 1979. xxxviii, 1097p. $14.95, paper.

The reprint of Brosol's translation will be of great help in the study and teaching of Dostoyevsky. The importance of *The Diary of a Writer* as a source of information and a commentary on Dostyevsky's later works, especially *The Brothers Karamazov*, is generally acknowledged. Brosol's translation is adequate. His commentary is helpful, but much more information is needed to follow many of the articles.

SR, 40:1:147-48

562. Dunlop, John B., et al., eds. **Alexander Solzhenitsyn: Critical Essays and Documentary Materials.** 2nd ed. New York: Collier Books, a division of Macmillan; London: Collier Macmillan, 1975 [1973]. 666p. $5.95, paper.
The first edition of this volume, which appeared before the publication of Solzhenitsyn's *August 1914*, contained a dozen critical essays. For the second edition, the editors have added articles that deal with *August 1914* and with the first volume of *Gulag Archipelago*. The new edition also includes an appendix containing document, a critical review of various English translations of Solzhenitsyn's work, and an excellent bibliography.
　　SR, 35:3:579-80

563. Erofeev, Venedikt. **Moscow to the End of the Line.** Translated by H. W. Tjalsma. Introduction by Vera S. Dunham. New York: Taplinger Publishing, 1980. 164p. $8.95.
One of the most interesting, inspired, and intensely visionary pieces of Russian prose to have appeared in *samizdat*, Erofeev's *Moskva-Petushki* was written in 1968. The book is a celebration of the Russian language, even the contemporary Soviet language, not as it appears in official print but as it is spoken. The book is full of literary allusions, both serious and absurd, and its ambience reinforces the author's use of *poema* to remind us of Chichilov in *Dead Souls*.
　　SR, 40:3:509

564. Field, Andrew. **Nabokov: His Life in Part.** New York: The Viking Press, 1977. xiv, 285p. Photographs. $15.00.
On the positive side, Field's latest book gives us a wealth of fascinating inforamtion, much of it new, most of it apparently quite reliable. What emerges is a vivid and instructive picture of Nabokov's life, personality, opinions, and interests. He also offers well-researched and worthwhile discussions of Nabokov's family background, his life as an émigré in Berlin, and several parallels between Nabokov and Pushkin. On the negative side, Field's book seems proudly haunted by the fear that the author is "too much like Vladimir Nabokov to judge him."
　　SR, 37:2:347-48

565. Grayson, Jane. **Nabokov Translated: A Comparison of Nabokov's Russian and English Prose.** New York and London: Oxford University Press, 1977. xii, 257p. $21.00.
This book examines Nabokov's translations of his own works, with particular attention to resulting alterations of characterization and style. It contains worthwhile discussions on the use of color in *Laughter in the Dark*, Nabokov's "false alarm device," and the "Thamara theme." The reader of this specialized, thorough study should know Russian.
　　SR, 37:2:347-48

566. Green, Michael, ed. and trans. **Michael Kuzmin: Selected Prose and Poetry.** Ann Arbor, MI: Ardis, 1980. xxviii, 416p. $22.50.
Kuzmin (1875-1936) was a prose writer, poet, essayist, musician, and playwright. He was an avowed and defiant homosexual, and his novel *Wings* created a scandal when published in 1906. This collection of Kuzmin's works is the largest to appear in English so far. It contains 13 short stories, the complete novel *Wings*, the complete *Alexandrian Songs, The Trout Breaks the Ice,* and the collection of pensées entitled *Fish-Scales in the Net*.

567. Jensen, Kjeld Bjornager.**Russian Futurism, Urbanism, and Elena Guro.** Arkus, Denmark: Arkona, 1977. iv, 204p. Paper.

Jensen distinguishes Guro, whom he calls an impressionist, from the other Futurists, whom he considers expressionists. His extensive analysis of her three urbanistic prose pieces suggests a sadomasochistic motivation for her increasing hostility to the city. The book includes a useful bibliography.

SR, 38:1:159

568. Khlebnikov, Velimir. **Snake Train: Poetry and Prose.** Edited by Gary Kern. Introduction by Edward J. Brown. Translated by Gary Kern, et al. Ann Arbor, MI: Ardis, 1976. 388p. $4.95, paper.

Selected works of Velimir Khlebnikov, Russia's outstanding modernist writer, have at long last appeared in English. In *Snake Train*, Kern has included his own and others' annotated renditions of long and short poems, experiments, dramatic works, prose fiction, and visions and theories. Three appendices provide a chronology of Khlebnikov's life, a memoir by his Futurist friend Dmitrii Petrovskii, and a Russian text of some of the poems. Translations of the shortest poems included in an appendix appear together with the translations. One would also welcome a select bibliography of secondary material available in English.

SR, 37:2:349-51

569. Klyuev, Nikolai. **Poems.** Translated by John Glad. Published by the Iowa Translation Series, International Writing Program, University of Iowa. Ann Arbor, MI: Ardis, 1977. xx, 96p. $2.95, paper.

Faced with the unenviable and formidable problem of Klyuev's hodge-podge of styles, twisted syntax, and heavy use of diminutives, Glad has opted for fairly literal translations that are generally faithful to the originals, although sometimes at the expense of poetic grace or fluidity. Anyone truly interested in Klyuev is well advised to take a look at this volume.

SR, 37:4:717-18

570. Livshits, Benedikt. **The One and a Half-Eyed Archer.** Translated, annotated, and with an introduction by John E. Bowlt. Newtonville, MA: Oriental Research Partners, 1977. 272p. Illus. $25.00.

Livshits' interpretation of Russian Futurism must be understood in the context of 1933, when a 47-year-old Jewish artist and critic recanted his youthful mistakes under party pressure. Livshits himself wrote that his memoir was intended to "expose these political prejudices of an erroneous aesthetics — in the formation of which I took an immediate part." Readers should thus approach this memoir with some caution because Livshits has, in part, translated a political anti-Westernism of 1933 into a remembered cultural anti-Westernism of 1911-1914. He perished during the purges in 1939. This book remains a crucial source on Russian Futurism.

SR, 37:2:353-54

571. Mamleyev, Yuri. **The Sky above Hell and Other Stories.** Translated by H. W. Tjalsma. New York: Taplinger Publishing, 1980. 160p. $7.95.

Mamleyev, a recent émigré, is one of the most original representatives of the Russian literary avant-garde of the last two decades. The collection of essays is fairly representative of his artistic method, defined by the author as "metaphysical realism."

SR, 40:3:508-509

572. Mandelstam, Nadezhda. **Hope Abandoned.** Translated from the Russian by Max
      Hayward. New York: Atheneum, 1974. xii, 687p. $13.95.

In *Hope Abandoned*, Mandelstam attempts a reevaluation not only of the 1920s – which
are usually idealized both in the Soviet Union and in the West – but of the Silver Age as
well. The book's greatest significance lies in its perceptive analysis of the ways intellectuals
change under a totalitarian system. The inevitable result – a loss of one's identity – is seen
by the author as an illness of our age. The English translation by Max Hayward is very
accurate. In addition to an index, a chronology and a very useful appendix are provided.
This book has its place among the best memoir literature of the century.
      SR, 36:1:156-57

573. Mandelstam, Osip. **50 Poems.** Translated by Bernard Meares, with an introductory
      essay by Joseph Brodsky. New York: Persea Books, 1977. 117p. $7.95.

Brodsky's essay is certain to be an attraction for Bernard Meares' volume. His appreciation
of Mandelstam and his ability to articulate his feelings for another poet suggests a special
relationship and makes one wish for a fuller critique. The translations which follow are
true representations of Mandelstam, even though they are unfortunately variable in
quality.
      SEER, 57:3:439-40

574. Mandelstam, Osip. **Journey to Armenia.** Translated by Sidney Monas. With a
      critical essay, "Mandelstam and the Journey," by Henry Gifford. San Francisco:
      George F. Ritchie, 1979. 77p. $32.00.

Gifford's essay in this volume pertains in its implications to Mandelstam's entire creative
work so that, in effect, there are two journeys – to Armenia and across Mandelstam's
mind. Both offer a gratifying and an instructive experience. The translation by Sidney
Monas is skillful and smooth, indeed, witty.
      RR, 40:1:85

575. Mandelstam, Osip. **Osip Mandelstam: Selected Essays.** Translated by Sidney
      Monas. The Dan Danciger Publication Series. Austin and London: University of
      Texas Press, 1977. xxvi, 245p. $15.95.

Monas' translations vary considerably in their precision and excellence; by far the best in
this volume is *Journey to Armenia*. As for the selection of items included in this volume,
Professor Monas has chosen to limit himself to what must be regarded as "basic
Mandelstam."
      SR, 36:4:721-22

576. Mandelstam, Osip. **Selected Poems.** Bilingual edition. Translated and annotated by
      David McDuff. New York: Farrar, Straus & Giroux, 1975 [1973]. xxiv, 182p. $3.95,
      paper.

Among the recent collections of Mandelstam's poems, McDuff's volume is unique in
several ways. The translator worked alone, the Russian originals are printed *en face*, and
the paperback edition is the cheapest. The selection is a good one, and it is preceded by an
introduction that acquaints the reader with essential background information, marred only
occasionally by an uncritical or uninformed repetition of certain of the numerous myths
that becloud Mandelstam's life.
      SR, 35:3:580-81

577. Nabokov, Vladimir. **Details of a Sunset and Other Stories.** Translated from the Russian by Dmitri Nabokov in collaboration with the author. New York: McGraw-Hill, 1976. 179p. $8.95.
The present short story collection contains 13 stories, the last batch of his stories "meriting to be Englished." Only some 7 remain untranslated. The volume is special because it contains not only some of Nabokov's earliest prose (written in Berlin in 1924-35) but some of his finest Russian stories ("Christmas," "The Return of Chorb," "The Passenger," "The Doorbell"). This collection brings Nabokov's work into particularly sharp focus.
SR, 35:4:778-79

578. Nabokov, Vladimir. **Tyrants Destroyed and Other Stories.** Translated by Dmitri Nabokov in collaboration with Vladimir Nabokov. New York and London: McGraw-Hill, 1975. xii, 238p. $8.95.
This book is a collection of 13 short stories. All but "The Vane Sisters" (1951) were written in the 1920s and 1930s in Berlin, Paris, and Meuton. The book is indeed a welcome addition to Nabokov's literary *oeuvre* in English.
SR, 35:1:182

579. Nikitin, Nikolai. **Night and Other Stories.** Edited and translated by Victor Peppard. Royal Oak, MI: Strathona Publishing Co., 1978. 136p. $11.50.
Nikitin's stories, now translated for the first time, are not first-rate since the atmosphere of his stories, though effectively conveyed, remains insufficiently buttressed. Notwithstandin these criticisms, Nikitin's stories are required reading for anyone interested in Russian prose of the early 1920s. The translations of the stories are excellent, and the introduction provides an objective assessment of Nikitin's work.
SR, 38:3:533

580. Pachmuss, Temira, ed. and trans. **Between Paris and St. Petersburg: Selected Diaries of Zinaida Hippius.** Urbana, Chicago, London: University of Illinois Press, 1975. xvi, 329p. $12.50.
Pachmuss has diligently selected, translated, edited, and annotated the seven diaries of Zinaida Hippius that make up this volume. The diary contains a great many fascinating details about Hippius' life at that time and about a number of people with whom she was closely associated (such as Kartashev, Marietta Shaginyan, and Boris Savinkov).
SR, 35:2:388-89

581. Panichas, George A. **The Burden of Vision: Dostoevsky's Spiritual Art.** Grand Rapids, MI: William B. Eerdmans Publishing Co., 1977. 216p. $5.95, paper.
With this book, the case for Dostoyevsky as a metaphysician, prophetic mind, and spiritual pathfinder, who must be taken seriously as a thinker and moralist, has been stated with so much intellectual forcefulness, persuasiveness, and self-evident truth that this manner of approach to the Russian visionary's work has definitely arrived to stay. The book represents the most welcome enrichment of the body of Dostoyevsky studies.
SR, 38:1:157

582. Pavlova, Karolina. **A Double Life.** Translated and with an introduction by Barbara Heldt Monter. Ann Arbor, MI: Ardis, 1978. xxii, 111p. $10.00.
Dvoinaia zhizn' (1848) is not exactly a novel but a Romantic hybrid, part "physiological sketch" in prose, part Romantic idealism in poetry. Each of the 10 chapters narrates with irony a day in the life of Cecilia von Lindenborn, who is duped into marrying a man who only wanted her for her money. In general, the translation is accurate.
SR, 38:2:352-53

583. Pilnyak, Boris. **The Naked Year.** Translated with an afterword by Alexander R. Tulloch. Ann Arbor, MI: Ardis, 1975. 204p. $3.95, paper.

Tulloch replaces Brown's 1928 rendition's occasional looseness with meticulous attention to the Russian original that frequently constitutes a flaw in itself. Indeed, because of this methodical exchange of English words for Russian, there are instances where the sense is almost completely garbled in transit. Such awkwardness deprives the work of Pilnyak's verbal verve and zest. Despite its flaws, Tulloch's translation stands up to close scrutiny as well as many. It is certainly a useful volume.

SR, 35:4:777-78

584. Platonov, Andrey. **The Foundation Pit.** Translated by Mira Ginsburg. New York: E. P. Dutton, 1975. 141p. $71.50.

Platonov's strenuous language and the starkness of his landscape make *The Foundation Pit* painful but moving reading. Ginsburg smooths it out, shortening the sentences and emphasizing the formality of bureaucratic jargon rather than its absurdity.

SR, 35:1:181-82

585. Pushkin, A. S. **Eugene Onegin.** 4 vols. Translated from the Russian with a commentary by Vladimir Nabokov. Revised edition. Bollingen Series 71, Princeton, NJ: Princeton University Press, 1975. xxviii, 390p.; xvi, 547p.; xvi, 341p.; v, 428p. $60.00.

Reappearing now (first edition in 1964), 12 years later, in a "complete revised" version, *Eugene Onegin* is unlikely to arouse new passions. Apart from a few minor corrections in the commentary, the revision is confined to the translation itself, and here readers will find as before that, in his own words, the translator has sacrificed "to completeness of meaning every formal element including the iambic rhythm, whenever its retention hindered fidelity ... everything that the dainty mimic prizes higher than truth." Nabokov's homage to Pushkin is a uniquely important work and deserves a place in every arts library in the Western world.

SEER, 55:99-100

586. Pushkin, Alexander. **Eugene Onegin.** Translated by Charles Johnston. London: Published by the Translator, 1977. 226p. £5.85.

This translation comes nearer than any existing version to an adequate rendering of that distinctive gamut of authorial tones that gives the original its unique vitality. This version should become the standard English *Onegin* for our time.

SEER, 58:1:111-12

587. Różewicz, Tadeusz. **"The Survivor" and Other Poems.** Translated with an introduction by Magnus J. Krynski and Robert A. Maguire. Princeton, NJ: Princeton University Press, 1976. xx, 160p. $12.50.

With the publication of these latest collections (the other is *Selected Poems*, translated by Adam Czerniawski [1976]), Różewicz is sure to attract the attention of young American poets in search of a "naked poetry." He is a deceptively easy poet. His "anti-aesthetic" and "anti-poetic" stance can distract too easily from what is paradoxically a layered, and at times even-mannered, style. The translations, accompanied by the originals *en face*, are a model of painstaking fidelity, both visually and verbally.

SR, 36:3:541-42

588. Saltykov-Shchedrin, M. E. **The History of a Town.** Translated and with an introduction by I. P. Foote. Oxford: Willem A. Meeuws, 1980. xvi, 192p. £9.00.

This is the first English translation of Saltykov's satire. Foote's rendering of the text is complete, faithful to the original, and contains many happy formulations. The blemishes of the translation are minor. Foote has provided an excellent English version of one of Saltykov's principal works. Regrettably, the introduction and commentary are only of limited value.

SEEJ, 25:3:111-13

589. Saltykov-Shchedrin, M. E. **Saltykov-Shchedrin, M. E.: Selected Satirical Writings.** Edited by I. P. Foote. Oxford: Clarendon Press, 1977. vi, 284p. $21.00.

The Russian texts in this volume are reprints from the recent collected edition of M. E. Saltykov-Shchedrin's works (*Sobranie sochinenii* [Moscow, 1965-76]). The collection includes a substantial introduction by Foote, introductory notes to the individual items, commentaries to all the texts, a glossary of rare words, and a select bibliography, all of which provide reliable information on Saltykov's life and work as well as on the historical background of mid-nineteenth-century Russia. The collection has little or no appeal to specialists, although it may be useful as a review source for Saltykov's satires.

SR, 27:2:345

590. Sokolov, Sasha. **A School for Fools.** Translated by Carl R. Proffer. Ann Arbor, MI: Ardis, 1977. 288p. $10.00.

Sokolov, born in 1943, studied at the Military Institute of Foreign Languages and later at the School of Journalism at Moscow State University, left the Soviet Union in 1975. In his book, the chief narrator is a former inmate of a school for retarded and disturbed children. The book eschews the epigonic-realistic narrative techniques that predominate, in quantity if not quality, in contemporary Soviet prose fiction as well as in Russian literature of dissent.

SR, 37:3:538-39

591. Sologub, Fyodor. **The Created Legend.** 3 vols. Translated by Samuel D. Cioran. Ann Arbor, MI: Ardis, 1979. Vol. 1: *Drops of Blood.* 217p. Vol. 2: *Queen Ortruda.* 247p. Vol. 3: *Smoke and Ashes.* 134p. $45.00, cloth, for 3 volumes.

Sologub's trilogy serves as a period piece, and, illustrative of Russian Symbolist prose, it abounds in those Romantic dualisms that are derived from the contrast between heaven and hell. Cioran has provided the first complete and reliable translation of the trilogy; his introduction consists of a short biography with a history of the text and Russian criticism.

SR, 40:1:148-49

592. Solzhenitsyn, Alexander I. **The Gulag Archipelago 1918-1956: An Experiment in Literary Investigation, III-IV.** Translated from the Russian by Thomas P. Whitney. New York: Harper & Row, 1975. vi, 712p. $15.00, cloth. $2.50, paper.

Solzhenitsyn seeks to demonstrate that Stalin was merely a symptom of a profound ethical and spiritual sickness that began in 1917. He insists upon the central role of Lenin in the creation of the terror and the camp system, quoting an August 1918 telegram in which Lenin urged that "doubtful" elements should be locked up in a "concentration camp." He quotes other documents to show that Lenin took the lead in urging and implementing "merciless mass terror." Volumes III-IV, like volumes I-II, provide a detailed account of what it was like inside the camps, but Solzhenitsyn argues that life "on the outside" shared many of the same features. *The Gulag* is a major intellectual and moral achievement. (Volumes I-II were published in 1974-1975; see Horak, p. 259.)

SR, 36:1:119-20

593. Solzhenitsyn, Aleksandr I. **The Oak and the Calf: Sketches of Literary Life in the Soviet Union.** Translated by Harry Willetts. New York: Harper & Row, 1980. viii, 568p. $15.95.

Solzhenitsyn's memoirs, added to over the years and taken through his expulsion from the Soviet Union, trace his transformation into a world-renowned writer. Despite the disturbing tendency toward myth-making, the details of Solzhenitsyn's struggle for the survival of his works are of major importance. The translation admirably preserves Solzhenitsyn's verbal energy and mordant wit. Solzhenitsyn's works remain of special importance for all readers interested in literature and politics.

LJBR, 1980:291

594. Suslov, Ilya. **Here's to Your Health, Comrade Shifrin!** Translated by Maxine Bronstein. Foreword by Maurice Friedberg. Bloomington and London: Indiana University Press, 1977. xviii, 204p. $8.95.

Even if Suslov's book is not a major literary event, it is still the personal statement of a man with a good mind, a good face, a sharp ear for cant, and a fine sense of irony. He tells us the saga of Tolia Shifrin's struggle to survive in the system with unfailing humor. It deserves to be read.

SR, 37:1:172-73

595. Tertz, Abram [Andrei Sinyavsky]. **A Voice from the Chorus.** Translated from the Russian by Kyril FitzLyon and Max Hayward. Introduction by Max Hayward. New York: Farrar, Straus & Giroux, 1976 [1973]. xxiv, 328p. $10.00.

The history of this text — mainly Sinyavsky's communications to his wife — clarifies the lack of any discussion of the political and moral implications of his imprisonment. It imparts many things to the reader, particularly a sense of humility and a deep skepticism with regard to all purely man-made attempts at self-redemption. Hayward's explanations of little-known Russian terms, turns of speech, and specific realia of Soviet Russian life in its less publicized, largely unexplored aspects prove to be a useful aid to the Western reader. The English version, on the whole, reads well.

SR, 37:1:171-72

596. Tolstoy, L. **Letters, 1828-1910.** Selected, edited, and translated by R. F. Christian. 2 vols. London: The University of London, The Athlone Press, 1978. xvi, 737p. £20.00.

Christian's edition of Tolstoy's letters is a major contribution to Tolstoy's English reputation and a worthy memorial to him on the 150th anniversary of his birth. From more than 30 volumes of Tolstoy's works — and from elsewhere — Christian has selected for translation just over 600 letters. He has furnished valuable introductions to the principal phases in Tolstoy's life and has given admirably concise and informative biographical data for Tolstoy's correspondents, as well as ample annotation to the letters themselves. This is a biography with the difference that here we have the personality of Tolstoy more directly illuminated than biographers have on the whole allowed.

SEER, 57:3:425-28

597. Tsvetaeva, Marina. **A Captive Spirit: Selected Prose.** Edited and translated by J. Martin King. Ann Arbor, MI: Ardis, 1980. vi, 491p. $22.50.

This volume is composed of about one-third of Tsvetaeva's entire prose output, and it is representative of her genius at its peak. The volume consists of 16 individual works organized in three sections according to genre — literary portraits, autobiography, and literary criticism. These sections are supplemented by a critical introduction, copious notes and commentaries, and two appendices. The translations are lucid and quite good.

SEEJ, 25:1:105-108

598. Tsvetaeva, Marina. **The Demesne of the Swans.** A bilingual edition, including the definitive version of the Russian text, established by the edition, with introduction, notes, commentaries, and translation, Robin Kemball. Ann Arbor, MI: Ardis, 1980. 211p. $15.00.

A valuable feature of Kemball's work is the definitive version of the Russian text established on the basis of the manuscript deposited by Tsvetaeva in the Manuscript Division of the Basel Library. The editor's scrupulous eye makes this edition the one Tsvetaeva specialists will turn to rather than to the 1957 and 1971 editions of the same work. The chief merit of this volume, however, is the English translation.

SEEJ, 25:1:105-108

599. Zinoviev, Alexander. **The Yawning Heights.** Translated by Gordon Clough. New York: Random House, 1979 [Switzerland: Editions L'Age d'Homme, 1976]. 829p. $15.00.

The paradoxical title of this book beautifully conveys its dismal thesis—that the "shining height" of socialism, the "radiant future which has recently dawned," is actually a bottomless abyss of human ugliness and banality, and that, in fact, it could not have been otherwise. The action is set in a country of uncertain geography and whose name is Ibansk, a coinage which goes easily into English as "Fuckupia." The translation is excellent.

SR, 39:4:672-74

Special Studies, Censorship

600. Gladilin, Anatoly. **The Making and Unmaking of a Soviet Writer: My Story of the "Young Prose" of the Sixties and After.** Translated by David Lapeza. Ann Arbor, MI: Ardis, 1979. 166p. $10.00.

The author of this personal statement on the recent history of Soviet prose is one of a group of young writers who surfaced in the early sixties and seemed to offer the promise of a new vitality and variety in Soviet literature. In this volume, Gladilin reports in detail on the travails in the Soviet Union of a young man with a somewhat heterodox pen. The book is largely a report on the several varieties and "levels" of censorship with which such a writer must somehow cope. The evidence presented here suggests—to no one's surprise—that the process does succeed in emasculating literature.

RR, 39:1:119-20

PHILOSOPHY AND POLITICAL THEORY

General Surveys

601. Berlin, Isaiah. **Russian Thinkers.** Edited by Henry Hardy and Aileen Kelly. Introduction by Aileen Kelly. New York: The Viking Press, 1978. xxiv, 312p. $14.95.

Under Sir Isaiah's pen, Russia's intelligentsia and literary elite come to life—the reader can recognize men of emotion and commitment, with all their human weaknesses and spiritual glory. He shows how these emotions, lives, friendships, and dislikes were diffracted in the ideas of these men and in the ideas of succeeding generations. For him the importance and greatness of the fathers of the Russian intelligentsia—Herzen and Belinskii—and of the two writers—Ivan Turgenev and Leo Tolstoy—reside in the individual quality of their search for moral truthfulness. This collection of essays on Russia's intellectual past offers many a lesson for the thoughtful reader in the so-called Western world.

SR, 38:1:106-107

602. Ulam, Adam B. **Ideologies and Illusions: Revolutionary Thought from Herzen to Solzhenitsyn.** Cambridge, MA, and London: Harvard University Press, 1976. x, 335p. $15.00.

In this book, Ulam takes a stroll through the garden of his past research. He touches on the birth of Russian radicalism, utopia and socialism, the roots of Marxism, the personalities of the founders of Russian Social Democracy, Lenin and the Bolsheviks, Stalin and Stalinism, and Titoism before lingering over Soviet foreign policy. Ulam traces the influence of a number of what he regards as significant ideas shaping Russian history. This book, though rambling, is both perceptive and, as always with this author, good reading.

CSP, 20:1:122-24

603. Walicki, Andrzej. **A History of Russian Thought from the Enlightenment to Marxism.** Translated by Hilda Andrews-Rusiecka. Stanford: Stanford University Press, 1979 [1973]. xx, 456p. $25.00.

This book's interpretive narrative takes the form of 18 chapters combining chronological progression with concentration on specific topics in different periods. Walicki is at his best in the fundamental analysis of thought, whether the specific subject of investigation is Chaadaev's total world view and the relationship of that view to his celebrated *Letter*, the manifold Hegelian influences in Russia, or the different kinds of positivism. Every specialist will welcome this work. It will also be very useful to students of the specialists, for whom the English edition has extensive references to materials and studies available in English.

SR, 40:1:102

Non-Marxist Movements

604. Acton, Edward. **Alexander Herzen and the Role of the Intellectual Revolutionary.** Cambridge and London: Cambridge University Press, 1979. x, 194p. $18.95.

What Acton has achieved in his study of Herzen is a sympathetic, cogent, and illuminating portrait of the intellectual revolutionary's dilemma. It is freshly written and open-minded work of scholarship that will undoubtedly attract new interest to Herzen as man and thinker.

SEER, 58:1:114-15

605. Bakunin, Mikhail. **The "Confession" of Mikhail Bakunin.** With the marginal comments of Tsar Nicholas I. Translated by Robert C. Howes. Introduction and notes by Lawrence D. Orton. Ithaca, NY, and London: Cornell University Press, 1977. 200p. $12.50.

Bakunin wrote his celebrated *Confession* in 1851, at the behest of Tsar Nicholas I, while imprisoned in the Peter and Paul Fortress. Speaking as "a prodigal, alienated, depraved son before his outraged and wrathful father," he recounted his activities and impressions from his departure for Berlin in 1840 to his arrest in 1849 following the abortive Dresden uprising. The *Confession* is an important psychological as well as historical document. It is among the most absorbing of all Bakunin's writings, and the tsar read it with care, giving it to the tsarevich, Alexander II, for his edification.

SR, 37:1:125-26

606. Brower, Daniel R. **Training the Nihilists: Education and Radicalism in Tsarist Russia.** Ithaca, NY, and London: Cornell University Press, 1975. 248p. $12.50.
This book provides a historical interpretation of the sociology of the radical intellectuals in mid-nineteenth-century Russia. The author argues that in Russian higher education, a "recruitment" system developed that fed a steady, if small, stream of committed revolutionaries into the life of the country, and that the radical intelligentsia was drawn from much the same social strata as university students in general.
SR, 35:1:129-30

607. Cochrane, Stephen T. **The Collaboration of Nečaev, Ogarev and Bakunin in 1869, Nečaev's Early Years.** Osteuropastudien der Hochschulen des Landes Hessen, series 2. Marburger Abhandlungen zur Geschichte und Kultur Osteuropas, vol. 18. Giessen: Wilhelm Schmitz Verlag, 1977. x, 365p. DM 70.00, paper.
This is one of the few scholarly examinations of Necaev's career and, by any measure, the most generous of the recent ones. The author has made excellent use of the materials made available by B. P. Koz'min, newer documentary collections published by Arthur Lehning and Michael Confino, and other materials provided by helpful scholars. He has painstakingly tracked down the NMecaev materials available in the West and has sifted the evidence meticulously, rejecting errors made by previous students of Necaev.
SR, 38:3:489-90

608. Copouya, Emile, and Keitha Thompkins, eds. **The Essential Kropotkin.** New York: Liveright, W. W. Norton, 1975. xxiv, 296p. $12.50.
This new anthology of Kropotkin's writings contains seven of his most famous essays: "The Spirit of Revolt," "An Appeal to the Young," "Law and Authority," "Prison and Their Moral Influence on Prisoners," "Modern Science and Anarchism," "The Wage System," and "Anarchism." It is a welcome Kropotkin primer, perhaps the best collection for the general reader.
SR, 35:3:534

609. Engel, Barbara Alpern, and Clifford N. Rosenthal, eds. and trans. **Five Sisters: Women against the Tsar.** Foreword by Alix Kates Shulman. New York: Alfred A. Knopf, 1975. xxxvi, 261p. $8.95.
This is a collection of translations of memoirs of five women who were members of Russian revolutionary populist organizations in the 1870s and 1880s, including Figner, Zasulich, and Praskovia Ivanovskaia. Taken together, these memoirs are of great interest to students of women's history, Russian social history, and the history of revolutionary movements.
SR, 35:3:533

610. Gleason, Abbott. **Young Russia: The Genesis of Russian Radicalism in the 1860s.** New York: The Viking Press, 1980. xvi, 437p. $16.95.
Gleason focuses on what is Russia's most crucial decade before 1917. Unlike most conventional treatments of the reform era, his analysis probes below the surface to see why and how certain individuals came to their particular ideas. What is their contribution to the radical aim of liberating the people from the state, and how do they — young, ardent, and dedicated — relate to that people and the state? Writing with the American radical protest of the 1960s very much in mind, Gleason's examination of the Russian scene a century ago provides provocative contrast. This is a scholarly, lively, readable book.
LJBR, 1980:191

611. Hardy, Deborah. **Petr Tkachev, the Critic as Jacobin.** Seattle and London: University of Washington Press, 1977. xiv, 339p. $12.50.

Unlike A. L. Weeks, the first Western biographer of Tkachev, Hardy eschews, for the most part, any attempt to link Tkachev with Lenin. Instead, she provides a detailed account of his social background, copious writings, and revolutionary activities at home and abroad, which were fairly typical of prominent Russian revels in the 1860s and 1870s. Tkachev emerges as a lonely and secretive man, better at wielding the pen than at organizing resistance to authorities or making converts among fellow revolutionaries. This book tells us all we need to know about Tkachev and his impact during his lifetime.

SR, 37:2:296

612. Lukashevich, Stephen. **N. F. Fedorov (1828-1903): A Study in Russian Eupsychian and Utopian Thought.** Newark and London: University of Delaware Press and Associated University Presses, 1977. 316p. $18.50.

Fedorov was a complex and daring thinker. A Promethean who believed in controlling nature for man's benefit and in the "self-creation" of man, he desired to transform the "will to procreation" into the "will to resurrection." He advocated the gathering of the world's peoples by the autocrat of Russia, their conversion to Russian Orthodoxy (by force if necessary), psychogenetics, colonies in space, and a Central Learned Commission to supervise all human activity, all art and science, until man achieved perfection.

SR, 38:1:131-32

613. Miller, Martin A. **Kropotkin.** Chicago and London: University of Chicago Press, 1976. x, 342p. $15.00.

Miller's book is based on an impressive range of manuscripts and printed sources in Russian and other languages, including those available in Soviet archives. An extensive research has enabled Miller to throw light on Peter Kropotkin's intellectual development during his adolescence, his role in the influential Chaikovskii Circle in the 1870s, and his involvement in the debates among Russian anarchist exiles at the time of the 1905 revolution. In these areas, Miller adds to what is available from *The Anarchist Prince* by George Woodcock and Ivan Avakumovic.

SR, 36:2:296-97

614. Osofsky, Stephen. **Peter Kropotkin.** Boston: Twayne Publishers, 1979. 202p. $11.95.

The purpose of this book on the Russian anarchist is "to gauge his contribution to anarchist theory and, beyond this, to modern political theory." It is a synthetic work, that effectively utilizes the various specialized studies on Kropotkin toward this end. The author believes that Kropotkin's social criticism retains a significance for contemporary political problems, to which he addresses himself in the final chapter. There is a biographical sketch that succinctly restates the major themes of Kropotkin's career. The heart of the book is a presentation and critical assessment of Kropotkin's world view. Osofsky has also included a chronology, a bibliography, and a wide-ranging list of references in his notes.

RR, 40:1:62-63

615. Pereira, N. G. O. **The Thought and Teachings of N. G. Černyševskij.** Slavistic Printings and Reprintings, 308. Paris and The Hague: Mouton, 1975. xii, 144p. Dfl. 29.00.

Pereira adds little that is unexpected to Cernysevskij but offers an intelligent, if brief, review of his interaction with his cultural milieu. After a short introduction to

Cernysevskij's life and historical situation, the author provides a summary of Russian radical premises in the chapter entitled "Epistemology, Ethics, and Aesthetics."
    SR, 39:4:678-79

616. Perrie, Maureen. **The Agrarian Policy of the Russian Socialist-Revolutionary Party: From Its Origins through the Revolution of 1905-1907.** New York and London: Cambridge University Press, 1976. xii, 216p. $15.95.
Perrie's discussion of the formative influences on the early Socialist-Revolutionary Party is interesting but sketchy. The emphasis is primarily on political behavior of the Social Revolutionists and on their programmatic statements, as shaped by the challenge of Marxism and Chernov's inspiring political contacts with the peasants of Tambov and Saratov in the 1890s. The most valuable research in this book relates to the Revolution of 1905, when Social Revolutionists were confronted with a vastly expanded arena for revolutionary political activity. Perrie focuses upon an analysis of the social composition of the Socialist-Revolutionary Party and the peasant movement in 1905-1907.
    SR, 37:2:294-95

617. Pipes, Richard. **Struve: Liberal on the Right, 1905-1944.** Cambridge, MA: Harvard University Press, 1980. xix, 526p. $32.50.
Peter B. Struve (1870-1944) was the intellectual leader in 1905-1907 of the nonradical minority in the Constitutional-Democratic Party; pioneered in 1906 the study of modern totalitarianism by stressing similarities between right- and left-wing radicalism and tracing their common intellectual roots; was in charge in 1915-1917 of "economic warfare" against Germany; was a member of General Wrangel's government in 1920 and, for a few months, was the chief representative of non-Communist Russia in negotiations with the Allies; was the foremost ideologist of the White side in the civil war and of militant anti-Communism among Russian émigrés in the 1920s. In Pipes' study, Struve emerges as a genius, a man with an extraordinary range of intellectual interests and accomplishments, an outstanding scholar, and a superb journalist. The author discusses extensively Struve's economic theory.
    RR, 40:2:158-62

618. Pipes, Richard, ed. **Bibliography of the Published Writings of Peter Berngardovich Struve.** Ann Arbor, MI: University Microfilms Interantional, 1980. xii, 220p. $20.25.
This bibliography traces, identifies, and collects in one volume all Struve's writings, unpublished archival materials, both in Russia and abroad. Also sources that deal directly with Struve (mainly contemporary press and reminiscences) are included.

619. Pomper, Philip. **Sergei Nechaev.** New Brunswick, NJ: Rutgers University Press, 1979. x, 273p. $18.00.
Pomper's biography of Nechaev presents a historically accurate prototype, drawn from meticulous archival research on Nechaev's life and from astute psychoanalytic speculation on the sources of Nechaev's pathological behavior. The key to understanding Nechaev's career, Pomper hypothesizes, was his single-minded pursuit of "both martyrdom and revenge," motivated by a "particularly extreme form" of ego-defensive strategy that Anna Freud calls "identification with the aggressor." This is a skillfully written, well-produced, and thought-provoking book; it makes for spell-binding reading.
    RR, 39:1:78-79

620. Putnam, George F. **Russian Alternatives to Marxism: Christian Socialism and Idealistic Liberalism in the Twentieth-Century Russia.** Knoxville: University of Tennessee Press, 1977. xii, 233p. $13.50.

This book is a serious, balanced work without a hero or a scheme for retroactively saving Russia from Communism. Putnam's aim is to learn more about "what was lost or repressed in Russian culture, what needs or desires may lie unfulfilled" in Soviet Russia. The structure of the book hinges on the selection of two men to focus upon—Serge Bulgakov and Paul Novgorodtsev. The author declares that the period produced three Russian alternatives to Marxism—God-seeking (Merezhkovskii, Hippius, Rozanov), Christian socialism (Bulgakov, Berdiaev), and idealistic liberalism (Novgorodtsev, Struve, Frank)—and proceeds to concentrate on the last two approaches. The period under discussion has much to tell present-day Russians of all political and cultural shadings, and others as well.

SR, 38:1:111-12

621. Sapir, Boris, ed. **Lavrov: Gody emigratsii: Letters and Documents in Two Volumes.** Russian Series on Social History, 2. International Institute of Social History, Amsterdam. Dordrecht and Boston: D. Reidel, 1974. Vol. 1: *Lavrov and Lopatin (Correspondence 1870-1883).* 603p. Vol. 2: *Other Correspondence of Lavrov, and Varia (Russian Text).* 669p. Dfl. 345.00. $125.00 for 2 vols.

Lavrov's career is the organizing principle for the collection, and his correspondence with a number of revolutionary socialists—both Russian and non-Russian—comprises the bulk of the documents. In addition, there are a number of documents that shed light primarily on the appearance of terrorism and the struggles of dedicated populists against divisive Marxist and liberal tendencies in the movement during the 1880s and 1890s. Lavrov, during his emigration (1870 until his death in 1900), became a kind of barometer of the changes in the revolutionary movement. Scholars will be delighted not only with Sapir's annotations but with a voluminous index of names and periodicals included in the second volume.

SR, 35:2:331-32

622. Schneiderman, Jeremiah. **Sergei Zubatov and Revolutionary Marxism: The Struggle for the Working Class in Tsarist Russia.** Ithaca, NY, and London: Cornell University Press, 1976. 401p. $18.50.

Schneiderman has written a most scholarly, detailed, and objective history of the undertaking by a brilliant policeman, S. V. Zubatov, who aimed at influencing the emerging labor class in Russia. The author has marshaled an impressive volume of material to support his arguments, mostly from printed sources because the Soviet authorities denied him access to the archives. Schneiderman considers that in the decade prior to 1905 "the government could have evolved a labor policy capable of satisfying the working class," and Zubatovism was the most significant effort in that direction.

SR, 36:2:298-99

623. Shestov, Lev. **In Job's Balances: On the Sources of the Eternal Truths.** Translated from the German by Camilla Coventry and C. A. Macartney. Introduction by Bernard Martin. Athens, OH: Ohio University Press, 1975. 379p. $12.00.

This book by Shestov, the Russian existentialist philosopher and critic (1866-1938), is now available in English in addition to previously published volumes by the Ohio University Press. Students of Russian thought will welcome this work and the next volumes announced for publications.

SR, 35:4:752-53

624. Stephan, John J. **The Russian Fascist: Tragedy and Farce in Exile.** New York: Harper & Row, 1978. xxiv, 450p. + 24pp. plates. $15.00.

Russian fascism emerges in this book as an émigré political movement of the 1930s without roots in any society. As would-be imitators and collaborators of Hitler and the Japanese, the Russian fascists adopted their coloration while claiming to represent vaguely defined Russian national interests. The most representative groups of Russian fascists emerged in the Harbin colony and in Thompson, Connecticut. The author has unearthed, through great diligence, a story of exile intrigue long buried in Japanese, American, and German archives. His research is formidable, and his story is well told for the general reader as well as for the specialist.

    SR, 38:1:116

625. Ulam, Adam B. **In the Name of the People: Prophets and Conspirators in Prerevolutionary Russia.** New York: The Viking Press, 1977. xiv, 418p. Illus. $15.00.

The period under discussion is comparatively brief—from the emancipation of the serfs in 1861 until the collapse of the People's Will organization in about 1883 after the repression that followed the assassination of Alexander II. The immense and scattered literature, much of it contemporary, some dating from the Soviet period, has been thoroughly combed. The main thread of the narrative runs from publicity and propaganda to terrorism, from Herzen to the People's Will; and Professor Ulam's chief preoccupation is with the character and causes of the change.

    SR, 37:1:126-27

626. Walicki, Andrzej. **The Slavophile Controversy: History of a Conservative Utopia in Nineteenth Century Russian Thought.** Translated by Hilda Andrews-Rusiecka. Oxford: Clarendon Press, 1975. viii, 609p. $43.95.

Walicki, Polish historian of the Warsaw School, defines the Slavophile utopian model in terms of its consistencies as well as its vagaries; he brings out the connection between this and other variants and the interdependence between the Slavophile model and the Westernizers' alternatives; finally, he explains not only intellectually, but sociologically and psychologically, the genesis of this model and its attraction for so many nineteenth-century Russians. As historical narrative, Walicki's book will satisfy most readers. He confirms the Slavophiles were in large measure reactionary noblemen worried about how capitalism would affect their traditional positions.

    CSP, 19:1:94-95

627. Yanov, Alexander. **The Russian New Right: Right-Wing Ideologies in the Contemporary USSR.** Berkeley: Institute of International Studies, University of California, 1978. xvi, 185p. $3.95, paper.

Yanov chronicles the mid-1960s rise of a new Russian nationalist movement that shows potential for repeating what the author asserts is the paradox of nineteenth-century Russian nationalism—it is passing from opposition to the Soviet regime to "fraternal union" with the regime. Yanov is at his best when describing events and personalities he was professionally and personally close to in the USSR. Policy makers and planners who are concerned about the incipient Soviet leadership change will especially profit from Yanov's labors.

    RR, 39:1:93-94

Marxism in Russia and the USSR

628. Grier, Philip T. **Marxist Ethical Theory in the Soviet Union.** Dordrecht, Holland, and Boston: D. Reidel Publishing Company, 1978. xviii, 276p. Dfl. 65.00.

One of the central problems of Marxism has been whether Marxism can have an ethics. Grier presents the views of those leading Soviet philosophers who interpret Marx's writings as implying a definite ethical standpoint. He properly situates Soviet ethical theory within the vast context of Marxist thought, assigning it a unique place and relating it to its past. In his conclusion, Grier finds a conflict in Soviet ethical theory between a philosophy of history according to which human action is denominated "progressive" or "reactionary," and an ethical theory according to which it is "right" or "wrong." The philosophy of history is "Marxist-Leninist historical science," which, in fact, is not a science but rather a metaphysical theory. Any student of Marxism will find valuable information and perceptive interpretations in this book.

SR, 39:1:136-37

629. Knei-Paz, Baruch. **The Social and Political Thought of Leon Trotsky.** Oxford: Clarendon Press, 1978. xxii, 629p. $34.95.

The author has produced a most useful volume free from polemics and critical but not unfair. He offers a painstakingly detailed analysis of Trotsky's social and political ideas in the context of historical events. The inquiry is organized into a coherent framework centered around the theory of permanent revolution, its practice, and "betrayal." A section on Trotsky's ideas on art, literature, philosophy, and the Jewish question is of interest.

SR, 38:4:678-79

630. **Selected Writings of Alexandra Kollontai.** Translated and with an introduction by Alix Holt. Westport, CT: Lawrence Hill & Co., 1977. 335p. $12.95.

This collection of Kollontai's writings is the only anthology available in English. The selections illustrate her major concerns, and they supplement, rather than duplicate, translations already in print. The book will be particularly useful to general-study students who do not read Russian.

SR, 39:1:120-21

631. Tucker, Robert C., ed. **The Lenin Anthology.** New York: W. W. Norton, 1975. xiv, 764p. $18.95.

Tucker offers a well-edited collection with an index for easy use. He has prefaced the collection with an excellent essay on Lenin's emergence as the revolutionary leader who singlemindedly combined Marxist thought with Russian revolutionary tradition. Regrettably, Tucker has not provided citations for the various extracts from Lenin's writings. The Lenin that emerges from Tucker's collection—with the help of his introduction—is the familiar charismatic messiah of the Russian Revolution.

SR, 35:2:335-36

Intellectual and Cultural Histories

632. Rozanov, Vasily. **The Apocalypse of Our Time and Other Writings.** Edited by Robert Payne. Translated by Robert Payne and Nikita Romanoff. Afterword by George Ivask. New York: Praeger Publishers, 1977. 301p. $10.95.

The present volume is a new manifestation of an emerging interest in Rozanov's writings. The well-written and sympathetic introduction by Robert Payne combines a useful

biographical sketch with a sensitive presentation of the characteristics of this highly original Russian writer.
SR, 38:2:324

633. Rozanov, Vasily. **Four Faces of Rozanov: Christianity, Sex, Jews and the Russian Revolution.** Translated and with an introduction by Spencer E. Roberts. New York: Philosophical Library, 1978. vi, 310p. $10.00.
V. Rozanov (1856-1919) was a highly idiosyncratic and provocative writer on religion and literature. Roberts' new selection of Rozanov's writings is a welcome contribution to the history of Russian intellectual thought of the generation preceding the Revolution of 1917. Rozanov, a Christian conservative at the outset, later began attacking the church, then the New Testament, and Christ himself, only to recant at the end of his life. He made a name for himself with his hysterical attacks upon Jewish "blood murderers" at the time of the Beilis case.
SR, 38:2:323

PSYCHOLOGY AND PSYCHIATRY

634. Krippner, Stanley. **Human Possibilities: Mind Exploration in the USSR and Eastern Europe.** Garden City, NY: Anchor Press & Doubleday, 1980. ix, 348p. $14.95.
This is an extensive study of the status, development, and application of psychology in the Soviet Union as personally observed by Dr. Krippner during his trip to the USSR in 1971. Subjects and material include parapsychology, hypnosis, suggestopedia, problems of the unconscious, and holographics. Each chapter is supplemented with a reading list comprising Western and Soviet literature. Students of psychology studying its application under the totalitarian regime will appreciate this report, written by an expert for learning purposes.

635. Lur'e, A. R. **The Selected Writings of A. R. Luria.** Edited and with an introduction by Michael Cole. White Plains, NY: M. E. Sharpe, 1978. xxii, 351p. $22.50.
Cole has assembled several articles by the eminent Soviet psychologist, A. R. Lur'e (1902-1977). The papers focus on child development, language acquisition, mental imagery, mental ability, and neuropsychology. The book is strongly recommended to scholars in Soviet studies, psycholinguistics, child development, and cognitive and social psychology.
SR, 39:4:697

RELIGION

History

636. Alexeev, Wassilij, and Theofanis G. Stavrou. **The Great Revival: The Russian Church under German Occupation.** Minneapolis: Burgess Publishing Co., 1976. xvi, 229p. Illus. $21.95.
This work embodies Alexeev's doctoral dissertation, detailing by geographical region the experiences of Russian Orthodox hierarchs and parishes. Relying primarily on refugee interviews and German reports, Alexeev presents accounts of church services in a number of localities, indicating the sweep of the religious movement that affected most of the German-occupied region and played its part in convincing Stalin to come to terms with the church at home.
SR, 36:3:501-503

637. Brostrom, Kenneth N., ed. and trans. **Archpriest Avvakum: The Life Written by Himself.** Introduction by Kenneth N. Brostrom. Michigan Slavic Translations, no. 4. Ann Arbor: Michigan Slavic Publications, Department of Slavic Languages and Literatures, University of Michigan, 1979. x, 278p. Illus. $7.00, paper.

Brostrom has filled a major gap by providing an excellent translation of the *Life of Archpriest Avvakum*, accompanied by a historical introduction that includes a brief discussion of the textual history of the *Life*; annotations; a translation of V. V. Vinogradov's seminal article, "On the Tasks of Stylistics: Observations Regarding the Style of the *Life*;' and his own "Further Remarks on the *Life*." The volume is adorned with copious illustrations from the material, liturgical, and religious culture of seventeenth-century Muscovy, including an icon of Avvakum.

SR, 39:4:713-14

638. Fedotov, George P. **St. Filipp Metropolitan of Moscow — Encounter with Ivan the Terrible.** Translated by Richard Haugh and Nickolas Lupinin. Edited by Richard Haugh, Nickolas Lupinin, and Michael Meerson-Aksenov. Belmont, MA: Nordland Publishing Co., 1978. 207p. $22.50.

George P. Fedotov (1886-1951), a religious historian famous for his two-volume *The Russian Religious Mind*, uses the sparse material on the churchman as a frame for a discussion of Russian history during his subject's lifetime (1507-1568), especially church-state relations. Filipp was born Fedor Kolychev. The biography traces Filipp's career in as much detail as possible, concentrating on his egomaniacal construction works during his 18-year tenure as hegumen of the Solovki Monastery and then on his brief term as metropolitan, a position that led to his conflict with Ivan the Terrible's *Oprichnina* and subsequently to Filipp's murder. The translation is generally superb, highly literate, and unstilted.

SR, 39:2:301-302

639. Freeze, Gregory L. **The Russian Levites: Parish Clergy in the Eighteenth Century.** Russian Research Center Studies, 78. Cambridge, MA, and London: Harvard University Press, 1977. xvi, 235p. $15.00.

Freeze's book is a brilliantly researched and thoughtful study of the ways in which the Russian parish clergy fared, as a group, in the increasingly secular environment of eighteenth-century Russia. The author's central argument is that the policies of Peter the Great and his successors transformed this lay clergy from a relatively open social group into a closed "caste-estate" that was both impoverished and culturally removed from the rest of society. As a consequence, the Orthodox church was left without the kinds of local priests who could make the church a vital part of public life.

SR, 37:1:121-23

640. Nichols, Robert L., and Theofanis George Stavrou, eds. **Russian Orthodoxy under the Old Regime.** Minneapolis: University of Minnesota Press, 1978. xiv, 261p. + 8pp. plates. $16.50.

This volume consists of papers read at a symposium at the University of Minnesota in April 1976 — four on the Russian church, society, and culture; five on church and state; and two bibliographical aids. Among the contributors are: Donald Treadgold, James Cracraft, Robert L. Nichols, Marc Szeftel, Alexander Muller, John Meyendorff, Paul Valliere, and Edward Kasinec on bibliography. The book's contents are too varied and disconnected, but, if a student wants to know what is being done on that subject and what the possibilities are for research in this field, this is a good place to start.

SR, 38:1:110-11

Special Studies

641. Bourdeaux, Michael, and Michael Rowe, eds. **May One Believe — in Russia? Violations of Religious Liberty in the Soviet Union.** London: Darton, Longman & Todd, 198?. xiii, 113p. £3.45.
This is a collection of documents, some relating to the laws on religious liberty in the Soviet Union, most being about the experiences and fate of the orthodox, evangelical, and Catholic churches in the USSR.

642. Dunn, Dennis J. **The Catholic Church and the Soviet Government, 1939-1949.** East European Monographs, 30. Boulder, CO: *East European Quarterly*, 1977. viii, 267p. $17.00. Distributed by Columbia University Press, New York.
This work attempts to shed light on the crucial era 1939-1949 by examining a heretofore seldom explored aspect of this period — Soviet Catholic relations. It reveals Soviet and papal motivation in the elaboration of war and postwar policy; Soviet rationale in the elaboration of war and postwar policy; Soviet rationale in the formulation of domestic religious policy after the war in Lithuania, West Ukraine, Carpatho-Ukraine, and, finally, Soviet and Catholic attitudes in the evolution of governmental policies in those regions. This massive study attains an impressive bibliographical depth.
  NP, 7:2:239-40

643. Dunn, Dennis J., ed. **Religion and Modernization in the Soviet Union.** Boulder, CO: Westview Press, 1977. x, 414p. Illus. $21.75.
This excellent symposium on the governmental administration and politics of religion in the USSR presents the well-documented, thoughtful findings of 12 competent scholars. Both a substantive contribution and a valuable interpretation of the contradictions of Soviet society, it deserves a wide audience. The book deals with three major topics — underlying forces and values; policies and practices in the control of religion, including the use of antireligious satire; and the status of various religions. The work has value for the student, the academician, and the policy maker.
  SR, 39:2:326

643a. Lane, Christel. **Christian Religion in the Soviet Union: A Sociological Study.** Albany: State University of New York Press, 1978. 256p. $25.00.
The author has collected a large part of the available sociological information and reported it systematically in chapters dealing in turn with all the major categories of religious organization. The study makes a valuable contribution to the subject discussed.
  SR, 39:2:327

644. McKown, Delos B. **The Classical Marxist Critiques of Religion: Marx, Engels, Lenin, Kautsky.** The Hague: Martinus Nijhoff, 1975. x, 174p. Dfl. 40.00.
All four writers asserted that the true understanding of religion, as of any social institution, could be acquired only in the study of actual conditions, which, in the last analysis, meant a society's mode of production. The book offers a valuable contribution to a subject that has long needed attention.
  SR, 35:3:541-42

645. Read, Christopher. **Religion, Revolution and the Russian Intelligentsia, 1900-1912: The Vekhi Debate and Its Intellectual Background.** Totowa, NJ: Barnes & Noble, 1980. x, 221p. $25.00.

Though this discussion is focused on the *Vekhi* Debate, the author has thrown his net wide to include all kinds of people and ideas, which brings to mind the two views of a net as a contrivance for either catching or as an object through which things slip. Read has obviously done his work with care and application and has related the matter studiously and methodically. The most suggestive section of the book is probably on the "God-builders." The most useful section is on the "Continuing Debate," where Solzhenitsyn's epigonian move to retrieve the *Vekhi* cause is discussed. The work, as a whole, gives the impression of a *précis* on the highest level of most published materials, not a recreation of ideas and representative figures, nor an assessment of the climate of opinion and its causes.
SEER, 59:3:458-59

SCIENCE AND RESEARCH

646.   Heiliger, William S., comp. **Bibliography of the Soviet Sciences, 1965-1975.** 2 vols. Troy, NY: Whitston, 1978. v, 996p. $65.00/set.
The more than 9,300 entries, which have been culled from the *Ezhegodnik izdanii* of the Soviet Academy of Sciences, are given in English translation and are grouped by year within each institute or journal. A name and subject index is appended.

647.   Hutchings, Raymond. **Soviet Science. Technology, Design: Interaction and Convergence.** London: Oxford University Press, 1976. xiv, 320p. + 8pp. plates. Tables. $27.50.
Hutchings' book supplies a competent, original, and fascinating analysis of these three categories as applied to the scientific-industrial complex in the Soviet Union. The basic thesis of the book is that although Soviet science, technology, and design depend heavily on borrowing from the West, they are not without distinct national characteristics which, in their own way, illuminate some of the vital components of the Soviet political system, social arrangements, and cultural values. Hutchings has produced a pioneering study in a field that is both fascinating and important. In addition to rich material, his book offers many carefully documented generalizations and valuable hints for further research.
SR, 36:2:321-22

648.   Lewis, Robert. **Science and Industrialization in the USSR.** Studies in Soviet History and Society Series. London: Macmillan, 1979, in association with the Centre for Russian and East European Studies, University of Birmingham. xiv, 211p. Tables. $30.00.
This is a fairly detailed study of the historical evolution of the structure and subordination of Soviet research and development establishments. Broadly speaking, it provides the historical background within the 1920s and 1930s to the longer OECD study, *Science Policy in the USSR* (Paris, 1969), which itself, despite its title, was concerned mainly with scientific organization. There are also chapters on research planning, science at the factory, and industrial research and innovation. The aircraft industry is singled out for more detailed inspection. Brief but useful appendices cover expenditures, costs, and manpower.
SEER, 59:1:122-23

649.   Lubrano, Linda L., and Susan Gross Solomon, eds. **The Social Context of Soviet Science.** Boulder, CO, and Folkestone, England: Westview Press and William Dawson & Sons, 1980. xvi, 240p. $24.50.
This collection of essays begins with a chapter by Solomon on the state of Western studies of Soviet science. Besides reviewing the changing pattern of these studies over the last 30 years, she suggests that future work should be directed particularly toward two topics that

currently are neglected: 1) to focus more on science itself as distinct from its political, cultural, and social environment; 2) to focus more on the relationship between science and politics. It is unfortunate that such a useful volume lacks an index.

SR, 40:1:125-26

650. Medvedev, Zhores A. **Nuclear Disaster in the Urals.** Translated by George Saunders. New York: W. W. Norton, 1979. vii, 214p. $12.95.

Medvedev, a Russian biologist exiled in 1973 and now in London, has written a book on a nuclear disaster in the Ural mountains that occurred in the winter of 1957-1958. The book has the merit of drawing attention to an event that appears to be both real and important. Since that time, the Soviet Union has published many details of peaceful uses of nuclear explosives, for example, extinguishing a resistant gas-well fire.

RR, 40:1:69-70

651. Medvedev, Zhores A. **Soviet Science.** New York and Toronto: W. W. Norton and George J. McLeon Limited, 1978. xii, 262p. + 12pp. photographs. $10.95.

Medvedev's book is an interpretative, historical account of the changing conditions in Soviet science since the Bolshevik Revolution. It is not an institutional analysis, focusing instead on individual scientists affected by the needs and demands of a political system more concerned with its own security than with the advancement of knowledge. The author characterizes the development of Soviet science as uneven, contradictory, and often misdirected because of incompetent political leaders and other factors outside the scientific community. The book is informative and well written and appeals to a wide audience.

SR, 38:4:692-93

652. Rigby, T. H., and R. F. Miller. **Political and Administrative Aspects of the Scientific and Technical Revolution in the USSR.** Department of Political Science, Research School of the Social Sciences, Australian National University, Occasional Paper, no. 11. Canberra: Australian National University Press, 1976. iv, 115p. $4.95, paper.

The Soviet leadership has recognized the significance of what it calls the "scientific-technical revolution," and it has taken steps to control, or at least to manipulate, that process as much as possible. This is not always successful, as Rigby and Miller aptly demonstrate. Their papers document a situation of tension and accommodation between the CPSU and the complexities of technological development.

SR, 37:2:310-11

653. Thomas, John R., and Ursula M. Kruse-Vaucienne, eds. **Soviet Science and Technology: Domestic and Foreign Perspectives.** Washington, DC: The National Science Foundation and the George Washington University, 1977. xiv, 455p.

This book contains 19 papers presented at a workshop held in November 1976 and sponsored by the National Science Foundation. It is divided into five sections: 1) Soviet science policy and organization; 2) the interaction of Soviet science with the Soviet system; 3) the interaction of Soviet science and technology with the economy; 4) the impact of foreign technology on the Soviet economy; and 5) cooperation between the United States and the USSR in science and technology. Overall, participants at the workshop reached a consensus that Soviet leaders are concerned about the level of their technology but are politically unprepared to reform the economy in major ways.

SR, 38:4:690-92

SOCIOLOGY

Bibliographies

654. Matthews, Mervyn, in collaboration with T. Anthony Jones. **Soviet Sociology, 1964-75: A Bibliography.** New York and London: Praeger Publishers, 1978. xvi, 269p. $37.95.

This work provides a bibliography (unannotated) of some 2,500 sociological books, collections, articles, and *avtoreferati* published between 1964 and 1975 (in Russian and occasionally in Ukrainian). The largest sections pertain to social structure and mobility and to sociology as a discipline. There are also sizable sections on labor and education. Other topics include youth, marriage and the family, religion, mass communications, culture, and the arts. The introduction also outlines the history of sociology in the USSR. The bibliography will be a welcome addition to Western sociologists' reference shelves.

SR, 38:3:507-508

General Studies

655. Vucinich, Alexander. **Social Thought in Tsarist Russia: The Quest for a General Science of Society, 1861-1917.** Chicago and London: University of Chicago Press, 1976. xi, 294p. $15.50.

This volume presents a comprehensive picture of the impact of scientific thought and the development of a rationalistic tradition in Russia. It is an encyclopedic endeavor and possesses all of the strengths and defects of such a project. While presenting interesting surveys of several schools of thought, Vucinich tends to slight the complex issues and tensions in the individual thinkers studied. The author has done well to make some of Russia's thinkers accessible to nonspecialists.

SR, 36:1:117-18

Medical Care and Social Welfare

656. McAuley, Alistair. **Economic Welfare in the Soviet Union: Poverty, Living Standards, and Inequality.** Madison and Herts, England: University of Wisconsin Press and George Allen & Unwin, 1979. xx, 389p. $25.00.

This book makes an important contribution to the knowledge about an area of Soviet life about which Soviet sources are notably reticent and published data obscure. The author first assembles and evaluates available data relating to trends in total money incomes and earnings from wages and the prevalence of poverty in the USSR as a whole. The evidence shows that the government's new approaches have met with considerable success, but that the Soviet welfare state has a long way yet to go before it can match even its own internal criteria, to say nothing of levels of living achieved in the West. A series of appendices explains in detail the derivation of the estimates that underline the discussion in the text.

657. Ryan, Michael. **The Organization of Soviet Medical Care.** Oxford: Basil Blackwell, 1978. 168p. £10.00.

This book carefully describes advances in Soviet medical care as well as its weaknesses and problems. We learn that this care is not exactly a single monolithic system; that disregard for policies announced at the center is widespread; that in many ways medicine is business (with "second-economy" features); and that the gap in expenditures between republics widened during the 1960s, suggesting differences in qualitative levels. The most striking finding is that total expenditures have not risen relative to national wealth.

RR, 39:3:380-81

Social Problems and Social Change

658. Juviler, Peter H. **Revolutionary Law and Order: Politics and Social Change in the USSR.** New York and London: The Free Press and Collier Macmillan, 1976. xiv, 274p. $13.95.

In this wide-ranging review of Russian and Soviet responses to the phenomenon of crime from 1864 to the present day, Juviler seeks to identify the basic patterns of and trends in criminal policy, with emphasis upon the post-Stalin era. He has produced a solid, reflective exploration of a highly pertinent facet of Soviet life and experience.

659. Matthews, Mervyn. **Privilege in the Soviet Union: A Study of Elite Life-Styles under Communism.** London: George Allen & Unwin, 1978. 197p. $17.25.

In this admirable sociological study, the author addresses the touchy question of Soviet privilege, its extent, and its recipients. The first section defines the Soviet elite and describes its material privileges, both in money and kind. The legal underpinnings and historical evolution of privilege and its recipients are examined in the second section. The final chapters assess mobility into the Soviet elite and compare it to the elites of Eastern Europe (especially Poland) and the United States. This book is a lively and painstaking documentation of a dusky corner of Soviet society, with all the force that modern analysis can add and, blessedly, none of its jargon.

SR, 39:3:509-510

660. Yanowitch, Murray. **Social and Economic Inequality in the Soviet Union: Six Studies.** White Plains, NY: M. E. Sharpe, 1977. xvii, 197p. Tables. $15.00.

Yanowitch brings together findings that illuminate many facets of social inequity in the USSR. After first reviewing changes in Soviet conceptions of the social structure, he examines income differentials, the inequality of access to education, patterns of social mobility, authority relations in the work place, and aspects of sexual inequality. Extensively documented and lucidly written, the book will be of interest to many Russian area specialists and to social scientists concerned with these problems. It is suitable as a supplementary text for undergraduate or graduate courses on Soviet society, social stratification, or social policy.

SR, 38:2:317

Women, Family, Youth

661. Blekher, Feiga. **The Soviet Woman in the Family and in Society: A Sociological Study.** New York: John Wiley, 1979. ix, 234p. $37.95.

The author simultaneously presents a historical survey, while describing marriage and family problems, women's work, and the way women experience everyday life. No less than 37 topics are discussed in four chapters, almost exclusively via massive use of Soviet writings. No use is made of recent publications by Western scholars. The book has considerable value in that it brings together a lot of material and organizes it in quite an orderly fashion around the topics discussed. The author is also to be commended for recognizing that "women's problems" reflect many aspects of life.

RR, 40:3:348-49

662. Lapidus, Gail Washofsky. **Women in Soviet Society: Equality, Development, and Social Change.** Berkeley: University of California Press, 1978. x, 381p. Tables. $17.50.

This work is commendable for its originality. The research is centered around a major theme: the relationship between different institutions and the social values that play a part in promoting the equalization of women's status and certain stages of development in Soviet society. The author's investigation starts from a historical perspective — the birth in Russia of the "woman question," the influence of radical ideologies for which women's liberation postulates a social revolution, and how economic independence gained through work is considered to be the guarantee of equality.

　　SR, 39:1:127-28

663. Liegle, Ludwig. **The Family's Role in Soviet Education.** Translated from German by Susan Hecker. Foreword by Ure Bronfenbrenner. New York: Springer Publishing Co., 1975. xiv, 186p. $9.95.

The author focuses primarily on Soviet family life, the work careers of Soviet females, and the intertwined relationship between the family and the state as competing educational institutions. He observes wide gaps between espoused Marxist ideology and the everyday realities of family, female work, and the educational system. His conclusion: Soviet society has failed to transfer the family's and the female's traditional household and educational activities to society at large. Household work falls to the mother or wife, not the father or husband.

　　SR, 35:4:749-51

664. Mazour, Anatole G. **Women in Exile: Wives of the Decembrists.** Tallahassee, FL: The Diplomatic Press, 1975. x, 134p. $15.00.

Fourteen of 18 Decembrist wives went to Siberia with their exiled spouses. Ninety-five pages of narrative in this book are followed by a brief epilogue and 13 documents — mainly extracts from letters and official orders. Biographical notes on 30 Decembrists and a select bibliography are included in the book.

　　SR, 35:2:327

665. O'Dell, Felicity Ann. **Socialization through Children's Literature: The Soviet Example.** New York and London: Cambridge University Press, 1978. x, 278p. Tables. $32.50.

The author's attempt to assess the success of character education in the Soviet school is the most important aspect of her book. This well-researched study reaffirms the assumption that only an education in which there is no disparity between the textbook and real life, and in which there is a measure of tolerance for dissenting views, is able to bring out the best in young individuals.

　　SR, 39:1:139

Special Studies

666. Bailes, Kendall E. **Technology and Society under Lenin and Stalin: Origins of the Soviet Technical Intelligentsia, 1917-1941.** Princeton, NJ: Princeton University Press, 1978. xiii, 469p. $32.00.

Bailes uses the terms "technology" and "society" to cover the social and political problems of an important professional group in Soviet society. He is concerned with the selection of young people for technological jobs, the problems they face at work, their collective relations with the regime, and a number of related matters. Bailes suggests that the technologists abandoned earlier efforts "to influence public policy through autonomous professional societies, and tried to do so from within the Party itself." This is a most worthwhile and readable book.

SEER, 58:2:307-308

667. Brine, Jenny, Maureen Perrie, and Andrew Sutton, eds. **Home, School and Leisure in the Soviet Union.** London: George Allen & Unwin, 1980. xiv, 279p. $28.50.
With its main theme the study of daily life in Soviet society, the three main sections of this book are devoted to topics that are of intrinsic value in people's everyday lives: housing, the family, and the role of women; education and child care; and recreation. Most of the authors sympathize with the Soviet system, but their essays reflect a balanced approach.

668. Chalidze, Valery. **Criminal Russia: Essays on Crime in the Soviet Union.** Translated from the Russian by P. S. Falla. New York: Random House, 1977. xiv, 241p. $10.00.
Chalidze is a prominent human rights activist. Deprived of his Soviet citizenship, he now lives in New York City where he edits a journal on matters concerning the Soviet human rights movement he helped to found. The book opens with a brief essay on the Russian criminal tradition. Toleration of crime, glorification of brigands, disrespect for property, and widespread violence and cruelty in the pre-Soviet era are noted. According to the author, the Soviet criminal tradition absorbed many features of this earlier period. Various forms of violence and lawlessness are discussed in detail. The bibliographic notes indicate that the book is based entirely on indigenous sources. The book concludes with a good index.

SR, 37:3:511

669. Cox, Terence M. **Rural Sociology in the Soviet Union: Its History and Basic Concepts.** New York: Holmes & Meier, 1979. vi, 106p. $17.00.
According to the author, rural society in the Soviet Union is rich empirical ground for testing the concepts of Marxist sociology. A basic tenet of Soviet and Marxist sociology is that property relations define class structure and nourish its antagonisms. In the Soviet Union, only rural society contains the two property relationships allowed by Soviet law: collective and state ownership. Differences in rural and urban settlements, age, ethnicity, sex, and education have also emerged to complement the relations based on property. Whereas rural society was once divided into workers and peasants, it is now separated into several more categories: mental and physical workers, skilled and unskilled workers, and intelligentsia and professionals.

SR, 39:2:323-24

670. Lubrano, Linda L. **Soviet Sociology of Science.** Columbus, OH: American Association for the Advancement of Slavic Studies, 1976. vi, 102p. $4.95, paper.
This is a survey of Soviet writings on *naukovedenie* (the science of science) and, in somewhat more detail, on Soviet sociology of science. Essentially it is a work of reportage rather than criticism and provides a good description of a burgeoning activity, the results of which will help to shape Soviet scientific efforts.

SR, 37:1:143

671. Smith, R. E. F., ed. **The Russian Peasant: 1920 and 1984.** Library of Peasant Studies, no. 4. Totowa, NJ: Frank Cass & Co., 1977. 120p. $17.50.

The still scarce English literature on Russian peasantry is enhanced by this volume comprising a translation of three essays—Maxim Gorky's *On the Russian Peasantry*; A. M. Bolshakov's *The Soviet Countryside 1917-1924* (in extract); and Ivan Kremnev's (pseud. of A. V. Chaianov) *The Journey of My Brother Alexei to the Land of Peasant Utopia*. Smith provides information about the authors and critically analyzes the essays, which offer three different dimensions of the peasants' life and behavior.

Chapter 9
NON-RUSSIAN REPUBLICS, JEWS, OTHERS

GENERAL STUDIES

672. Azrael, Jeremy R., ed. **Soviet Nationality Policies and Practices.** New York and London: Praeger Publishers, 1978. xii, 393p. $25.00.
The essays in this volume "share a common concern with the character, functioning and development of the USSR as a multi-national polity and society." Contributors concentrate mainly on three issues—elites, planning, and identity. The methodology of modern social science, including its mathematical elements, is equally characteristic of their approach. This is one of the pioneering solid contributions to the understanding of Soviet nationality policy and the role of non-Russian peoples of the USSR. The work should be available to any study of the USSR regardless of the field of specialization.

673. Clem, Ralph S., ed. **The Soviet West: Interplay between Nationality and Social Organization.** Foreword by Edward Allworth. New York: Praeger Publishers, 1975. xvi, 161p. $15.00.
The Soviet West, which includes Estonia, Latvia, Lithuania, Belorussia, Ukraine, and Moldavia, is an area of major political and economic importance to the Soviet Union, as well as an area with traditional ties to Europe and with a record of national dissent. This collection of articles focuses on the interaction between the efforts of national groups to preserve their identities and the pressures for integration from the Party, the press, the schools, and the economy. The work contributes to a better understanding of the Soviet nationality problem.
SR, 35:1:145

674. d'Encausse, Helene Carrère. **Decline of an Empire: The Soviet Socialist Republics in Revolt.** Translated by Martin Sokolinsky and Henry A. LaFarge. New York: Newsweek Books, 1979. 304p. $10.95.
This book is representative of a relatively recent multiple trend in scholarly writing on Soviet nationality relations, a trend away from the focus on single nationalities and away from highly partisan polemical treatments. A particular merit of the work is its emphasis on historical context. The first chapter is a detailed consideration of the historical roots of Soviet nationality problems; the author is careful to give proper consideration to the theoretical views and enunciated aims of the Bolsheviks of all nationalities in the period up to and immediately after the Revolution. Her lengthy discussion of birth rates, migration, language adherence, and labor supply is accurate and highly readable.
NP, 9:2:242-43

675. Grimsted, Patricia K. **Archives and Manuscripts Repositories in the USSR, Estonia, Latvia, Lithuania, and Belorussia.** Princeton, NJ: Princeton University Press, 1980. 782p. $40.00.

A landmark survey of institutions in Soviet Estonia, Latvia, Lithuania, and Belorussia with archival and manuscript materials is offered in this work. It has appendices on archival organization and access requirements, geographical names, maps, and a glossary of archival terms. The Inter Documentation Company in Switzerland has produced the volume's major finding aids, manuscript catalogues, and other reference materials on microfiche.

676. Hodnett, Grey. **Leadership in the Soviet National Republics: A Quantitative Study of Recruitment Policy.** Oakville, Ontario: Mosaic Press, 1978. xx, 410p. Tables. $20.00.

This volume is a "strictly quantitative" study that examines recruitment policies and practices for the top Communist Party and governmental positions in the Soviet non-Russian republics between 1955 and 1972. The 50 republic positions that are analyzed range from the first secretaryship and the other republic Party secretaries to the Central Committee department heads, the chairman and key members of the council of ministers, the chairman of the Presidium of the Supreme Soviet, the president of the Academy of Sciences, and the chairman of the Union of Writers. Data were collected on these positions from the newspapers in each of the 14 union republics and resulted in 1,182 biographies as well as positional files for each of the top positions of each republic.

NP, 8:2:241-42

677. Horak, Stephan M., ed. **Guide to the Study of the Soviet Nationalities: Non-Russian Peoples of the USSR.** Littleton, CO: Libraries Unlimited, 1982. 265p. $30.00.

Compiled for the purpose of bringing a better balance to Western scholarship concerning Soviet studies, this bibliography annotates over 1,300 monographs and articles (in English and foreign languages) dealing with the non-Russian nationalities of the Soviet Union, with introductions to each nationality section and references to reviews in scholarly journals. The *Guide* concerns itself mainly with the areas of social sciences and humanities. Contributors are: Marjorie Mandelstam Balzer, David M. Crowe, Kenneth C. Farmer, Stephen Fischer-Galati, Sidney Heitman, James L. Heizer, Vitaut Kipel, Isabelle Kreindler, Edward J. Lazzerini, Joseph D. McCadden, and Shimon Redlich.

678. Kamenetsky, Ihor, ed. **Nationalism and Human Rights: Processes of Modernization in the USSR.** ASN Series in Issues Studies (USSR and East Europe), no. 1. Littleton, CO: Libraries Unlimited for the Association for the Study of the Nationalities (USSR and East Europe), 1977. 246p. $18.50.

This volume offers a sampling of some of the better works now being done in the West on Soviet nationality policy by historians, sociologists, and political scientists. The volume's 14 articles are arranged under three broad headings: "the historical-theoretical background, the broader all-Union issues related to nationalities and human rights, and an evaluation of trends in the case of selected non-Russian nationalities and minorities."

CRSN, 6:1:117-20

679. Katz, Zev, Rosemarie Rogers, and Frederic Harned, eds. **Handbook of Major Soviet Nationalities.** New York: Free Press, 1975. 481p. $25.00.

This handbook offers a general survey of major Soviet nationalities divided into five groups: Slavs, Baltics, Transcaucasians, Central Asians, and other nationalities such as Jews, Tatars, and Moldavians. In each case, the information includes history, economy, demography, culture, and a selected bibliography. Numerous tables related to basic data, income, trade, and demography. All of these topics are discussed for each nationality in relationship to the Russian who, in 1970 constituted 53% of the population of the USSR.

As an introduction to the nationalities of the USSR, the book is a welcome addition to a growing list of good works.

SR, 35:4:751-52

680. Luckyj, George S., ed. **Discordant Voices: The Non-Russian Soviet Literatures, 1953-1973.** Oakville, Ontario: Mosaic Press, 1975. viii, 149p. $9.95.

The six essays included here are: Leon Mirkitichian on Armenian literature, Stanislau Stankevich on Belorussian literature, Rolf Ekmanis on Latvian literature, Gustav Burbiel on Tatar literature, and George Luckyj on Ukrainian literature. Valuable lists for further study in Western languages, Russian, and the vernacular languages are also included.

SR, 37:3:539-40

681. Nekrich, Aleksandr M. **The Punished Peoples: Deportation and Fate of Soviet Minorities at the End of the Second World War.** New York: W. W. Norton, 1978. xii, 238p. $10.95.

The Punished Peoples was prepared in the USSR before Nekrich immigrated to the United States in 1976. He makes excellent use of very restricted access to the sources, which are extensively discussed. The Crimean Tatars, Chechens, and Kalmyks are most fully treated. Human aspects come through forcibly without detriment to the high scholarly level of the book. Nekrich estimates that over one million people belonging to non-Russian nationalities were deported. This is not simply a case study—it offers new insights on wartime collaboration, Soviet nationality policies in the past and today, and the fate of peoples under a totalitarian Communist regime.

682. Szporluk, Roman, ed. **The Influence of East Europe and the Soviet West on the USSR.** New York: Praeger Publishers, 1976. x, 260p. Tables. Figures. $17.50.

The book consists of seven papers presented at a conference on the influence of Eastern European and Western areas of the USSR on Soviet society, held at the University of Michigan in 1970. The volume proves beyond any doubt that in many borderland areas and satellite countries things are done and problems are solved differently from what is done in the Soviet Union itself. Several essays bring forth information about the Soviet West, an area still largely unexplored by American scholars.

SR, 35:4:754-75

BALTIC REPUBLICS

Bibliographies, Encyclopedias

683. Kantautas, Adam, and Filomena Kantautas, comps. **A Lithuanian Bibliography: A Checklist of Books and Periodicals Held by the Major Libraries of Canada and the United States.** Edmonton: University of Alberta Press, 1975. 725p. $10.00.

This valuable reference tool has 10,168 entries that describe and locate an extensive list of books, journals, pamphlets, articles, and other items in 43 Canadian, 458 American institutions, and 11 depositories in Europe. The items are listed under various topical headings.

684. **Supplement to a Lithuanian Bibliography.** Edited by A. Ulpis, et al. Edmonton: University of Alberta Press, 1980. 728p. + 16pp. illus.

The *Supplement* lists over 4,000 books and other items added by the surveyed libraries between 1972 and 1977.

685. Ziplans, Emilija, et al., comps. **Baltic Material in the University of Toronto Library.** 2nd ed. Toronto: University of Toronto Press for the Association for the Advancement of Baltic Studies, 1978. 267p. $8.00, paper.

This is a finding aid to the impressive, growing collection of Baltica in the University of Toronto Library. The current guide, a revision of the 1972 edition, lists 3,288 books, pamphlets, government records, serials, and machine-readable titles in 15 languages. It covers a wide range of subjects and disciplines and is an excellent general survey of available Baltic materials in the West.

History

686. Christiansen, Eric. **The Northern Crusades: The Baltic and the Catholic Frontier, 1100-1525.** London: Macmillan, 1980. xxii, 273p. Maps. £12.50.

This book describes the extension of Christianity and feudal government in the Baltic area through the Crusades. Because it is intended for an undergraduate readership, the *apparatus criticus* is reduced to a minimum, and the book does not claim to be a work of original research. Nevertheless, a synthesis of medieval Baltic history has never been attempted before. The author's many insights give this book an importance far beyond the circle for which it was intended.

    SEER, 59:3:433-34

687. **The Lithuanian Statute of 1529.** Translated and edited with an introduction and commentary by Karl von Loewe. Leiden: E. J. Brill, 1976. xiii, 206p. Dfl. 68.00.

This intelligent and readable translation brings this first of the three great codifications of Lithuanian legal practice into the reach of all interested parties. The detailed commentary adds variations and comparative readings from the newly (re-)discovered Firleyevsky and Zamoyski MSS in Warsaw to the standard texts of the Dzialynski MS at Kórnik and the Slutsky MS at Leningrad.

    SEER, 55:4:576-77

688. Senn, Alfred Erich. **The Emergence of Modern Lithuania.** New York: Columbia University Press, 1959. 272p. Reprint: Westport, CT: Greenwood Press, 1975. 272p. $16.50.

Lithuania's efforts to achieve independence involved complex diplomatic and military struggles. This history details, chronologically, efforts by the Lithuanians during 1917 through 1919, particularly against Soviet Russia, to obtain nationhood. Senn draws his sources from an impressive array of primary and secondary materials.

689. Senn, Alfred Erich. **Jonas Basanavičius: The Patriarch of the Lithuanian National Renaissance.** Newtonville, MA: Oriental Research Partners, 1980. 93p. $9.50.

The historical significance of Basanavičius is summed up in his leading part in the publishing in 1883 of the first journal of the national awakening; his chairmanship of the Grand Diet of Vilnius of 1905, from which the history of Lithuanian representative institutions begins; his founding of the Lithuanian Learned Society; and his honorary chairmanship of the meeting of the Council of Lithuania when it declared the restoration of the independent Lithuanian state in 1918. Senn's is a biography almost wholly of a public life. Little is available to evoke the inner spirit within the public man.

    RR, 40:2:191-93

690. Vardys, Stanley V., and Romuald J. Misiunas, eds. **The Baltic States in Peace and War 1917-1945.** Published with the cooperation of the Association for the

Advancement of Baltic Studies. University Park and London: Pennsylvania State University Press, 1978. viii, 240p. $12.50.
This volume includes papers presented at a number of conferences organized by the Baltic Institute in Scandinavia and the AABS, and it conveniently summarizes current Western research on Baltic history between 1917 and 1945. Ten of the fourteen articles are concerned with the relations of the Baltic States with the Great Powers, while the remaining four articles deal with internal developments.
> SR, 39:2:331-32

691.   Ziedonis, Arvids, Jr., et al., eds. **Baltic History.** Publication of the Association for the Advancement of Baltic Studies, 5. Columbus, OH: Association for the Advancement of Baltic Studies, Ohio State University, 1974. x, 341p. $16.00.
This volume comprises proceedings of the two conferences of the AABS and includes 28 historical papers, loosely organized around the topics of the medieval Baltic states, the eighteenth century, the period between the two world wars, and Baltic foreign relations during World War II.
> SR, 34:4:845-46

Government and Politics

692.   Allworth, Edward, ed. **Nationality Group Survival in Multi-Ethnic States: Shifting Support Patterns in the Soviet Baltic Region.** Published in cooperation with the Program on Soviet Nationality Problems, Columbia University, New York and London: Praeger Publishers, 1977. xvi, 302p. Tables. $21.00.
Focusing on Lithuania, Latvia, and Estonia, this collection of essays is concerned with determining what factors are important for the survival of nationality groups, especially in a modernizing, multinational, and authoritarian society. The individual studies explore various aspects of the problem, including the possible defenses of groups, the roots of nationality differences, the significance of culture and religion, the importance of national leadership in politics and economics, social distance between groups, and the special problem of Baltic Jews. The collection constitutes a valuable addition to the understanding of ethnic processes in the Soviet Union and the world.
> SR, 37:4:692

Foreign Relations

693.   Kaslas, Bronis J. **The Baltic Nations: The Quest for Regional Integration and Political Liberty.** Pitton, PA: Euramerica Press, 1976. 319p. $12.00.
An enlarged, revised edition of the author's (then Bronius Kazlauskas) *L'Entente Baltique* (1939), the study traces the evolution first of Poland's, then Estonia's, Latvia's, and Lithuania's efforts to form a viable Baltic Entente. The author feels their efforts were successful in several diplomatic, economic, and administrative areas, though the three nations failed to stop Soviet aggression.
> *Guide*, p. 32

694.   Rodgers, Hugh I. **Search for Security: A Study in Baltic Diplomacy, 1920-1934.** Hamden, CT: Shoe String Press, 1975. xi, 181p. $12.00.
Rodgers' account of frantic Latvian diplomacy, in the period between World War I and the rise of Hitler, presents a special case study for a small nation caught between two great powers. Although there was really no escape for the Latvian frog trapped in the German-

Russian-Polish snake pit, it was only natural for statesmen Meierovics and Cielēns to act the role of mini-Talleyrands. Their survival-oriented ploys included such schemes as political union among the Baltic states and Poland; an Eastern Locarno, involving agreements between Germany and Russia and the Baltic countries, which failed largely because neither Russia nor Germany intended to play fair with the little states. This is an outstanding contribution to East European diplomatic history.

CSP, 17:4:678-79

Religion

695. Vardys, V. Stanley. **The Catholic Church, Dissent and Nationality in Soviet Lithuania.** East European Monographs, 43. Boulder, CO: *East European Quarterly*, 1978. xiii, 336p. $18.00. Distributed by Columbia University Press, New York.
Catholic efforts to full civil rights is examined by Vardys deeply and broadly in the Lithuanian frame of reference, a praiseworthy attempt since Lithuania's Catholic struggle remains very closely intertwined with national dissent and constitutes a considerable part of the general Soviet civil rights movement. Thus, while focusing attention on the goals, scope, and social dynamics of Lithuanian Catholic dissent, the author examines it in the perspective of Lithuania's modern development.

NP, 7:2:238-39

Language and Literature

696. Ekmanis, Rolfs. **Latvian Literature under the Soviets 1940-1975.** Belmont, MA: Nordland Publishing Co., 1978. 533p. $27.50.
Ekmanis describes his perspective as not being "conventionally" literary but, rather, concerned with "the policy of the Communist Party of the Soviet Union as, in its shifting formulations, it has affected Soviet Latvian literature and culture." He is particularly successful in his selection and presentation of various samples of mutilated art as they correspond to shifting Party policies, but the total argument of the book lacks sufficient force and coherence. Nonetheless, the author has presented a significant piece of mosaic in the total picture of Soviet cultural and political imperialism.

NP, 8:2:250-51

697. Straumanis, Alfreds, ed. **Confrontation with Tyranny: Six Baltic Plays with Introductory Essays.** Prospect Heights, IL: Waveland Press, 1977. 363p. $15.00.
This is a collection of two Estonian, two Latvian, and two Lithuanian plays. Three were written by authors in the Soviet Baltic Republics, while the others were composed by exiles. Each play has been translated, with commentary. The selection is well balanced. The range of responses to the central theme is broad—from political to abstract, from realistic to symbolic.

SR, 40:1:152-53

698. Straumanis, Alfreds, ed. **The Golden Steed: Seven Baltic Plays.** Prospect Heights, IL: Waveland Press, 1979. 383p. $15.00.
Straumanis introduces this book with an easy philosophical essay on custom and ritual in their historical connection to theater in general and to their relevance to the development of Baltic drama in particular. Each play is prefaced by an informative or critical essay. The playrights, translators, and essayists are all of Baltic descent and include dramatists, scholars, and theatre practitioners of note. The seven plays have been well chosen to

present the range of sophistication with which each dramatist embodies folkloric motifs. Represented are Estonian, Latvian, and Lithuanian plays. Translations are satisfactory.
JBS, 11:3:267-68

The Society, Sociology

699. Parming, Tönu, and Elmar Järvesoo, eds. **A Case Study of a Soviet Republic: The Estonian SSR.** Foreword by Edward Allworth. Boulder, CO: Westview Press, 1978. xxvi, 432p. $22.00.
This is a purposefully planned in-depth study of a Soviet republic, edited and produced by scholars especially competent in the area of Estonian affairs. In a heavily statistical essay on demographic development, Parming predicts a further decrease in the percentage of ethnic Estonians in the republic. Rein Taagepera offers valuable insights into Estonian attitudes toward Soviet rule. Jaan Pennar analyzes the party leadership, and Järvesoo concludes that the Estonian standard of living is the highest in the USSR. This is an indispensable book for students of Baltic affairs and of the Soviet nationality question.
SR, 39:1:143-44

700. Rank, Gustav. **Old Estonia: The People and Culture.** Translated by Betty and Felix Oinas. Bloomington: Indiana University Press, 1976. 152p. $12.00.
This represents another title in Indiana University's Ural-Altaic series. The book, which discusses all aspects of early Estonian life and the peasantry, is by an outstanding Estonian ethnographer.

BELORUSSIA

701. **Letter to a Russian Friend.** London: The Association of Byelorussians in Great Britain, 1979. 64p. £1.00.
The Belorussian dissent movement has been strikingly quiescent before the *Letter* appeared, and, for this reason, the appearance of this work in the West at the present time is an event of considerable interest and significance. The document is published in its original somewhat shaky Russian, with a short but informative introduction, and an English translation to which a number of helpful notes have been appended. Its publication at this time is an important event, serving to highlight many of the present linguistic and cultural tendencies of the Soviet Union. It should be of interest to students of sociolinguistics and cultural politics.
SEER, 59:1:151-53

702. Mayo, Peter J. **A Grammar of Byelorussian.** Sheffield: Anglo-Byelorussian Society in association with the Department of Russian and Slavonic Studies, University of Sheffield, England, 1976. 66p. £1.50.
The first part of the *Grammar* acquaints the reader with the alphabet, stress, pronunciation, and spelling; the remainder of the book deals with the morphology of Belorussian. A bibliography of works in Belorussian, Russian, and English is also given.

703. McMillin, Arnold B. **A History of Byelorussian Literature: From Its Origins to the Present Day.** Giessen: Wilhelm Schmitz, 1977. 447p. DM 60.00, paper.
This book is a general survey of Belorussian literature from the twelfth century to 1975. In spite of numerous shortcomings, the book has merit, since it is a summary of serious studies. Its value as a reference work would have been greater had the author cited his sources and had he allotted more space to contemporary Belorussian writers.
CSP, 20:2:275-76

704. Pashkievich, Valentina. **Fundamental Byelorussian. Book I; Book II.** Toronto: Byelorussian-Canadian Coordinating Committee, 1974-78. Book 1: 312p.; Book 2: 422p.

This is a textbook for Belorussian and non-Belorussian-speaking students. It covers the fundamentals of grammar, offers a short but complete course of phonetics and morphology, indicates stresses, presents written and oral drill exercises, and contains an extensive Belorussian-English dictionary. Book II contains an appendix with grammatical tables summarizing the declensions of nouns, adjectives, and pronouns, conjugations of verbs, and tables of numerals. The dictionary lists over 20,000 words.

705. Wexler, Paul. **A Historical Phonology of the Belorussian Language.** Historical Phonology of the Slavic Languages, III. Heidelberg: Carl Winter Universitätsverlag, 1977. 192p. DM 185.00.

The author presents 51 sound changes from the late Common Slavonic period to the present. In identifying the specifically Belorussian linguistic territory, Wexler follows Shevelov in dividing East Slavonic into two dialect areas, Polack-Ryazan' and Kiev-Poleśsie, thereby avoiding the need to posit a united *'drevnerusskiy yazyk'* for the purpose of historical phonology as V. V. Ivanov does in his *Istoricheskaya fonologiya russkogo yazyka* (Moscow, 1968).

        SEER, 57:3:414-15

UKRAINE

Bibliographies, Encyclopedias

706. Pidhainy, Oleh S., and Olexandra I. Pidhainy, comps. **The Ukrainian Republic in the Great East-European Revolution: A Bibliography.** Part II. Toronto, Ontario: New Review Books, 1975. xv, 357p. $34.50.

The first volume of this bibliography was published in 1966. Part II lists articles and books covering the period from March 1917 to April 1920. It is divided into five sections and subdivided into alphabetical sections for works in Ukrainian, Russian, and Western languages.

707. Wynar, Bohdan S., with the assistance of S. Holte, comps. **Doctoral Dissertations on Ukrainian Topics in English: Prepared during the Years 1928-1978.** Englewood, CO: Ukrainian Research Foundation, 1980. 20p. $3.50, paper.

The entries are arranged by broad subject categories, with the larger number of dissertations in history, politics, and international relations. This list serves not only as a bibliography of dissertations completed but also to point out significant gaps in the literature and to propose guidelines for future research on Ukrainian topics.

History

708. Doroshenko, Dmytro. **A Survey of Ukrainian History.** Edited and updated by Oleh W. Gerus. Winnipeg: Humeniuk Publication Foundation, 1975. xiii, 873p. $25.00.

Dmytro Doroshenko (1882-1951), noted Ukrainian historian, authored approximately 600 historical studies, including his academic survey of Ukrainian history *Narys istorii Ukrainy,* 2 vols. (1932). The first English edition of this work was edited by G. Simpson (1939). The present revised edition is based on the Ukrainian text as well as on its earlier English edition. Gerus has updated Doroshenko's text by the addition of six new chapters, new maps, bibliography, and pictorial materials. Also, he has included a separate chapter

on Ukrainian historiography and a brief biographical sketch on Doroshenko. The work covers all periods of Ukrainian history beginning with prehistory.
CSP, 19:2:248-49

709. Dushnyck, Walter, ed. **Ukraine in a Changing World.** New York: Ukrainian Congress Committee of America, 1977. 300p. $10.00.
This book is a conference volume, consisting of papers presented at a special conference held in 1974 in observance of the thirtieth anniversary of the founding of *The Ukrainian Quarterly.* Fourteen Ukrainian, American, and Canadian scholars took part, and their papers deal with a variety of themes pertaining to Ukrainian history, culture, politics, and activities in the diaspora. Several papers deal with the conditions in Soviet Ukraine, the dissent movement, oppression, and the religious situation in Ukraine. This volume is unique because it offers a scholarly examination of issues from the Ukrainian standpoint.

710. Gajecky, George, ed. **The Cossack Administration of the Hetmanate.** Harvard Ukrainian Research Institute, Sources and Documents Series. Cambridge, MA: Harvard Ukrainian Research Institute, 1978. 2 vols. xvi, 775p. Maps. $18.50.
This book consists of the first comprehensive description of the structure of the Ukrainian Cossack State of the seventeenth century. It includes a list of all officers at both regimental and company levels, and an index of the names of more than 3,000 Cossack officers.

711. Hunczak, Taras, ed. **The Ukraine, 1917-1921: A Study in Revolution.** Assisted by John T. Von der Heide. Introduction by Richard Pipes. Cambridge, MA: Harvard University Press, 1977. viii, 424p. $15.00.
This is a collection of essays by 14 American and Canadian specialists in modern Ukrainian history. The book is arranged more or less in chronological order. The collection offers precious little that is genuinely new and thought-provoking in terms of interpretation or documentation. One is puzzled by the absence of Galicia (West Ukraine). However, from the perspective of an undergraduate student of history, the book is a welcome addition.
CSP, 21:1:131-33

712. Kortschmaryk, Frank B. **The Kievan Academy and Its Role in the Organization of Education in Russia at the Turn of the Seventeenth Century.** Shevchenko Scientific Society, Ukrainian Studies, English Section, vol. 13. New York: Shevchenko Scientific Society, 1976. 95p. $7.50.
This study tells of the widespread but generally unacknowledged significant influence and contribution of the Kievan Academy as the model for education in Russia.

713. Magocsi, Paul Robert. **The Shaping of a National Identity: Subcarpathian Rus',** **1848-1948.** Cambridge, MA, and London: Harvard University Press, 1978. xvi, 640p. Maps. $25.00.
The theme of this book is that Subcarpathian Rusyns failed to develop into an independent nationality because their intelligentsia suffered from a sense of inferiority vis-à-vis other closely related nationalities. Magocsi illustrates his point by dividing his discussion into three sections: the historical background up to 1919, the cultural setting, and political developments to 1948. He also realizes that, in some respects, the issue of the identity of the Subcarpathian Rusyns has become academic since their incorporation into the Ukrainian SSR in 1944.
NP, 7:2:221-22

714. Palij, Michael. **The Anarchism of Nestor Makhno, 1918-1921: An Aspect of the Ukrainian Revolution.** Institute for Comparative and Foreign Area Studies, Publications on Russia and Eastern Europe, no. 7. Seattle and London: University of Washington Press, 1976. xiv, 248p. Photographs. $14.50.

In the treatment of the historical background related to the movement, which Makhno brought into life, Palij focuses upon three phases of Ukrainian history: the later stage of the Ukraining Cossack State, the history of the Ukrainian people through the nineteenth century, and the period from the beginning of the twentieth century to the Revolution of 1917. The author draws the political, ideological, and military profile of Makhno and describes his impact on the Revolution by analyzing his attitudes and relations to the Bolsheviks, to various Ukrainian governments, and to the White Guards under the command of Denikin and Wrangel. The book is composed in a scholarly and highly readable form.

NP, 6:1:75-79

715. Sirka, Ann. **The Nationality Question in Austrian Education: The Case of Ukrainians in Galicia 1867-1914.** European University Studies: Series III, History and Allied Studies, vol. 124. Frankfurt/Main, Bern, Switzerland, and Cirencester, England: Peter D. Lang, 1980. viii, 230p. Tables. S.Fr. 43.00, paper.

This is the only study on the role of education in Austria-Hungary as related to a national issue, in particular, the case of Ukrainians in Galicia. Vienna's rather benevolent attitude toward the Ukrainian initiative to develop their own educational facilities contributed significantly to the rise of Ukrainian national consciousness and the foundation of the Shevchenko Scientific Society in Lviv (Lemberg). It also aided in the introduction of higher education for the Ukrainian clergy, which only promoted Ukrainian national rebirth.

716. Subtelny, Orest, ed. **On the Eve of Poltava: The Letters of Ivan Mazepa to Adam Sieniawski, 1704-1708.** Preface by Oleksander Ohloblyn. New York: The Ukrainian Academy of Arts and Sciences in the United States, 1975. 159p.

This collection of 54 of Hetman Mazepa's letters to A. Sieniawski provides the missing links in the historian's attempt to better understand Mazepa's strategy, intention, and secret diplomacy, all of which were clearly aimed at regaining Ukraine's independence and at ending Russian encroachment as a result of the Pereiaslav Treaty of 1654. The letters, housed in the Czartoryski Library in Cracow, are written in the Polish language and are here provided with only brief English summaries.

SR, 36:1:137-38

717. Sydorenko, Alexander. **The Kievan Academy in the Seventeenth Century.** University of Ottawa Ukrainian Studies, no. 1. Ottawa: University of Ottawa Press, 1977. xvi, 194p. + 34pp. plates. Paper.

The Kievan Academy originated as a school of the Kiev Brotherhood in 1615 and 16 years later underwent a major education reform by Petro Mohyla. After the 1630s the academy became the major intellectual and education center in East Europe, following the pattern of Western academic institutions. The author provides adequate background relating to the political and cultural setting in seventeenth-century Ukraine and emphasizes the strenuous Polish-Russian-Ukrainian relationships and the struggle of the Ukrainian Orthodox Church with Polish Catholic influences. The academy also supplied a large number of the clergy for Russia.

NP, 7:1:106-107

718. Wynar, Lubomyr R., ed. **Habsburg and Zaporozhian Cossacks: The Diary of Erich Lassota von Steblau, 1594.** Translated by Orest Subtelny. Published for the Ukrainian Historical Association, Inc. Littleton, CO: Ukrainian Academic Press, 1975. 144p. $9.00.

Emperor Rudolf II wanted to enlist Cossack military forces against the Turks and their allies, the Tatars. With the Cossacks joining the Holy Roman Empire against the Turks, increased tension between Poland the Ottoman Empire would result and encourage a more friendly attitude of the Poles toward the Habsburgs. An alliance with the Cossacks would also strengthen the pro-Habsburg candidate for the Polish crown should that throne become vacated. The editor of this book provides the reader with a worthwhile lengthy introduction explaining the historical context of the diary within the cross-currents of Eastern European history at that time.

SR, 36:4:698-99

Government and Politics

719. Boris, Jurij. **The Sovietization of Ukraine: The Communist Doctrine and Practice of National Self-Determination.** Edmonton, Toronto: Canadian Institute of Ukrainian Studies, 1980. 488p. $19.95. Distributed by University of Toronto Press.

This is the second revised edition of the author's work originally published in Stockholm in 1960 under the title *The Russian Communist Party and the Sovietization of Ukraine.* The work's originality lies in its emphasis on sociological and economic elements. The section on political parties in Ukraine has been updated and chapters have been reorganized.

720. Farmer, Kenneth C. **Ukrainian Nationalism in the Post-Stalin Era: Myth, Symbols and Ideology in Soviet Nationalities Policy.** The Hague: Martinus Nijhoff, 1980. 253p. $36.50.

This study provides a history of Ukrainian nationalism from Khrushchev's consolidation of power to the demise of Petro Shelest, simultaneously developing and employing a conceptional framework useful for the study of nationalism under the Soviet Russian regime. This framework is symbolic politics, and the study of the manipulation of the myths and symbols that form ideological discourse. Ukraine, because of its size, historical realities, and deep national tradition, is a barometer of national discontent in the Soviet Union. For this reason, the study of Soviet nationalities policy must always begin with the study of Ukrainian nationalism.

721. Motyl, Alexander J. **The Turn to the Right: The Ideological Origins and Development of Ukrainian Nationalism, 1919-1929.** East European Monographs, 65. Boulder, CO: *East European Quarterly*, 1980. 212p. $15.00. Distributed by Columbia University Press, New York.

To explain the origin, complexities, and formation of ideological Ukrainian nationalism, the author went to original sources, newspapers, and periodicals published by the respective Ukrainian political parties, groups, and organizations that were active in the immediate post-World War I period in Galicia, Austria, Czechoslovakia, and Germany. He also consulted memoirs of individuals who helped to shape Ukrainian thought, views, and actions during that period. Motyl's extensive documentation, a 10-page comprehensive bibliography, and objectivity make this excellent study an indispensable reading for the expert of modern East European history.

722. Potichnyj, Peter J., ed. **Ukraine in the Seventies**. Papers and Proceedings of the McMaster Conference on Contemporary Ukraine, October 1974. Oakville, Ontario: Mosaic Press, 1975. x, 355p. $12.95.

Eighteen essays are divided into six parts in this book: Resource Development; Economics; Sociology and Demography; Non-Ukrainian Nationalities; Party, State, Society; and Ukrainian Studies in the West: Problems and Prospects. The symposium offers analytical and objective insights into the internal development of Ukraine in the 1970s.

723. Rakhmanny, Roman. **In Defense of the Ukrainian Cause**. Edited by Stephen D. Olynyk. North Quincy, MA: The Christopher Publishing House, 1979. 297p. $12.95.

This volume is a collection of 44 political commentaries and essays on diverse aspects of the contemporary Ukrainian situation by a Ukrainian-Canadian journalist. Topics discussed are: Insurgency in the Ukraine: Ukrainian Nationalism and Soviet-West Relations; Ukrainian Nationalism: Intellectual Dissent in Ukraine; International Communism and Ukrainian Nationalism; and Ukrainians in Diaspora. Specialists in Ukrainian affairs will find no surprises, but they, as well as any other reader, will find here a rich reservoir of information on the complexities of the Ukrainian national movement since the end of World War II.

    RR, 39:4:512

Foreign Relations

724. Margolin, Arnold. **Ukraine and the Policy of the Entente**. Translated by V. P. Sokoloff. Los Angeles: L. A. Margolina, 1977. 261p.

This is the first English translation of Margolin's reflections on the Bolshevik Revolution and civil war in Ukraine, first published in 1921. Following the Bolshevik coup, Margolin lent his support to the Ukrainian national movement as a jurist and diplomat. He thus treats many aspects of the Ukrainian problem from firsthand experience. The book offers some points of interest to anyone considering developments in Ukraine between 1917-1921.

    RR, 38:3:369-70

725. Potichnyj, Peter J., ed. **Poland and Ukraine: Past and Present**. Edmonton: The Canadian Institute of Ukrainian Studies, 1980. 364p. $14.95.

This is an informative guide to the history of Polish-Ukrainian relations, past and present, discussed in 18 essays, 17 of which were presented at the eleventh conference on Communist and East European Affairs at McMaster University, held in 1977. The contributions are divided into five chapters: Historical Legacy; Cultural Relations; Economic Ties and Communications; World War II and After; and Political Problems. The collection is selective and the contributors concentrated on positive aspects of Ukrainian-Polish relations, hoping to contribute to accommodations and more friendly relations in the future.

726. Sawczuk, Konstantyn. **The Ukraine in the United Nations: A Study in Soviet Foreign Policy, 1944-1950**. East European Monographs, 9. Boulder, CO: *East European Quarterly*, 1975. 158p. $10.00. Distributed by Columbia University Press, New York.

This is a study of how Ukraine came to be a founding member of the United Nations in 1945; its political role and activities in the early years, especially the impact of the U.N. delegate Dmytro Manuilsky; and the complicated question of the juridical status of the Ukrainian SSR in the international community.

Religion

727. Labunka, Miroslav, and Leonid Rudnytzky, eds. **The Ukrainian Catholic Church, 1974-75.** A Symposium held at La Salle College, Philadelphia, PA. Philadelphia: St. Sophia Religious Association of Ukrainian Catholics, 1976. 162p.

The papers in this symposium are divided into three sections: the Soviet government and the Ukrainian Catholic Church; the Vatican and the Ukrainian Church; and the Ukrainian Catholic Church and Eastern spirituality.

Economics

728. Koropecky, I. S., ed. **The Ukraine within the USSR: An Economic Balance Sheet.** New York: Praeger Publishers, 1977. xxi, 316p. $26.95.

Two important conclusions flow from this volume — Ukraine is a region of "relative decline," and there is a definite drain of resources and revenues from the Ukrainian SSR. There is unanimity among the contributors in estimating the costs incurred by Ukraine's economy and population and on the role of Ukraine's economy within the USSR. The book provides reliable information and offers a variety of arguments for interpretation.

Language, Literature, Folklore

729. Altbauer, Moshe, and Horace G. Lunt, eds. **An Early Slavonic Psalter from Rus'.** Vol. I: *Photoreproduction.* Harvard Ukrainian Research Institute, Sources and Documents Series. Cambridge, MA: Harvard Ukrainian Research Institute, 1979. 181p. $15.00. Distributed by Harvard University Press, Cambridge, MA.

This is a photoreproduction of an old Rus' manuscript written approximately A.D. 1100. It is the oldest version of the Psalter text that was standard in Ukraine but not in Russia. The volume also includes photoreproductions of portions of a mid-twelfth century Psalter that is the second oldest witness to this text.

730. Babiński, Hubert F. **The Mazeppa Legend in European Romanticism.** New York: Columbia University Press, 1974. xii, 164p. $12.00.

The Mazeppa legend arose in Ukraine but reached its highest development in the West. Though the legend was widely known long before 1819, it took Byron's treatment in the long poem *Mazeppa* to give it genuine life. The work is a useful addition to Mazeppa literature. The bibliography is extensive and catholic — even strictly nationalistic studies are included.

SR, 34:4:871

731. Čyževs'kyj, Dmytro. **A History of Ukrainian Literature (From the Eleventh to the End of the Nineteenth Century).** Translated by Dolly Ferguson, Doreen Gorsline, and Ulana Petyk. Edited and with a foreword by George S. N. Luckyj. Littleton, CO: Ukrainian Academic Press, 1975. xii, 681p. $25.00.

This work represents a milestone in Ukrainian literary criticism in general and among historical works of Ukrainian literature in particular because it presents in an original way, based on scholarly research methods, a comprehensive description of the literary periods with their principal trends and an analysis of the works of their representatives. The extensive bibliography and the index of names and titles effectively complete this first scholarly and comprehensive history of Ukrainian literature.

SR, 36:2:355-57

732. Franko, Ivan. **The Master's Jests.** Translated by Roman Tatchyn. New York: Shevchenko Scientific Society, 1979. 133p. $10.00.
Ivan Franko's popularity as a poet rests in no small measure upon his deep understanding of human nature expressed with compassion and humor in a manner both expansive and succinct. The combination of these qualities imparts a uniqueness to his style that is very difficult to recreate in a foreign language and as partly proven in the case of *The Master's Jests.* The excellent content footnotes to be found throughout the text are ne of the positive aspects of this translation and are helpful in better understanding the story.

733. Humesky, Assya A. **Modern Ukrainian.** Edmonton and Toronto: The Canadian Institute of Ukrainian Studies, 1980. 438p. $8.00, paper.
This text covers the basics of Ukrainian phonology and morphology as well as some elements of sentence structure and intonation. There are 20 lessons that include dialogues and narrative passages, grammar notes, explanatory notes, and exercises. The text is accompanied by tapes and can be used for independent study by both the beginning and the advanced student. Tapes (12 cassettes) are also available at $60.77.

734. Kitch, Faith C. M. **The Literary Style of Epifanij Premudryj: Pletenije sloves.** Slavistische Beiträge, Band 96. Munich: Verlag Otto Sanger, 1976. 298p. DM 34.00.
This book consists of a study of the *Life of Stefan of Perm'*, attempting to analyze the style and structure of the *Life* and to place it in perspective against the background of the Kievan and South Slavic rhetorical *vita.* The strongest point of the book is the constant comparison of Epifany with Evtimy and Domentian, a comparison that both brings out Epifany's uniqueness and tells us a good deal about thirteenth- and fourteenth-century *pleteniye sloves.* Kitch rightly suggests that *Life of Stefan* has its roots in Kievan literature.

735. Kulish, Mykola. **Sonata Pathetique.** Translated by George S. N. Luckyj and Moira Luckyj. Introduction by Ralph Lindheim. Littleton, CO: Ukrainian Academic Press, 1975. 110p. $11.50.
This is the first English translation of Mykola Kulish's 1930 play, one of the representative works of modern Ukrainian literature. The plot deals with the 1917-1920 revolution as reflected in a small Ukrainian town where the characters symbolize Ukrainian nationalist aspirations, Russian chauvinism, and Communism. The qualities of the play are well retained in this translation.

736. Luckyj, George S. N., ed. **Shevchenko and the Critics, 1861-1980.** Translations by Dolly Ferguson and Sophia Yurkevych. Introduction by Bohdan Rubchak. Toronto: University of Toronto Press, 1980. xii, 522p. $30.00.
This book contains 27 articles and essays by 24 authors, from P. Kulish's "Graveside Oration" of 1861 to an article of 1980 by G. Grabowicz. Rubchak's extensive introduction, with a penetrating survey of the whole range of ideas presented in the book, is excellent. The criticism of Taras Shevchenko's works could be classified into three major approaches: 1) the poet as a prophet and leader of the struggle for national liberty, 2) the poet as a fighter for social justice, and 3) the poet as a great master in literature.
CSP, 23:3:355-61

737. Prokopiw, Orysia. **The Ukrainian Translations of Shakespeare's Sonnets.** Ottawa: University of Ottawa Press, 1976. 334p.
This book consists of translations of Shakespeare's sonnets into Ukrainian by 11 Ukrainian authors of the nineteenth and twentieth centuries. Prokopiw focuses attention on single sonnets translated by most authors and arrives at a detailed analysis of the metric form,

vocabulary, and semantics of each of them. Her book is a valuable addition to Ukrainian literary criticism and a useful contribution to the study of problems in comparative literature.

CSP, 19:3:392-93

738.   Shankovsky, Igor. **Symonenko: A Study in Semantics.** Munich: Ukrainisches Institut für Bildungspolitik, 1977. 212p. $8.00.

This is a study about Vasyl Symonenko, one of the best-known Ukrainian poets of the 1960s, and his literary works that initiated a new renaissance of Ukrainian literature under the Soviet regime. A comprehensive bibliography, an index, and an appendix with several poems and extracts from Symonenko's *Diary* are included.

739.   Smyrniw, Walter, ed. **Ukrainian Prose Manual: A Text for Intermediate Language Studies.** Oakville, Ontario: Mosaic Press, 1977. v, 192p. $5.00, paper.

This book offers samples of contemporary colloquial Ukrainian prose from recent issues of Soviet Ukrainian periodicals. The text provides various oral and written exercises that should enable the student to acquire the knowledge of the basic lexical, syntactical, and idiomatic features of contemporary Ukrainian. The last seven passages are serious articles on topics in Ukrainian culture, to be read with a dictionary.

740.   Struk, Danylo Husar. **Ukrainian for Undergraduates.** Oakville, Ontario: Mosaic Press (for the Canadian Institute of Ukrainian Studies), 1978. xxv, 350p. o.p.

The method employed in this textbook is one of "basic explanations and rule," the objective being "to correct the student defects but also to provide them with a firm set of rules." The book is "divided into twenty-three chapters and an introduction to phonetics." Each lesson in the book contains a rather extensive vocabulary list with English equivalents. Good explanations of grammatical rules and usage are given. This is one of the best textbooks on Ukrainian language available yet.

CSP, 22-3:445-46

741.   Sverstiuk, Ievhen. **Clandestine Essays.** Translated and with an introduction by George S. N. Luckyj. Harvard Ukrainian Research Institute Monograph Series. Littleton, CO: Ukrainian Academic Press, 1976. 100p. $7.50.

The author of these essays is one of many Soviet Ukrainian intellectuals now being confined for alleged political offenses. This volume presents two of his longer essays in a very readable translation, and George Luckyj's lucid introduction relates the author to major Ukrainian literary trends. The essay, "A Cathedral in Scaffolding," interprets Oles Honchar's novel, *Sobor* (1968), and the essay, "Ivan Kotliarevsky Is Laughing," places the father of modern Ukrainian literature in the context of literary development, dissent, and *samvydav*.

SR, 38:2:358

742.   **Ukrainian dumy: Original Texts.** Translated by George Tarnawsky and Patricia Kilina. Introduction by Natalie K. Moyle. Toronto: Canadian Institute of Ukrainian Studies, 1979. 219p. $5.95.

Thirty-three Ukrainian *dumy*, or epics, are here translated into English. Natalie Moyle compares the heroes of the Ukrainian epics with those in *Chanson de Roland* and *Niebelungenlied*. The translations are good and inclined more to poetic criteria than to exact rendering. Since *dumy* have verse of different length, the translators tried, often quite successfully, to reflect this in English, while omitting peculiar rhyming observed in the originals.

CSP, 22:3:443-44

743. Zilyns'kyj, Ivan. **A Phonetic Description of the Ukrainian Language.** Translated by Wolodymyr T. Zyla and Wendell M. Aycock. Cambridge, MA: Harvard Ukrainian Research Institute, 1979. xii, 212p. $12.50, paper.

This is a translation of the author's work published in 1932 in Polish, *Opis fonetyczny języka ukraińskiego.* It contains much valuable material on Ukrainian dialects at a stage in their development, especially due to the fact that in the meantime some of the dialects discussed disappeared altogether as a result of political events.

Dissent Movement

744. Khodorovich, Tatyana, ed. **The Case of Leonid Plyushch.** Boulder, CO: Westview Press, 1976. xvii, 152p. $10.75.

To the reader of this dossier, it remains a mystery: How this "convinced Marxist" graduate of Kiev State University and member of the cybernetics institute of the Ukrainian Academy of Sciences came to ask embarrassing questions, at age 25, regarding Stalinist survivals and a nationalities policy that was cast in the "tsarist pattern"; then how he found the inner resources to withstand 30 months in psychoprison; then, when asked that he render a token recantation of his *samizdat* essays as a "deviation from the norm," how he was able to make the flat reply, "I won't write anything for them." Clearly, this is an extraordinary case. The eloquence of his witness should bestir physicians in the West to intercede for the thousand or so others who remain in Soviet psychoprisons for the unorthodoxy of their beliefs.

CSP, 19:3:381

745. Liber, George, and Anna Mostovych, comps. **Nonconformity and Dissent in the Ukrainian SSR, 1955-1975: An Annotated Bibliography.** Harvard Ukrainian Research Institute, Sources and Documents Series, no. 3. Cambridge, MA: Harvard Ukrainian Research Institute, 1978. xxxix, 245p. $8.50.

This bibliography, impressive in many ways, includes 1,242 items and stresses national, religious, and civil rights movements in Ukraine, covering the uncensored material published during the years 1955 to 1975 in numerous *samvydav* publications, including letters, appeals, petitions, reports, accounts of political events, essays, monographs, belles-lettres, in addition to books and articles published abroad prior to June 15, 1976. The material is arranged by names and subjects with a complete bibliographical description and a short pertinent annotation. The volume includes also abbreviations of political terms and a comprehensive index.

NP, 7:2:242-43

746. Osadchy, Mykhailo. **Cataract.** Translated and edited by Marco Carynnyk. New York: Harcourt Brace Jovanovich, 1976. xxiii, 240p. $8.95.

Osadchy's literary memoir about repression and the spirit of resistance in Ukraine of the 1960s and 1970s joins such better-known works on recent experience of imprisonment, camps, and exile in the USSR as those of Solzhenitsyn, Marchenko, Amalrik, and others. Still, his is a unique work. Conceived as a testimony, *Cataract* has highly artistic expression yet reaches at times Koestler's insight into sociopolitical analysis of the police state. The all-pervading theme of this work is the national resistance in the Soviet Union and a plea for cultural and political freedoms for Ukraine. The price of writing the *Cataract* after release from his first imprisonment was Osadchy's second arrest in 1972, with a new sentence of seven years.

CSP, 19:4:534-35

747. Plyushch, Leonid. **History's Carnival: A Dissident's Autobiography.** Edited, translated and with an introduction by Marco Carynnyk. New York and London: Harcourt Brace Jovanovich, 1979. xvii, 429p. $14.95.

This is the autobiography of one of the best-known dissidents, now living in Paris, who spent two years in the notorious Dnipropetrivsk psychoprison for his political views. This is a moral and philosophical autobiography revealing the Soviet system as the inhuman and most oppressive regime of the twentieth century. The book also contains little-known information about the Democratic movement in the USSR, especially in Ukraine. Plyushch's encounter with the KGB offers new insights into the practices of this organization. His wife, Tatiana Zhitnikova, recounts her activities on behalf of her husband.

748. Stern, August, ed. **The USSR vs. Dr. Mikhail Stern.** Translated from Russian by Marco Carynnyk. New York: Urizen Books, 1977. 267p. $10.00.

A unique document, this is an account of the investigation and trial of Dr. Mikhail Stern, based on tape recordings smuggled out of the USSR. Soviet police interrogated more than 2,000 of Stern's patients in rural Ukraine, intimating that the Jewish doctor was ritually murdering Gentile children and poisoning patients. Despite this official anti-Semitism, many of the Ukrainian peasants demonstrated considerable heroism by defying the prosecution and rejecting falsified pretrial testimony being passed in their names.

749. Symonenko, Vasyl. **Granite Obelisks.** Translated and edited by Andriy Freishyn-Chirovsky. Jersey City, NJ: "Svoboda" Press, 1976. 143p. $5.00.

This is a collection of some of the poetry and the *Diary* of Symonenko. The *Diary*, especially the circumstances of its transmission to the West, occasioned the beginning of harsh repression of Ukrainian intellectuals in the 1960s.

750. **The Ukrainian Herald, Issue no. 6: Dissent in Ukraine.** Translated and edited by Lesya Jones and Bohdan Yasen. Toronto: Smoloskyp Publishers, 1977. 215p. $6.95.

This issue includes commentary by V. Chornovil, an article on the circumstances of Ukrainian-language instruction in Kiev's schools, five documents on Valentyn Moroz's case and a collection of appeals on his behalf, and a number of short essays on and by individual Ukrainians who represent the movement for human and national rights in Ukraine.

751. **The Ukrainian Herald, Issue no. 7-8 (Spring 1974), An Underground Journal from Soviet Ukraine: Ethnocide of Ukrainians in the U.S.S.R.** Compiled by Maksym Sahaydak. Introduction by Robert Conquest. Translated and edited by Olena Saciiuk and Bohdan Yasen. Baltimore: Smoloskyp Publishers, 1976. 9v. 209p. $6.95.

This is a competent and faithful English translation of the combined issue 7 and 8 of the Soviet Ukrainian *samvydav* journal *Ukrains'kyi visnyk*. Issue 7-8 appeared after the 1972 wave of KGB arrests of intellectuals and dissidents and it shows a virulent separatism that is reminiscent of an earlier era of Ukrainian nationalism. The first part offers statistical analysis of the imposed denationalization of Ukraine through linguistic Russification. The second part consists of discussion of the purge in Ukraine during the early 1970s and of the repression of Ukrainian national culture.

CAUCASIAN REPUBLICS AND PEOPLES

752. **Agathangelos' History of the Armenians.** Translated and edited by R. W. Thomson. Albany: State University of New York Press, 1976. xcviii, 527p. $50.00.
Thomson offers a complete translation of Agathangelos' *History* that purports to be an eyewitness account of the conversion to Christianity of Greater Armenia, although its surviving Armenian recension was probably compiled some 150 years after the fact (about A.D. 460). The translation is accompanied by a useful introduction, extensive notes, a bibliography, and a valuable index of biblical quotations and allusions. The text used is that of the Tiflis 1914 Lukasean edition.
    SR, 38:4:699-700

753. Der Hovanessian, Diana, and Marzbed Margossian, eds. and trans. **Anthology of Armenian Poetry.** New York: Columbia University Press, 1978. xxii, 357p. $20.00.
This fine collection includes all periods and types, from folk and early Christian to Soviet and diaspora. Brief biographical notes are included. The date of composition is given; sources are not. The smooth translations, in modern American poetic idiom, have immediacy but at some sacrifice of stylistic identity and diversity.

754. Lang, David Marshall. **Armenia: Cradle of Civilization.** Revised edition. London: George Allen & Unwin, 1978 [1970]. 320p. + 8pp. plates. Illus. $29.00.
Focusing primarily on prehistorical, classical, and early Christian Armenia, Lang's work provides the nonspecialist with pertinent information and an easy narrative, accompanied by an abundance of photographs. (For a review of the first edition, see SR, 27:1:133-35.)
    SR, 38:4:700

755. Mepisashvili, Rusudan, and Vakhtang Tsintsadze. **The Arts of Ancient Georgia.** New York: Thames & Hudson, 1977 and 1979. 309p. $29.95.
The authors present a visual and verbal display of the artistic, principally architectural, achievements of the Georgians. This work chronicles not only the arts of the most ancient past but the full range of the more prolific medieval and even the early modern periods. Rich in fine photographs, plans, and explanatory text, the book is a handsome contribution to the study of Caucasian art.
    RR, 39:3:274

756. Rustaveli, Shota. **The Lord of the Pantherskin: A Georgian Romance of Chivalry.** Translated with an introduction and notes by R. H. Stevenson. Afterword by A. G. Baramidze. Albany: State University of New York Press, 1977. xxix, 240p. $17.00.
Rustaveli's great medieval romance follows a difficult idiom, and textual problems abound. Stevenson's continuous prose translation, based on the 1669-quatrain Georgian Academy of Sciences text of 1957, seeks to be intelligible, while retaining the original's formalized expression and vitality. Stevenson's introduction discusses the poem in an international context.

757. Walker, Christopher J. **Armenia: The Survival of a Nation.** London: Croom Helm; New York: St. Martin's Press, 1980. 446p. $30.00.
This historical survey of Armenia and the Armenians, starting with ancient and medieval times, covers Armenia under the Russian and Ottoman Empire occupations, along with the attempts to establish a republic after each empire collapsed, and ends with the history of the Armenian SSR within the USSR. This text is recommended for undergraduate students and lay readers.

CENTRAL ASIAN REPUBLICS AND PEOPLES

758. Allworth, Edward, comp. **Soviet Asia: Bibliographies.** New York: Praeger Publishers, 1975. 687p. $35.00.

This massive bibliography with the subtitle, "A Compilation of Social Science and Humanities Sources on the Iranian, Mongolian, and Turkic Nationalities," contains approximately 5,200 entries published in Russia between 1850 and 1970. The following areas are considered: Soviet Asia in general, the Black Sea and West Caspian littoral, the Volga basin, Central Asia, Siberia, and Mongolia. Each region is divided by chapters comprising general works and works relating to specific national groups. This attractive volume is a must for all research libraries.

759. Bennigsen, Alexandre A., and S. Enders Wimbush. **Muslim National Communism in the Soviet Union: A Revolutionary Strategy for the Colonial World.** Chicago: The University of Chicago Press, 1979. 267p. $20.00.

This book begins with an account of the experiences and aims that by 1917 had led various Muslim leaders in the Russian empire to look to the Bolshevik party as a means for the national liberation of their peoples. However, as the book recounts, these dreams were frustrated as early as 1928, and most of the leading national Communists (like Mir Said Sultan Galiev) were physically purged soon after that. The conflict between Muslim and Russian Communists had two main sides, one organizational and the other doctrinal. This book has a substantial appendix that includes translations of documents crucial to the study of the subject, as well as capsule biographies of the most important persons mentioned. There is also a chronology of events and an extensive bibliography that is unfortunately marred by minor inaccuracies in the spelling of non-English titles.

NP, 9:1:139-40

760. McCagg, William O., Jr., and Brian D. Silver, eds. **Soviet Asian Ethnic Frontiers.** New York: Pergamon Press, 1979. xx, 280p. $22.50.

This is a collection of papers first presented at a conference held in February 1977 at Michigan State University and updated through spring 1979. Focusing on the nationalities that straddle the volatile Soviet frontiers with Afghanistan, China, Iran and Turkey, the papers cut across disciplines and "fiefs" of area studies. Several papers add new information and insights on the area and its peoples and also contribute to the basic conclusions that emerge from this volume surveyed by the editors in their excellent introduction. The book is equipped with six helpful maps and author and subject indexes.

RR, 39:4:511

JEWS

Bibliographies, Biographies

761. Bykovsky, Lev. **Solomon I. Goldeman: A Portrait of a Politician and Educator (1885-1974). A Chapter in Ukrainian Jewish Relations.** New York, Toronto, Munich: Ukrainian Historical Association, 1980. 98p. $8.00.

Bykovsky's contribution is a noble attempt to enrich the knowledge about Ukrainian-Jewish relations. The upheavals of 1917 brought Goldeman to the leadership of the Ukrainian National Committee of Poalei Zion and started him on his important work in the area of Jewish-Ukrainian political cooperation. Subsequently, he represented Ukrainian Jews in the Ukrainian *Rada* until his emigration in 1920. While abroad, Goldeman continued to work with and on behalf of the Ukrainian cause.

762. Fluk, Louise R., comp. **Jews in the Soviet Union: An Annotated Bibliography.** New York: The American Jewish Committee, Institute of Human Relations, 1975. 44p. $1.50.

This bibliography contains a selection of the most significant and accessible writings, both scholarly and popular, on Soviet Jewry published in English between January 1967 and 1974. There are 314 entries — books, pamphlets, and articles.

763. Portnoy, Samuel A., ed. **Vladimir Medem: The Life and Soul of a Legendary Jewish Socialist.** New York: KTAV Publishing House, 1979. xxxvi, 583p. + 12pp. photographs. $20.00.

Medem's memoirs are a good focal point for a study of the Bund, for he was deeply involved in its activities. Medem served on the central committee of the Bund and was a participant and observer at Bund, Russian, and European socialist congresses. Not the least of these was the famous Second Congress of the RSDWP in 1903 in Brussels and London, where the Bund was written out of the Russian party. Medem also helped to develop for the Bund a comprehensive position on the Jewish national question in Russia.
NP, 7:2:224-25

Education

764. Greenbaum, Alfred Abraham. **Jewish Scholarship and Scholarly Institutions in Soviet Russia, 1918-1953.** Jerusalem: Centre for Documentation and Research of East European Jewry, The Hebrew University, 1978. 224p.

The author claims that Jewish "bourgeois" and Soviet-sponsored scholarship still coexisted until the late twenties. Growing limitations and pressures in the sphere of Soviet nationalities policies after 1928 resulted in the disappearance of the former; and World War II and Stalin's liquidation of Jewish scholarship and institutions in the USSR brought Jewish culture to an end.

765. Halevy, Zvi. **Jewish Schools under Czarism and Communism: A Struggle for Cultural Identity.** Foreword by George Z. F. Bereday. New York: Springer Publishing Company, 1976. vi, 298p. $14.50.

This book deals only tangentially with wider questions of Jewish education in imperial Russia, while treating in detail the fate of the Soviet state-supported, Yiddish-language secular school system. There were virtually no non-Russian-language Jewish secular schools in Russia prior to 1917. The author attempts to explain the creation of the Yiddish school system in the 1920s, the reason for its subsequent elimination, and the way this was accomplished. The schools declined because of governmental policy.
SR, 38:2:322-23

Emigration

766. Shindler, Colin. **Exit Visa: Détente, Human Rights and the Jewish Emigration Movement in the USSR.** London: Bachman & Turner, 1978. 291p. £7.50.

This is a compact, carefully researched, accurate, and compelling history of the emergence from silence of Soviet Jews. Written by a veteran of the campaign for Soviet Jewish rights, the book traces the campaign's origins and its course through the suffering of its activists (often related in their words).
SJA, 9:1:72

History

767. Brym, Robert J. **The Jewish Intelligentsia and Russian Marxism: A Sociological Study of Intellectual Radicalism and Ideological Divergence.** New York: Schocken Books, 1978. viii, 157p. Figures. $16.95.
The central question this book addresses is: Why were members of the Russian Jewish intelligentsia in the late nineteenth and early twentieth centuries drawn to one or another of four distinct but related radical organizations – the Poalei Zion, the Bund, the Menshevik Party, and the Bolshevik Party? The choices made depended upon a variety of situational factors but, above all, the degree of "embeddedness" of each *intelligent* of East European Jewry, and also on the particular sociocultural characteristics of the population among whom each worked.
SR, 38:4:671-72

768. Frankel, Jonathan. **Prophecy and Politics: Socialism, Nationalism and the Russian Jews, 1867-1917.** Cambridge: Cambridge University Press, 1980. 650p. $49.50.
This book discusses the Jewish Socialist movements in Russia before 1917 and emphasizes the importance of the 1881 pogroms as a turning point in the history of modern Jewish politics. The book also traces the development of these movements and their ideologies among the émigrés in the United States and Palestine. Particular emphasis is placed on leading ideologists and how they reconciled their socialist internationalist convictions with Jewish interest and nationalism.

769. Kochan, Lionel, ed. **The Jews in Soviet Russia since 1917.** 3rd ed. London: Oxford University Press, Published for the Institute of Jewish Affairs, 1978. 440p. £2.95.
This is the third updated edition of a most significant collection of essays on various aspects of Soviet Jewry. All the essays in the volume point to one common fact – the anomalous position of Soviet Jews in the USSR.

Language and Literature

770. Bergelson, David. **When All Is Said and Done.** Translated and with an introduction by Bernard Martin. Athens: Ohio University Press, 1977. xxii, 310p. $13.50.
First published in 1913, Bergelson's story of an indecisive educated woman's quest for a place under the sun is a minor classic of modern Yiddish writing.
SR, 39:4:720-21

771. Howe, Irving, and Eliezer Greenberg, eds. **Ashes out of Hope: Fiction by Soviet-Yiddish Writers.** New York: Schocken Books, 1977. vi, 218p. $10.95.
This is the best small anthology of Soviet Yiddish prose in English translation. It contains three finely wrought novellas by David Bergelson, one by Der Nister, and a short novel by Moshe Kulbak.
SR, 39:4:720

772. Howe, Irving, and Eliezer Greenberg, eds. **A Treasury of Yiddish Poetry.** New York: Schocken Books, 1976. 378p. $5.95, paper.
This English anthology of modern Yiddish poetry includes a section on Yiddish poets in the Soviet Union. Seven poets are represented here, together with a brief introduction on Yiddish poetry in the USSR.

773. Lvov-Rogachevsky, V. **A History of Russian Jewish Literature.** Edited and translated by Arthur Levin. Essay by B. Gorev. Ann Arbor, MI: Ardis, 1979. 213p. Photographs. $14.00.

This is a stimulating potpourri of useful information on the Jews in Russia, hitherto available only in fairly inaccessible Russian periodicals. The volume consists of an essay on the treatment of the Jews in Russian literature, written by B. Gorev in 1917, followed by an extended essay on Jewish writers in the Russian language, published by V. Lvov-Rogachevsky in 1922. The work is smoothly translated by Arthur Levin, who provides useful, copious notes.

   SR, 39:4:719

Dissent Movement and Anti-Semitism

774. **Antisemitism in the Soviet Union: Its Roots and Consequences.** 2 vols. Jerusalem: Centre for Documentation and Research of East European Jewry, The Hebrew University. Vol. 1: 1979. 332p.; Vol. 2: 1980.

These two volumes contain the proceedings of two symposia on anti-Semitism in the USSR; one was held in Jerusalem in April 1978, the other in Paris in March 1979. The contributions indicate that contemporary Soviet anti-Semitism has its roots in pre-1917 Russia and is used by the regime today for various purposes. A list of anti-Semitic and anti-Israeli publications published in the USSR in the 1960s and 1970s supplements the discussions.

775. Grossman, Leonid. **Confession of a Jew.** Translated with an introduction and notes by Ranne Moab. New York: Arno Press, A New York Times Company, 1975. viii, 189p. $12.00.

Dostoyevsky devoted half of the March 1877 issue of his *Diary of a Writer* to "the Jewish Question," that is, the question of his own anti-Semitism, of which he was accused by a reader, Avraam Kovner. As a consequence, a correspondence developed between Kovner and Dostoyevsky, and later between Kovner and V. V. Rozanov (another anti-Semite). Grossman in this study examines Kovner's life and writings, which appeared first in Russian in Leningrad in 1924. This is the first English translation.

   SR, 35:4:753-54

776. Kuznetsov, Edward. **Prison Diaries.** Translated by Howard Spier, with an introduction by Leonard Schapiro. New York: Stein & Day, 1975. 254p. $8.95.

Kuznetsov's diaries add to the growing dissent literature emanating from the Soviet Union. This translation consists of prison stories and memoirs from the labor camps.

777. Rass, Rebecca. **From Moscow to Jerusalem: The Dramatic Story of the Jewish Liberation Movement and Its Impact on Israel.** New York: Shengold, 1976. 256p. $8.95.

Rass has chosen an attractive and informative style of presentation. She presents events in chronological order, which enables her to discuss the political background as well as the obstacles awaiting the would-be emigrant. The distinct, abrupt sentences draw the reader into a world in which one can live only armed by idealism.

   SJA, 7:2:75-79

778. Svirsky, Grigory. **Hostages: The Personal Testimony of a Soviet Jew.** Translated from the Russian by Gordon Clough. New York: Alfred A. Knopf, 1976. 305p.; London: Bodley Head, 1976. £4.95.

Svirsky has made a reputation as a novelist but cannot reconcile himself to the pernicious influence of anti-Semitism. The bitterness of rejection is shared by many Soviet Jews and flavors every chapter of *Hostages*. In squandering such patriotism and talent, Soviet society is losing much more than it seems to know.

     Guide, p. 144

779. Taylor, Telford, et al. **Courts of Terror: Soviet Criminal Justice and Jewish Emigration.** New York: Alfred A. Knopf, 1976. xi, 187p. $6.95.

The authors have concentrated on a limited aspect of the wide range of Soviet Jewry's problems – the use of judicial procedure as a means of repression against the Jewish emigration movement.

     SJA, 7:2:75-79

Others: Tatars, Germans

780. Fisher, Alan. **The Crimean Tatars.** Studies of Nationalities in the USSR, vol. 1. Stanford: Hoover Institution Press, Stanford University, 1978. xiv, 264p. Photographs. $14.95.

Fisher's work is the first in which a historian has approached the history of the Tatar nation as a whole, from the foundation of the Khanate in the fifteenth century to the present. The book is perfectly balanced between the three main periods of Tatar history: 1) the glorious era of the Crimean Khanate, 2) Crimea as a province of the tsarist empire (1783-1917), and 3) the Crimean Soviet Republic, the genocide of 1943, and the struggle for survival. Fisher's understanding of Tatar history is profound and original.

     SR, 38:2:329-30

781. Giesinger, Adam. **From Catherine to Khrushchev: The Story of Russia's Germans.** Battleford, Sask.: Marian Press, 1974. 443p. Maps.

The Russian Germans are an interesting case study in the history of provincial Russia since most of them had migrated to the Volga, the Black Sea region, Volhynia, and other parts of the Russian Empire. Russia's rulers considered them useful subjects. Eventually, almost all foreign colonizers were exposed to some form of Russification. The Russian Germans lived in scattered settlements, were mainly farmers, and rarely received more than a basic elementary education. Disruption of families, forced labor, loss of property, and the experience of total terror characterized the history of the Germans after 1917. This work is of great value for the student of migration history.

     SR, 35:4:733

Part III

EASTERN EUROPE
(Including the GDR and the Balkan Peninsula)

Chapter 10
EAST EUROPEAN COUNTRIES – GENERAL STUDIES

GENERAL REFERENCE WORKS

782. Dillon, Kenneth J. **Scholars' Guide to Washington, D.C. for Central and East European Studies: Albania, Austria, Bulgaria, Czechoslovakia, Germany (FRG and GDR), Greece, Hungary, Poland, Romania, Switzerland, Yoguslavia.** Woodrow Wilson International Center for Scholars. Washington, DC: Smithsonian Institution Press, 1980. 329p. $25.00.

This guide describes and evaluates research resources available to individuals with scholarly or practical needs. Individual entries describe the size, content, and organizational format of each collection's holdings, and evaluate their subject/country most distinctive materials. The volume concludes with a number of useful appendices and indexes.

783. Dimadis, K. A., ed. **Balkan Bibliography.** Vol. 5. Thessaloniki: Institute for Balkan Studies, 1979. xvi, 520p. Paper.

This continuous publication of the Institute for Balkan Studies, like the previous volumes, includes, in addition to works in the Greek language, publications in all major Western languages pertaining to Balkan studies. An extensive use of this bibliography, however, requires knowledge of the Greek language.

784. Horecky, Paul L., and David H. Kraus, eds. **East Central and Southeast Europe: A Handbook of Library and Archival Resources in North America.** Joint Committee on Eastern European Publication Series, no. 3. Santa Barbara, CA: ABC-Clio Press, 1976. xii, 466p. $35.75.

A total of 43 different institutions are included in this book, from the Library of Congress and major university libraries to such little-known collections as the Noli Library of Albanian and Eastern Orthodox Culture in South Boston. Singled out for separate treatment, where appropriate, are holdings relating to Albania, Bulgaria, Czechoslovakia, East Germany, Greece, Hungary, Judaica, Poland, Rumania, and Yugoslavia. The index is regrettably meager for a reference book. This should not be considered an end product; therefore, further efforts are needed to make all holdings in the United States and Canada known and more readily accessible to the research public if study of these areas is to receive the increased attention it deserves.

SR, 37:1:146-48

785. Nowak, Chester Michael, comp. **Czechoslovak-Polish Relations, 1918-1939: A Selected and Annotated Bibliography.** Hoover Institution Bibliographical Series, 55. Stanford: Hoover Institution Press, 1976. xii, 219p. $10.00.

This work contains 869 citations to bibliographies and published primary and secondary sources. Literature published up to 1972 is included; all items are annotated. Also included are items on particular areas such as Teshen, Spis, Orava, Eastern Galicia and Carpatho-Ruthenia (Ukraine). Use of the book is facilitated by cross-references and an author index.

786. Sanders, Irwin T., Roger Whitaker, and Walter C. Bisselle, comps. **East European Peasantries: Social Relations: An Annotated Bibliography of Periodical Articles.** Boston: G. K. Hall, 1976. vi, 179p. $12.00.

This volume is divided into eight parts with articles on each of the East European states, with the exception of Albania and East Germany but including Greece. Within each section, the articles and unpublished studies are arranged in alphabetical order according to the author's last name. Such bibliographical information as title, journal name, volume, date published, and page numbers are included. In non-English titles, the title is always translated. A large number of the articles and studies included in the volume are annotated with a brief summary. The strongest part of the volume deals with Poland and Yugoslavia.
    SR, 36:2:332-33

GEOGRAPHY

787. Kostanick, Huey Louis, ed. **Population and Migration Trends in Eastern Europe.** Boulder, CO: Westview Press, 1977. xiv, 247p. $17.50.

The articles in this collection derive from a conference held at the University of California, Los Angeles, in February 1976. They provide a reasonably thorough introduction to the study of migration in Eastern Europe. The authors are principally concerned with the unusually rapid industrialization and urbanization that have occurred since the "demographic watershed" of 1945. Conscious planning has automatically raised questions of optimum population distribution and the government policies required for its achievement.
    SR, 38:3:513-14

788. Mellor, Roy E. H. **Eastern Europe: A Geography of the Comecon Countries.** New York: Columbia University Press, 1975. x, 358p. Illus. Tables. $17.50.

This book is divided into three main parts—the first deals with physical environment and political geography, the second with the demographic and economic framework of the region, and the third with Comecon and the national economies. The subject of towns and villages is given limited treatment, and little space is devoted to the important topic of urbanization. Despite a few flaws, the book is well written.
    SR, 35:2:367-68

789. Pitcher, Donald Edgar. **An Historical Geography of the Ottoman Empire: From Earliest Times to the End of the Sixteenth Century.** Leiden: E. J. Brill, 1972. x, 171p. + 36 maps. Dfl. 275.00.

Pitcher's work consists of an introduction, 9 chapters, 36 maps, and an index of place names. The introduction is bibliographical, citing the 303 titles, maps, and atlases used as sources and references. Carefully grouped by time periods and regions, this introduction is a good and basic introductory bibliography for Ottoman studies. Each of the chapters is devoted to a specific period in Ottoman history and consists of a well-written brief description of major events and specific references to relevant maps.
    SR, 35:3:571-72

790. Turnock, David. **Eastern Europe: Studies in Industrial Geography.** Boulder, CO, and Folkestone, England: Westview Press and William Dawson & Sons, 1978. xii, 273p. Illus. $19.50.

This work treats all eight Communist states of Eastern Europe, excluding the USSR. The author has chosen to treat industrial geography separately in a historical context. The material is organized in a framework that is traditional in studies of economic geography.

Accompanying the text are 37 maps. The footnotes and bibliography are helpful, as is the index, which includes references to place names as well as subject topics. An extraordinarily broad and difficult topic has been treated comprehensively, yet in sufficient detail, to be useful to a wide range of readers.

HISTORY

791. Jelavich, Charles, and Barbara Jelavich. **The Establishment of the Balkan National States, 1804-1920.** A History of East Central Europe, vol. 8. Edited by Peter F. Sugar and Donald W. Treadgold. Seattle and London: University of Washington Press, 1977. xvi, 358p. Maps. $18.95.

The general theme of this volume is the emancipation of the Balkan nations from Ottoman rule and the involvement of the Great Powers in the process. Each nation receives its own chapter or chapters, but there are also chapters that surmount the narrow boundaries of one nation. Among the latter are: a survey of Balkan cultural development and an account of the Balkan nationalities in the Habsburg Empire.

    CSP, 20:3:443-44

792. Kann, Robert A. **A History of the Habsburg Empire, 1526-1918.** Berkeley: University of California Press, 1974. xiv, 646p. Maps. $25.00.

The author surveys in a style that is clear and succinct the development of both the Austro-German and the Hungarian parts of the monarchy from the Turkish and religious wars of the sixteenth and first half of the seventeenth centuries through the First World War. The non-German nationalities are generally dealt with in cursory fashion. The book, as a whole, is a useful addition to the literature in English on the Habsburg monarchy.

    SR, 35:1:157-58

793. Kann, Robert A., Béla K. Király, and Paula S. Fichtner, eds. **The Habsburg Empire in World War I: Essays on the Intellectual, Military, Political and Economic Aspects of the Habsburg War Effort.** East European Monographs, 23. Boulder, CO: *East European Quarterly*, 1977. xiv, 247p. $14.00. Distributed by Columbia University Press, New York.

This collection is unusual in that it treats the impact of war on the Habsburg Monarchy without presenting the topic as a prelude to the monarchy's inevitable disintegration. Rather than dwelling on the fatal weakness of a multinational empire in the twentieth century, the implicit emphasis in a number of essays is on the resilience of some of its structures. No doubt, the process by which the war fueled the "ethnic nationalisms of the Habsburg peoples" would be a crucial issue in the empire's wartime history. Nonetheless, the case studies raised in this book invite further research, and the book as a whole serves as a reminder of the triumph of particular nationalisms.

    SR, 37:2:329-30

794. Király, Béla K., and Gunther F. Rothenberg, eds. **War and Society in East Central Europe.** Vol. 1: *Special Topics and Generalizations on the 18th and 19th Centuries.* New York: Columbia University Press, 1979. 461p. $18.50.

This impressive collection of some 23 essays summarizes the impact of warfare in the relatively backward agrarian societies of Poland, Hungary, Serbia, Rumania, Cossack Ukraine, and the eastern Habsburg Empire. The book provides a unique appraisal of the lesser-known aspects of wars in the history of Eastern Europe. The essays are highly informative, and the book should be of interest primarily to the military historian.

795. Orton, Lawrence D. **The Prague Slav Congress of 1848.** East European Monographs, 46. Boulder, CO: *East European Quarterly*, 1978. vii, 185p. $13.50. Distributed by Columbia University Press, New York.

Orton stresses that when the Danubian Slavs organized a congress in Prague in the spring of 1848, they aimed to develop a common platform and policy to protect and enhance their national well-being, calling their meeting expressly a "Slav," not a "Pan-Slav" congress, "wanting to stress to their suspicious, indeed, hostile, neighbors that their enterprise was not Russian-imported or guided." The Bibliographical Essay and Selected Bibliography of this book are unique, providing an impressive amount of historical information.

    NP, 8:1:132

796. Polonsky, Antony. **The Little Dictators: The History of Eastern Europe since 1918.** London and Boston: Routledge & Kegan Paul, 1975. xii, 212p. Maps. Statistical appendix. $16.50.

The author introduces the reader to the many political, economic, social, demographic, ideological, and international problems that rocked the East European countries. He then outlines the extent to which some of these problems persist today, while others have been alternated or replaced by new ones. Particularly neat is his stitching together of domestic failures in interwar East Central Europe with the collapse of the French alliance system and the erosion of the democratic ideological model. The best single chapter is the one on Rumania.

    SR, 35:4:757

797. Sugar, Peter F. **Southeastern Europe under Ottoman Rule, 1354-1804.** A History of East Central Europe, vol. 5. Edited by Peter F. Sugar and Donald W. Treadgold. Seattle and London: University of Washington Press, 1977. xviii, 365p. Maps. $16.95.

Sugar's overall conclusion is that the empire's greatest strength was, at the same time, its greatest weakness. The early empire was founded on the twin pillars of loyalty to the sultan and belief in Islam. The author sees the mature empire as consisting of two sorts of regions — the core provinces in which the central government had or aspired to direct control — and tribute-paying vassal states, such as the Rumanian Principalities, Transylvania, and Dubrovnik. Dissolution of the empire came about as a result of the breakdown of two basic Ottoman institutions, the timar and the millet. When the center began to disintegrate, the mosaic nature of Orthodoxy began to assert itself, as it had done in medieval times. This book offers a unique interpretation of the entire Ottoman experience in the Balkans.

    SR, 37:2:332-34

798. Winters, Stanley B., and Joseph Held, eds. **Intellectual and Social Developments in the Habsburg Empire from Maria Theresa to World War I: Essays Dedicated to Robert A. Kann.** East European Monographs, 11. Boulder, CO: *East European Quarterly*, 1975. x, 304p. $14.00. Distributed by Columbia Press, New York.

These 10 chapters, by 10 American and Austrian scholars, were a tribute to the distinguished American and Austrian historian, Professor Robert A. Kann, for his seventieth birthday in 1976. Their wide range, from social to diplomatic history, over the last 200 years, reflects the range of interest of this fruitful and versatile historian. Several contributions deal with Hungarians, Czechs, Serbs, Croats, and Rumanians.

    SR, 37:2:328-29

GOVERNMENT AND POLITICS

799. King, Robert R., and James F. Brown, eds. **Eastern Europe's Uncertain Future: A Selection of Radio Free Europe Research Reports.** New York and London: Praeger Publishers, 1977. xxii, 360p. Tables. $25.00.
This volume is a collection of revised Radio Free Europe background reports written originally for the RFE research series in 1976 and 1977. The compilation consists of five parts: external influences; foreign economic relations; domestic economies; political and social developments; and church and state relations. Introductions to the respective parts by the editors are supposed to integrate the chapters into larger themes. The volume provides a mosaic of the problems facing both Eastern Europe as a whole and the individual states in the region.
   SR, 38:3:509-510

800. Seton-Watson, Hugh. **The "Sick Heart" of Modern Europe: The Problem of the Danubian Lands.** Seattle and London: University of Washington Press, 1975. xii, 76p. $4.95.
The Danubian lands have been the sick heart of twentieth-century Europe. This Seton-Watson's fundamental point depends on his threefold analysis that World War I grew out of the "clash of conflicting nationalisms in Central Europe," that World War II grew out of "the national and social conflicts in the Danube lands," and that the current situation in Eastern Europe is one of "national humiliation" for eighty million Europeans.
   SR, 35:3:548

801. Volgyes, Ivan, ed. **The Peasantry of Eastern Europe.** Vol. 1: *Roots of Rural Transformation.* Comparative Rural Transformation Series. New York: Pergamon Press, 1979. xii, 192p. $18.50.
All nine essays in this volume are based on extensive investigation of archival or published sources, and all, with perhaps one or two exceptions, make valuable contributions to their respective subjects. The main theme of the volume might be called "peasants and politics," for agrarian problems were an object of constant concern to governments and parties, as at least six articles make evident. Essays discuss agrarian problems in Bulgaria, Yugoslavia, Poland, Hungary, and Czechoslovakia.
   SR, 39:3:514-15

FOREIGN RELATIONS

802. Barker, Elisabeth. **British Policy in South-East Europe in the Second World War.** New York: Barnes & Noble, Harper & Row. London and Basingstoke: Macmillan, 1976. viii, 320p. Maps. $27.50.
Barker, an accomplished journalist-historian, has produced the best short account to date of the British wartime role in southeast Europe as a whole. Part 1 deals with the war from its outbreak to the Balkan military campaign of 1941. Part 2 covers the longer period that ensued but, except in broad terms of British-Soviet rivalry until the end of the war, stops with the region's liberation by the end of 1944. The author's basic thesis is that British effort in southeast Europe is "a story of last-minute improvisations and the undertaking of commitments without the resources to fulfill them." The thesis is indisputable, supported by new documentation, and even-handedly elaborated.
   SR, 36:3:706-707

803.   Boia, Lucian. **Relationships between Romanians, Czechs and Slovaks (1848-1914).**
        Biblioteca Historica Romanie Studies, no. 54. Bucharest: Editura Academieei
        Republicii Socialiste România, 1977. 157p. Lei 7.50.
Boia has written an overview of the primarily political relations among Rumanians,
Czechs, and Slovaks during the latter phase of their campaign for autonomy within the
Habsburg Empire. The work is reflective of its sponsorship — Rumanians are given center
stage, and the vantage point is Translyvania rather than the Regat. Of the non-Rumanians,
the Slovaks receive the bulk of the author's attention. In the early Dualist era, Rumanians
and Slovaks made sporadic attempts to establish a united front against Magyar oppression,
but only the Rumanians were able to retain parliamentary representation, and then only
ineffectively. The absence of a bibliography is partially recompensed by ample footnotes
and a useful name index.
        SR, 39:2:339-40

804.   Calder, Kenneth J. **Britain and the Origins of the New Europe, 1914-1918.**
        International Studies Series. Cambridge: Cambridge University Press, 1976. x,
        268p. $19.95.
This study deals with east-central Europe as it was reconstructed after the dissolution of the
Habsburg Monarchy and the demise of the Romanov empire. Calder's book centers on the
collaborative relations that evolved in the context of World War I between the British
government and émigré organizations claiming to represent the national aspirations of the
Poles, Czechs, Slovaks, and South Slavs. This account draws primarily on the official
records of government departments in London and on the private papers of British
officials. The book is most useful where it illustrates the operation of the bureaucracy in its
exploitation of the subject nationalities, that is, in fighting the war.
        SR, 36:2:327-28

805.   Hovi, Kalervo. **Cordon Sanitaire or Barrière de l'Est?: The Emergence of the New
        French Eastern European Alliance Policy 1917-1919.** Turun Yliopiston Julkaisuja,
        Annales Universitatis Turkuensis, series B, vol. 135. Turky, Finland: Turun
        Yliopisto, 1975. 244p. Paper.
One of the outstanding merits of this minograph is its utilization of many previously
unavailable archival documents. The material from the French archives is especially
significant because it only recently was made accessible to researchers. Hovi refers to the
origins of these two concepts, analyzes their meanings, and discusses their use in several
works in various periods. The work will be of significant value to historians of the period in
their attempts to understand this complicated subject.
        SR, 36:4:697-98

806.   Lundestad, Geir. **The American Non-Policy towards Eastern Europe 1943-1947:
        Universalism in an Area not of Essential Interest to the United States.** Oslo:
        Universitetsforlaget, 1978. 654p. $18.00, paper. Distributed by Columbia University
        Press, New York.
Lundestad's study, deliberately limited to U.S. policy in Eastern Europe and not wandering
all over the East-West scene, is well organized and, above all, thorough. The material
comes mainly from the U.S. National Archives and from a large number of manuscript
collections, interviews, and oral history material, as well as from the voluminous amount
of published material. The views from the field are presented clearly — including the
activism of Arthur Bliss in Poland and of Maynard Barnes in Bulgaria and their impatience
with the State Department's immobility, caution, and appeasement — but what lies behind

the gray anonymity of "the Department" is a bit harder to fathom. The work offers the sober exposition of the views and actions of official Washington.
    SR, 38:4:696-97

807.   Remington, Robin Alison, ed. **The International Relations of Eastern Europe.** Detroit: Gale Research Co., 1979. xvi, 273p. $22.00.
The first part of this annotated bibliography covers titles that relate to Communist Eastern Europe as a whole, and the second part identifies and describes sources and books relating to Albania, Bulgaria, Czechoslovakia, GDR, Hungary, Poland, Rumania, and Yugoslavia.
    NP, 8:1:133

COMMUNISM

808.   Bahro, Rudolf. **The Alternative in Eastern Europe.** Translated by David Fernbach. London: NLB, 1979 [1977, under the title *Die Alternative*]. $19.50. Distributed by Schocken Books, New York.
As a Marxist militant, Bahro proposes for Eastern Europe some kind of a cultural revolution that will shake the foundations of bureaucratic rule. He advocates liquidation of bureaucratic corruption at high levels of administration, abolition of piecework and work norms, planned periodic participation of the entire managerial and intellectual staff of society in simple operative labor, and a systematic revision of wage scales in order to abolish the present inequalities and injustices. Bahro takes the position—very appealing to many Western leftists—that Communism is not only necessary but also possible.
    SR, 39:4:700-702

809.   Fischer-Galati, Stephen, ed. **The Communist Parties of Eastern Europe.** New York: Columbia University Press, 1979. viii, 393p. $20.00.
This is a solid collection of eight "case study" essays. The research in these articles takes the stories of the East European Communist parties up to 1976-1977. The following countries are covered: Poland, Albania, Bulgaria, Rumania, Czechoslovakia, and Yugoslavia.
    SR, 39:4:699-700

810.   McCauley, Martin. **Communist Power in Europe 1944-1949.** New York: Barnes & Noble, Harper & Row, 1977. xxvi, 242p. $21.50.
This book is a collection of thirteen papers presented at the University of London between 1974 and 1976. Five essays deal with the mechanics of Communist Party take-overs in Soviet-occupied Europe, four examine Communist parties that failed to come to power despite substantial support, one deals with the Baltic States, and three are general surveys of Eastern Europe during and after the war. The book has a coherent theme. Some of the papers are very good, and only a few are extremely poor.
    SR, 39:2:329-30

811.   Rakowska-Harmstone, Teresa, and Andrew Gyorgy, eds. **Communism in Eastern Europe.** Bloomington and London: Indiana University Press, 1979. x, 338p. $17.50.
This symposium of 12 essays stresses the importance of two conflicting forces shaping political life in postwar Eastern Europe: 1) the diverse historical, political, economic, and cultural traditions of East European people and 2) the determination of the Soviet Union to integrate them and subject them to Moscow's control. The volume is primarily concerned with the 1964-1979 post-Khrushchev period and with projections for the 1980s.
    NP, 9:1:158-59

ECONOMICS

812. Bryson, Phillip J. **Scarcity and Control in Socialism: Essays on East European Planning.** Lexington, MA: Lexington Books, D. C. Heath, 1976. xiv, 202p. Figures. Tables. $16.50.

This is a slender volume best described as a cross between a textbook and a scholarly monograph. It is organized topically like a text, each section dealing with a different aspect of planning and control. Themes discussed are: decentralization, information theory, pricing, investment criteria, and CMEA decentralization. Like a monograph, the embellishments introduced in each chapter are intended as serious contributions to the pertinent literature.

    SR, 35:4:759

813. Granick, David. **Enterprise Guidance in Eastern Europe: A Comparison of Four Socialist Economies.** Princeton, NJ: Princeton University Press, 1975. xvi, 505p. $27.50.

This is an intriguing study of contemporary industrial management in Rumania, East Germany, Hungary, and Yugoslavia. The importance of the book rests in its descriptive-empirical content as well as in its presentation of clearly stated judgments. Management of industry, defined by Granick to include all levels of the national managing apparatus, is analyzed in terms of managerial theory. This book is mandatory reading for all who enjoy the penetrating persuasion of someone with clear vision.

    SR, 37:3:515-17

814. Höhmann, Hans-Hermann, et al., eds. **The New Economic Systems of Eastern Europe.** Berkeley and Los Angeles: University of California Press, 1975. xxiv, 585p. $22.50.

This is a very useful and handy reference, for it covers the broad features of contemporary industrial and agricultural systems in all East European nations, including Albania and Yugoslavia, and it contains much information, particularly on laws, decrees, and regulations, that is not readily available elsewhere. The book, the fruit of English-German cooperation, updates Morris Bornstein's (ed.) *Plan and Market: Economic Reforms in Eastern Europe* (1973).

    SR, 35:3:546-48

815. Mieczkowski, Bogdan. **Personal and Social Consumption in Eastern Europe: Poland, Czechoslovakia, Hungary, and East Germany.** New York: Praeger Publishers, 1975. xxiv, 342p. Tables. $21.50.

This study consists of three parts. The first part is a discussion of the theory and the political economy of consumption in Marxist thought and in socialist East Europe. Part 2 consists of studies of consumption in each of the four countries; comparisons among these and conclusions make up part 3. The serious student of consumption and/or East Europe, if sophisticated and patient, will find much here that is interesting and illuminating.

    SR, 35:3:549

816. Mieczkowski, Bogdan. **Transportation in Eastern Europe: Empirical Findings.** East European Monographs, 38. Boulder, CO: *East European Quarterly*, 1978. xvi, 221p. Tables. Figures. $14.50. Distributed by Columbia University Press, New York.

This volume represents the first study in English to provide a comprehensive view of transport in East European countries covering the period between 1945 and 1975. It is based on statistical materials not easily obtainable in the West. Among the modes of transport covered are railroad, road, water, pipelines, and air. It is both a systematic evaluation of the transport system in Eastern Europe as a whole and a detailed study of transport of each individual country. The aspects covered here are: geographic and economic determinants; national planning of transportation; growth of transportation since World War II; the cost of transport and its international implications.

NP, 7:2:230-31

LANGUAGE AND LITERATURE

817. de Bray, R. G. A. **Guide to the South Slavonic Languages.** 3rd ed. revised and expanded. Columbus, OH: Slavica Publishers, 1980. Part 1: 399p. $24.95; Part 2: 483p. $27.95; Part 3: 254p. $22.95.

This book has been a standard reference work since the publication of the first edition 30 years ago.

CSP, 23:2:230-31

NATIONAL MINORITIES

818. Dawidowicz, Lucy S. **The War against the Jews, 1933-1945.** New York: Holt, Rinehart & Winston, 1975. xviii, 460p. $15.00.

In addition to discussing Nazi extermination of Jews, the author analyzes prevailing forms of anti-Semitism in East European countries. Her stirring, yet at the same time impeccably scholarly, account should be read by all interested in recent history of Central and Eastern Europe.

SR, 34:4:821-23

819. Sugar, Peter F., ed. **Ethnic Diversity and Conflict in Eastern Europe.** Santa Barbara, CA: ABC-Clio Press, 1980. xii, 400p. Tables. $20.75.

Ten contributors describe the influence of ethnicity on the development of Eastern Europe, strongly underscoring the importance of Eastern Europe in the sociological investigation of ethnicity. This volume documents the role of language and the influence of government, religion, and economic factors on class structures, ethnic minorities, and nationality.

820. Vago, Bela. **The Shadow of the Swastika: The Rise of Fascism and Anti-Semitism in the Danube Basin, 1936-1939.** Published for the Institute of Jewish Affairs, London. Westmead, Farnborough, Hants, England: Saxon House, D. C. Heath, 1975. vii, 431p. $18.95.

Vago has used British Foreign Office material either directly or closely relevant to the precarious position of Jews in Rumania, Czechoslovakia, and Hungary, within the general framework of domestic political developments, from 1936 until August 1939. Until now, German material has provided the main external evidence on prewar political developments in this area. Of the documents, 164 are printed in part or in full. The work is necessarily intended for specialists.

SR, 35:2:374

DISSENT MOVEMENT

821. Tökés, Rudolf L., ed. **Opposition in Eastern Europe.** Baltimore and London: The Johns Hopkins University Press, 1979. xiv, 306p. $22.50.
The aim of this volume is to present, on the one hand, the chronological development of regime-opposition in Czechoslovakia, Poland, the G.D.R., and Hungary since 1968, while, on the other hand, locating this development within a political sociology of the working class, the intelligentsia, and the peasantry. The individual nation studies by Kusin, Rupnik, Volkmer, and Schöpflin are excellent accounts in their own right.
SEER, 59:1:136-38

THE SOCIETY, SOCIOLOGY

822. Byrnes, Robert F., ed. **Communal Families in the Balkans: The Zadruga Essays by Philip E. Mosely and Essays in His Honor.** Introduction by Margaret Mead. Notre Dame, IN, and London: University of Notre Dame Press, 1976. xxxii, 285p. $14.95.
This volume is a fitting tribute to Philip Mosely. It represents a genuine contribution to knowledge in an area that deeply interested Mosely at an early stage in his career—the changing socioeconomic structure of the peasant household, the extended family commune, or *zadruga*, in southeastern Europe. Mosely's conclusion that the *zadruga* was most viable in a pioneer setting where new lands were to be cleared was not entirely borne out by subsequent studies.
SR, 35:4:762-63

823. Faber, Bernard Lewis, ed. **The Social Structure of Eastern Europe: Transition and Process in Czechoslovakia, Hungary, Poland, Romania, and Yugoslavia.** New York: Praeger Publishers, 1976. xvi, 419p. $25.00.
Faber has produced a solid and useful volume on the sociology of Eastern Europe, which quite properly relies heavily on contributions from East European sociologists. It includes also contributions on the family, urban life, and factory organization. This book is of interest to political scientists, sociologists, and area specialists.
SR, 36:3:514-15

824. Obrebski, Joseph. **The Changing Peasantry of Eastern Europe.** Edited by Barbara and Joel Halpern. Cambridge, MA: Schenkman Publishing Co., 1976. 102p. Illus. $11.25, paper.
It is fortunate that at least some of the writings of the Polish ethnographer and sociologist Joseph Obrebski (1905-1967) have now been reprinted. Obrebski's field research included studies on peasant agriculture in Dobrudzha, Bulgaria, European Turkey, Macedonia and Serbia; on peasant communities in a part of interwar central-eastern Poland (the region of Polesie), as well as on the changing socio-cultural scene in Jamaica after 1945. Thirty excellent photographs portraying peasant life and village surroundings in Polesie constitute sociological evidence *sui generis*, each one being almost a document in itself.
SEER, 55:4:555-56

825. Sanders, Irwin Taylor, et al., comps. **East European Peasantries: Social Relations: An Annotated Bibliography of Periodical Literature.** Boston: G. K. Hall, 1976. vi, 179p. $12.00.
See entry 786 for annotation.

826. Volgyes, Ivan, ed. **Political Socialization in Eastern Europe: A Comparative Framework**. New York: Praeger Publishers, 1975. xvi, 201p. $16.50.
This symposium presents generally sound and informative descriptions of the formal and informal structures, or agencies, of socialization in five East European states. The editor has provided a consistent framework within which data from individual countries are treated, as well as an overall conceptual framework, which is a survey of the roles and nature of socialization agencies in socialist countries.
   SR, 35:2:366

THE ARTS AND CULTURE

827. Bialostocki, Jan. **The Art of the Renaissance in Eastern Europe: Hungary, Bohemia, Poland**. The Wrightsman Lectures, vol. 8. Ithaca, NY: Cornell University Press, 1976. xxvi, 312p. Illus. $25.00.
This book introduces to the English-speaking reader material that until now has been inaccessible because of the language barrier. The exhaustive bibliography indicates that Polish, Hungarian, Czech, and Slovak researchers are interested in the art of the Renaissance, but their publications are generally found only in their respective languages. The 351 illustrations and 20 drawings are an excellent and inseparable counterpart to the text.
   SR, 38:1:162-63

828. Liehm, Mira, and Antonin J. Liehm. **The Most Important Art: East European Film after 1945**. Berkeley: University of California Press, 1977. viii, 467p. Illus. $23.50.
This book is a good reference work to East European films. An appendix on Socialist Realism and a short but useful bibliography follow the text.
   SR, 38:2:360-61

829. Skendi, Stavro. **Balkan Cultural Studies**. East European Monographs, 72. Boulder, CO: *East European Quarterly*, 1980. x, 278p. $20.00. Distributed by Columbia University Press, New York.
The first of 4 sections of this study is comprised of 4 essays on the Balkan languages, while the 5 essays of the second section deal with the Balkan epic. The third section is devoted to Balkan history, and the final section consists of brief biographies of Philip E. Mosely and Alois Schmans, both friends and close associates of Skendi. This very informative volume concludes with a short selected bibliography. The 17 chapters which comprise this book have all been published earlier in various journals and edited books, and their availability in one physical volume is a welcome contribution to Balkan studies.

GENERAL STUDIES

830. **Balkanistica: Occasional Papers in Southeast European Studies**, vol. 2, 1975. Edited by Kenneth E. Naylor and Craig N. Packard. Published for the American Association for Southeast European Studies. Cambridge, MA: Slavica Publishers, 1976. iv, 153p. $6.95, paper.
Four of five parts of this book consist of essays on minority politics; the Albanians in Yugoslavia; education of the Albanian minority in the Socialist Republic of Macedonia; the image of the Turk in Mazuranić's Smrt Smail-Age Čengića; voices from the mountain: the image of the Ottoman-Turk in Bulgarian literature; Turkish loanwords as an element of Ivo Andric's literary style in *Na Drini Ćuprija*; Macedonian language and nationalism during the nineteenth and early twentieth centuries; "Young Bosnia' in the light of a generation-conflict interpretation of student movements; local sociopolitical organizations and public policy decision-making in Yugoslavia. Part 5 contains the constitution and bylaws of the AASES.

Chapter 11
INDIVIDUAL COUNTRIES

ALBANIA

831. Kondis, Basil. **Greece and Albania, 1908-1914.** Tsessaloniki: Institute for Balkan Studies, 1976. 151p.

Kondis argues that Greece favored the creation of an autonomous Albania. After 1908, the chaotic conditions in the Ottoman Empire and the threat of Bulgarian and Serbian expansion made the Albanians and Greeks natural allies. For the period 1908 to 1912, Kondis' well-documented and moderately pro-Greek presentation of Albanian-Greek relations is unquestionably the best study on this subject in any language.

SR, 38:1:151-52

832. Logoreci, Anton. **The Albanians: Europe's Forgotten Survivors.** Boulder, CO: Westview Press, 1978. 230p. + 8pp. plates. $16.00.

Approximately one-third of this work consists of an overview of Albanian history from the fourteenth-century Ottoman invasions to the end of World War II. This account provides a reliable survey of Albanian history prior to the establishment of the present regime. The major portion of the book is devoted to a discussion and analysis of political, diplomatic, economic, social, and cultural developments from 1945 to the early 1970s. The author has produced a lucid and balanced introduction to contemporary Albania that will be especially useful to students and nonspecialists.

CSP, 23:1:107

833. Marmullaku, Ramadan. **Albania and the Albanians.** Translated from Serbo-Croation by Margot and Boško Milosavjević. Hamden, CT: Archon Books, 1975. x, 178p. $12.50.

The author, a Yugoslav Albanian from Kosovo, is a senior adviser on Balkan Affairs in the Commission on International Relations of the Presidency of the Yugoslav League of Communists. The author's perspective is that of an orthodox Party intellectual. He takes for granted the socialist developmental aspirations of the Albanian leadership and basically approves of their techniques for "building socialism" in Albania. This brief but cogent historical survey of Albania's past is not seriously encumbered by Marxist perspective, except at a superficial level. The special section on the Albanians of Kosovo also contains some valuable critical insights.

CSP, 18:3:350-52

834. Prifti, Peter R. **Socialist Albania since 1944: Domestic and Foreign Developments.** Studies in Communism, Revisionism, and Revolution, 23. Cambridge, MA: The MIT Press, 1978. 311p. $25.00.

Prifti bases his information mostly on Albanian sources and offers the most up-to-date reference work on the development in that country. The author also provides information on Albanians in Yugoslavia.

BULGARIA

835. Anastasoff, Christ. **The Bulgarians: From Their Arrival in the Balkans to Modern Times. Thirteen Centuries of History.** Hickesville, NY: Exposition Press, 1977. 380p. $20.00.

This is a popular history of the Bulgarians from the ancient time to 1944, with special emphasis on the Bulgarian Renaissance of the eighteenth century and the emergence of modern Bulgaria and the fate of its people. Included are an appendix with 11 documents, chronology of the history of Bulgaria, an extensive bibliography, and an index. Several maps and photos enhance the usefulness of this book, which is aimed at students and general readers.

836. Bell, John D. **Peasants in Power: Alexander Stamboliski and the Bulgarian Agrarian National Union, 1899-1923.** Princeton, NJ: Princeton University Press, 1977. xiv, 271p. $16.50.

Bell has carefully combed most of the available sources in Western languages, Bulgarian, and Russian, and the result is a comprehensive scholarly analysis of the great experiment, that is, the first peasant government in Europe. He pays special attention to agrarian ideology and its implementation when the agrarian government was in power — from 1919 to 1923, and he provides a valuable counterbalance to the only other extensive account in English, a rather negative one, appearing in Joseph Rotschild's *The Communist Party of Bulgaria.* This is now the definitive account of the Stamboliski era in English.

SR, 37:1:161-62

837. Butler, Thomas, ed. **Bulgaria Past and Present: Studies in History, Literature, Economics, Music, Sociology, Folklore and Linguistics.** Proceedings of the First International Conference on Bulgarian Studies Held at the University of Wisconsin, Madison — May 3-5, 1973. Columbus, OH: American Association for the Advancement of Slavic Studies, 1976. xiv, 397p. $7.00, paper.

The collection comprises 37 contributions organized into 5 subjects.

838. Devedjiev, Hristo H. **Stalinization of the Bulgarian Society, 1949-1953.** Philadelphia: Dorrance, 1975. 216p. $7.95.

This is a personal account by a knowledgeable émigré who had lived in Bulgaria until his defection in the 1960s. His account shows that during the Stalinist period, the Bulgarian police was the most odious in the Balkans. Indeed, the purges in Bulgaria were by their scope and sheer wickedness the most revolting anywhere in Soviet Eastern Europe, with the possible exception of Czechoslovakia.

SEER, 55:2:268-70

839. Miller, Marshall Lee. **Bulgaria during the Second World War.** Stanford: Stanford University Press, 1975. xiv, 290p. $10.95.

The author investigates the political history of Bulgaria during its involvement in the Second World War, skillfully interweaving threads of domestic and foreign politics. He pays relatively little attention to the purely military history. He reveals that Nazi Germany exercised little control over the policies of its satellite, and the rather humane treatment of the Bulgarian Jews provides a good illustration of this point. This is a very worthwhile contribution to American scholarship on Bulgaria.

SR, 35:3:565-66

840. Moser, Charles A. **Dimitrov of Bulgaria: A Political Biography of Dr. Georgi M. Dimitrov.** Thornwood, NY: Caroline House Publishers, 1979. xxii, 360p. $14.95.

Dimitrov, heir to Alexander Stamboliski's mantle of leadership of the Bulgarian Agrarian Party, was one of the country's most important twentieth-century political figures. The strength of this volume is the clear presentation of Dimitrov's analysis of the Bulgarian events that he witnessed and in which he participated. Moser also includes an important final chapter presenting Dimitrov's agrarian ideology—an elucidation of Stambolinski's.

SR, 40:3:497-98

CZECHOSLOVAKIA

General Reference Works

841. Hejzlar, Zdeněk and Vladimir V. Kusin. **Czechoslovakia 1968-1969: Chronology, Bibliography, Annotation.** New York and London: Garland Publishing, 1975. 316p. $28.00.

The authors have performed an important service by putting order into this increasingly unwieldy body of source material. Their contribution is a useful reference for students of Eastern Europe, and an invaluable timesaver for historians, sociologists, and political scientists attempting to use the Czechoslovak case for purposes of comparative analysis. In addition to chronology of events, there is a worldwide bibliography of books published from 1968 to 1974.

SR, 35:1:156-57

842. Zeman, Jarold K. **The Hussite Movement and the Reformation in Bohemia, Moravia and Slovakia (1350-1650): A Bibliographical Study Guide (with Particular Reference to Resources in North America).** Reformation in Central Europe, no. 1. Published under the auspices of the Center for Reformation Research by Michigan Slavic Publications. Ann Arbor, MI: 1977. xxxvi, 389p. $14.00.

The material covered in this study includes manuscripts, microfilms of manuscripts, rare books (before 1700), unpublished theses, editions of sources, and literature, with special attention to periodical articles. The data were collected between 1972 and 1977. There are about 3,853 entries in 14 languages, arranged with several thousand cross-references in four major parts: Historical Development (1350-1650); Biographical Studies; Topical Studies; Study Aids. Intended for students and scholars at all levels and of varying interests, the guide is also envisaged as a useful work of reference for librarians.

SEER, 58:3:469-70

843. Zeman, Zbyněk. **The Masaryks: The Making of Czechoslovakia.** New York: Barnes & Noble, Harper & Row, 1976. 230p. $16.50.

This is a dual biography of Thomas G. Masaryk and of his son Jan Masaryk. The book is aimed at a popular market and offers the layperson interesting reading on historic personages and events.

SR, 36:2:337-38

Government and Politics

844. Kaplan, Frank L. **Winter into Spring: The Czechoslovak Press and the Reform Movement 1963-1968.** East European Monographs, 29. Boulder, CO: *East European Quarterly*, 1977. viii, 208p. $14.00. Distributed by Columbia University Press, New York.

Kaplan has gathered solid evidence in support of the fact that Czechoslovakia's communication media, especially the press and cultural periodicals, played a major role in the liberalization process that culminated in the "Czechoslovak Spring" of 1968. Appended to the volume are several tables of statistical data about Czechoslovak newspapers and other periodicals from 1948 to 1970 and a select bibliography of books and articles.

SR, 38:1:140-41

845. Kusin, Vladimir V. **From Dubček to Charter 77: A Study of 'Normalization' in Czechoslovakia, 1968-1978.** Edinburgh, England: Q Press, 1978. x, 353p. £8.50.
Kusin distinguishes four stages in the process of normalization: the first, covering the aftermath of the invasion until April 1969 when Dubček ceded the Party leadership to Husák; the second, lasting until May 1971 when the new Party Secretary believed that he had consolidated his rule; the third, which investigates the political equilibrium of normalization; and the final one, from the end of 1976, which deals with the issue of human rights. This study is written in a fresh and lively language; the author makes an intelligent use of otherwise colorless Communist Party statements by emphasizing their most ambivalent sentences.

SEER, 58:3:467-68

846. Loebl, Eugen. **My Mind on Trial.** New York and London: Harcourt Brace Jovanovich, 1976. xiv, 235p. $8.95.
This book is a great contribution as primary source material for anyone who wishes to understand the mechanics of thought control in the judicial systems of Communist regimes in Eastern Europe. Some new light is thrown on the tortuous psychology of the decent believer who becomes a pitiful victim of the faith to which he was prepared to sacrifice his life and the lives of others. This is the story of Eugen Loebl, the former deputy minister of foreign trade in Communist Czechoslovakia in 1949. In 1952, during the spectacular Slansky trial, he was sentenced to life imprisonment. Loebl's rehabilitation only came at Dubček's hands in 1963. After the latter's downfall, Loebl chose exile in the West. The book provides firsthand evidence of the detailed way in which the Kremlin exercised its mastery over its satellites.

SR, 37:2:323-25

847. Mlynář, Zdeněk. **Night Frost in Prague. The End of Humane Socialism.** London: C. Hurst & Co., 1980. 300p. £9.50.
The author's detailed and vivid eye-witness account of what happened at the meeting of the Czechoslovak party presidium on the night of the Warsaw Pact invasion of Czechoslovakia in August 1968, and the negotiations (if they can be called that) between the Czechoslovak leaders and their counterparts in Moscow a few days later, should attract a wide readership to these political memoirs. The author is extremely well qualified to speak on all these issues, and the book recounts his political experiences as a member of the Czechoslovak Communist establishment.

SS, 33:4:619-22

848. Paul, David W. **The Cultural Limits of Revolutionary Politics: Change and Continuity in Socialist Czechoslovakia.** East European Monographs, 48. Boulder, CO: *East European Quarterly*, 1979. x, 361p. $18.50. Distributed by Columbia University Press, New York.
The concept of political culture is the author's key. Drawn to its utility as the most promising link between micro and macro objects, it represents roughly the modal pattern of orientation toward specified political objects. Marshaling evidence, ranging from survey

research data to history, the author presents a complex case, which revolves around the view that the achievements of the Communist revolution have "been severely limited by the resistance of factors that are firmly embedded in the political culture." This commendable study should be consulted by all concerned with the future of Czechoslovakia.

SR, 39:2:338-39

849. Pravda, Alex. **Reform and Change in the Czechoslovak Political System: January-August 1968.** Beverly Hills, CA, and London: Sage Publishers, 1975. 96p. $3.00.
This monograph on the interaction of reform and change in Czechoslovakia in 1968 is concise and useful. Pravda does pinpoint the gap between theory and reality, and has summarized the core of the experiment in reform, placed it within a theoretical framework, and dealt with some of the toughest problems involved in moving from a closed authoritarian system toward democratic socialism.

SR, 35:3:562

850. Riese, Hans-Peter, ed. **Since the Prague Spring: Charter '77 and the Struggle for Human Rights in Czechoslovakia.** New York: Vintage Press, 1978. xiv, 208p. $10.00.
This collection of primary documents by dissidents in Czechoslovakia offers a wide-ranging selection, including political criticism, letters in behalf of political prisoners, demands for cultural autonomy, condemnation of Soviet domination, and the first 10 statements of Charter '77. With its informative background notes by Arthur Miller and useful set of biographical data, the volume should be of major interest to students of Communist affairs.

NP, 8:1:131

851. Ulč, Otto. **Politics in Czechoslovakia.** Foreword by Jan F. Triska. San Francisco: W. H. Freeman, 1974. xiv, 181p. $9.00.
This is a refreshing survey of Communist politics in Czechoslovakia since 1948, drawing upon a wide assortment of primary sources. The discussion is organized around political topics such as policy making, participation, recruitment, and political socialization. It is a valuable addition to the literature on contemporary Eastern Europe.

SR, 35:1:155-56

852. Valenta, Jiri. **Soviet Intervention in Czechoslovakia 1968: Anatomy of a Decision.** Baltimore: The Johns Hopkins University Press, 1979. xii, 208p. $12.00.
See entry 209 for annotation.

Communism, Communist Party

853. Hrubý, Peter. **Fools and Heroes: The Changing Role of Communist Intellectuals in Czechoslovakia.** Oxford, New York, Toronto: Pergamon Press, 1980. xx, 265p. $30.00.
Scores of disappointed Czechoslovak Communist intellectuals now wander throughout the Western world calling themselves reformed Communists or democratic socialists. Generally, they are accepted as innocent victims of Soviet aggression, but many of them had enthusiastically helped to impose the Soviet regime on their homeland during and after the 1948 coup. The author depicts the gradual transformation of the political and moral principles of a group of well-known Czechoslovak Communist intellectuals who in 1948 cast themselves in the role of saviours of the nation and its proletariat.

CSP, 23:3:359-60

854. Suda, Zdenek L. **Zealots and Rebels: A History of the Communist Party of Czechoslovakia.** Stanford: Hoover Institution Press, 1980. xi, 275p. $8.95, paper. Among the Communist parties that have had the opportunity to implement their own programs, the Communist Party of Czechoslovakia occupies a very important place. Its experiences and that of the Czechoslovakian population over the last 30 years are of special significance because of several unique circumstances, the geopolitical location of the country, and Czechoslovakia's traditionally Western political culture. This volume, in many regards, is a pioneering study of the Communist regime in a unique setting and time.

History

855. Beld, Antonie van den. **Humanity: The Political and Social Philosophy of Thomas G. Masaryk.** Issues in Contemporary Politics, Historical and Theological Perspectives, 1. The Hague and Paris: Mouton, 1975. x, 162p. Dfl. 25.00.
This study examines Masaryk's thought, taking as its starting point the concept of *humanita*, the fundamental norm of morality in Masaryk's system. The author concludes that Masaryk upheld two mutually incompatible views on the relationship between human nature and morality. A concluding chapter deals with the question of revolution in Masaryk's thought: Can the goals of humanity be attained by means of force or revolutionary violence?
    SR, 36:3:522-23

856. Brisch, Hans, and Ivan Volgyes, eds. **Czechoslovakia: The Heritage of Ages Past: Essays in Memory of Josef Korbel.** East European Monographs, 51. Boulder, CO: *East European Quarterly*, 1979. viii, 239p. $13.50. Distributed by Columbia University Press, New York.
This is a collection of 10 essays on various aspects of Czech and Slovak history and culture, 2 essays on the career of Joseph Korbel, an introduction by the editors, and several appendices. It is valuable not because it contains new or startling insights into Czech and Slovak history and politics, but because it brings together under one cover essays on several important subjects written by scholars from different disciplines. This book should be useful in advanced undergraduate and introductory graduate courses.
    SR, 39:4:705-706

857. Brock, Peter. **The Slovak National Awakening: An Essay in the Intellectual History of East Central Europe.** Toronto and Buffalo: University of Toronto Press, 1976. x, 104p. $12.50.
This book covers the essential facts of the evolution of Slovak linguistic and political consciousness from the latter decades of the eighteenth century to the revolution of 1848. The first stage was inaugurated in the 1780s by Anton Bernolák and his followers who devised and promoted the use of a Slovak written language that was distinct from Czech. In the 1820s and 1830s came the contributions of Protestant intellectuals. In the next decade, Ludovit Štur and his supporters asserted the existence of a Slovak political nation outside the traditional context of the *natio Hungarica*. This work is the most complete account of the subject available in English.
    SR, 36:2:336-37

858. Eidlin, Fred H. **The Logic of "Normalization": The Soviet Intervention in Czechoslovakia of 21 August 1968 and the Czechoslovak Response.** East European Monographs, no. 74. Boulder, CO: *East European Quarterly*, 1980. 278p. $20.00. Distributed by Columbia University Press, New York.

The nearly unanimous response of Czechoslovakia's population, rulers, and institutions to the 1968 Soviet invasion was to reject the intervention and freeze authority along the lines of legitimacy prevailing before the invasion. The study explains how the outlines of a stalemated political situation emerged as both the occupation and the Czechoslovak response to it became consolidated.

859. El Mallakh, Dorothea H. **The Slovak Autonomy Movement, 1935-1939: A Study in. Unrelenting Nationalism.** East European Monographs, no. 55. Boulder, CO: *East European Quarterly*, 1979. xvi, 260p. $16.00. Distributed by Columbia University Press, New York.

The most significant conclusion of this study is that the Slovak People's Party was "the largest and most defined political movement in Slovakia" — a fact historians have thus far failed to appreciate. Historians have likewise failed to realize that the influence of the Slovak People's Party extended far beyond its own immediate political ambience. Having moved the Party to center stage, the author can ask some new, probing questions. In preparing her study, El Mallakh was able to consult the unpublished pre-1939 police reports on the People's Party, which lend a special value to the work.
   AHR, 85:3:678-79

860. Garver, Bruce M. **The Young Czech Party, 1874-1901, and the Emergence of a Multi-Party System.** New Haven, CT, and London: Yale University Press, 1978. xv, 568p. $20.00.

Garver has produced what is, to some extent, a history of the Czech Lands in the period 1874-1901. To understand the rise and decline of the Young Czech Party, it is essential to appreciate the economic development of Bohemia, Moravia, and Silesia in the late nineteenth century and the social differentiation that went with it, as well as the constitutional intricates of Austria-Hungary. Future textbook writers will frequently refer to this monograph for its careful statistics of population or landholding, or for its explanation of provincial government or attitudes to state rights.
   SEER, 59:2:308-309

861. Jelinek, Yeshayahu. **The Parish Republic: Hlinka's Slovak People's Party, 1939-1945.** East European Monographs, 14. Boulder, CO: *East European Quarterly*, 1976. viii, 206p. $11.50. Distributed by Columbia University Press, New York.

Jelinek's description of the Slovak state is one of the most balanced records available. He uses evidence drawn from a wide range of sources, including archival material from Germany, the United States, and Israel. He observes that there was relative freedom in the cultural sphere, the lower-middle class gained economically, and there was a considerable increase in Slovak consciousness. This made a return to the pre-1938 administrative system unwise after World War II. Anyone dealing with this period of Slovak history will find this book required reading.
   SR, 39:4:706-707

862. Korbel, Josef. **Twentieth-Century Czechoslovakia: The Meanings of Its History.** New York: Columbia University Press, 1977. xiv, 346p. $14.95.

Korbel first describes the roots of the new state that emerged in 1918 and tells the history of the First Republic (1918 to 1938). The years of progress are followed by the years of darkness (1938 to 1945), the years of hope and fears (1945 to 1948), the years of shame (1948 to 1962), and, finally, the Sisyphean years (1962 to 1968). The book culminates in a mastery description of the Prague Spring of 1968 and its sad consequences. This is a very valuable book that can be recommended to all students of modern history.

SR, 32:2:322-23

863. Skilling, Gordon. **Czechoslovakia's Interrupted Revolution.** Princeton, NJ: Princeton University Press, 1976. xvi, 924p. $45.00.

The author's extensive research, persuasive interpretations, and detailed biographical footnotes combine to make this the best volume available on the subject. This may well be the most comprehensive history of the Dubček era that we have until new primary sources become available. The study's detailed treatment of 1968 presents a vast amount of information and conveys the complexities and contradictions of the reform movement.

SR, 37:1:152-53

864. Vyšný, Paul. **Neo-Slavism and the Czechs 1898-1914.** Soviet and East European Studies. Cambridge: Cambridge University Press, 1977. xiv, 287p. $21.95.

This interesting, well-written volume offers a valuable treatment of Neo-Slavism, a short-lived but significant movement that sought to promote Slavic cooperation, particularly between Czechs and Russians. Its creator and main driving force was the Czech politician, Karel Kramář. This is an impressive piece of research and a thoughtful analysis that illuminates a crucial area of politics and diplomacy in prewar Eastern Europe.

SR, 34:4:701-702

865. Wallace, William V. **Czechoslovakia.** London and Tonbridge, England: Ernest Benn, 1977. xv, 374p. Plates. £9.95; Boulder, CO: Westview Press, 1976. xvi, 374p. Illus. Maps. $24.00.

This is a straight history of the Czechs and Slovaks from 1849 until the present time. It is good and informative on economic history of the nineteenth century and has many interesting things to say on the resulting social developments. It gives the Slovaks their proper place in the story before and during the creation of their common state with the Czechs. Wallace's *Czechoslovakia* provides a comprehensive guide for the general reader.

SEER, 56:1:133-34

Foreign Relations

866. Campbell, Gregory F. **Confrontation in Central Europe: Weimar Germany and Czechoslovakia.** Chicago and London: University of Chicago Press, 1975. xvi, 383p. $15.00.

This original contribution to scholarship is the first comprehensive and analytical study of Czechoslovak-German relations from 1918 to 1933. The author stresses almost exclusively the diplomatic aspects of the Czechoslovak-German relationship, discussing economic aspects occasionally and cultural and scientific developments hardly at all. He neatly places that relationship in the context of European foreign relations and reveals how it was affected by every important international crisis or conference from 1919 to 1933. The bibliographical essay on archival and printed sources is well done.

SR, 37:9:326-27

867. Kalvoda, Josef. **Czechoslovakia's Role in Soviet Strategy.** Washington, DC: University Press of America, 1978. x, 382p. $8.75, paper.

This book begins with the encounter of the Czecho-Slovak Legion with the Bolsheviks in Russia in 1918 and ends with the events revolving around the "Prague Spring" in 1968, including the description and analysis of the manifold activities of Czechoslovak nationals

and the Prague-trained professional revolutionaries in Latin America and other countries. Most especially valuable is chapter VIII, "Beneš and the Question of East Central Europe," based on declassified or published literature or other sources, giving more details on Beneš's role in the process of the Communist seizure of power in East Central Europe.
NP, 7:2:240

868. Smelser, Ronald M. **The Sudeten Problem, 1933-1938: Volkstumspolitik and the Formulation of Nazi Foreign Policy.** Middletown, CT: Wesleyan University Press, 1975. x, 324p. $16.00.
Smelser's book is well researched, particularly on the earlier period. He comes to the conclusion that it was not only Hitler's aggressive foreign policy that led to Munich, but, of equal importance, were the factional rivalries among the Sudeten Germans themselves, further complicated by the competition between various Reich institutions and agencies intervening in the issue of German ethnic groups, which helped to mold Hitler's ambitions towards Czechoslovakia. Smelser significantly contributes to the knowledge of how Nazi foreign policy worked in practice.
SEER, 59:1:125-26

869. Ullmann, Walter. **The United States in Prague, 1945-1948.** East European Monographs, 36. Boulder, CO: *East European Quarterly*, 1978. x, 205p. $12.00. Distributed by Columbia University Press, New York.
This book is based primarily on State Department archives since Czech sources are not available. In essence, the book deals with the Prague ambassadorship of Laurence Steinhardt. The author's conclusions are not very favorable. He states that Steinhardt may have been adequate for a conventional station, but he was hardly a counterweight for the diplomatic efforts of the USSR. The ambassador's, as well as Washington's, good wishes and hopes were not enough then, nor are they enough today.
SR, 38:3:517-18

Economics

870. Rudolph, Richard L. **Banking and Industrialization in Austria-Hungary: The Role of Banks in the Industrialization of the Czech Crownlands, 1873-1914.** Cambridge: Cambridge University Press, 1976. xii, 291p. Tables. $28.00.
On the basis of original calculations, Rudolph demonstrates that significant industrial growth took place in the 1880s and 1890s before banks seriously turned their interests to industry. While he admits that social attitudes may have played a role in the extreme cautiousness of bankers, he also points to the rational, that is, economic, sources of such attitudes. The author's details and interpretations clarify the picture of Austrian banking and open up new areas for research.
SR, 36:2:339-40

Language and Literature

871. Kirschbaum, J. M. **Slovak Language and Literature: Essays.** Readings in Slavic Literatures, 12. Edited by J. B. Rudnyckyj. Winnipeg and Cleveland: University of Manitoba, Department of Slavic Studies, 1975. xvi, 336p. Plates.
This book does serve two very useful and important purposes (aside from the fact that it is the largest compilation of information on Slovak literature available in English) — it emphasizes the fact that, in the course of their development, Slovak language, literature, and culture were much more independent of Czech influences than many Westerners,

including Czechs, have been wont to think; and it emphasizes the importance of Bernolák's version of standard Slovak, showing that it was not entirely abortive. The book has, however, hundreds of misprints.
SR, 36:1:160-61

872. Matejka, Ladislav, and Irwin R. Titunik, eds. **Semiotics of Art: Prague School Contributions.** Cambridge, MA, and London: The MIT Press, 1976. xxi, 298p. $17.95.
The Structuralist Prague Linguistic Circle grew largely out of the Moscow Linguistic Circle and Russian Formalism, but it also had Czech philosophical roots — Matejka points out that the early Revival Prague professor, Bernard Bolzano, speculated about signs and signs of signs, but one will also find germs of Structuralist semiotic theory in late nineteenth-century critics like H. G. Schauer and F. X. Šalda. This is an anthology of 21 essays by Czech and Russian members of the prewar Prague school and their postwar followers, published between 1933 and 1973.
SEER, 56:4:614-16

873. Novák, Arne. **Czech Literature.** Translated from the Czech by Peter Kussi. Edited and with a supplement by William E. Harkins. Ann Arbor, MI: Michigan Slavic Publications, 1976. x, 375p. $8.00.
The main thesis of Novák's book is that, although Czech is the oldest of Slavic literatures, few works have received recognition outside of Czechoslovakia, and those works htat have been noticed are recognized through the strength of their ideas, not artistic qualities. One reason, he maintains, is that lyricism (the favorite form of Czech authors) reaches the world maimed by translation, as "butterflies shorn of color." Another reason is the fact that the Czechs have been a nation without a state for many centuries — literature was the mirror of national life, the printed word its life line.
SR, 36:4:723-24

874. Trensky, Paul I. **Czech Drama since World War II.** Introduction by William E. Harkins. Columbia Slavic Studies. White Plains, NY: M. E. Sharpe, 1978. xii, 250p. $20.00.
Trensky's book is by far the most comprehensive treatment of the subject in any language, a work that will be of great value not only to Slavicists but to anyone interested in modern drama in general. It is a vivid and inspired account of one of the most captivating epochs (1960s) in the history of the Czech stage.
SR, 39:1:167-68

The Society, Sociology

875. Kansky, Karel Joseph. **Urbanization under Socialism: The Case of Czechoslovakia.** New York: Praeger Publishers, 1976. xviii, 313p. Tables. Maps. Figures. $22.50.
This study proposes a general synthesis and a precise terminology for socialist urbanization. The emphasis is on the spatial aspects of city development, and the approach is geographical and demographic. The great asset of the volume is a mass of housing and population data relating to East Central Europe that will be of use to scholars in a half-dozen disciplines. The 57 tables, 17 maps, and assorted diagrams and graphs provide detailed information on everything from the inhabitable floor space per dwelling unit to the proportion of in-commuters by city size. With its thorough documentation and comprehensive index, it should also serve as a valuable reference for Slavic specialists.
SR, 37:2:327-28

GERMAN DEMOCRATIC REPUBLIC

876.   Haase, Herwig E. **Development Trends in the GDR Economy during the 1980s: A Prognosis of Its Problems.** Berlin: Berichte des Osteuropa Instituts an der Freien Universität, 1980. 100p. DM 12.00.
This concise study begins with an examination of the challenge facing the GDR economy – declining growth, over-employment, price increases, and rising foreign trade burdens. It then considers the factors impeding growth – wasteful use of inputs, technological lag, financial problems, supply shortages. It concludes that major reforms are unlikely.

877.   Klein, Margrete Siebert. **The Challenge of Communist Education: A Look at the German Democratic Republic.** East European Monographs, no. 70. Boulder, CO: *East European Quarterly*, 1980. 200p. $19.50. Distributed by Columbia University Press, New York.
Klein's study shows how, by making their goals explicit and by acknowledging that education must serve society, the German Democratic Republic has registered a gain over the more undirected compulsory education of the West. Yet, the regimented educational system is not free from serious shortcomings affecting a nation's creative abilities.

878.   Legters, Lyman H., ed. **The German Democratic Republic: A Developed Socialist Society.** Boulder, CO: Westview Press, 1978. xiv, 285p. $20.00.
This volume of 11 essays emerged, in part, from a series of papers presented at the Rocky Mountain Association of Slavic Studies in 1972. Unfortunately, it contains very little analysis of the GDR that is of any lasting quality. The work is not without some merit, however. The main thesis of the study is interesting and deserves serious consideration. The authors collectively suggest that the forces of change that have had an impact on the GDR's political and social arrangements have been the product of the complex interplay between the German tradition blending into an international Communist system and the process of modernization and development itself.
        SR, 39:2:333-34

879.   Leptin, Gert, and Manfred Melzer. **Economic Reforms in East German Industry.** London: OUP, 1978. xxv, 200p. £12.00.
The much publicized New Economic System (NES) introduced in 1963 receives here well-deserved attention, together with the controversial changes in the NES introduced in the post-1970 period. The authors argue that the basic problem of planned economies, that of decentralization of decision making while maintaining planners' prerogatives, has not been solved in the GDR, either by the NES or by any of its successors such as the most recent 1975 "mini-reform." This is a meticulous and well-researched work. It will encourage further research on one of the most challenging and successful planning systems in existence today.
        SS, 32:1:138-41

880.   McCauley, Martin. **Marxism-Leninism in the German Democratic Republic: The Socialist Unity Party (SED).** London: Macmillan, 1979. xix, 267p. £12.00.
McCauley has produced a well-written, generally reliable, and useful addition to the small number of English-language volumes on the GDR. Based on a wide variety of GDR, West German, American, and British sources, the book draws together information, some of which has not been previously available in English. It also contains a useful bibliography and brief biographies of over 60 SED functionaries. Some oversimplifications and

statements made in the book would surprise East Germans if they were able to read them. For instance, he tells us that the DBD was successful among the peasants.
SS, 33:2:316-18

881. Moreton, N. Edwina. **East Germany and the Warsaw Alliance: The Politics of Détente.** Boulder, CO: Westview Press, 1979. xvi, 267p. $18.00.
The author shows that East Berlin has had an important, if negative, influence on the Soviet Union's European policies, and that it has been a force to reckon with within the Warsaw Pact. In analyzing the role of GDR foreign policy over the past 30-odd years, Moreton places primary emphasis on the "German problem," with special attention to the period since 1967. This is probably the most important book on GDR foreign policy to appear in English to date.
SR, 39:4:703-704

882. Schneider, Eberhard. **The GDR: The History, Politics, Economy and Society of East Germany.** London: C. Hurst & Co., 1978. xii, 121p. £6.50.
This is a concise but comprehensive general survey of most aspects of the society of the GDR, covering economic geography, history, party and state structure, the economy, social services and trade unions, education and training, ideology and, finally, foreign policy and attitudes to the German question. This book offers to the reader with no previous knowledge of the GDR a sound basic picture of the country and its society.

883. Schweigler, Gebhard Ludwig. **National Consciousness in Divided Germany.** London and Beverly Hills, CA: Sage, 1975. vii, 287p. $11.00, paper.
Schweigler concludes that the single *Bewusstseinnation* characterizing Germany before 1945 has been replaced by two states, each with its own national consciousness. This view is particularly strong among younger Germans in both the FRG and the GDR. Moreover, present trends point to the probability that the chasm between the two identifications will widen in the future.
SR, 37:3:519-20

HUNGARY

General Reference Works

884. Harvard University. Library. **Hungarian History and Literature: Classification Schedule, Classified Listing by Call Number, Chronological Listing, Author and Title Listing.** Widener Library Shelflist, 44. Cambridge, MA: Harvard University Press, 1974. 186p. $25.00.
This volume includes 6,550 titles in Hungarian and other languages, available in one of the most important Hungarian collections in North America.

885. Kerek, Andrew, comp. **Bibliography of Hungarian Linguistic Research in the United States and Canada.** Hungarian Reference Shelf, No. 5. New Brunswick, ME: Hungarian Research Center, American Hungarian Foundation, 1979. 28p. $3.50.
The 255 items listed in alphabetical order in this attractively produced booklet "represent the work of American (and some Canadian) linguists, regardless of places of publication or dissemination." Kerek has excluded dictionaries, adequately dealt with in I. Halász de Bēky's *Bibliography of Hungarian Dictionaries 1410-1963* (Toronto, 1966), as well as word-lists, phrase-books, readers, and the like, since these do not generally supply explicit information on grammar.
SEER, 59:1:79-80

886. Sinor, Denis, ed. **Modern Hungary: Readings from the 'New Hungarian Quarterly.'** Bloomington and London: Indiana University Press, 1977. xxi, 424p. $17.50.

This is a selection of articles published in *The New Hungarian Quarterly*, a useful journal that gives access to Hungarian intellectual output to those who do not read Hungarian. The journal, of course, seeks to create a favorable image of Hungary. Nevertheless, the idea to publish this collection is a good one, offering an insight into official Hungarian thinking.

Geography

887. Enyedi, György. **Hungary: An Economic Geography.** Translated by Elek Helvei. Revised and edited by Mary Völgyes. Boulder, CO: Westview Press, 1976. xi, 289p. $22.75.

This is the first economic geography of Hungary written by a Hungarian author for English readership abroad. In its depth of analysis and breadth of perspective, it surpasses other previously published works. Innovative in structure as well as in topics, the book presents exciting new material and ideas culled from recent geographical literature in Hungarian.
CSP, 19:3:396-98

888. Enyedi, György, ed. **Rural Transformation in Hungary.** Studies in Geography of Hungary, 13. Budapest: Akadémiai Kiadó, 1976. 116p. $7.00.

The six essays integrated by Enyedi into one volume on rural transformation deal with various components of the transformation process that created a new landscape in rural areas. The contributors discuss the demographic characteristics of transformation, the development of rural industries, and other pertinent aspects of the development.
SR, 38:1:145-46

Communism, Communist Party

889. Kovrig, Benneth. **Communism in Hungary: From Kun to Kadár.** Histories of Ruling Communist Parties, Hoover Institution Publication, no. 211. Stanford: Hoover Institution Press, 1979. xviii, 525p. $10.95.

Kovrig's volume takes the chronological approach and deals with Hungarian history in six parts: from the formation of the socialist movement to 1919; 1919 to 1944, 1944 to 1948; 1948 to 1955; 1955 to 1957; 1957 to 1963; and from 1963 to the present. His divisions are logical and conceptually he is correct in breaking down the history in this manner. The most interesting part of the book is where the author deals with the contemporary development of Kadár's policies and his attempts to modernize both Hungary and the apparatus necessary to rule the country. The book is lucid, well written, and thorough in its analysis of the most pragmatic rule Hungary has ever experienced.
AHR, 85:3:677-78

890. Molnár, Miklós. **A Short History of the Hungarian Communist Party.** Boulder, CO: Westview Press; Folkenstone, England: Wm. Dawson & Sons, 1978. 168p. $16.50.

Molnár's book deals with the history of the Hungarian Communist Party and its natural interrelatedness with Hungarian social history. Only a few months after it had come into being (November 1918), the Party assumed power over Hungarian society (21 March 1919), bringing an end to the parliamentary regime in the Western sense. During the interwar period, the Party was insignificant, with membership ranging from no more than a few dozen members to several hundred; all in all, it could in no way be considered a workers' party. The book is based almost exclusively on official party documents produced in Hungary.

SEER, 58:3:459-60

History

891. Bartha, Antal. **Hungarian Society in the Ninth and Tenth Centuries.** Translated by K. Balázs. Studia Historica, Academiae Scientiarum Hungaricae, 85. Budapest: Akadémiai Kiadó, 1975. 147p. $9.00.

Bartha's work appeared in 1968. It shows an impressive acquaintance with sources, ancient and modern, Eastern European and Western. The first chapter describes in broad terms the conditions in Eastern Europe at the time when the Hungarians resided in the regions north of the Black Sea. The second part describes the life of the Hungarian tribes in the ninth century, and the final chapter deals with the changes that followed the conquest of the Carpathian Basin and the creation of the Hungarian medieval state. This is an excellent book, especially in its original Hungarian version. Unfortunately, the English translation is often awkward and unclear.

SR, 35:4:761

892. Deák, Istvän. **The Lawful Revolution: Louis Kossuth and the Hungarians, 1848-1849.** New York: Columbia University Press, 1979. xxi, 415p. $16.95.

Deák's finely argued and highly readable book emphasizes the specificity of Hungary in 1848 and the inapplicability of many cosmopolitan labels. He focuses on the revolutionary leadership of the Hungarian nobility. This nobility was also to a greater degree unrivaled by other social classes than any other in Europe. The same goes to Kossuth himself, for he was far more a Mirabeau or a Danton than he was a Blanqui or Napoleon III. Deák, on point after point, marshals evidence to show Kossuth and the nobility as stable and centrist in their ideology. The book includes extensive footnotes, a fine bibliography, and a helpful index.

NP, 9:2:252-53

893. Decsy, János. **Prime Minister Gyula Andrássy's Influence on Habsburg Foreign Policy during the Franco-German War of 1870-1871.** East European Monographs, no. 52. Boulder, CO: *East European Quarterly*, 1979. 177p. $12.00. Distributed by Columbia University Press, New York.

The work is basically a reassessment of Andrássy's role in Austria-Hungary's foreign policy during the Franco-Prussian War. Based partially on printed and archival sources, and partially on some earlier major works on Andrássy, Decsy has produced a balanced account of his diplomacy and has also drawn a number of balanced conclusions about the considerations that motivated this diplomacy. This is a welcome addition to the growing number of American scholarly works on some of the great Hungarian statesmen of the nineteenth century.

NP, 9:1:156-58

894. Deme, Laszlo. **The Radical Left in the Hungarian Revolution of 1848.** East European Monographs, no. 19. Boulder, CO: *East European Quarterly*, 1976. x, 162p. $12.00. Distributed by Columbia University Press, New York.

The role of the Radical Left — their involvement in the March Revolution in Pest notwithstanding — was, on the whole, peripheral. Deme's book is the first comprehensive English-language study of this question. He has made an honest and respectable attempt to portray the significance of the Radicals. The work is supplemented by brief biographical sketches of the most significant personalities, a chronology of the Revolution, a list of primary and secondary sources, as well as by a brief index.

SR, 38:1:143-44

895. Frank, Tibor. **The British Image of Hungary, 1865/1870.** Theses in English and American, Department of English, L. Eötvös University, Budapest. Budapest: L. Eötvös University, 1976. 375p. 20 Ft., paper.

The impressive broad scope of Frank's sources includes archival material, contemporary journals and periodicals, and respectable secondary sources. His clear and objective analysis of his title topic, his original research, and his presentation of it — all deserve warm commendation. Readers will be enriched by his work.

SR, 37:1:156-57

896. Hidas, Peter I. **The Metamorphosis of a Social Class in Hungary during the Reign of Young Franz Joseph.** East European Monographs, no. 26. Boulder, CO: *East European Quarterly*, 1977. xvi, 140p. $12.00. Distributed by Columbia University Press, New York.

This is a well-documented, though greatly abbreviated, report concerning a few years of Hungarian and Habsburg domestic policy, complete with statistical tabulations and economic charts. The text effectively demonstrates that the society as a whole changed between 1849 and 1853, the period discussed here.

SR, 37:3:526-27

897. Ives, Margaret C. **Enlightenment and National Revival: Patterns of Interplay and Paradox in Late Eighteenth-Century Hungary.** With a selection of documents in translation. Ann Arbor, MI: Published for SSEES by University Microfilms International, 1979. 270p. $23.85.

This is a much needed study in English of the enlightenment in Hungary, whose aims and aspirations were similar to those of the German *Aufklärung*. Ives' main argument — that "the situation [in Hungary] became very complex in that progressive ideas seemed to entail unqualified support of Vienna while patriotic leanings verged towards backsliding and retreatism" — is a fair statement of the generally accepted Marxist view whose vocabulary contains no concepts like "national interest." The patterns of interplay of the above two components produce the paradox to which the title refers.

SEER, 58:4:577-78

898. Kabdebo, Thomas. **Diplomat in Exile: Francis Pulszky's Political Activities in England, 1849-1860.** East European Monographs, no. 56. Boulder, CO: *East European Quarterly*, 1979. 208p. $13.00. Distributed by Columbia University Press, New York.

The author has intended to bring together in this book references undiscovered so far in the context of the study of Louis Kossuth and the Hungarian emigration in London, consequent upon the collapse of the Hungarian War of Independence 1848-1849. The role of Lord Palmerstone in connection with the events of 1848-1849 and with Pulszky's and other Hungarian emigrants in London is seen in sharper light after the reading of references gleaned by Kabdebo. The volume is a very informative study that will become a standard work of reference for students of Kossuth and his era.

NP, 9:2:253-54

899. Király, Béla K. **Ferenc Deák.** Twayne's World Leader Series. Boston: Twayne Publishers, 1975. 243p. $8.50.

Ferenc Deák was the Hungarian statesman who negotiated the Compromise of 1867 that resulted in the emergence of the Austro-Hungarian Monarchy. The liberalism of Deák and those who worked with him gave Hungarian politics a steady line from the calling of the Diet of 1830 to the Compromise of 1867, in spite of the violent upheavals and oppression of the events of 1848-1849 and the Bach period. From Király's book, the general reder learns why Deák's work deserves to be remembered, though the specialist will not learn much new.

SR, 36:1:145-46

900. Lomax, Bill, ed. **Eyewitness in Hungary: The Soviet Invasion of 1956.** Nottingham, England: Spokesman Books, 1980. 183p. £8.50.

This is a collection of accounts by people who were present in Hungary during the 1956 uprising—all were Communists and all were greatly shaken by the events they witnessed but nevertheless remained "committed communists or socialists." Most of the accounts were written and first published shortly after 1956 but have since become inaccessible.

901. Pastor, Peter. **Hungary between Wilson and Lenin: The Hungarian Revolution of 1918-1919 and the Big Three.** East European Monographs, no. 20. Boulder, CO: *East European Quarterly*, 1976. viii, 191p. $13.00. Distributed by Columbia University Press, New York.

Focusing on the relationship between victors and vanquished, this study is a detailed account of Hungary's attempts to evade the territorial consequences of a punitive peace during the five-odd months between the dissolution of the Habsburg Empire and the coming to power of Bela Kun. Magyar leaders of this period emerge as naive visionaries, united in their determination to avoid the consequences of a lost war and out of touch both with the aspirations of their national minorities and with the mood of the victorious Allies.

SR, 36:3:523-24

902. Spira, György. **A Hungarian Count in the Revolution of 1848.** Translated by Thomas Land. Translation revised by Richard E. Allen. Budapest: Akadémiai Kiadó, 1974. 346p. $14.00.

Among the talented representatives of Hungary's post-World War II generation of historians, G. Spira stands out as the leading expert on the Louis Kossuth-led anti-Habsburg struggle for Magyar national independence. His study deals with six most dramatic months of Count Stephen Széchenyi's political career—from the March revolution of 1848 to his spiritual collapse in September, when Hungary was on the threshold of civil war. Spira provides a panoramic view of the Hungarian scene woven of minute, meticulously researched day-to-day details, many of which are drawn from archival sources hitherto unpublished or unused.

SR, 36:4:705-706

903. Stroup, Edsel Walter. **Hungary in Early 1848: The Constitutional Struggle against Absolutism in Contemporary Eyes.** Foreword by Steven Béla Várdy. State University of New York at Buffalo. Program in East European and Slavic Studies Publication Number 11. Buffalo and Atlanta: Hungarian Cultural Foundation, 1976. 261p. $8.80.

Stroup's intention, brilliantly executed, is to show that there was far more to the Hungarian 1848 revolution than the breakdown of the feudal economic system; that the main motivation of the famous April Laws was the Hungarian noblemen's desire to restore the country's traditional liberties and to modernize Hungary; that the Hungarian reform

movement well preceded the events of 1848; and that, therefore, the April Laws were not an offspring of the European turmoil of that year.
SR, 36:4:704

904. Szabad, György. **Hungarian Political Trends between the Revolution and the Compromise (1849-1867).** Studia Historica, no. 128. Budapest: Akadémiai Kiadó, 1977. 184p. $11.00.

This book is well written; it gives a convincing and comprehensive account of Hungarian political development between 1849 and 1867; and it avoids obsessive concentration on constitutional detail. The Compromise was not a compact freely arrived at by a free nation. Rather, it was a political deal made by the Deák group with Franz Josef and approved by a parliament that had been elected under the greatest possible government pressure. It is little wonder, the reviewer states, that the final arrangements were not submitted to the people for their approval at a free election.
SEER, 56:3:464-65

905. Tihany, Leslie Charles. **The Baranya Dispute, 1918-1921: Diplomacy in the Vortex of Ideologies.** East European Monographs, no. 35. Boulder, CO: *East European Quarterly*, 1978. xii, 138p. $11.00. Distributed by Columbia University Press, New York.

Between 1919 and 1921, the Serbian administration of Pecs attempted to use novel means to detach Baranya—during Kun's Soviet republic, they encouraged rightists, and later, during Horthy's "white terror," left separatists, to shape Baranya into a Serbian protectorate. Allied insistence on the observation of the terms of the Treaty of Trianon forced Serbia to return the country to Hungary in August 1921. This brief essay is the first study in any language to deal exclusively with this fascinating episode in East European history.
SR, 38:3:519-20

906. Vardy, Steven Bela. **Modern Hungarian Historiography.** East European Monographs, no. 17. Boulder, CO: *East European Quarterly*, 1976. xii, 333p. $16.50. Distributed by Columbia University Press, New York.

Following a survey of Hungarian historiography from its origins, Vardy concentrates on the modern period. He analyzes the roots of the changing outlook of Hungarian historians in the vicissitudes of Hungarian society and in the shifting currents of European thought, pointing out the political implications of the positions taken by Hungary's interwar historians. An appendix lists individually all the volumes in the several collections of historical sources published in Hungary during the dualist and interwar periods.
SR, 37:1:155-56

Foreign Relations

907. Juhász, Gyula. **Hungarian Foreign Policy, 1919-1945.** Translated by Sándor Simon. Budapest: Akadémiai Kiadó, 1979. 356p. $29.00.

One of the great merits of Juhász's study is his recognition that not only internal factors but also external factors helped shape Hungarian foreign policy. The author admits that the unwise peace settlement of 1919-1920 created universal resentment in Hungary. He is realistic in acknowledging that the forces of the political left were very weak in interwar Hungary, even among the workers. This work is recommended reading for all historians of modern Eastern Europe.
SR, 40:1:139

908. Sakmyster, Thomas L. **Hungary, the Great Powers and the Danubian Crisis 1936-1939.** Athens: University of Georgia Press, 1980. 284p. $20.00.
The author begins with a lengthy, though valuable, examination of interwar Hungarian politics. What used to once be described as "Horthy's Fascist dictatorship" emerges from these pages not very fascist and not much of a dictatorship. Except for the four years of Gömbös' premiership (1932-1936), the dominance of the conservative element went virtually unchallenged. This was particularly true in the field of foreign policy where Kánya, Bethlen, and even Horthy generally agreed that caution, rather than reckless adventurism, would best serve Hungary's interest. This caution was clearly shown in Hungary's behavior during the Munich crisis. This book is a valuable compendium of recent research and contains much archival material that was unavailable to scholars in the 1950s. As such, it is a useful addition to the diplomatic history of the prewar years.
CSP, 23:1:111-12

Economics

909. Benet, Iván, and János Gyenis, eds. **Economic Studies on Hungary's Agriculture.** Translated by Jenö Racz. Budapest: Akadémiai Kiadó, 1976. 194p. $12.00.
Nine papers incorporated in this book outline the goals of current agricultural policy. The elimination of discrepancies between town and country, as well as between agricultural and industrial labor, is a prominent goal of national policy; the convergence of two forms of socialist property is another target. This book also offers an evaluation of the basic factors of production — land, labor, and capital — and includes projections until 1985.
SR, 38:1:145-46

910. Held, Joseph, ed. **The Modernization of Agriculture: Rural Transformation in Hungary, 1848-1975.** East European Monographs, no. 67. Boulder, CO: *East European Quarterly*, 1980. 400p. $19.50. Distributed by Columbia University Press, New York.
This study analyzes the difficult process of rural modernization in Hungary, 1848-1975. It identifies the impediments to modernization, both cultural and technological; describes the process itself, achieved by force and coercion; and addresses the nature of the change that took place in the peasantry as a result.

Language and Literature

911. **Ararát: A Collection of Hungarian-Jewish Short Stories.** Translated and with an introduction and notes by Andrew Handler. Rutherford, NJ, and London: Feirleight Dickinson University Press and Associated University Presses, 1977. 157p. $10.00.
This anthology introduces to the reader a translator of high artistic qualities as well as a very knowledgeable scholar of modern Hungarian history — Andrew Handler — who, in his introduction and notes, elucidates convincingly the cultural and sociopolitical problems of Hungarian Jewry during the last decades of the nineteenth and the first decades of the twentieth centuries. Handler limits his choice to authors who, in addition to their Jewish origin, emphatically displayed their "Jewish identity," wrote short stories, and dealt mainly with Jews living in their traditional environment and life-style.
SR, 39:2:357-58

912. George, Emery, ed. and trans. **Miklós Radnóti: The Complete Poetry.** Ann Arbor, MI: Ardis, 1980. 400p. $7.50, paper.

One of the most gifted poets of the Hungarian interwar period, Miklós Radnóti, was merely 35 years old when in 1944 he became a victim of Fascism. In an incisive introduction, George acquaints the reader with the historical and intellectual background of Radnóti's poems. He then translates more than 300 poems in a faithful and graceful English volume. The translations follow closely the organization of the last complete edition in Hungarian. The book contains rich and well-arranged iconographic material, with copious notes illuminating the individual poems.
CSP, 23:1:112-13

913. Vajda, Miklós, ed. and introduction. **Modern Hungarian Poetry.** Foreword by William J. Smith. New York and Budapest: Columbia University Press and Corvina Press, 1977. xxxv, 289p. + 12pp. photographs. $11.95.

With the help of an impressive array of distinguished poet-translators, Vajda succeeds in presenting a wide and attractive picture of contemporary Hungarian poetry or, at least, parts of it. Sensitively registering the tremors of both history and the soul, the translators render the poems into vivid, colorful, and poetic English. Regrettably, the poets who left Hungary after 1956 are not included.
SR, 37:2:358-59

National Minorities

914. Braham, Randolph L. **The Hungarian Labor Service System, 1939-1945.** East European Monographs, no. 31. Boulder, CO: *East European Quarterly*, 1977. x, 159p. Illus. $11.00. Distrubuted by Columbia University Press, New York.

This brief, well-documented, and thorough study is the first detailed history of the auxiliary labor service into which Hungarian Jews were compelled during the Second World War. Hungary's treatment of Jews throughout the war was as contradictory as the entire participation of Hungary in World War II. The introduction, administration, and operation of the Jewish labor service bore these very marks of contradiction. The original purpose of legislation introduced between 1938 and 1941 was to remove the "unreliable" Jewish elements from fighting while compelling them to undertake incredibly hard physical labor. The author devotes most of his attention to the fate of Hungarian Jews sent to work in Ukraine and Yugoslavia, where most of them perished.
SR, 38:3:520

915. Handler, Andrew. **Blood Libel at Tiszaeszlar.** East European Monographs, no. 68. Boulder, CO: *East European Quarterly*, 1980. x, 273p. $20.00. Distributed by Columbia University Press, New York.

On April 1, 1882, a young Christian servant girl from the village of Tiszaeszlar was sent on a shopping errand to the nearby village of Öfalu. She never returned. The rumor spread that she became a victim of ritual murder. This "murder" of a girl gave occasion to one of the most sensational trials of dualist Hungary, and stands as a landmark in the history of Hungarian anti-Semitism. This study will be received as a major study of the first of these waves of anti-Jewish outbursts in modern Hungarian history.
CSP, 23:2:228-29

916. Lambert, Gilles. **Operation Hazalah.** Translated by Robert Bullen and Rosette Letellier. Indianapolis and New York: Bobbs-Merrill Co., 1974. xi, 235p. $6.95.

This book relates the story of the courageous and desperate Jewish resistance movement, organized in Budapest, Hungary in 1944 by young Zionists, which helped save tens of thousands of Jewish lives in the face of the awesome and efficient death machine commanded by Adolf Eichmann. With forced documents, they released condemned Jews from prison or from trains heading for death camps, and guided escapees over borders.

SR, 35:1:163-64

917. Spira, Thomas. **German-Hungarian Relations and the Swabian Problem: From Károlyi to Gömbös 1919-1936.** East European Monographs, no. 25. Boulder, CO: *East European Quarterly*, 1977. xii, 382p. $18.50. Distributed by Columbia University Press, New York.

Spira has given more in this book than the title indicates since the three introductory chapters cover "Hungary's Minority Policy before World War I," "Minorities 'Conciliated'—Education and Cultural Policy 1918-1919," and "The Early Horthy Era: Swabians, Austrians and Germans—The Seeds of a Dilemma (1919-1922)." The remaining chapters cover historical surveys of the difficulties between the Magyars and the Swabians, the latter being the largest and most vocal minority remaining in Trianon Hungary.

NP, 6:1:89-90

The Society, Culture, Sociology

918. Ferge, Zsuzsa. **A Society in the Making: Hungarian Social and Societal Policy, 1945-1975.** Preface by S. M. Miller. White Plains, NY: M. E. Sharpe, 1980. 288p. $22.50.

This thorough study provides much new data about the contemporary structure of Hungarian society. The author provides a personal report on conditions in Hungary, and his inside knowledge makes this book a distinctive contribution to the knowledge of Eastern Europe and social policy in general.

919. Hann, C. M. **Tázlár: A Village in Hungary.** Changing Culture Series. Cambridge: Cambridge University Press, 1980. xii, 206p. £12.00.

The author, a British anthropologist, spent the 10 months from October 1976 to August 1977 in continuous residence in the village after a previous year in Budapest learning Hungarian and about Hungary. The focus of interest in this book is changing culture—the ways in which a traditional peasant society adapted to socialism. Some historical background is provided, but it is basically a study of a contemporary Hungarian rural community.

SS, 33:2:321

POLAND

General Reference Works

920. Czachowska, Jadwiga, and Roman Loth, comps. **Przewodnik Polonisty: Bibliografie, Slowniki, Biblioteki, Muzea Literackie** (A Polonist's Guide: Bibliographies, Dictionaries, Libraries, Literary Museums). Wroclaw: Ossolineum, 1974. 642p. 120.00 zl.

This guide, like its twin volume *Warsztat badawczy polonisty* (A Polonist's Workshop), is intended primarily to help the graduate student in Polish literary studies. It supplies information on what bibliographical literary sources are available and where they can be found. Thus, *A Polonist's Guide*, both exhaustive and well organized, will also prove useful to advanced researchers.

SR, 35:1:185-86

921. Davies, Norman, comp. **Poland, Past and Present: A Select Bibliography of Works in English.** Newtonville, MA: Oriental Research Partners, 1977. xxi, 185p. $13.00. This is a bibliography of almost 1,800 items in English and French dealing with all aspects of Polish history, culture, politics, ethnic groups (Jews), religion, immigration, architecture, law, economy, international relations, and East-West trade. It contains a glossary of Polish historical terms, place names, and periodicals.
　　CSP, 19:4:548

922. Hoskins, Janina W. **Tadeusz Kosciuszko, 1746-1817: A Selective List of Reading Materials in English.** Washington, DC: Library of Congress, 1980. 24p. This list includes books, pamphlets, articles, and other available material located in the Library of Congress, Harvard University, Duke University, and Cornell University libraries. Each entry is identified by the call number and location. Some 200 entries are listed.

Government and Politics

923. Piekalkiewicz, Jaroslaw. **Communist Local Government: A Study of Poland.** Athens: Ohio University Press, 1975. xiv, 282p. $10.00. This book, resulting from many years of research (including long stays in Poland), is guided by the proposition that "an understanding of communist politics will never be complete without an investigation of the political process at the local level." Its most important assets are rich factual material on how the councils function, an interesting presentation of public complaints raised in the local press, and movement from a simplified interpretation of the Communist political system to the interpretation of this system in terms of an interplay of social groups and interests.
　　SR, 35:3:558-59

Communism, Communist Party

924. Dziewanowski, M. K. **The Communist Party of Poland: An Outline of History.** 2nd ed. Cambridge, MA: Harvard University Press, 1976. 419p. $20.00. After 17 years, Dziewanowski's work has finally been updated to the events of 1974. This is still the best monographic study on the Polish Communist movement.
　　NP, 5:2:231-35

History

925. Brock, Peter. **Polish Revolutionary Populism: A Study in Agrarian Socialist Thought from the 1830s to the 1850s.** Toronto and Buffalo: University of Toronto Press, 1977. viii, 125p. $10.00. The four essays, reprinted here with some stylistic revisions, originally appeared between 1959 and 1961 in various journals. The notes and bibliography have been updated. The Polish populists generally agreed that agrarian socialism could not be introduced until Poland was free from foreign domination, but, in this struggle, they would have to rely on the gentry no less than the peasantry.
　　SR, 38:2:330-31

926. Cottam, Kazimiera Janina. **Boleslaw Limanowski (1835-1935): A Study in Socialism and Nationalism.** East European Monographs, no. 41. Boulder, CO: *East European Quarterly*, 1978. xviii, 365p. $18.50. Distributed by Columbia University Press.

Boleslaw Limanowski, of gentry origin, organized a Polish patriotic demonstration in Warsaw in 1861 for which he was punished by five years of exile in the Russian far north. In Paris in 1892, he presided over the founding congress of the Polish Socialist Party, remaining with that group's right wing for the rest of his long life. Cottam has produced an excellent guide to his life and thought, a historical biography that reveals much about the interrelationship of socialism and nationalism in Poland in the late nineteenth and early twentieth centuries.

    SR, 39:3:517

927. Dziewanowski, M. K. **Poland in the Twentieth Century.** New York: Columbia University Press, 1977. xvi, 309p. + 16pp. photographs. $14.95.

This survey of the modern history of Poland is written in a lively style and language and is aimed at the student and general reader. It offers a balanced treatment of politics, the economy, culture, education, and social issues. The author shows a preference for empirical interpretation. His excellent analyses of events affecting Poland since 1918, together with the stresses of geopolitical factors, are a welcome contribution to a better understanding of that nation's fate. Several illustrations, an index, and quite extensive notes and bibliography enhance the quality of the book.

928. Fedorowicz, J. K. **England's Baltic Trade in the Early Seventeenth Century: A Study in Anglo-Polish Commercial Diplomacy.** New York: Cambridge University Press, 1980. xiv, 334p. Maps. $35.00.

The principal subject of this book is the Eastland Company, whose activities have been studied in light of Polish as well as British archives. This has enabled Fedorowicz to correct and amend the picture of the Company presented over 20 years ago by R. W. K. Hinton. The author has drawn a careful line between commercial affairs and political matters that were also of concern to the two countries, but inevitably the two overlap, as in the case of the negotiations between Sweden and Poland in 1629, in which English diplomats sought to play a mediating role. The conclusion briefly sketches the relations of the two countries during the English civil war and interregnum period.

    SEER, 59:3:443

929. Fountain II, Alvin Marcus. **Roman Dmowski: Party, Tactics, Ideology, 1895-1907.** East European Monographs, no. 60. Boulder, CO: *East European Quarterly*, 1980. xiii, 240p. $16.00. Distributed by Columbia University Press, New York.

Roman Dmowski's actions and writings had a truly historical impact on modern Poland, and for many years (1904-1919) he was the leading Polish statesman. This book deals with the earlier part of his life. It starts with an introductory chapter on the situation in Poland after 1864 and then presents, with many details, Dmowski's background and political beginnings. In sum, it is a concise but rather complete history of the earlier part of Dmowski's life. The author cites not only English, German, and French texts but also almost everything that has been published in Polish.

    PR, 25:3-4: 126-27

930. Garliński, Józef. **Fighting Auschwitz: The Resistance Movement in the Concentration Camp.** London: Julian Friedman Publishers, 1975. xii, 327p. Photographs. $12.50.

The concentration camp in Auschwitz was not only a place of inhuman crimes – struggle and charity became the fulfillment of life for many of the camp's inmates, those who conquered fear and then offered resistance. This book is carefully written and documented, and includes an extensive bibliography, indexes, and illustrations. It is generally a factual account.

SR, 34:5:759-60

931. Giergielewicz, Mieczyslaw, ed., in cooperation with Ludwik Krzyzanowski. **Polish Civilization: Essays and Studies.** New York: Polish Institute of Arts and Sciences and New York University, 1979. 318p. $16.00.

Fourteen essays and studies and a two-page introduction written by Ludwik Krzyzanowski take up the anthology's 318 pages. Contributions vary in length, covering various aspects of the Polish culture and history. The material selected by the editor was originally intended for native Polish readers.

CSP, 22:3:432-33

932. Gross, Jan Tomasz. **Polish Society under German Occupation: The General-gouvernment, 1939-1944.** Princeton, NJ: Princeton University Press, 1979. xviii, 343p. $20.00.

This book represents an attempt at sociological synthesis of numerous works on German occupation of Poland. As such, this is a praiseworthy undertaking, although it is unfortunately marred by omission of some sources, especially those published by the Parisian Institut Litteraire.

NP, 9:1:153-56

933. Hagen, William W. **Germans, Poles, and Jews.** Chicago: University of Chicago Press, 1980. ix, 406p. $17.50.

With certain reservation, it is fair to say that this work, for its size, gives a very full picture of the topic. Its greatest strength is in the detail with which the economic and political backgrounds of Prussia and the partitioned lands are integrated into a consistent whole. The chronological ebb and flow of Prussia's *Polenpolitik* is very well traced in relation to overall domestic policy in Prussia. The book is extremely well documented and clear in its presentation of the major issues of German-Polish relations in the Prussian partition of Poland.

CSP, 23:3:366

934. Korboński, Stefan. **The Polish Underground State: A Guide to the Underground, 1939-1945.** Translated by Marta Erdman. East European Monographs, no. 39. Boulder, CO: *East European Quarterly*, 1978. x, 268p. $16.00. Distributed by Columbia University Press, New York.

Korbonski was one of the most important figures of the resistance movement in Poland during World War II. In his desire to offer a complete portrait of both the structure and the dynamics of the Polish underground, Korbonski has divided his book into 27 separate chapters dealing with educational and cultural activity, the legal system, press and information service, industry, commerce, agriculture, and others. He is especially effective in discussing the complex interplay of relationships among the various political groups. Also included are references to the relationship of the various non-Polish ethnoreligious groups to the underground, which are of particular interest, even if not always objective.

NP, 7:1:107-109

935. Kulski, Julian Eugeniusz. **Dying, We Live: The Personal Chronicle of a Young Freedom Fighter in Warsaw (1939-1945).** New York: Holt, Rinehart & Winston, 1979. 304p. $16.95.

This is a personal memoir, based upon a journal the author wrote shortly after World War II in an effort to record his harrowing experiences as a young Polish freedom-fighter. When the war began, J. E. Kulski was ten years old. By the time he was twelve, he became a member of the Polish Home Army—at first as a courier, later, as a full-fledged combatant of the 9th Commando Company which operated against the Germans in the Zoliborz section of Warsaw. His baptism of fire came in the Warsaw Uprising of 1944.

PR, 25:3-4:125-26

936. Leslie, R. F., ed. **The History of Poland since 1863.** Soviet and East European Studies Series. Cambridge: Cambridge University Press, 1980. xxii, 494p. Tables. Maps. £25.00.

The book is written by four specialists, has carefully drawn maps, useful tables, and a good select bibliography but a poor index. The part written by Leslie covers the half-century before 1914. The book contains a good deal of useful material. Roughly one-third of the volume is devoted to the years 1948-75. As is often the case with collective works, it is impossible to endorse the entire volume unequivocally. The contributions by Polonsky, and especially Pelezynski, however, deserve high praise and recognition.

SEER, 59:3:452-53

937. Naimark, Norman M. **A History of the "Proletariat": The Emergence of Marxism in the Kingdom of Poland, 1870-1887.** East European Monographs, no. 54. Boulder, CO: *East European Quarterly*, 1979. 329p. $18.00. Distributed by Columbia University Press, New York.

This well-researched work attempts to provide a link between the earliest emergence of Marxist thought in Poland and the present-day regime. It focuses mainly on the rise of the underground Marxist group "Great Proletariat" against the prevalent historical background in the Russian part of Poland (Congress Kingdom). Furthermore, Naimark analyzes the consequences of the collaboration of Polish socialist groups with Russian radicals from *Narodnaia Volia* and Marxists. The third and final aspect of this book examines the impact of industrialization upon the thinking of the Polish intellectuals within the context of nationalism and socialism. Sources for the study were secured in archives and libraries of Warsaw, Moscow, and the Hoover Institution. The author's conclusions are reflective and authoritative.

938. Polonsky, Antony, and Boleslaw Drukier, eds. **The Beginnings of Communist Rule in Poland.** Boston and London: Routledge & Kegan Paul, 1980. viii, 464p. Maps. $37.50.

This is an important collection of documents relating to the period December 1943 through June 1945. These previously unknown documents were delivered by Drukier, a former pro-rector of the Higher School of Social Sciences attached to the Central Committee of the PZPR(PUWP). The documents are notes he made in the course of research in secret Party archives. Only some of the documents have since been published in Poland. The collection is of special interest to experts on Poland's modern history.

939. Sutton, John L. **The King's Honor and the King's Cardinal: The War of the Polish Succession.** Lexington: University Press of Kentucky, 1980. vi, 250p. Notes. Maps. $19.50.

The fighting in the War of Polish Succession, little of which took place in Poland, was for the most part relatively trivial. Only two real battles were fought, both of them in Italy and neither of them giving clear-cut victory to either side. This is a subject inherently difficult to make exciting or perhaps even very interesting. Sutton's account is competent and thorough, though written in a rather wooden style. The French and Austrian archives have been extensively used, and a good deal of scholarly effort has gone into the making of this book.

SEER, 59:3:445-46

940. Thackeray, Frank W. **Antecedents of Revolution: Alexander I and the Polish Congress Kingdom, 1815-1825.** East European Monographs, no. 67. Boulder, CO: *East European Quarterly*, 1980. 197p. $15.00. Distributed by Columbia University Press, New York.

This study examines the Russian-sponsored Polish Congress Kingdom during the first decade of its existence, exploring the forces leading to the violent 1830 November Revolution. The author examines Alexander's desire to solve the Polish question in a way favorable to the Russian Empire, the new era of Russo-Polish relations he inaugurated, and the results of his attempts to bridge traditional enmity while maintaining Russian dominance.

941. Wandycz, Piotr S. **The Lands of Partitioned Poland, 1795-1918.** A History of East Central Europe, vol. 7, edited by Peter F. Sugar and Donald W. Treadgold. Seattle and London: University of Washington Press, 1974. xviii, 431p. Maps. $14.95.

This work is a thorough survey divided into four roughly equal parts—the aftermath of the Partitions (1795-1830), the age of insurrections (1830-1864), the age of organic work (1864-1890), and the road to independence (1890-1918). A discussion of social, economic, and political conditions opens each section, followed by an outline of major political and social developments. Chapters on cultural trends and achievements conclude each major era, and a very useful bibliographical essay ends the book. This work will facilitate and stimulate the study of East Central Europe.

SR, 36:3:518-19

942. Watt, Richard M. **Bitter Glory: Poland and Its Fate 1918 to 1939.** New York: Simon & Schuster, 1979. 511p. + 32pp. plates. $16.95.

This book consists of 18 chapters dealing with the rebirth of Poland in 1918, the struggle for its frontiers, domestic politics, economic problems, foreign policy, and the outbreak of World War II. The book is based on an excellent selection of secondary sources—mostly in English. The author presents a balanced and overall positive image of Poland between the wars, and the book is eminently readable and one of the least distorted books on interwar Poland that has so far been published in English.

SR, 40:2:300-301

943. Zawodny, J. K. **Nothing but Honour: The Story of the Warsaw Uprising, 1944.** Hoover Institution Publications 183. Stanford and London: Hoover Institution Press and Macmillan, 1978. 328p. + 8pp. plates. $12.95.

This book concentrates on a two-month tragic segment of the six-year war, the Warsaw uprising of 1944. It seems a most interestingly and assiduously documented book with a shattering logic of its own. It paints a picture of Western wartime leaders that is far from flattering, a picture traced in documents, quotes, and recollections. The author also offers well-documented analysis of factors, people, and events that bore on the epic story of the Warsaw uprising. The book is a "must" for any political scientist and historian who endeavors to understand the story of World War II.

NP, 8:1:101-115

Foreign Relations

944. Cannistraro, Philip V., Edward D. Wynot, and Theodore P. Kovaleff, eds. **Poland and the Coming of the Second World War: The Diplomatic Papers of A. J. Drexel Biddle, Jr., United States Ambassador to Poland, 1937-1939.** Foreword by Charles Morley. Columbus: Ohio State University Press, 1976. xvi, 358p. Photographs. $17.50.

Ambassador Anthony Drexel Biddle, Jr., was one of the few foreign diplomats to enjoy the complete confidence of Polish Foreign Minister Józef Beck. Precisely because Beck confided in Biddle on matters of policy and frequently sought his views, the publication of the "Biddle Report" on the fall of Poland in September 1939 and a selection of his diplomatic correspondence provide an interesting source for the study of Polish diplomacy and domestic affairs during the years 1937-1939. This well-edited work is a substantial addition to the existing primary source material on Polish foreign policy.

SR, 36:2:335-36

945. Kacewicz, George V. **Great Britain, the Soviet Union and the Polish Government in Exile (1939-1945).** Studies in Contemporary History, 3. The Hague: Martinus Nijhoff, 1979. 255p. $45.80.

This book offers an account of the political, constitutional, and legal questions that arose in the transfer to and operation of the Polish government in exile and its armed forces on foreign soil, with a detailed analysis of the politics of the Grand Alliance that led to its decline. The turmoil within the Polish government and the struggle of Sikorski and Mikolajczyk to reach a *modus vivendi* with Moscow and London are brought to light and discussed in detail. The book includes appendices, bibliography, and an index.

946. Kulski, W. W. **Germany and Poland: From War to Peaceful Relations.** Syracuse, NY: Syracuse University Press, 1976. xxii, 336p. $22.50.

Kulski, former member of the Polish diplomatic corps between 1928 and 1945, has written a valuable book on the relations between Poland and West Germany since World War II. Ultimately, it is a study of the territorial changes (and their consequences) between Germany and Poland that resulted from the war. Kulski traces the history of the Oder-Neisse boundary from its diplomatic origins up through Willy Brandt's *Ostpolitik* and the Warsaw Treaty of 1972. Additionally, he provides a brief summary of Polish-German prewar history and develops the role that the Soviet Union and the Soviet bloc play in contemporary Polish-German affairs. The central thesis is that the German-Polish nexus has come a long way since the war, but that the "bitter history of their relations ... cannot be swept under the carpet by the fiat of two governments."

CSP, 19:4:521-22

947. Lerski, George J., comp. **Herbert Hoover and Poland: A Documentary History of a Friendship.** Introduction by George J. Lerski. Foreword by Mark O. Hatfield. Hoover Archival Documentaries, Hoover Institution Publication 174. Stanford: Hoover Institution Press, Stanford University, 1977. xvi, 128p. $10.95.

This book presents Hoover in his role as director of the American Relief Administration during the First World War. Lerski briefly describes Hoover's relations with Poland throughout his presidency and concludes with a discussion of Hoover's actions as honorary chairman of the Commission for Relief in Poland, created a few weeks after the Nazi invasion. This work provides some valuable insights into the motives of a statesman who played an important role in Polish-American relations.

SR, 38:2:332

948. Lukas, Richard C. **The Strange Allies: The United States and Poland, 1941-1945.** Knoxville: University of Tennessee Press, 1978. viii, 230p. $12.50.

This book is not only thoroughly researched but also well written and organized. The author's style is concise, which intensifies the drama of the events that he describes. He ably traces the interaction among the main factions involved: the Roosevelt administration, the Polish government-in-exile in London, the American *Polonia*, the Soviet government, and the Lublin Committee sponsored by Stalin. The desperate efforts of American politicians to resolve this problem, which, unfortunately, bordered on duplicity at times, are reviewed in some detail. (Given Stalin's determination to subjugate Poland, it is quite possible that a more moderate Polish stance would not have helped, and the outcome would have been the same.)

SR, 38:4:700-701

949. Newman, Simon. **March 1939, the British Guarantee to Poland: A Study in the Continuity of British Foreign Policy.** Oxford: Clarendon Press, 1976. viii, 253p. $14.25.

Newman has written a detailed account of the British guarantee to Poland, which was issued on March 31, 1939. His well-documented study, based on the newly opened materials in the British Public Record Office, is an important revisionist interpretation of the reasons and circumstances that led to the guarantee. Newman contends that, in essence, World War II was started by Lord Halifax and others in the Foreign Office who recognized the risk and accepted the inevitability of war.

SR, 36:4:700-701

950. Polonsky, Antony, ed. **The Great Powers and the Polish Question, 1941-45: A Documentary Study in Cold War Origins.** London: The London School of Economics and Political Science, 1976. 282p. Maps. £5.00.

This collection of documentary source materials, mostly hitherto unpublished, should stimulate further discussion of the topic, while simultaneously resolving many unanswered questions and illuminating many unclear issues. The documents are well chosen, skillfully arranged, and superbly edited by Professor Polonsky, who in many cases has provided footnotes more carefully researched than some previous studies on the subject. The picture that emerges is one of confusion and division—with resulting inconsistencies—within the British, American, and Polish leadership circles over the proper approach to the Polish question.

SR, 36:2:336

951. Wandycz, Piotr S. **The United States and Poland.** Cambridge, MA: Harvard University Press, 1980. 465p. $25.00.

Based primarily upon published works, this study is a survey and synthesis of the political relations between the United States and Poland during the past two centuries. Divided into seven chapters and a section containing the author's reflections, the book primarily deals with American-Polish relations in the twentieth century, the period which witnessed the most significant and sustained contacts. The American image of Poland was no more realistic than the Polish image of the United States. These distortions contributed to frustration and disappointment on both sides. The author is at his best when he discusses the policies of Roosevelt toward Poland during World War II. This book will remain essential reading for a long time for anyone interested in United States-Polish relations.

PR, 26:1:120-23

952. Woytak, Richard A. **On the Border of War and Peace: Polish Intelligence and Diplomacy in 1937-1939 and the Origins of the Ultra Secret.** East European Monographs, no. 49. Boulder, CO: *East European Quarterly*, 1979. 141p. $11.00. Distributed by Columbia University Press, New York.

"Enigma" was a machine enabling the Poles to decode German ciphers used in radio communications; it was handed over to the British in 1939 and has been recognized as a major contribution to the war effort. Its story is a part of this study. Unlike others, Woytak emphasizes not so much the significance of Slovakia as the importance of Carpatho-Ukraine that was becoming a center of Ukrainian nationalism. Polish intelligence was soon engaged in subversive activity to help the Hungarians annex this country. Woytak's book deals more with diplomacy than with intelligence.

Economics

953. Feiwel, George R. **The Intellectual Capital of Michal Kalecki: A Study in Economic Theory and Policy.** Foreword by Lawrence R. Klein. Knoxfille: University of Tennessee Press, 1975. xxii, 583p. $22.50.

Kalecki was the continental, socialist Keynes. Embodied in his intellectual capital were Tugan-Baranovsky, Rosa Luxemburg, engineering, and the statistical description of the Polish economy. This is a very useful book that presents an accurate account of Kalecki's ideas. The author has succeeded in giving the reader some appreciation of the controversies in which Kalecki became involved. Perhaps this book serves best as a supplement to Kalecki's own basic works, now available essentially in English.

SR, 35:4:755-56

954. Kula, Witold. **An Economic Theory of the Feudal System: Towards a Model of the Polish Economy 1500-1800.** Translated by Lawrence Garner. Introduction by Ferdinand Brandel. London and Atlantic Highlands, NJ: NLB and Humanities Press, 1976 [Warsaw: Państwowe Wydawnictwo Naukowe, 1962]. 191p. $13.00.

Kula, Polish Marxist and professor of economic history, discusses here with admirable clarity the socioeconomic forces that were at play in Poland during the period from the sixteenth to the seventeenth centuries. He claims the method that he uses is not only appropriate to the study of Poland at that time but may also be applied to the understanding of any society as it passes from premodern to modern conditions. He offers useful and provocative suggestions to others who would join him in that examination, claiming only that his work is initiative, not definitive.

SR, 37:2:320-21

Language and Literature

955. Brooks, Maria Zagorska. **Polish Reference Grammar.** The Hague: Mouton, 1975. xvi, 580p. Dfl. 120.00.

This volume contains rich material on all aspects of Polish grammar. It consists of two main sections−part 1 discusses grammar; part 2 provides review exercises. In addition, there is a useful Dictionary of Verbs at the end of the book. In general, the major contribution of the work lies in Brook's somewhat novel methodological approach to Polish grammar.

CSP, 19:4:542-43

956. Gerould, Daniel, ed. **Twentieth-Century Polish Avant-Garde Drama: Plays, Scenarios, Critical Documents.** Introduction by Daniel Gerould. Translated by

Daniel Gerould in collaboration with Eleanor Gerould. Ithaca, NY, and London: Cornell University Press, 1977. 287p. Illus. $15.00.

Gerould in this work has revealed to American literary scholarship an original and sharply outlined phenomenon—the contemporary experimental drama of Poland. The drama is closely watched and intelligently interpreted on the stage *hic et nunc*, thanks, largely, to the efforts of Gerould, its translator, explicator, and propagandist. The work is well conceived and thoughtfully structured. It is an anthology of six selected playwrights—Witkacy, A. Trzebiński, Galezyński, J. Afanasjew, S. Mrozek, and T. Różewicz—who are represented by some creative works and some theoretical pronouncements and personal confessions. A bibliography of the topic, containing more than 100 items, concludes the book.

SR, 37:2:356-57

957. Leach, Catherine S., ed. and trans. **Memoirs of the Polish Baroque: The Writings of Jan Chryzostom Pasek, A Squire of the Commonwealth of Poland and Lithuania.** Berkeley: University of California Press, 1976. xxxiv, 327p. $20.00.

This important Polish literary and historical document has been well known in Europe from the beginning of this century and in Poland since its original publication in 1836. It appears now for the first time in English. The work describes the very complex period of the Polish-Lithuanian Commonwealth. The exploits of Pasek, an old yarn-spinning braggart, lived on long after his death at the beginning of the eighteenth century, to spark a fire in the national temperament and offer some solace in the bleak days following the unsuccessful Polish uprising of 1830. The *Memoirs* have been acclaimed ever since as an historical epic romance. Useful appendices include a key to Polish pronunciation, a glossary of state and provincial offices, and a summary of the main historical events of the period.

CSP, 20:1:133

958. Segel, Harold B., ed. **Polish Romantic Drama: Three Plays in English Translation.** Edited, selected, and with an introduction by Harold B. Segel. Ithaca, NY, and London: Cornell University Press, 1977. 320p. Photographs. $17.50.

The works of three Polish poets are offered here in translation—Mickiewicz's *Forefathers' Eve*, Krasinski's *The Un-Divine Comedy*, and Slowacki's *Fantasy*. All three works, however, suffer from a shortage of notes.

959. Stone, Rochelle Heller. **Boleslaw Leśmian: The Poet and His Poetry.** Berkeley: University of California Press, 1976. xii, 364p. $15.95.

The author has carefully mapped out the philosophical background of Leśmian's poetry and has devoted considerable attention to his links with later Russian Symbolist poetry. The study of these connections is the most valuable part of the book. When trimmed of its wild exaggerations, Stone's investigation of Leśmian's links with late Russian Symbolism is a contribution to Leśmian scholarship. Her analyses can help American students get acquainted with a highly idiosyncratic and difficult poet. The book, however, should be used with great caution.

SR, 36:2:357-58

960. Welsh, David. **Jan Kochanowski.** Twayne's World Authors Series, no. 330. New York: Twayne Publishers, 1974. 160p. $7.50.

Kochanowski (1530-84) was Poland's greatest Renaissance poet, a reformer of verse in his own time, and a seminal influence on Polish poetry to the present. This book is the first English-language account of Kochanowski's poetry. The poet is consistently viewed within the framework of contemporary Polish culture, enabling the reader to gain some insight into the overall scope of sixteenth-century Polish literary development.

SR, 35:3:583-84

961. Witkiewicz, Stanislaw Ignacy. **Insatiability: A Novel in Two Parts.** Translated and with an introduction and commentary by Louis Iribarne. Urbana: University of Illinois Press, 1977. xvi, 447p. $15.00.

Insatiability (written in 1927 and published in 1930) describes a world that has yielded to regressive impulses. Toward the end of the book, individualism has given way to collectivism, and a society has emerged in which "each could do as he pleased, as long as he went about it in a prescribed manner." This futuristic scenario focuses heavily on sex. Above all, however, *Insatiability* is an orgy of words. This is not a typical novel by the standards of the 1920s (or of the 1970s), but it is fascinating.

SR, 37:3:541-42

The Society, Sociology

962. Goldfarb, Jeffrey C. **The Persistence of Freedom: The Sociological Implications of Polish Student Theater.** Boulder, CO: Westview Press, 1980. xii, 169p.

This book is about what has happened with these theaters under the impact of the liberal and patriotic traditions of the Polish intelligentsia. These theaters became the institutional vehicles for independent expression soon after their establishment, while, at the same time, the important centers of opposition against Party efforts to transform Poland into an obedient society on the Soviet model. It is precisely this vital need of the Party to maintain a link with the youth that has been widely utilized by the creative and innovative theatrical groups in order to secure for themselves some modicum of free expression, according to the reviewer of this book.

PR, 25:3-4:123-24

963. Slomczyński, Kazimierz, and Tadeusz Krauze, eds. **Class Structure and Social Mobility in Poland.** Translated by Anna M. Furdyna. White Plains, NY: M. E. Sharpe, 1978. x, 211p. $17.50. Published simultaneously as vol. 7, nos. 3-4 of *International Journal of Sociology.*

This book makes available to English-speaking readers an interesting selection of papers written by some of the best-known Polish sociologists. The quality of the papers is uniformly high, and so is the quality of the translation. The volume contains a highly useful bibliography of Polish studies dealing with the various issues related to problems of class structure and social mobility in Poland.

SR, 39:1:148-49

National Minorities

964. Heller, Celia S. **On the Edge of Destruction: Jews of Poland between the Two World Wars.** New York: Columbia University Press, 1977. xi, 396p. $14.95.

Against the historical perspective of some six centuries, Heller unfolds a panorama of definitions, forms, patterns, confrontations, struggles for survival, internal conflicts, and desperation affecting the broad strata of Jewish society. The great majority of Jews had welcomed Poland's independence and, their position secured by the Minorities Treaty of 1919 and Constitution of 1921, looked confidently to the future. However, the Jews soon faced the growing indifference of the state and a spreading anti-Semitism among the Poles.

These experiences are the subject of the bulk of this study, with a concentration on the pattern of oppression, use of terror and abuses, and the responses of Jewish groups and parties to the worsening situation.

RUMANIA

Government and Politics

965. Nelson, Daniel N. **Democratic Centralism in Romania: A Study of Local Commun-ist Politics.** East European Monographs, no. 69. Boulder, CO: *East European Quarterly*, 1980. 186p. $15.00. Distributed by Columbia University Press, New York.

As a study of politics in a Communist party state, this work uniquely applies hypotheses concerning developing politics in non-Communist Western and Third World nations to the experience of an East European state. Focusing on local politics, the author analyzes the interaction of Rumanian political institutions and society at that level where there is close and continuous contact.

Communism, Communist Party

966. King, Robert R. **History of the Romanian Communist Party.** Stanford: Hoover Institution Press, 1980. 190p. $8.95.

This is the first history of the Rumanian Communist party to appear in any language. It will serve only as a point of departure for further extended investigations when access to Rumanian archives is far more possible than at present. There is, however, too much reliance on official Rumanian publications and materials, making some of the author's observations less convincing.

History

967. Bobango, Gerald J. **The Emergence of the Romanian National State.** East European Monographs, no. 58. Boulder, CO: *East European Quarterly*, 1979. 307p. $17.00. Distributed by Columbia University Press, New York.

This book presents Rumanian history from 1829 to 1866, with concentration on internal political events and on foreign reactions regarding Rumanians' drive towards nationhood. Issues discussed include Cuza's double election, efforts towards international recognition, internal social, economic, and political development, and church-state relations, together with Cuza's methods of governing a newly created and unified state. The author did extensive research and offers a well-balanced and interesting study on an important period of Rumania's history.

968. Hitchins, Keith. **Orthodoxy and Nationality: Andreiu Şaguna and the Rumanians of Transylvania, 1846-1873.** Harvard Historical Studies, 94. Cambridge, MA: Harvard University Press, 1977. x, 332p. $14.00.

To chart the course of Şaguna's life is to follow the political and cultural development of the Rumanians of Transylvania during the quarter of a century that preceded the creation of the Dual Monarchy. Perhaps the dominant figure of the period, Andreiu Şaguna (1809-73), bishop and later metropolitan of the Rumanian Orthodox Church, gave his people a realization of their identity. The metropolitan's activity, in all facets, is admirably described and explained in this study that will no doubt establish itself as the standard work on the major figure of this period in Rumanian political life in Transylvania.

SEER, 57:4:599-601

Foreign Relations

969. Braun, Aurel. **Romanian Foreign Policy since 1965: The Political and Military Limits of Autonomy.** New York and London: Praeger Publishers, 1978. xvi, 217p. $20.00.

This book analyzes in some detail Rumania's unorthodox foreign policy objectives. There are basic limitations within which Rumania's leaders know they must live. They cannot allow much domestic dissent or criticism of the USSR or the Communist Party, the reviewer states. Nor can they quit Comecon or the Warsaw Pact outright, make military alliances that would appear to threaten the integrity of the Soviet bloc, or disavow responsibility for the East European "commonwealth." This book is a useful contribution to East European studies.

SR, 39:2:344-45

Language and Literature

970. Alexandrescu, Sorin, ed. **Transformational Grammar and the Rumanian Language.** PDR Press Publications on Rumanian, 1. Lisse: The Peter de Ridder Press, 1977. 97p. $9.25.

Initiating a new series on Rumanian linguistics along with a new journal, *The International Journal of Rumanian Studies*, this slim volume appears to fill the need for a survey in English of recent transformational contributions to the study of Rumanian. James E. Augerd's introduction, with its useful five-page bibliography, promises a collection of studies that are concerned principally with the Rumanian language and are conducted within the framework of transformational grammar.

SEER, 57:2:270-71

971. **Selected Poems of Tudor Arghezi.** Translated by Michael Impey and Brian Swann. The Lockert Library of Poetry in Translation. Princeton, NJ: Princeton University Press, 1976. xxvi, 223p. $16.50.

This volume presents a selection of Arghezi's poems in original Rumanian, with an English version on the opposite page. Impey has provided an introduction to Arghezi's life and work, and his poet-collaborator joins him in a "Translator's Introduction." This book for students of Rumanian will be a useful aid.

SEER, 56:1:122-23

972. Stolojan, Sanda. **Duiliu Zamfirescu.** Twayne's World Authors Series, 551. Boston: Twayne Publishers, G. K. Hall, 1980. 156p. $12.95.

Duiliu Zamfirescu (1858-1922) is not a major figure on the European literary scene. It is significant that only one of his works has been translated into English. His importance in the history of Rumanian literature, however, is beyond dispute. Stolojan's book has a chapter on Zamfirescu's life (he was a career diplomat) and his controversial role in the Rumanian literary scene; three chapters on his novels; one each on his stories and memoirs, his plays, his poetry, his correspondence; and one very short one on his language. This book, the first study of Zamfirescu to be published outside Rumania, is an informative and very welcome introduction to his work.

SEER, 59:3:421

973. Tsantis, Andreas C., and Roy Pepper. **Romania: The Industrialization of an Agrarian Economy under Socialist Planning.** Washington, DC: The World Bank, 1979. xxxvi, 707p. Illus. $30.00. Distributed by Johns Hopkins University Press, Baltimore, MD.

This is the first basic report on fundamental economic conditions in Rumania since it joined the World Bank in 1972. The book provides a virtual cornucopia of basic data about economic sectors, economic planning since 1950, and techniques of Rumanian socialist planning. Nearly 300 pages are devoted to appendices on government operation, stages of growth, banking, and social welfare. The work adds much to the fundamental understanding of the specific operation of the Rumanian economy in a readily usable form.

SR, 40:2:310-11

The Society, Sociology

974. Gilberg, Trond. **Modernization in Romania since World War II.** New York: Praeger Publishers, 1975. xiv, 261p. Tables. $13.50.

The main body of this text consists of a well-argued and amply documented review of Rumanian achievements and effectiveness of the work of the agents of modernization, that is, the Communist Party and its affiliated organizations, to progress in such areas as education, industrialization, agriculture, communication and social services, and integration of ethnic minorities. Gilberg propounds the optimistic solution that the forces of modernization will eventually overcome those of retardation.

SR, 35:1:171-72

975. Jowitt, Kenneth, ed. **Social Change in Romania, 1860-1940: A Debate on Development in a European Nation.** Institute of International Studies, Research Series, no. 36. Berkeley: Institute of International Studies, University of California, 1978. xii, 207p. $4.50, paper.

Jowitt, editor of this collection, describes Rumania's development in terms of Max Weber's distinction between class and status societies. This suggestive analysis is complemented by Andrew Janos, who comes to the arresting conclusion that neither communism nor fascism have to do primarily with industrialization, since the imperatives for survival in a changing world system generate pressures for this in any event. Instead, they are efforts of the peasant periphery or the middle-class semiperiphery, respectively, to find original paths out of dependency.

SR, 38:3:525-26

976. MacKendrick, Paul. **The Dacian Stones Speak.** Chapel Hill: University of North Carolina Press, 1975. xxii, 248p. Illus. $12.95.

This work covers most of Rumania from the Neolithic era to the Slavic conquest of Histria in the seventh century A.D. Initially, the treatment is chronological, but, in the Roman era, chapters are topographical or topical (as on religion and the arts). Almost half the pages are given to illustrations and plans. The work is a pleasant perambulation over ground not often trodden by classical scholars.

SR, 34:4:860

YUGOSLAVIA

General Reference Works

977. Hocevar, Toussaint. **The Economic History of Slovenia, 1828-1918: A Bibliography with Subject Index.** New York: Society for Slovene Studies, 1978. vii, 49p.

This well-researched bibliography lists 55 books and 179 journal articles relating to the economic history of the Slovene lands from the introduction of mechanized industry in 1828 until the fall of Austria-Hungary and the formation of Yugoslavia in 1918. Hocevar's concept of economic history is a broad one—works included deal with agrarian history, demography, economic geography, finance, transportation and commerce, as well as with specific industries, manufacturers, and enterprises such as mining, metallurgy, textiles, papers, chemicals, leather, etc.

NP, 7:2:241-42

978. Horton, John J. **Yugoslavia.** World Bibliographic Series. Oxford: Clio Press, 1977. xvi, 195p. $25.25.

The purpose of this selective bibliography on Yugoslavia, according to the compiler, is to "identify those particular contributions, irrespective of length, which appear to be more than usually helpful in illuminating Yugoslav life in its various aspects." The 617 items included are primarily citations to books and articles in English; each entry is annotated in detail. A useful index provides access to citations by author, title, and subject.

SR, 38:3:547

979. Milenkovitch, Michael M., comp. **Milovan Djilas: An Annotated Bibliography, 1928-1975.** Ann Arbor, MI: University Microfilms International, 1976. v, 45p. $9.00.

This bibliography describes 11 books that Djilas wrote between 1952 and 1973, 3 edited volumes of his major works. Part 2 consists of 472 entries covering the prewar period, and part 3 covers 17 items written by persons who have known Djilas.

980. Terry, Garth M. **Yugoslav Studies: An Annotated List of Basic Bibliographies and Reference Works.** London: A. C. Hall, 1977. xi, 89p. £4.20.

This bibliography is divided into three sections. The first lists general reference works; the second, general bibliographies under the headings of 'Yugoslavia' and each of the six republics; the third, under like headings, comprises subject bibliographies and subject reference books. The great majority of works listed are in one of the Yugoslav languages or English. *Yugoslav Studies* will serve as a useful handbook to researchers, scholars, and librarians.

SEER, 56:3:478

Government and Politics

981. Denitch, Bogdan Denis. **The Legitimation of a Revolution: The Yugoslav Case.** New Haven and London: Yale University Press, 1976. xiv, 254p. $15.00.

The author sees Yugoslavia's "self-management" system as an ideal laboratory for the analysis of the legitimation of a revolutionary elite. He is confident that without outside intervention "the continued process of change" will produce "a model of a democratic socialist society—a model with no real precedent." He is also confident that the LCY can overcome the crises engendered by nationality conflicts, local issues, and divergent group interests.

SR, 36:2:342-43

982.　Dragnich, Alex N. **The Development of Parliamentary Government in Serbia.** New York: Columbia University Press, 1978. 138p. $10.00.

Beginning with the Serbian revolt against the Turks in 1804, Dragnich describes what he considers the three stages of Serbia's national political development: nation building (1804-1868), the struggle for parliamentary government (1868-1903), the parliament in action (1903-1918). Dragnich tends to exaggerate Serbia's political achievements and to gloss over her shortcomings in both domestic and international affairs. Readers seeking a more balanced presentation might consult Michael B. Petrovich's *A History of Serbia, 1804-1918* (1976).

983.　Horvat, Branko, Mihailo Markovic, and Rudi Supek, eds. **Self-governing Socialism: A Reader.** White Plains, NY: International Arts and Sciences Press, 1975. Vol. 1: xiv, 490p.; Vol. 2: viii, 327p. $19.00, paper.

This is a collection of writings not only by Yugoslav authors but also of classics (Marx, Lenin, Gramsci, Owen, Proudhon, etc.) and the Western experts on Yugoslav socialism. The book offers good insight into what the leading Yugoslav social scientists expect from self-management, how they would like to deal with its problems, and how it is related to Western thinking.

NP, 5:2:235-37

984.　Ra'anan, Gavriel D. **Yugoslavia after Tito: Scenarios and Implications.** Boulder, CO: Westview Press, 1977. xiv, 206p. $14.50.

This study treats the most difficult problem in political science, namely, the prediction of future political behavior. To this end, the author divides his work into two parts—the first of which concentrates on the internal politics of Yugoslavia, while the second probes the international politics of Yugoslavia's special position, from both geopolitical and military points of view. Ra'anan's evolution of Yugoslav political prospects is fairly dismal on both scores. He concludes that the country is vulnerable due to its many internal ethnic frictions. Ra'anan feels that Yugoslavia's internal and external brittleness might present the Soviets with an almost irresistible temptation to intervene.

NP, 8:2:254-56

985.　Robinson, Gertrude Joch. **Tito's Maverick Media: The Politics of Mass Communications in Yugoslavia.** Urbana, Chicago, London: University of Illinois Press, c1977. 263p. $12.95.

The author concentrates on describing the sources of Yugoslav news coverage utilized by the mass media as well as describing *Tanjug*, the Yugoslav national news agency, both in terms of structure and news-gathering capabilities. Unlike the other Communist presses, *Tanjug* does not have an internal monopoly on news dissemination. Yugoslav mass media are not subjected to precensorship, and the editorial staffs are relatively free to choose their sources regardless of origin. A major portion of their material originates with the Western news agencies. This book does display marked deficiencies in the political area due to the author's lack of sophistication in understanding the Yugoslav political scene. She takes at face value most of the information supplied by the Yugoslavs.

NP, 8:2:256-57

986.   Zukin, Sharon. **Beyond Marx and Tito: Theory and Practice in Yugoslav Socialism.** New York: Cambridge University Press, 1975. x, 302p. $15.50.

Zukin's purpose in this book is to describe the reality and theory of Yugoslav self-management and socialism from the point of view of the Yugoslavs themselves. By observing participants in local meetings in Belgrade and interviewing 10 Belgrade families, Zukin presents her interpretation of the reality of self-management and socialism. Between practice and theory, she discovers, there is an extraordinary wide gap. Anyone who chooses to defend the self-management model in its present form will have to respond to this work. And that will be no easy task, for this is an excellent study, well conceived, well researched, and well presented.

CSP, 19:4:526

History

987.   Despalatović, Elinor Murray. **Ljudevit Gaj and the Illyrian Movement.** East European Monographs, no. 11. Boulder, CO: *East European Quarterly*, 1975. vii, 271p. $12.00.

Gaj's role in and his contributions to the Illyrian Movement are amply evidenced and well presented in this book. However, more emphasis could have been placed on the financial problems that seemed to have plagued Gaj all his life. Yet, the present study may be considered one of the most important and comprehensive biographical studies of Gaj the man, journalist, editor, publisher, and pseudopolitician. Through Gaj, the author also examines the major aspects of the early nineteenth-century movement—as the cultural renaissance in which Croatian vernacular was made into a modern literary language and as an attempt to establish cultural unity among all Southern Slavs.

CSP, 19:1:110-11

988.   Djilas, Milovan. **Wartime.** Translated by Michael B. Petrovich. New York and London: Harcourt Brace Jovanovich, 1977. x, 470p. Plates. $14.95.

The wartime memoirs of Djilas are of special importance because they come from a man who, while once prominent as a participant on one side of the conflict, is no longer a blind protagonist of that side. Djilas sheds additional light on controversial points that have divided the two camps for over 30 years. He confirms that the war against the internal enemy was, at least in the spring of 1943, more on the minds of the Partisan leaders than the war against the occupier. Djilas' book is also revealing in many other respects. It gives us an intimate portrait of leading Partisan personalities, including Tito. He describes the senseless brutality of the war—the hundreds of thousands of deaths and executions attributed more to the internal than to the external conflict.

SR, 37:3:491-94

989.   Eekman, Thomas, and Ante Kadić, eds. **Juraj Križanić (1618-1683), Russophile and Ecumenic Visionary: A Symposium.** Slavistic Printings and Reprintings, 292. The Hague and Paris: Mouton, 1976. viii, 360p. Dfl. 108.00.

The 13 studies included in this volume are grouped thematically. The first section deals mainly with the literature available on Križanić, his biographical study, and development of his outlook. The second section includes articles on Križanić's contact and responses to the Slavic idea. The book is rounded off (third section) by a full bibliography of Križanić's works and of secondary literature.

SR, 37:1:157-58

990. Hehn, Paul H. **The German Struggle against Yugoslav Guerrillas in World War II: German Counter-Insurgency in Yugoslavia 1941-43.** East European Monographs, no. 57. Boulder, CO: *East European Quarterly*, 1979. 153p. $10.00. Distributed by Columbia University Press, New York.

Hehn presents a good introductory survey of the guerrilla struggle in the Balkans and an equally sound conclusion. The bulk of the work is a translation of a German military document prepared for the High Command in Berlin in 1943. As such, it takes the reader into the world of the professional soldier, trained to think in terms of victory or defeat, but not equipped to comprehend the continued resistance of a people after the surrender of their government. Scholars interested in the military history of wartime Yugoslavia will find this work useful for its details on troop movements, planning, and various negotiations.

NP, 9:2:255-56

991. Milazzo, Matteo J. **The Chetnik Movement and the Yugoslav Resistance.** Baltimore: The Johns Hopkins University Press, 1975. xii, 208p. $12.00.

Milazzo's primary concern is the question of collaboration by the Chetniks. This study is useful, particularly for the author's attention to the response to the Italian occupation, but he virtually ignores the non-Mihailović "Chetnik" movements and consequently fails to give his topic a balanced treatment.

SR, 35:2:375-77

992. **Patriot or Traitor: The Case of General Mihailovich. Proceedings and Report of the Commission of Inquiry of the Committee for a Fair Trial for Draja Mihailovich.** Introductory essay by David Martin. Foreword by Frank J. Lausche. Hoover Institution Publication, no. 191. Stanford: Hoover Institution Press, Stanford University, 1978. xviii, 499p. $19.00.

This volume allocates most of its pages to the testimonies of former American airmen shot down over Yugoslavia during the Second World War and rescued by the forces of General Draja Mihailovich. The airmen came to New York to bear witness on his behalf in May 1946 at the instigation of the "Committee for a Fair Trial for Draja Mihailovich." They were prepared to go to Belgrade, but the Tito regime had no wish to hear their voices, and on July 17, 1946, Yugoslav officials executed the foreordained sentence of death on Tito's chief rival for power. The Hoover Institution has rendered a service to history by publishing the witnesses of those ordinary Americans.

SR, 39:2:342-43

993. Petrovich, Michael Boro. **A History of Modern Serbia, 1804-1918.** New York and London: Harcourt Brace Jovanovich, 1976. Vol. 1: 33, 359p. + 8pp. plates. Maps; Vol. 2: xi, 372p. (pp. 360-731) + 8pp. plates. Maps. $49.50. for 2-vol. boxed set.

Petrovich's interpretation of Serbian history in the first half of the nineteenth century is traditional. He believes that the church preserved the memory of Serbia's medieval past during Turkish times, that the folk epics reinforced the resulting sense of national identity, and that local autonomy under the Turks prepared the Serbs for political democracy. His treatment of the second half of the nineteenth century remains traditional, too, but with significant nuances. He makes it clear that whereas the idea of Yugoslavism was always present among the Serbs, its fluctuating importance never rose to the level of the other goals. This long-awaited work has immediately become the standard account of its subject in any Western language.

SR, 36:4:707-709

994. Rogel, Carole. **The Slovenes and Yugoslavism, 1890-1914.** East European Monographs, no. 24. Boulder, CO: *East European Quarterly*, 1977. viii, 167p. $12.00. Distributed by Columbia University Press, New York.

Rogel traces the evolution of this small nation from its middle period from 1890 to 1914 with skill and considerable success. The book fills an important gap in the English historiography of the Slovene nation. It is meant to be an introductory study and, as such, it serves its purpose well.

SR, 38:1:147

995. Rusinow, Dennison. **The Yugoslav Experiment, 1948-1974.** Published for the Royal Institute of International Affairs, London. Berkeley and Los Angeles: University of California Press, 1977. xxii, 410p. $16.50.

Rusinow's political history of the Yugoslav regime is based in part on the study of a wide selection of the literature, but it rests primarily on the reports he wrote and the interviews he undertook while serving as an American University field service representative in Yugoslavia from 1963 to 1973. The book's principal contribution is the new insight it gives into the process by which ethnic conflict returned to the Yugoslav state and again came to dominate its political life. This presentation is flawed by the author's failure to place the development he traces in its international context. Nonetheless, for what it does accomplish, it is a very useful book.

SR, 37:2:335

996. Stokes, Gale. **Legitimacy through Liberalism: Vladimir Jovanović and the Transformation of Serbian Politics.** Publications of Russia and Eastern Europe of the Institute for Comparative Foreign Area Studies, 5. Seattle and London: University of Washington Press, 1975. xvi, 279p. $11.00.

V. Jovanović belonged to the first generation of Serbia's foreign-educated intellectuals. An eclectic compiler and popularizer, he was a foremost exponent of West European liberalism, which he adapted to Serbian conditions. His purpose was to forge a constitutional and parliamentary alternative to the traditional state-craft of Miloš and Mihailo. This volume is based on solid archival work and considerably complements the knowledge of the earliest influences on Jovanović's thought.

SR, 35:4:764-65

997. Tomasevich, Jozo. **War and Revolution in Yugoslavia, 1941-1945: The Chetniks.** Stanford: Stanford University Press, 1975. x, 508p. $20.00.

The Chetnik movement in Yugoslavia first received attention in Walter J. Roberts' *Tito, Mihailovic, and the Allies, 1941-1945* (1973). Tomasevich's study is the most ambitious effort published as the first volume of a projected series *War and Revolution in Yugoslavia*. This work is primarily a political-diplomatic history of the Draža Mihailović Chetnik movement. It deals as briefly as possible with the military aspects of the war and omits much consideration of its social background.

SR, 35:2:375-77

998. Wilson, Duncan. **Tito's Yugoslavia.** New York and London: Cambridge University Press, 1979. xvii, 269p. Map. $27.50.

The death of Tito marked the end of the most important phase so far in Yugoslavia's history. It is now possible to assess the impact of his career on the evolution of present-day Yugoslavia. Wilson's book, written and published before Tito died, makes an excellent start and, though addressed to the general reader, is so full of information, careful judgments, and specialized knowledge that it will be essential reading for all future historians of this subject. The author served as a diplomat in Belgrade in the fifties and sixties. The book has a chapter on nationalities problems that gives special attention to the situation of Croatia and interregional rivalries. This book is essential reading for all interested in present-day Yugoslavia.
    SEER, 59:1:130-31

Foreign Relations

999. Auty, Phyllis, and Richard Clogg, eds. **British Policy towards Wartime Resistance in Yugoslavia and Greece.** New York: Barnes & Noble; London: Macmillan, in association with the School of Slavonic and East European Studies, University of London, 1975. xii, 308p. $27.50.
This "piece of microhistory" deals mainly with the formulation of the British attitude toward Yugoslavia and Greece within the Special Operations Executive, the SOE. Countless facts, previously unknown, are being revealed here in addition to views expressed by the former members of the SOE.
    SR, 35:3:570-71

1000. Campbell, John C., ed. **Successful Negotiation: Trieste 1954. An Appraisal by the Five Participants.** Princeton, NJ: Princeton University Press, 1976. x, 181p. Maps. Appendices. $11.50.
All five former participants of the successful Conference on Trieste seem to agree that the main elements that contributed to the final outcome were the secrecy of the proceedings; the free hand for the middlemen; the use of implicit threats; and the implicit offer of rewards. Under the adroit probing of John Campbell, assisted by Joseph E. Johnson, these five diplomats appraise their actions in a candid and revealing way.
    SR, 37:2:336-37

1001. Clissold, Stephen, ed. **Yugoslavia and the Soviet Union, 1939-1973.** London: Oxford University Press, 1975. xxiii, 318p. $29.25.
This useful collection underscores the range and vitality of the Soviet-Yugoslav relationship during the past 40-odd years. Of the 238 documents or parts thereof printed here, about 30 relate to Soviet relations with either the prewar Yugoslav government or the government in exile. Many of the rest are communications between Tito or the Yugoslav Communist government and the Comintern, Stalin or the Soviet government. Some are statements, protest notes, agreements, declarations, and treaties. Generally, chronological order is followed. Clissold has provided an excellent aid to research on Soviet-Yugoslav relations. The entire enterprise has been carefully carried out.
    CSP, 20:3:430-31

1002. Larson, David L. **United States Foreign Policy toward Yugoslavia, 1943-1963.** Washington, DC: University Press of America, 1979. viii, 380p. $11.75, paper.
This book provides a useful, detailed, and mainly chronological survey of American-Yugoslav relations between 1943 and 1963, including the difficulties Americans had in reconciling themselves to having any such relations at all. It quotes extensively from a

number of official statements and speeches and cites many English-language sources. It contains little, if any, original research or, for that matter, analysis.

SR, 39:3:521

1003. Micunovic, Veljko. **Moscow Diary.** London: Chatto & Windus, 1980. xxvi, 474p. £12.50.

See entry 271 for annotation.

1004. Nord, Lars. **Nonalignment and Socialism: Yugoslav Foreign Policy in Theory and Practice.** Publications of the Political Science Association in Upsala, 69. Stockholm: Rabén & Sjörgren, 1974. x, 306p. Paper.

Nord makes several valuable contributions to the analysis of Yugoslav foreign policy. His rigorous comparative treatment of these diplomatic events forms an important supplement to traditional descriptions of nonalignment. The explicit differentiation of several facets of Yugoslav foreign policy provides the first step toward an assessment of this important question. Nord's quantification techniques should also be of interest to all students of Communist foreign policy.

SR, 34:4:858-59

1005. Wheeler, Mark C. **Britain and the War for Yugoslavia, 1940-1943.** East European Monographs, no. 64. Boulder, CO: *East European Quarterly*, 1980. iv, 351p. Map. $18.50. Distributed by Columbia University Press, New York.

Wheeler's book shows a detailed yet coherent grasp of the vast mass of confusing, contradictory, and irritatingly incomplete British documents dealing with Anglo-Yugoslav relations in the period 1940 to 1943. In particular, his research into the War Office papers bearing on the Mihailović-Tito controversy has enabled him to produce facts and to suggest interpretations not previously published. This applies especially to the messages sent by the two British liaison officers with Mihailović in the crucial period of the autumn of 1942 and early months of 1943, when British policy towards Yugoslav resistance was in the melting pot. The footnotes to this book are exceptionally full and useful.

SEER, 59:3:466-67

Economics

1006. Farkas, Richard P. **Yugoslav Economic Development and Political Change: The Relationship between Economic Managers and Policy-Making Elites.** New York: Praeger Publishers, 1975. xii, 133p. $13.50.

In this penetrating essay, Farkas focuses upon enterprise "directors" as a key to understanding the interrelationships between the political and economic systems in Yugoslavia. Also, the implications of Yugoslavia's external economic relations for domestic policy are considered. In fact, the business elites have become most influential in the myriad micropoliticoeconomic decisions that shape everyday life.

SR, 35:1:169

1007. Moore, J. H. **Growth with Self-Management: Yugoslav Industrialization 1952-1975.** Stanford: Hoover Institution Press, 1980. xvi, 334p. $17.95.

According to Moore, industrial policy in Yugoslavia has "amounted to a Yugoslav version of forced-draft industrialization." The implementation of self-management has been illusory because of the dominance of the director in enterprise decision making and the continued control over the banking system by the central authorities. This book will be of great interest to those who wish to follow the detailed, quantitative course of industrial development in Yugoslavia.

SS, 33:4:628-29

1008. Obradović, Josip, and William N. Dunn, eds. **Workers' Self-Management and Organizational Power in Yugoslavia.** Pittsburgh, PA: University Center for International Studies, University of Pittsburgh, 1978. xvi, 448p. Tables. $9.95.

The editors have assembled 21 articles and essays on the theory and practice of WSM by Yugoslav specialists, primarily from the most heavily industrialized northern republics of Slovenia and Croatia. The translations are, on the whole, quite good, although they are less successful in the theoretical articles. The book can be recommended to those interested in the strengths and weaknesses of the well-known Yugoslav approach to industrial democracy.

SR, 39:4:707-708

1009. Sirc, Ljubo. **The Yugoslav Economy under Self-Management.** London: Macmillan, 1979. xix, 270p. Tables. £15.00.

Sirc's aim is "to show the Yugoslav economy under self-management as it appears to Yugoslavs who have to live with it, so as to help outside observers to comprehend better what is happening there." This means relying predominantly on the opinions of Yugoslav observers, on the grounds that "those who run an economy know best whether the system functions or not." Sirc produces an impressive array of Yugoslav references at every stage of his highly critical appraisal. The study contains a large number of interesting insights and provides a useful basis for further discussion of a large number of aspects of Yugoslav economy.

SEER, 59:3:469-70

Language and Literature

1010. Andrić, Ivo. **The Bridge on the Drina.** Translated from the Serbo-Croatian by Lovett F. Edwards. Introduction by William H. McNeill. Chicago: University of Chicago Press, 1977 [1945, 1959]. iv, 314p. $4.95, paper.

The present edition of Andrić's most famous work, the novel which played a decisive role in his winning the Nobel Prize for literature in 1961, is a reprint of Lovett Edwards' 1959 English translation. Except for replacing John Simon's afterword by William McNeill's introduction and certain technical changes in general format and typeface, the present edition is the same as its predecessors.

SR, 37:3:543

1011. Ćosić, Dobrica. **A Time of Death.** Translated by Muriel Heppell. New York and London: Harcourt Brace Jovanovich, 1978. 437p. $10.95.

This is the latest work of the Serbian novelist, which is available now in English. A detailed account of the First World War in Serbia, this book should be of interest to a wider audience. Heppell has succeeded in producing a readable version despite the obvious pressures imposed by a work of such length. The second volume is due to appear in the near future.

SEER, 58:3:474

1012. Dordević, Mihailo. **Serbian Poetry and Milutin Bojić.** East European Monographs, no. 34. Boulder, CO: *East European Quarterly*, 1977. vi, 113p. Illus. Glossary. $10.00. Distributed by Columbia University Press, New York.
A five-chapter study on the life and work of Bojić and 26 translations of his most representative lyric poems constitute the major parts of this book. They are followed by an impressive bibliography and a glossary of important names, titles, places, and events mentioned in the book, which was compiled by Jelisaveta Stanojevich-Allen. The majority of the translations of poems are very successful and Dordević's reevaluation of Bojić's poetry is well argued and convincing.
SR, 38:3:536-37

1013. Friedman, Victor A. **The Grammatical Categories of the Macedonian Indicative.** Columbus, OH: Slavica Publishers, 1977. iii, 210p. $9.95.
This monograph attempts a semantic and syntactic analysis of the 10 tense forms of the Macedonian indicative. Chapter by chapter, Friedman builds a distinctive feature matrix, which he presents complete in his conclusion. The categories used are resultativeity, tense/reference, taxis (i.e., anteriority or not), status (affirmation or not), and aspect. The author is mostly concerned with modern literary Macedonian and draws on a wide variety of sources.
SEER, 57:3:416-17

1014. Groen, B. M. **A Structural Description of the Macedonian Dialect of Dihovo.** Lisse: The Peter de Ridder Press Publications on Macedonian, 2. 1977. viii, 307p. $17.00.
Groen follows, on the whole, the useful pattern set by Hendriks in his description of the Radožda-Vevčani dialect, with a brief introduction that places the dialect geographically and socially, sections on phonology and morphology, notes on syntax, 24 pages of fascinating texts, and a 52-page lexicon, which includes virtually all the words collected during the seven months' field work, mostly from three elderly informants whose command of the dialect was judged to be sufficiently uncontaminated by the standard language. The book makes some important contributions to Macedonian grammar.
SEER, 56:4:629-30

1015. Koljević, Svetozar. **The Epic in the Making.** Oxford: Clarendon Press, Oxford University Press, 1980. xvi, 376p. Appendices. £25.00.
This is an English version of the author's excellent book in Serbo-Croat *Naš junački ep* (Belgrade, 1974). It has been considerably expanded, with general information for the nonspecialist reader, and includes useful maps, appendices, and a valuable bibliography. The many quotations from the epic poetry are in English translation and fairly accurate, while the original is provided in footnotes. Perhaps the most interesting element in the book is the insistence on the individual quality of the various singers.
SEER, 59:3:417-19

1016. Mihailovich, Vasa D., ed. **Contemporary Yugoslav Poetry.** Iowa City: University of Iowa Press, 1977. xlviii, 242p. $12.50.
In addition to 237 pages of poems translated from Macedonian, Serbo-Croatian, and Slovenian, and brief notes on 43 contemporary Yugoslav authors, this newest collection of Yugoslav poetry contains a 40-page introduction entitled "The Poetry of Postwar Yugoslavia" by Gertrud Graubert Champe. There are 215 poems in the collection. The translations have been done by 31 translators. This is a valuable contribution to the field of

Yugoslav studies in the English-speaking world. The collection will be an indispensable tool to teachers of Serbian and Croatian literatures.

CSP, 20:3:436-37

1017. Mikasinovich, Branko, ed. **Five Modern Yugoslav Plays.** New York: Cyrco Press, 1977. xii, 339p. $15.00.

This book provides English-speaking readers with five representative samples of Yugoslav plays, representing Serbian, Croatian, Slovenian, and Macedonian ethnic backgrounds. In his introduction, the editor presents a survey of the history and development of Yugoslav drama from its beginnings until the present. The text of each play is preceded by a short biography of its author.

SR, 37:4:721-22

1018. Pekić, Borislav. **The Time of Miracles.** Translated by Lovett E. Edwards. New York and London: Harcourt Brace Jovanovich, 1976. 320p. $10.95.

This publication of an important work of Yugoslav literature in English is a sadly rare event, but the appearance of this first novel by one of the most interesting contemporary Serbian writers is particularly welcome. The essence of the work is irony—it examines the miracles of Christ from the point of view of those on whom they were wrought, those who were required by the Scriptures in order that their truth be experienced. Pekić's language is a subtle mixture of formal, stylized, colloquial, and lyrical elements arranged in compelling, varied rhythms.

SEER, 56:4:634-35

1019. Vidov, Božidar. **Croatian Grammar.** Toronto: Canada Multicultural Program, 1975. 119p.

This textbook is divided into four parts: phonetics, morphology, syntax, and orthography. At the end of the book, a small Croatian-English dictionary has been appended explaining the words used in the *Grammar*. The examples given to illustrate different kinds of compound and complex sentences are appropriate and well chosen. The same can be said about the different rules of this prescriptive grammar, which are set out in a very clear and systematic manner.

CSP, 20:3:439-40

Education

1020. Pervan, Ralph. **Tito and the Students: The University and the University Student in Self-Managing Yugoslavia.** Nedlands, Australia: University of Western Australia Press, 1978. xvi, 239p. $19.95. Distributed by International Scholarly Book Services, Forest Grove, Oregon.

This study represents a successful attempt to provide a sociopolitical analysis of the 1968 student disorders at Belgrade University. The author pays particular attention to the inadequacies of self-management as practiced at Belgrade University, the problems resulting from the unprecedented and uncontrollable growth in the university system, the deteriorating material situation of students, and the failure of youth organizations to articulate students' needs or to channel their energies. Pervan's use of Yugoslav sources is admirable, and his bibliography on higher education in Yugoslavia is superb.

SR, 39:1:151

Religion, Church

1021. Alexander, Stella. **Church and State in Yugoslavia since 1945.** Soviet and East European Studies Series. Cambridge: Cambridge University Press, 1979. xxii, 351p. £15.00.

Alexander takes the story of the Catholic Church's relations with state and party in Yugoslavia down to 1966 only (the signature of the protocol between the Vatican and the Yugoslav government). The relations of the Orthodox Church with state and party are covered to 1967 (the breakaway of the Macedonian dioceses from the Serbian Patriarchate). The author is notably objective in her treatment of the pressures on state and party in the early postwar period and of the resulting pressures on the churches.

SEER, 58:4:629-30

1022. Fine, John V. A. **The Bosnian Church: A New Interpretation. A Study of the Bosnian Church and Its Place in State and Society from the Thirteenth to the Fifteenth Centuries.** East European Monographs, no. 10. Boulder, CO: *East European Quarterly*, 1975. x, 447p. $17.50. Distributed by Columbia University Press, New York.

Fine takes a chronological approach to his subject. After examining religion in Bosnia's peasant society in chapter 1 and reviewing the sources in chapter 2, he surveys the development of Bosnia and its religious troubles from the end of the twelfth century to the Ottoman conquest in 1463 in chapters 3 through 6 and discusses the religious situation in Herzegovina from 1463 to 1481 and religion in Bosnia after the Turkish conquest in chapters 7 through 8. The book is carefully footnoted, has a good index, and a rich bibliography.

SR, 36:1:147-48

The Society, Sociology

1023. Doder, Dusko. **The Yugoslavs.** New York and Toronto: Random House, 1978. xiv, 256p. $10.00.

The author, reporter for the *Washington Post*, lived for three years in the 1970s in Yugoslavia while covering Eastern Europe. The book deals with several of the crucial, possibly contradictory, issues facing this unique land – national identity and the "ethnic key," socialist ideals and private goals, modernity and tradition, breadwinners abroad and dependents in Yugoslavia, political dictatorship, and self-management, constitutionalism, and other pertinent issues. Doder deals with all of this on both an intellectual and a commonsense level, presenting the true state of the country through rational arguments and references to individual human situations. The author discusses his talk with Djilas as well.

SR, 38:4:708-709

1024. Lockwood, William G. **European Moslems: Economy and Ethnicity in Western Bosnia.** New York: Academic Press/Harcourt Brace Jovanovich, 1975. xiv, 241p. Illus. $18.50.

This study is of an area in Bosnia encompassing three small towns (Bugojno, Donji Vakuf, and Gornji Vakuf) and their environs. The area is inhabited by Croat Catholics, Serb Orthodox, and Islamicized Slavs. This is a study of economics, ethnicity, and interethnic relations, past and present. The author examines nearly every aspect of the local society with which he is concerned.

SR, 35:3:568-69

Dissent Movement

1025. Djilas, Milovan. **Parts of a Lifetime.** Edited by Michael Milenkovitch and Deborah Milenkovitch. New York and London: Harcourt Brace Jovanovich, 1975. xiv, 442p. $15.00.

This collection represents a thorough sampling of Djilas' vast output. The most valuable, however, are the hitherto unpublished materials that the editors were able to procure directly from Djilas. Chronologically, the anthology spans the period from 1928 to 1973. The editors have been quite successful in their effort to present an adequate cross-section of Djilas work. Some selections are excerpted.

    SR, 35:3:569-70

1026. Sher, Gerson S. **Praxis: Marxist Criticism and Dissent in Socialist Yugoslavia.** Bloomington and London: Indiana University Press, 1977. xx, 360p. $15.00.

The author presents a sympathetic and thorough treatment of the dissenting Yugoslav Marxist intellectuals who came together around the journal *Praxis* during its short, precarious existence in 1964 to 1975. Basing their critiques on the writings of "the young Marx," these philosophers and social scientists — centered primarily in Zagreb and Belgrade universities — engaged in ideological combat with the state and party in an effort to further humanize Yugoslav socialism. Sher has produced an important book that is well written and documented with English, Serbo-Croatian, and other sources and interviews with many of the principals involved.

    SR, 38:3:524

National Minorities

1027. Freidenreich, Harriet Pass. **The Jews of Yugoslavia: A Quest for Community.** Philadelphia: The Jewish Publication Society of America, 1979. xiv, 323p. $14.95.

Following a brief introduction, this volume is divided into three parts, plus an epilogue. Part 1 traces the development of Jewish life; part 2 examines communal, organizational, and cultural activities, while part 3 deals with problems of national identity and political life and relations. On the whole, Yugoslav nationalism facilitated the acceptance of the Jews as a nationality, but it also made it more difficult for them to integrate into the mainstream of Yugoslav society. Zionism and Communism emerged as alternatives. About 80% of Yugoslavia's Jews perished in the Holocaust, and the majority of the survivors emigrated to Israel, leading to the situation where presently the Yugoslav Jewish community gradually is becoming extinct.

    CRSN, 8:1:181-82

AUTHOR/SHORT TITLE INDEX

SUBJECT INDEX

Aerospace, 394
Agrarian reform
 Poland, 925
 Russia, 341
Agriculture
 Eastern Europe, 18
 Hungary, 909-910
 USSR, 18, 21, 109-113
Agricultural history—USSR, 616
Akhmatova, Anna, 489, 554-55
Albania, 831-34
Alexander I, 348
Alexander III, 358
Angolan War, 290
Anti-Semitism
 Eastern Europe, 818, 820
 Hungary, 914-16
 Poland, 964
 USSR, 774-75, 778
Architecture—USSR, 76-78
Arghezi, Tudor, 971
Armenia, 752-54, 757
Art—Eastern Europe, 827-29
Auschwitz, 930
Avvakum, Archpriest, 637

Bakunin, Mikhail, 605
Balkan States, 791, 822, 829-30
Baltic Fleet, 368, 376
Baltic States, 685-86, 690-94
Baratynskii, El'genii A., 531
Barclay de Tolly, Michael, 343
Batiushkov, 532
Belorussia, 701-705
Bely, Andrei, 450, 557-58
Berlin Crisis, 252
Berngardovich, Peter, 618
Bessarabia, 342
Bestuzhev-Marlinsky, Alexander, 446
Blok, Aleksander, 454, 480, 487
Bolshevik movement, 212, 214, 303
Briusov, Valery, 523
Brik, Lili, 474
Brik, Osip, 467
Brothers Karamazov, 505
Bulgakov, Mikhail, 453, 457, 513
Bulgaria, 835-40
Bunin, Ivan, 542
Butkov, Jakov, 492

Catherine the Great, 312
Catholic Church
 Lithuania, 695
 Ukraine, 727
 USSR, 642
Censorship
 Russia, 333, 347
 USSR, 600
Černyševskij, N. G., 615
Chekhov, Anton, 444, 488, 491, 518, 521, 535, 539
Chetniks, 991, 997
Christian Socialism, 620
The Cold War, 246, 248, 249, 262, 267, 950
Comecon, 16, 26
Communism
 biography, 59
 comparative studies, 27-29, 31, 41, 52-53, 106, 143, 813
 Czechoslovakia, 853-54
 Eastern Europe, 808-811
 GDR, 880
 Hungary, 889-90
 international development, 43
 Poland, 923-24
 Rumania, 966
 sociology, 30, 48-53
 USSR, 210-11, 213
Concentration camps, 215, 216
Consumption
 Eastern Europe, 815
 USSR, 129
CPSU, 210-11, 213
Crime—USSR, 668
Crimean War, 337
Cuban Missile Crisis, 253
Cultural revolution—USSR, 139
Czechoslovak Legion, 362-63
Czechoslovak Spring, 844, 847, 852, 858, 863, 867
Czechoslovakia
 communism, 853-54
 dissent movement, 850
 economics, 870
 foreign relations, 866-69
 history, 855-65
 language and linguistics, 871-72
 literature, 873-74
 normalization, 845, 858
 politics, 851